THE UNTOLD STORY OF WESTERN CIVILIZATION

Vol. 2

THE UNTOLD STORY OF WESTERN CIVILIZATION

VOLUME 2

ANCIENT HISTORY

The Age of the Warrior Kings

Chuck and Tom Paprocki

Inner World Publications
San German, Puerto Rico
www.innerworldpublications.com

Copyright 2019 by Chuck Paprocki & Tom Paprocki

All rights reserved under International and
Pan-American Copyright Conventions

Published in the United States by
Inner World Publications

P.O. Box 1613, San German , Puerto Rico, 00683

Library of Congress Control Number:
2019933932

ISBN: 9781881717690

Cover Design: Tom Paprocki

All rights reserved. This book, or parts thereof, may not be reproduced in any form or by any means, electronic or mechanical, including photocopying, recording, or by any information storage or retrieval system, without the permission of the publisher except for brief quotations.

Cover photo: Gilgamesh, a Sumerian king who was the first man to achieve self-consciousness. In doing so he declared himself a god. His exploits inspired warriors in the Middle East for thousands of years.

Dedication

To the memory of Prabhat Rainjan Sarkar,
our spiritual guide.

Contents

Chapter One: The Ancient Middle East — 1

Mesopotamia: The Garden of Eden — 2
    Thus Spake the Lord — 5
    The Kings and Gods of Cities — 13
    The Coming of Enlil the Dark Lord — 17
The Emergence of Subjective Consciousness — 25
    Gilgamesh the God-King — 25
    The Priest Class — 29
    Lugalanda, the Greedy King — 30
    Urukagina and Basic Legal Rights — 31
    Lugalzaggesi and Scientific Warfare — 33
    The Akkadians and King Sargon — 34
    Ur-Nammu and the Code of Law — 39
    The Royal Tombs of Ur — 40
    The Babylonians and Marduk, the God of gods — 44
    The God of My Father — 46
    Hammurabi's Code — 48
The Minoans — 53
    The Last Great Matriarchal Civilization — 55
    The Volcano of Thera — 61
    The Gods Stop Talking — 64
    The Beginning of the "I-feeling" — 67
    The Threshold of Subjective Thought — 70
    Assyria and the Dark Age — 71
The Two-God Religion and the Emergence of Free Will — 76
    The Persians Arrive — 76
    Zoroastrianism — 78
    Alexander the Great: The Greeks Enter the Middle East — 89
    The Seleucid (Greek) Empire — 90

Chapter Two: Jews and the Rise of Monotheism — 92

Who is a Jew? — 92
Yahweh the Volcano God — 95
Who Are the Hebrews and From Where Did They Come? — 102
    The Hebrew Vagrants — 103
The Kingship of David — 104
The Kingdom Splits into Israel and Judah — 106
The Babylonian Captivity — 109
Greek Gods in Jerusalem — 112
The Jewish Revolts — 114
The Torah / Old Testament — 116
The Creation Myth and the Curse of Women — 125
The Jewish Prophets — 129
The Story of Samuel the Prophet and Saul the King — 133

Chapter Three: A Revolution in Human Consciousness — 140

Ecclesiastes — 140
The Jewish Mysticism of the Essenes — 142
God's Master Plan and the Role of the Chosen People — 144
The Traitor King and Wicked Priest — 149
The Teacher of Righteousness — 151
The Teacher of Righteousness and Jesus Christ — 159
The Suffering Servant and the New Covenant — 163
Early Jewish Christians and the Gnostics — 172
The Gospel of the Nazarenes — 174
The Naassenes — 180
The Gnostic Gospels — 186
    The Gospel of Thomas — 187
    The Gospel of Mary Magdalene — 194
    The Gospel of Philip — 197
Canonical Gospels — 204
Mithra — 206

Jesus Christ 209

Chapter Four: Religion and the Attack on Mysticism . . . 213

    The Church of Rome 213
    The Gospel of Matthew 213
    Paul the Apostle and the Church of Rome 219
    The Gentile Church of Rome 229
    Religion vs Mysticism 236
    Peter the First Pope 240
    The Bodily Resurrection of Jesus 243
    Desert Fathers and Desert Mothers 253
    Constantine and the Pax Deorum 260
        Constantine's Conversion to Christianity 262
        Constantine and the Church of Rome 264
    Arianism: The First of Many Heresies to Come 268

Appendix A: Major Gods and Goddesses in the Greek Pantheon . . . 275

Appendix B: Historical Timeline of the Jews . . . 280

Appendix C: Stories of the Desert Fathers . . . 281

Notes . . . 287

Illustration Credits . . . 307

About the Authors . . . 346

List of Figures

Map 2-1: Ancient Mesopotamia	3
Map 2-2: Eastern Mediterranean	54
Fig. 2-1: Great Goddess	58
Fig 2-2: Exterior of the Palace of Knossos	59
Fig. 2-3: Interior of the Palace of Knossos	59
Fig. 2-4: Bull-leaping fresco, found in Knossos palace, Crete, Greece dating around 1600-1450 BCE	60
Fig 2-5: A Volcanic Explosion	62
Map 2-3: Santorini: the Caldera Left From the Volcanic Explosion on Thera	63
Fig. 2-6: Altar with King Tukulti-Ninurta I Showing the Absent God	65
Fig. 2-7: Functions of the Left and Right Brain	68
Map 2-4: Expansion of the Assyrian Empire 824 to 671 BC	72
Map 2-5: Persian (Achaemenid) Empire 521 to 485 BC	77
Map 2-6: Alexander the Great's Empire 323 BC	89
Fig. 2-8: Egyptian Stele Placing the Israelites in Caanan ca 1200 BC	97
Fig. 2-9 - Small Figurine of a Goddess Worshiped by the Hebrews	100
Map 2-7: Kingdoms of Israel and Judah ca 921 BC	107
Fig. 2-10: Timeline of the Major Hebrew Prophets	130
Map 2-8: Location of Qumran	143
Fig. 2-11 Relationship Between Synoptic Gospels	205
Fig 2-12: Mithraic Alterpiece Found Near Fiano Romano, Near Rome, Now in the Louvre	206
Map 2-9: Spread of Christianity in Europe, Southwest Asia, and North Africa to the year AD 600	238

Chapter One: The Ancient Middle East

Ancient laws remain in force long after the people have the power to change them.
— *Aristotle*

By looking at the Indus Valley during the time of the matriarchy, we have learned many things. Likewise there is much to learn from the Middle East where developments brought the Aryans in contact with the Semitic peoples, the people of Mesopotamia and Assyria, as well as with the Egyptians and the ancient Greeks. The heritage of the Middle East has also had a profound impact on the collective subconscious, DNA, and social programming of Western civilization in general, and of the United States in particular. Most Americans trace their origins to the Greco-Roman civilization, not knowing that these societies were based on discoveries made long before they even existed. For example, to discover why the East is so different from the West, we must first look at the developments in the Middle East during the period of Ancient History.

There has long been a dividing line between East and West, between our respective beliefs and modes of behavior. At the crux of the difference is that the East, by virtue of its spiritual heritage, views the world as a single entity. To them, there is a Supreme Oneness within which everything exists. In the West, however, we do not think this way. Rather, we view everything as a competition between opposing forces—God vs the Devil, Man vs Nature, Man vs Woman, Good vs Evil, Left vs Right, White vs Black, etc. The dualism that conditions Western thought was born in the land of Iran and was propagated by Zoroaster and the Magi priest class at an extremely critical time in our human evolution. All of

Western history was shaped by their vision as it pervaded ancient Greece and Rome, as well as the Judeo Christian religions. Thus, in the United States today, our programming, which governs the very manner in which we interpret reality, is conditioned by this static dualism. Consequently, we are always at odds with whomever or whatever the "other" is. We need to dominate and conquer the other. Prejudice, dogma, and war are the inevitable consequences of our mindset. By examining the Middle East, we will see how this came about, as well as how the Jews and Christians came to mirror this mindset.

The dividing line between South Asia and the Middle East is the tableland of Iran. Iran means the land of the Aryans.[1]

While the Aryan tribes migrated east to the Indus Valley from their homeland in the Caucusus Mountains, they also went straight south to Iran and ultimately into Mesopotamia. The Aryan tribes in the Middle East were known as the Medes, Persians, and Hittites..

Eventually, under Cyrus the Great, the Persians would create the greatest empire of the then known world, but unlike in India where they rolled in through an open door, things were not so inviting in the Middle East. In fact, thousands of years before the Aryans reached battle strength, there had been an on-going struggle between the Sumerians and the Akkadians (indigenous Semite tribes). They fought over the rich delta land that lay between the Tigris and Euphrates rivers that even today is called Mesopotamia. The area lies within the border of present day Iran and Iraq.

Mesopotamia: The Garden of Eden

The earliest evidence of human activity in the ancient Middle East reveals that the people were nomadic hunters and shepherds. Artifacts found in the Shanidar cave in northeast Iraq and in the Wadi-en-Natuf area of Israel, dated around twelve thousand years ago, suggest the people were about five feet tall, were living in and around caves, and were skillful in fashioning tools from bone and flint. They drew pictures on cave walls and wore ornaments of shells and animal teeth. Clay figurines of the Great Goddess were also found. These people, were the early ancestors of the present Semitic peoples.[2]

By eleven thousand years ago, the people were burying their dead and adapting to a more settled life. They began to build permanent villages. In Israel, three such towns were discovered, each comprised of about fifty houses with reed roofs. "The houses were arranged around an open central area where many bell-shaped pits had been dug and plastered for the storage of food. Sometimes these pits were reused for burials."[3]

The transition from a nomadic lifestyle to living in a permanent town of two hundred people or more was the result of the discovery of agriculture. This fact is known by the discovery of an abundance of sickle blades, pounders, pestles, and other tools found in each house for the reaping and preparation of grains and legumes.

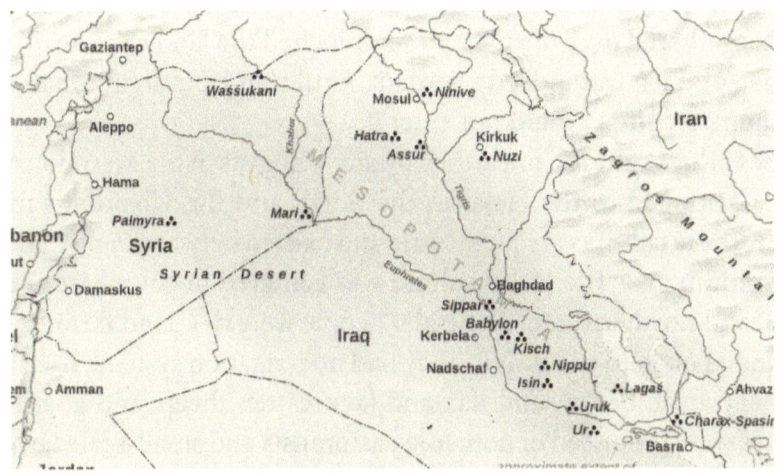

Map 2-1: Ancient Mesopotamia

In the beginning, we can assume that agriculture was primitive and only supplemented gathered vegetation, fishing, and the hunting of wild goats, gazelles, boars, fox, rabbits, and other animals. The transition from hunting and gathering to permanent agricultural settlements was a slow one, taking thousands of years to complete. Even today tribes of nomadic herdsmen still exist in the Middle East.

From 9,000 to about 4,900 years ago, different Semitic tribes grew side-by-side, occasionally expanding at the expense of their neighbors. Archaeologists identify successive cultures by the name of the most advanced town of that period. These are Qalat Jarmo in northeast Iraq (7000-6000 BC), Hassuna in northern Iraq (6000-5000 BC), Halaf in northeastern Syria (7,000 – 4300 BC), Ubaid in northern Iraq (5000-3500 BC), Uruk in southern Iraq (3500–3000 BC), and Jemdet Nasr in southern Iraq (3100-2900 BC).[4]

The earliest known towns began in the hilly areas to the east and west of the great plain of Mesopotamia. There the people grew einkorn, emmer wheat, and barley and raised sheep, goats, and pigs. Up until about seven thousand years ago, no towns had been established in the land between the two rivers, simply because the land was uninhabitable. Each year the low-lying plain was inundated by runoff from the hills and became a great shallow lake. When the water subsided, great swamps were left behind. In the summer, the swamps dried out, but thunderstorms gathered over the plains and drenched the land once again. The Garden of Eden was indeed a verdant, fertile land, but so uninhabitable that human beings would not enter it.

The earliest cultures, unearthed by archeologists in the Mesopotamian plain, belonged to the Halaf in the north and the Ubaidians in the south. These cultures are prehistoric and existed between eight and nine millennium ago. The Halaf culture was centered in southeast Turkey, Syria, and northern Iraq. The Halaf people were dry-land farmers who depended on natural rainfall. They had no irrigation system. They grew emmer wheat, barley, and flax and kept cattle, sheep, and goats. The culture was comprised of nomadic pastoralists and small-scale farmers. Archeologists have uncovered circular domed structures made of mud bricks with long rectangular anterooms that they believed were temples because of the large numbers of female figurines found in them.

Halaf also produced two-colored pottery, which was found throughout the area even centuries after the Halaf culture no longer existed.

It appears that around seven thousand to seventy-five hundred years ago the Halad culture began to transition into the Ubaidian culture, which existed in Mesopotamia to the south. Apparently, the transition was not caused by invasion but by general adoption of a superior culture.[5]

It was at this time that the Ubaidians began to extend their fields down to the edge of the land that was prone to flooding. The lure was a soil so rich that the yield in produce was many times that of mountain plots. The farmers learned to dig ditches and bank the sides of streams to control the amount of water that reached their fields. Satisfied by the success of this technique, they penetrated more deeply into the thick reeds, which grew over their heads, draining more and more swampland.

In time, the farmers reached the banks of the mighty Euphrates. They built embankments along the river and the land was theirs. The plains were turned into an enormous cultivated field that yielded rich harvests year after year. The Ubaidians built their towns along the Euphrates River. They hunted, fished, farmed, developed crafts, and sailed their boats along the river for trade. Rich harvests led to increased populations. The towns expanded. At first the people lived in huts made from the reeds. Later they formed the clay earth itself into lumps and built mud huts. Still later they learned to form bricks and bake them in the sun. Brick houses and temples were built that withstood the natural elements much better. Even the storms could no longer harm them. With such security, their tools, weapons, and pottery kept improving. As a result, the first cities in Mesopotamia appeared. The people bartered grain and crafts for their neighbor's products, including copper that came from the mountains in the North. The Ubaidians created the earliest known agricultural society in the Middle East.

Excavations of the oldest towns in the Land of the Two Rivers show that in each town a Temple was built to house a guardian god or goddess. The temple stood in the center of the town with its corners oriented to the cardinal points of the compass. Around these temples, the towns themselves developed. The oldest town in Mesopotamia was probably Eridu, a Ubaidian town. Here archaeologists found fourteen temples built one on top of the other, all dating before forty-nine hundred years ago.[6]

Thus Spake the Lord

Around five thousand years ago, a new people came to live in—and eventually dominate— the Ubaidian cities, as well as build their own. These new people came as traders, introducing new types of pottery made on a potter's wheel. They replaced the stamp seal with the cylinder seal. They built ziggurat temples. They made sculptures out of stone and introduced written records in a new language. Who were these sophisticated people, and where did they come from? These people called their new land Sumer and came to be known as the Sumerians. Evidence strongly suggests they came from India. Many of the artifacts and pieces of jewelry found in Sumerian rooms were made of materials derived from India and decorated with Indian patterns. "There are Sumerian seals with elephants and rhinoceroses in procession that are so like seals from India one cannot tell which is which."[7] Nonetheless, some archaeologists believe that the images on their pottery and seals look like people of the Mongolian race and could possibly have come from China. The Sumerians called themselves the "Black-Headed People" and were most likely of the Negroid race, descendants of ancient settlers of India, perhaps as far back as Homo erectus.

Apparently, the Sumerians came to Mesopotamia by boat. They sailed the seas between the mouths of the Indus and the Euphrates with the help of the monsoon winds.

In this ancient shipping lane lies the island of Bahrain. The Sumerians called it Dilman, the "Great Fish in the Eastern Sea," and told the tale of how it had originally risen from the sea off the Indian coast and had, with its half human and half fish inhabitants, floated westward to its present location in the Persian Gulf. From this island, tradition held, the creatures had gone ashore at Eridu and settled in the land of southern Mesopotamia and called their new land Sumer.

It is uncertain whether the Sumerians conquered Ubaidian cities by force or whether they became rulers in time by virtue of their superior culture. The early Sumerian King List contains Ubaidian (Semitic) and Sumerian names of Kings, indicating that racial strife was not a significant problem. Nonetheless a distinction between the two races was always noted. Mesopotamia became divided into two parts: Akkad, to the North, where the Semitic people known as Akkadians spoke an inflective language, and Sumer, in the South, where the Sumerians spoke an agglutinative language.

At the time the Sumerians arrived in Mesopotamia (the great plain between the Euphrates and Tigris rivers), they were in a transition from matriarchal to patriarchal values. We can observe this transition in the evolution of human consciousness in their religious myths.

The earliest records of the Sumerians in Mesopotamia revealed that their pantheon was tied linguistically to the Dravidian great goddess Kala Nath. Now, however, the deities had expanded to include male gods. The Great Goddess had changed into a pantheon of gods and goddesses, each representing an aspect of her being. This is a clear indication of the breakdown of matriarchy. As we mentioned in Volume 1, while some cultures stressed the word Kala, which became Kali, Kore, Kelly, etc., others stressed the word Anath or Ana. The Sumerians were in this latter camp.

The Great Goddess (Anath or Ana) had now become a male god called Anu, and his wife, who still had identical powers, was called Anata. Ana/Anath represented divinity in its highest sense, but now she had a female and male composition.

But Anu/Anata was not the only divinity. The deities of the Sumerians consisted of two major trinities, as well as the gods and goddess that represented five planets. A host of lesser divinities and household deities also existed and were worshipped. The household deities were worshipped from one generation to the next so that the sons always worshipped the "god of their father."

Anu/Anath represent the first pair of the first trinity. The titles of Anu included "the original chief," "the father of the gods," "king of the lower world," "the lord of darkness," and the "ruler of the far-off city." This indicates that Anu probably originated as a sacred king who went to the underworld to be sacrificed in order to generate life again on earth each spring. As such, Anu was revered as the first sacred king, (i.e., the first god and the father of all gods to follow). Anata is now only a reflection of Anu and so all his epithets apply to her.

The second pair of the first trinity is Bel/Beltis. Bel means "lord." This name is usually followed by a qualification, usually Nipru, which means to "pursue" or to "make to flee," thus he was the "Hunter Lord" or the "Conquering Lord." According to the immanent authority on the ancient Middle East, George Rawlinson, "Bel-Nipru is probably the Biblical Nimrod, the original Sumerian monarch, the "mighty hunter" and conqueror."[8] It was Nimrod who would later build Babylon, which in Assyrian times was still called "the city of Bil-Nipru." This leads us to believe that Bil-Nipru was originally a deified human—not a sacred king—but an actual strong man king. He is also called "father of the gods," "procreator," "king of all spirits," "lord of the world," and "lord of all the countries." The worship of Bil-Nipru, or Nimrod, as a god continued throughout the entire history of the Sumerian civilization.

Beltis was the wife of Bil-Nimrod. Unlike Anata, who was reduced to a shadow, Beltis was a force all her own. In fact, she became the form in which the Great Goddess was worshipped in Sumer. Her common title was in fact "the Great Goddess." She was also called "Mother of the Gods" and "the Mother of the Great Gods." Beltis was also the mother and wife of Nimrod's son, Nin, indicating that she was the Great Goddess who created sacred kings and married each new king or son of the previous king in annual rituals of rebirth. Beltis was the queen of heaven, the goddess who makes the earth fertile, the goddess of war and battle, and the goddess of hunting. Unlike the gods whose worship was confined to specific cities, Beltis was worshipped in her own temples everywhere. The existence of Nimrod indicates that the role of sacred king had now been replaced by the role of a monarch king. Nonetheless, while this indicates that we have entered the patriarchy period in the Middle East, the people still worshiped the Great Goddess and the tradition of the sacred king was still honored as a means to renew life each spring.

Hea or Hoa is the third god of the first trinity. He is a serpent god who "came up from the Persian Gulf to teach astronomy and letters to the first settlers on the Euphrates and Tigris." Hea is emblematic of superhuman knowledge. Hoa is "King of the rivers," "Lord of the abyss," "The great deep," "The intelligent guide," "The intelligent fish," and the "Teacher of mankind." His emblem is the wedge or arrowhead, which is used to create cuneiform writing. Thus, Hea is also the "Patron of the alphabet." Hea represented the serpent who had always been the companion of the Great Goddess. He was the serpent that every patriarch had to battle and defeat in order for the mantle of knowledge to be transferred to him and the men of his tribe. Hea is the dragon that must be killed. Hea is also the serpent that we find in the Jewish story of the Garden of Eden (Mesopotamia). As the Jewish patriarchs came to reject the knowledge of the civilizations that preceded them, it was also necessary to condemn the serpent of the goddess and blame the woman, Eve, who represented the great goddess, for being responsible for the downfall of humanity. Eve sinned in the eyes of the patriarchal god of the Jews because she offered man (Adam) fruit from the tree of knowledge. We can imagine that the Jewish priest class had to work very hard to sell this idea to the people.

Dav-Kina, wife of Hea had the same powers only differentiated by gender.

The first god of the second trinity is Sin or Hurki. He is the moon god. Ur, a city of the Sumerians, is dedicated to Sin. In Ur, Sin is known as "Chief," "lord of the spirits," "he who dwells in the great heavens," "chief of the gods of heaven and earth," "the bright," "the shining," "lord of the month," "the lord of building," etc. Sin's symbol is the crescent moon. The temple of Ur, which was begun by Nimrod's successor king Urukh, is dedicated to him.

There was also a moon goddess who was honored in her own "ark" or "tabernacle," but she was called "the lesser light," while Sin was called "the light."

San or Sansi was the second deity of the second triad. He was the sun god. His name means bright or shining. He is "the supreme ruler who casts a favorable eye on expeditions," "the vanquisher of the king's enemies," and "the breaker-up of opposition." San is worshiped in the cities of Larsa and Sippara. His symbol is the circle or cylinder.

Al, Gula, and Anuit are the three wives of the sun god. They represent the rising sun, peaked sun at noon, and setting sun. Gula, who represents the sun at its peak, is also called the mistress of life in that she provides life to everything that lives. She had temples independent of her husband.

Vul or Iva is the third member of second trinity. Vul is the god of the atmosphere or air. In Arabic, atmosphere is heva, the root of our word heaven. Vul is a destructive god, who was not worshiped until the time of the Assyrian conquest. His temple was in Asshur. Vul wielded the thunderbolt like Indra and Zeus and was also the "Destroyer of crops" and the "uprooter of trees."

In addition to this trinity of the moon, sun, and atmosphere, the Sumerians also worshipped five other gods that corresponded to the five planets—Saturn (Nin), Mars (Nergal), Jupiter (Marduk), Venus (Ishtar or Inanna), and Mercury (Nebo).

There is widespread acceptance among historians that the gods and goddesses played a major role in Mesopotamian consciousness as they did everywhere at this time of human history. We are told:

> ... it is well known that from an early period in Mesopotamian history, thinkers envisaged the world around them in theological terms. Individual deities were associated or, at times, totally identified with a part of the universe, such as a cosmic region, an astral body, meteorological phenomenon, vegetation, or animal or group of animals, a force of nature, or aspect of human social activity. In each city, one deity in particular was worshiped and was regarded as the tutelary deity of that city.[9]

How did such a worldview evolve? In our study of matriarchy, we showed that when the clan mothers first began to interpret reality, they believed that everything they came in contact with was alive. Everything was animated by a strange and mysterious force. Everything, they observed, had this force. It appeared in plants, animals, stars, the wind, etc. The spirits (as these forces came to be called) could express themselves in many ways. They could change their form at will. Most importantly, the spirit could be heard inside a person's mind in the form of a voice or, while sleeping, as a dream. Thus psychic forces were not confined to specific physical forms, per se, as we envision them today. Rather, any psychic force could inhabit even the simplest physical form, including rocks and other inanimate objects. Thus, anything, even an insect or plant, could be more intelligent than a human. It could curse or kill someone. There was no way for people to determine anything's motivation or to know the limits of its capabilities. Such a view created a fear and awe about everything and put humans at the mercy of the spirits. In time, as humans came to have a greater sense of themselves, the spirits became more humanlike (anthropomorphic) and the most powerful forces came to be understood as gods and goddesses. A spirit might occupy a tree, but the entire forest would be worshipped as a *god or goddess*. Such deities had total control over the minds of humans. People believed they were more powerful than themselves and had only created humans to serve them.

People in ancient societies, therefore, did not act out of individual volition. They had no sense of "I" to undergird or substantiate their actions. On the contrary, they had only the voices in their minds to command them. And these voices they called the gods or goddesses. These voices provided the impetus for human volition at that time. They were the masters of human destiny. Humans were their slaves.

According to Julian Jaynes, a psychologist, who studies the human brain, the right side of the brain, as it evolved, became responsible for synthesizing sensory stimuli and transmitting its findings to the left side of the brain where it was "heard"; that is, organized into language by the verbal hemisphere.

According to Jaynes, "the voice of the gods was directly organized in what corresponds to the Wernicke's area in the right hemisphere and "spoken" or "heard" over the anterior commissures to or by the auditory areas of the left temporal lobe."[10] In other words, there was a bridge between the right side of the brain that "interpreted" reality and the left side of the brain that "heard" it. Because our subjective sense of self had not yet evolved in these early days, what we "heard" was not attributed to our sense of I, but to "voices" in our mind. We originally called these voices spirits, and later, as our appreciation for larger forces developed, we called them goddesses and gods.

Experiments conducted by Jaynes, in which the Wernicke's area on the right hemisphere of the subject's brain is artificially stimulated, produce an experience of hearing commanding voices. Jaynes believes that the voices heard by schizophrenics today are identical to the voices heard by our ancient ancestors, in that they are not attributable to the self but rather to external forces. This mindset Jaynes calls the "bicameral mind." *Bicameral* meaning having two chambers. This state of the mind lacks integration by the "I." In human evolution it represents the mindset that immediately preceded an integrated self-awareness. Animals do not possess a subjective consciousness and, at the time, neither did we. According to Jaynes, the connecting bridge (anterior commissures) is no longer active is most people, yet vestiges of it remain in the brains of schizophrenics today.

The idea of the bicameral mind is consistent with Shrii P. R. Sarkar's Wheel of Creation theory. Shrii P. R. Sarkar, a modern day philosopher and spiritual master, says that mind evolves along with the evolution of species. It appears first as the Chitta (mental screen). Then the Ahamtattva (sense of doing) evolves, which is the sense of volition. And finally, the Mahatattva, literally the highest sense or sense of "I am," evolves. Therefore, only after such a sense of subjective consciousness evolves, is a human being able to say "I am" and, therefore, "I do," instead of "the goddesses or gods do."[11]

As we have discussed in Volume 1, it was Lord Shiva who first introduced the idea of subjective consciousness to humankind in his theory of Dharma and science of yoga. Shiva taught that every human, through certain physical and mental disciplines, could merge their subjective consciousness with a supreme deity, the macrocosmic subjective consciousness. The influence of Shiva on the Aryans is borne out by comparing writings in the Rig Veda (pre-Shiva) with the Aryan Upanishads (post-Shiva). As James observes, the "Indian hurtles from the bicameral Veda into the ultra subjective Upanishads. . . ."[12]

To put this biological and social upheaval in context, the transition of human consciousness at this time in the Middle East, not only embodied the transference of social power from women to men, which, in itself, was a profound cultural revolution, but it also occurred at a time when a significant biological change was occurring in the human brain. The left brain began to dominate the right brain. In such a transition, the voices of the ancestors, spirits, goddesses, and gods were being replaced by an internal logic and the emergence of a new voice, the voice of "I." So also, the magic of female birth-giving would be replaced in time by men's ability to create entirely new realities out of the written "Word." Men now learned how to "make a name" for themselves. They could write the tablets of destiny in stone. In this transition, the goddess's ability to transform blood into life, gave way to a god's ability to transform the Word into life. In the records of the Sumerians, we see the roots of this psychological process, which, by the time of the Hebrew prophets twenty-five hundred years later, would allow men to say, and allow all who heard to believe, that, "In the beginning was the Word, and the Word was made flesh." No longer was flesh made in the bodies of women.

Let us now look at the culture of the Sumerians to see how this inexorable process began to express itself in the West.

The Kings and Gods of Cities

One of the earliest records of Sumerian history, the Mem-lugal, or Sumerian King List, reveals that, "When kingship was lowered from heaven, the kingship was in Eridu."[13] This means that the sacred king had now evolved into the king as male ruler.

The chief deity of Eridu was Enki. If we analyze the meaning of this name in the context of other Sumerian writing, we discover that *en* means a kind of religious economic manager and *ki* means earth; so Enki meant the manager of the earth. Enki was the most powerful of Sumerian deities in the early days. This meant that Eridu was the most prosperous of the five Sumerian cities and that its temple was filled with grain. It also meant that the king (lugal) of Eridu was the most powerful of all the kings.

In all likelihood, Eridu was already a prosperous city when the Sumerians arrived in Mesopotamia. The Semitic Ubaidians, who built it, were already very sophisticated in the development of architecture, pottery, canal building, and civil administration. Perhaps Enki was even a translation of the name of a Semitic deity, Akki, the Great Goddess, who, after patriarchy was firmly established, became the Goddess of Demons whose kiss meant death. The indigenous Semitic tribes of northern Mesopotamia called themselves Akkadians indicating their worship of the Goddess. While Enki being a derivation of Akki is speculative, the qualities of Enki reflect the qualities of the more ancient Goddess than they do a male warrior God. Listen to this description of him from *The Land of Ur*:

> Enki was the god of wisdom, whose heart was unfathomable. He blessed the trees and the reeds, birds and men; he invented the plow and the pack, the molds to shape bricks; he framed laws and decrees. In his travels across the world, he visited the other gods and ordained the fates of various countries. He created healing herbs, he gave the winds their orders and he taught mankind how to construct canals that would serve both for irrigation and drainage.[14]

Such a description implies that either the Sumerians adopted Akki into their pantheon and changed her sex to male or, as an early Earth Lord of the Sumerians in Mesopotamia, he kept the qualities of the more ancient Great Goddess.

Additional stories of Enki reveal that Anu (sky god) and Inanna (goddess of love), the most ancient deities of the Sumerians, were envious of Enki's prosperity. As the ruling deities of Uruk, they plotted to steal the secrets of his success. It was decided that Inanna would sail down the river from Uruk to Eridu and pay Enki a visit. We are told that:

> Enki gave a banquet in her honor. At the feast he grew merry and he drank so much that he no longer knew what he was doing. Inanna so bewitched him with her loveliness that when she asked him to give her all the divine laws and powers, he made her a present of them. The craft of building; the skills of the tanner, the basket-maker, the smith and the carpenter; the arts of reading and calculating; he gave her them all, as well as the design of musical instruments and equipment to observe the stars – all human knowledge and all skills he presented to Inanna.[15]

This story continues to tell how Inanna, in great haste, left Eridu with her precious gifts. Although Enki sent sea monsters (keepers of knowledge) to pursue her, Inanna finally evaded them and, in doing so, became goddess of skills in the city of Uruk. Perhaps here we have the veiled story of jealousy between Sumerian kings, or perhaps an Ubaidian story that tells how the Sumerians were beholding to them for their skill base. It is impossible to tell.

By all accounts, Inanna was the principal deity in the city of Uruk. Her father, Anu, chief of the gods, could never control her. This indicates that the Queen of Uruk or the high priestess remained more powerful than the male priests. It was against Anu's advice; for example, that Inanna chose Dumuzi, a shepherd King to be her spouse, over Enkimdu, a farmer, who was her father's choice. We are told that Dumuzi and

Enkimdu fought fiercely for Inanna's hand, but that once she chose Dumuzi and enthroned him as king of Uruk, the two men became friends. Apparently the people understood that both the shepherd and the farmer were necessary for the success of Uruk.

In the tale of Inanna and Dumuzi, we have one of the earliest accounts of the ancient ritual of the Hieros Gamos (sacred marriage) in which the union of a sacred king with the Goddess confirms his right to rule. We can assume that the Queen of Uruk, the woman who embodied the voice of the Goddess, was still powerful enough politically to determine kingship. In the following extension of the Inanna/Dumuzi story, we can observe the ancient people's knowledge of annual cycles and their version of the Goddess and the sacred king. The story, taken from *In the Land of Ur*, goes like this:

> It was thanks to Inanna that Dumuzi was enthroned as king of Uruk, and because it was her doing, she felt herself all powerful. Dominion over the earth no longer satisfied her. She wanted to rule the underworld too, which was the domain of her older sister, Erishkigal. Inanna tied the divine laws to her girdle, placed the crown of the plains on her head, took a measuring rod of lapis lazuli in her right hand, placed a golden ring on her left hand, and bound a shield of stone to her breast. In order to conquer her sister, she then descended into the realm of the dead, saying to her chancellor: "if I have not returned to Uruk after three days and three nights, then go to the other gods, so that one of them may come to my aid."

Boldly Inanna entered her sister's underworld, which was guarded by seven gates. Pale with wrath, Erishkigal said to the keeper of the gates, "Fling open the gates so that Inanna may enter. But she shall come into my presence bowing low, stripped and naked shall she appear before me." And the keeper of the gates threw them open. At the first gate, the divine laws were taken away from Inanna and at the second gate, the crown from the plains. At each gate, yet another possession was removed from her until she stood at last defenseless before Ereshkigal, her sister and enemy. And Ereshkigal turned the eye of death on Inanna and spoke the word of doom. At once Inanna stiffened into a corpse. In vain did the people of Uruk wait for her return, but it never occurred to Dumuzi to go to Inanna's rescue. On the fourth day, therefore, the Chancellor went to Nippur and begged Enlil to go and help Inanna. Enlil refused. The Chancellor then went to Ur, to the god of the moon. The moon god also refused. At last the Chancellor went to Eridu where Enki listened to him, although Inanna had tricked him into giving her the laws of the gods. He sent two messengers into the underworld, and they took with them the bread of life and the water of life. They crumbled the bread over Inanna and sprinkled her with the water so that Inanna was restored to life. Ereshkigal then had to release her sister from the kingdom of the dead. But only on the understanding that someone else had now to leave the land of the living in her place, for such was the law. Dumuzi was chosen in exchange, but when he was confronted by the revived Queen and the ruthless ambassadors of Ereshkigal, he refused to lie down in the dust and so demons seized him by force and carried him off to the underworld.

In the Council of the gods, however, it was decided that Dumuzi would be allowed to return to life every year, to celebrate anew his marriage to Inanna, so that the land of Sumer would be fertile and not become a wilderness again. Ereshkigal, the goddess of death, agreed. She wanted to rule over as many dead as she possibly could. But as people had to be born before they could die, it was in her interest too to send Dumuzi back to the earth as the bringer of new life. Just as morning after morning, the sun god breaks out of his prison, the mountains of night, so Dumuzi would return to Uruk after every winter of death, to the city where stood the 'House of Heaven', the temple of Inanna.[16]

Here we have the classic tale of the sacred king, his marriage to the Goddess, and his return each year to fructify the land of Sumer. The people celebrated this event each spring. It was their New Year's celebration. To them, the Queen was Inanna and the King was Dumuzi, himself risen from the dead. They put their trust in him as God and felt secure in the protection of the Good Shepherd and in the grace and favor of the Queen of Heaven, who came to earth every year to meet him.

The Semitic people honored this same tradition as well. Akkadians, Babylonians, Assyrians, and later even the Hebrews would celebrate this same New Year. We are told that, "In the early period of the Hebrew monarchy, the central element of the annual New Year Festival was the ritual enthronement of Yahweh as king."[17]

So we see that within this tradition, each king of every city came to power by virtue of his marriage with the Goddess, and in his embodiment of a god, he was her divine consort. In such a manner, men and women had approximately equal power in this time in history. Both were required to bring life to the land and both were worshiped as deities.

The Coming of Enlil the Dark Lord

Around forty-nine hundred years ago, an event of nature occurred of such magnitude that life in Mesopotamia was thrown into an upheaval. Values shifted and a new super-deity came to power. His name was Enlil, lord of the atmosphere. From this point onward, life was no longer as simple as it once was. It took on a darker meaning. Doubt, lamentation, warfare, and the feeling of incompleteness grabbed the minds of the people. The event that triggered such a negative mentality was a "flood" of such proportions that it came to be known in the mythology of the Middle East as the Great Flood.

The Great Flood had a basis in fact. Archaeologists have noted "strata of clay apparently laid down by large inundations at Tel Fara (ancient Shuruppak, 50 km north of Uruk). Because, in Sumerian tradition, Shuruppak was the last ruling city before the flood, and Kish the first city thereafter, it was presumably the inundation attested to at Shuruppak and at Uruk and Kish at about the same time, that was the historic flood so long remembered."[18] This flood is dated between the Jemdet Nasr and Early Dynastic periods (about five thousand years ago). Abraham is dated about thirty-seven hundred years ago.

Aside from the reference to a flood in the Sumerian King List, the first real account of the event comes from Babylonian tablets. They say: "at the time when Utnapishtim was king in the old city of Shuruppak, the gods burned with anger against mankind. Enlil advised the gods in council that they should send a Great Flood to drown the human race and the gods agreed to this, promising that none of them would betray the terrible secret to any human being. But Enki, the God of the watery deeps, did not want the race of man to perish and he whispered to the reed hut where Utnapishtim lived: "Reed hut, hear me. A great flood is coming soon and Utnapishtim would be well advised to build himself a great ark and to go inside it with all his family, taking animals of every kind and leaving all his wealth behind. . . ."[19]

Utnapishtim understood Enki's words and he built the great ark, and made it watertight with bitumen. He stocked it with oil, meat, and flour, and also with wine to celebrate the feast of the New Year. And he led his family and animals of every species inside the ark and he locked the door from within. On the following day, a black cloud covered the vault of the sky. The gods beat against the sluice gates of heaven until they broke. The earth grew livid beneath the terrible flashes of lightning and the grounds splintered as a pot is shattered. The gods themselves grew afraid and slunk behind the clouds like dogs. Inanna, the goddess of love, screamed like a woman in travail: "Would that the day we decided to destroy mankind were turned to mud. My beloved people now fill the sea. It is choked with bodies as with fish spawn."[20]

For six days and seven nights the South wind raged and the deluge did not cease. It was only on the seventh day that silence returned to the earth. Utnapishtim opened the hatch in the roof of the ark and light fell upon his countenance. And he saw an island, the peak of Mount Nisir. The mountain held the ark fast and for seven days it would not let it sail away. Then Utnapishtim sent out a dove. The bird flew off and came back again, for it did find no place to rest. Next, Utnapishtim sent out a swallow and it too flew away only to return again, for it could find no resting place. Then Utnapishtim released a raven and the raven did not return. It saw a place where the waters had subsided and there it perched, ate carrion, cawed, and let its droppings fall.

So Utnapishtim and his family left the ark and made a sacrifice to the gods, who gathered like flies around the offering, drawn thither by the sweet savor of the sacrifice. Only one god was angry and that was Enlil. "There should have been no survivors," he declared. But Enki answered him: "You are too clever by half. You were too rash when you planned the total destruction of mankind. Let lions and wolves ravage them to keep their numbers down, for men are sinners. Let famine beset them. But there is one secret of the gods: they need men."

Then Enlil was won over. He stepped before Utnapishtim to thank him and he said: "'Utnapishtim was a child of men and destined to die. Now he shall be safe from death, immortal like us gods.' And the man through whom the human race was preserved was given an island at the mouth of the rivers to be his dwelling place for all time."[21]

Here we see a clear example of the bicameral mind at work. We also see here the source of the biblical story of Noah and the Great Flood from which the Hebrews, and thus Western religion, begin their account of human history. Yet there is a mystery at the very core of this story. Despite the archaeological evidence of inundation and despite the Babylonian tale of the Great Flood written at least one thousand years after the event, the Sumerian writings do not elaborate on it. Certainly, a cataclysmic event occurred which profoundly affected Sumerian thought and created another line of kingship. Yet, surprisingly, the fragments of Sumerian writings seem to indicate the cataclysm was, in fact, a firestorm and not a flood.

In his book, *The Rebel Lands: An Investigation into the Origins of Early Mesopotamian Mythology*, J. V. Kinnier Wilson makes a strong case that the personalities of the gods and goddesses of the Sumerians, which had come to shape the personalities of all subsequent Western deities and thus the temperament of Western thought in general, evolved out of an experience of a great earthquake in the Zagros Mountains, immediately east of the Mesopotamian plains.[22]

This quake, including its dust cloud and consequent oil eruptions, burning pillars of gas, winds filled with poison gas, and raging forest fires, killed many people, shook the faith of the living in their ruling deities, and gave birth to new and ominous deities who made their home in the Zagros Mountains, an area which came to be known as "the rebel lands."

The site of the earthquake, which Sumerians called Mt Ebih, is identified today as "a scar on the northern flank of the Kabir Kub" in the Sardmarreh Landslip, 160 miles east of Baghdad. Wilson says, "This scar, contained between the two jagged 'teeth' known as Filiman Kuh in the South East and Kuh Litanor in the Northwest, is 9 miles long from cliff to cliff. Between these points, a presumed earthquake has removed a mass of rock some 2 ½ miles wide and from three hundred to five hundred meters thick."[23]

The Sumerians could not understand what happened. They could only think that the mountain was being disrespectful to Inanna and that she destroyed it. In the tablet *Inanna and Ebih*, it is written that Inanna advanced against the mountain and threatened to destroy it if it did not show respect for her ("if it does not bring its nose to the earth for me," "if it does not rub its lips in the dust for me").

Apparently, the mountain remained rebellious for we are told that Inanna, "In her anger furiously she screamed, causing a great roar to break loose, the roar which filled heaven. Upon Ebih the su-stones began to move, they went thump down its side."[24]

In *Nin-me-sar ra*, Inanna is said to have also caused an oil flow: "In the form of the Great Serpent you (Inanna) deposited (oil) poison across the mountain land," and in *Inanna and Ebih*: "Now from the... great (oil) snakes began spilling forth poison one after another."

Apparently the earthquake caused great escapes of gas and oil in the foothills of the Zagros Mountains. The oil flows must have also been accompanied by combustion of escaping gas because the surrounding hills were also set on fire. In *Inanna and Ebih*, we find Inanna saying, "I will set fire to its surrounding forests, and up to its every lake will I cause Gibil, the purifier, to do his work."[25]

The people did not feel that Inanna was being presumptive in punishing the mountain. From *Enmerkar and the Lord of Aratta*, we know that the goddess held sway in the land at this time and thus would have demanded allegiance from all life from India to Mesopotamia.

Yet, in spite of Inanna's preeminence, the offense that caused the earthquake brought another deity to power in the minds of the Sumerians. This deity was Enlil. It was written:

> Enlil summons the storm; the people lament. He takes away the refreshing wind from the land; the people lament. The wind that makes men rejoice he removes from the land of Sumer and he sends the devastating

tempests. He summons the storm that destroys; the people lament. He sends the gale that lays waste. The thunderstorm that engulfs the ships like a tidal wave; the people lament. He fans the flame of the raging wind, the scorching breath of the desert. With the hurricane that destroys everything in its path, he covers the land with a black cloth. And the city falls in ruins. The narrow lanes and streets are littered with corpses like splinters of broken pots. Gates and walls gape wide; the dead lie in the squares and the fields, and the blood of the land fills the ditches as molten brass fills a mold.[26]

In the tale of the Great Flood we learned that it was Enlil who advised the Council of the gods to annihilate the human race. In stories concerning the rebel land, it is said of Enlil, "your *me* (ordinance) is a *me* which does not manifest as light. Your appearance is a divine (presence) which cannot be seen."[27] And again it is said, "when he moves (it is) by his own will in the form of a drifting cloud. Once more it is said, "In the form of a cloud along the horizon of the Great Mountain, Enlil started fire after fire."[28]

In the *Enlil Hymn* we find, "the depths of the mountain land, the sacred kissu, is your awesome residence; the Ekur, the shining house, is your vast, fear-laden dwelling place."[29]

As a consequence of this event, or events, the Sumerian people built the city of Nippur and installed Enlil as the tutelary deity. They called the ziggurat or god's house they built for him the Ekur. It represented the realm of the netherworld beneath the greatest pillar of fire, or burning jet of gas that was released by the earthquake. Perhaps here is the first reference to the underworld being a world of *fire and brimstone.* In such a way, the people paid worship to Enlil in hopes to appease his wrath. It also was a way for the priests of Enlil to share his power. In this way, they claimed the power of Enlil for their own and when their king went into battle, they told the people that he carried Enlil's weapons.

Apparently, there was more than one pillar of fire released by the earthquake because we read, "On the seven great lions you road, rising into heaven." Numerous texts refer to the seven Lion-heads of which

Ninurta, Enlil's eldest son, was the greatest of them all. Ninurta was called "primordial Lion-head, that greatly surpassed (all others)," and it was said of him, "you were the great Lion-head of the Enemy land."[30]

Ninurta, by virtue of an awesome display of unconquerable force, became in time the Sumerian's chief warrior God. The story was told how Ninurta (Ningirsu in Akkadian) gained his power by battling Anzu (Asag) who was appointed by Enlil to watch over the gates of his dwelling. Instead Anzu stole from him the Tablet of Destiny, which conferred upon its owner the office of "Enlilship" (supreme god), and made off with it to a mountain where Enlil could not reach him. One of the responsibilities of Enlil was to control the mighty nether powers that were capable of great destruction.

Put in this position, Enlil sought a champion among the gods. All declined. It was proposed that Ninurta serve as the god's champion against Anzu because Ninurta had the secret weapon, the *sibit gabli*, or the "Seven Battle Weapons." We can assume these were the seven pillars of fire caused by the earthquake.

The myth reveals how the opponents met face-to-face. In Tablet II, Anzu scorned the traditional arrows that Ninurta used against him. But in Tablet III things changed. Now we witness the result of Ninurta unleashing his secret weapon:

> The fiery brilliance (shown across the land)
> the dread fear of the Lion-head swept (over the mountain)
> Yea, the fury of its radiance enveloped the land,
> the fearfulness of it splendor swept the mountains and hills.
> (The light) by its intensity removed his sight,
> at the time that it removed it did the fire arise.
> Anzu it so disturbed, he then (easily) cut his throat,
> at the cry of the Lion-head had the fire ignited.

Who was Anzu? Anzu was described as "an enormous vulture floating with outstretched wings in the sky."[31] Archaeologists have traditionally equated him as "the thundercloud personified." Kinnier-Wilson, however, believes that he was "the dust cloud" released from the earthquake. He claims that the fact that Anzu was killed indicates that it disappeared from the sky. This seems logical for such a new force in the sky could easily have challenged Enlil and its disappearance could easily be attributed to the new force of the pillars of fire.

By comparing mythological tales, like those above, with geological findings, archaeologists have been able to determine that mythology was, like history, a means to describe real events. Unlike history, however, which does not attribute conscious motivation to nonhuman forces, mythology does. In fact, it attributes superior consciousness to natural forces because in fact, they were superior forces and humans could only understand their reason for being human in the context of these superior forces. The gods and goddesses were the immortals. By having the power to speak to humans, generation after generation, their power was enormous. By the time of the Sumerians, the gods and goddesses had come to be worshiped as an aristocracy that owned all the physical resources of the earth. Men and women were merely their serfs who worked their estates for them. The deities were endowed with human emotions and were unpredictably capricious, capable of good or evil as the mood seized them. Such spiritual helplessness describes the condition of humans who were unable to gain control of their own actions because they lacked the subjective consciousness necessary to undergird their own will. Here we can see how ancient is the impulse of human beings to blame others for our own inadequacies.

If we were able to ask the Sumerians what their reason for being human was, they would surely have said it was only to serve the gods and goddesses. This alone was why they were on earth. Such spiritual pessimism was made all the more bleak when Enlil came to power. Enlil was a ruthless god to whom human life meant nothing. It was ironic, therefore, that the worship of Enlil would lead eventually to human beings freeing themselves from being controlled by the gods. In our review of Mesopotamian history, which follows, we will witness the attempt by certain individuals to overthrow the influence of the gods and stand on their own two feet; that is, to stand on their own subjective consciousness. Unfortunately, the validation of one's subjective consciousness came about through man's attempt to mirror the ruthlessness of their chief

God, Enlil. Enlil's ruthlessness validated ruthlessness on the part of men. It was at this time, in contradiction to the established order and method of making kings, strong men emerged to seize power by virtue of their own strength. They became the first true kings, as history would understand it. As the kings justified their rule in the name of Enlil, they fought each other for territorial dominance, each impelled by his thirst for limitlessness to become Emperor of all of Sumer, then Babylonia, and ultimately the Middle East and beyond.

We will now look at some specific incidents that reveal the change in human consciousness, the consolidation of male power, the creation of fortified city-states, class struggle, and scientific warfare in the Middle East.

It is written in the Sumerian King List that after, "the Flood swept over the land, kingship again was lowered down from heaven." The King List records fourteen dynasties in Sumerian cities, which existed from 4,900 to 4,373 years ago. The size of the cities now ranged between ten and twenty thousand people. The first dynasty to be established after the "flood" was the city of Kish.

In Kish, Etana, a shepherd, became the first king. The story is told how he consulted Enlil to discover the secret of childbirth. Enlil told him that the "plant of birth" was kept in heaven. Etana was not discouraged by this answer, however. He convinced an eagle, whom he had once saved from a snake, to take him to heaven. The eagle took Etana high into the sky, but when they rose above the place where the earth could no longer be seen, Etana panicked and returned to earth without his prize. Upon entering Enlil's temple, he was told that not only must mortals work for the gods to whom they owed their existence, but they must also suffer for them. Etana bowed his head and accepted his destiny.

Exactly what this tale means cannot be determined. It may have shown the fruitlessness of men trying to know women's secrets (the plant and the snake are both matriarchal symbols), or it may have shown the futility of men trying to achieve divine powers. Whatever its intent, two things are clear from this tale. Men now were very curious about childbirth and Enlil was now the God whom men consulted. As for Etana, he gained a reputation for great wisdom, so that even Solomon in the Bible was compared to him. Little else is known about the first dynasty of Kish except that the last two kings dedicated new temples to the god Enlil.

The Emergence of Subjective Consciousness

Gilgamesh the God-King

In the first dynasty of Uruk, which followed that of Kish, many tales were told of a strong man named Gilgamesh (forty-eight hundred years ago), the son of Lugalanda, who achieved great deeds and was even so bold as to seek immortality for himself, a status which his contemporaries knew was only reserved for the deities. In the *Epic of Gilgamesh*, it is possible to see a man who overcame the bicameral consciousness of his day and achieved an integrated sense of his own self (i.e., a subjective consciousness). The deeds of Gilgamesh lived in the memory of the Mesopotamian people for more than two thousand years. Gilgamesh became a hero not only to the Sumerians but also to the Babylonians, Assyrians, Hurrians, and Hittites.

The *Epic of Gilgamesh* opens with a lament by the people of Uruk over the hardships they endured for decades in the building of a great wall around the city. Gilgamesh wanted to make the city impregnable to attack. So strong were the walls of Uruk that contemporary archaeologists were astonished to find the city of Uruk with the walls still standing. They reached more than eight miles in length, are twenty feet high and fifteen feet wide.[32] Here was no small undertaking dated nearly twenty-eight hundred years before Christ.

So great was Gilgamesh in strength and ferocity that the people believed he was two-thirds a god and only one-third human. So relentless was he in his demands of the people that they complained directly to Anu, the god of the skies, to stop Gilgamesh. In answer to their supplication, it was said, Anu created a man equal in stature to Gilgamesh, a man named Enkidu, who dwelt in the steppes as a hunter. He was uncivilized, however, and considered a wild man. A priestess was sent to him and she presented herself to him naked. He was aroused by her and made love to her. This was the ancient way of saying that he had the virility to be a king. She took him back to Uruk and taught him the ways of the city. One day at a marriage ceremony, in which Gilgamesh as king had first rights to the bride on her wedding night, Enkidu chose this opportunity to challenge Gilgamesh to a fight. During a vicious brawl in which neither succumbed, they stopped to marvel at the other's strength and became fast friends. Enkidu finally admitted that it was right that Enlil had given kingship to Gilgamesh.

This episode sanctioned in the minds of the people the transference of the male role of sacred king under matriarchy to the new role of monarch under patriarchy. Men of both beliefs could be friends, and kings were now accepted as rulers on earth by virtue of their own right, not simply as a consort to the goddess.

As the story continues, Gilgamesh led Enkidu to his mother, Ninsun, and said, "Here is another son for you, who is invincible." Emboldened by his new friendship, Gilgamesh then proposed the idea to Enkidu that they enter the *rebel land* and kill the monster Humbaba, who was one of the seven pillars of the fire unleashed by the earthquake.

We know from an early composition called the *Lugalbanda hurrumkurra*, that Lugalbanda, who was Gilgamesh's father and predecessor as the King of Uruk, had led an army into the rebel land only to die there, apparently from gas poisoning. The composition tells how the Army advanced into the rebel land:

> Uruk's advance (re-created) the Flood storm,
> Kullab's advance was the cloud covered heaven;
> as the dense cloud (of dust) at the time of the landslide
> so their dust rose to heaven.

And of Lugalbanda's death it is written:

> His eyes which kept filling from the swollen tear ducts
> the brave Lugalbanda was still opening and shutting
> Yet he died
> They lifted up his dropping neck but there was no sign
> of breath.[33]

When Gilgamesh suggested a return to the rebel land, Enkidu balked. He said, "When I used to wander through the cedar forest with the beasts, I saw Humbaba. His roar is like the deluge, his jaws are fire, his breath is death. No one can overcome him. Why do you seek certain death for your portion. Enlil himself has commanded Humbaba to guard the cedars. Whoever enters that forest will be paralyzed with fear. His grave is dug."[34]

Gilgamesh's response to Enkidu was classic. It inspired kings and warriors for millennia. He said, "Which of us can climb to heaven? That is only for the gods who reign there forever. Man is but a breath of wind that blows. But is that a reason to shrink away from death and to shun danger? I shall challenge Humbaba to fight me, I shall fell the cedars that are his pride. And if I fall, my name will endure. I want to make a name for myself."[35]

Hearing this, Enkidu agreed to go. Gilgamesh went to his mother, the priestess Ninsun, and she offered sacrifice and beseeched the Sun God to intercede on her son's behalf. The men also offered sacrifices before they departed. Upon reaching the forest, Gilgamesh had a series of dreams, all of which were interpreted by Enkidu as indications that Gilgamesh would be victorious over Humbaba.

It is written that as the men approached Humbaba, they cut down a great tree to enrage him. Shaken by his appearance, however, they shrunk back. The Sun God encouraged them to fight, however, and eight winds seized Humbaba and trapped him so he could not move. Then Gilgamesh and Enkidu threw a net over the monster and killed him. Exactly what this means is unclear, but apparently, Gilgamesh was able to extinguish one of the burning pillars. In fact, Shulgi, the King of Ur (4029 - 3982 BC) credits him with extinguishing all the fires. He addresses Gilgamesh by saying:

> Oh mighty one of the battle array, who destroyed the rebel city,
> Who struck down the Battle Weapons one after the other,
> Against that Asag who with his (oil) poison
> infested the pure ranges of the mountain land,
> Even against the house of Kish you send forth your Weapon

> (Yea), that seven-headed Lionhead you took your
> stand upon his corpse,
> Even Enmebaragesi, King of Kish,
> You set your foot upon his head as upon a snake.[36]

Gilgamesh's conquest of Humbaba so impressed Inanna, the goddess of love, that she said to him, "be my husband and your country will prosper." But Gilgamesh spurned the goddess, accusing her of being unfaithful to her husband Dumuzi. He said, "to which husband are you faithful? You are an unfinished door that does not keep out the wind, you are pitch that defiles the carrier, you are a jewel that entices the enemy into the land."[37]

Such disrespect for Inanna, most likely the high priestess of Uruk, indicates that Gilgamesh came to power not as a representative or son of Dumuzi in an annual marriage of the sacred king with Inanna as Queen, but instead, out of his own power justified as the will of Enlil. Here we recognize a clear departure from the tradition of matriarchy and the rise of patriarchal political power based upon "might makes right."

We are told that Inanna was outraged by these words and she called Gugalanna, the Bull of Heaven, to attack Uruk. When he snorted great fissures opened up in the ground and many people fell into these chasms and were crushed to death. But despite people's fear and suffering, Gilgamesh remained unbowed. In another attack, however, it is said that Inanna struck Enkidu with a grave illness and he died cursing his fate.

Gilgamesh mourned his friend's death for seven days and seven nights and after Enkidu was buried, Gilgamesh had a vision of his friend returned from the kingdom of the dead with only ghastly things to report. Gilgamesh became horror stricken by looking at the putrefied flesh of his dead friend, and in a panic he resolved to find Utnapishtim, the immortal survivor of the Flood and discover from him the secret of everlasting life. He was not successful, however. Apparently, even though Gilgamesh and his followers had seized political power, they were still unable to develop a worldview strong enough to challenge the matriarchal culture.

We are told that after many adventures, Gilgamesh found Utnapishtim, who told him that only he had been granted immortality for having saved the human race. Gilgamesh insisted that he know the secret of immortality too. When Utnapishtim relented, it was only to reveal to Gilgamesh the magic "Rose" of eternal life. But the Rose was stolen from Gilgamesh on his journey home by a serpent. Here again we find reference to the matriarchal symbol of the Goddess and the belief that only the serpent was immortal because it had the ability to shed its skin and thus be reborn without having to sojourn into the land of the dead.

Also revealing, it is written that on his travels to meet Utnapishtim, Gilgamesh met the Goddess disguised as an innkeeper, (i.e., the one who dispenses the Wine of Immortality to the gods). She counseled him to abandon his search for immortality and to take pleasure in the good things of life while he could—to eat and drink, to play with his children, to make love to his wife and to "make every day a festival."[38] This is what Gilgamesh ultimately did. He returned to Uruk and seeing the walls of the city that he had built, joy returned to his heart.

The strength and fearlessness of Gilgamesh, his willingness to challenge the established order and to seek immortality for himself, inspired the warrior kings for millennia. We even find a part of the Gilgamesh epic in the Bible (Eccl 9:7-9). Ironically, it refers to the counsel that the Goddess had given Gilgamesh concerning how to enjoy the good life.

Undoubtedly, male scribes romanticized the legend of Gilgamesh over the course of time. Evidence also suggests that the tale became more personalized and more self-conscious.[39] Even so, Gilgamesh was clearly an exception to the way people thought in his day about life, death, and immortality. This will become obvious as we now examine the evidence discovered from the first dynasty of Ur, which followed Gilgamesh's dynasty of Uruk.

The Priest Class

By the end of the Early Dynastic Period, around forty-four hundred years ago, a male priesthood had emerged to help the king carry out his religious and civic duties. As we have seen everywhere, this group of male intellectuals in the name of a divinity came to organize themselves as a separate social class. In Sumer, we are told, ". . . they controlled the taxes and the produce of the harvest, they were responsible for work in the fields, along with canals and in the workshops and they laid down the penalties for any shortcomings or failure to perform one's duty. For it was considered a sin; that is, an offense against the divine order of things, if someone was lazy or secretly obtained an advantage at someone else's expense. The priests distributed the new 'lots' to decide which field would be allocated to whom for cultivation, and they threatened the disobedient with terrible punishments, the most dire of which would be inflicted after death. All this they did in the name of the King."[40] In doing so they created the mold for all the priest classes to follow. Now the priests had the power to punish people in the afterlife and thereby control their souls.

By now, most kings of the city-states were driven to become supreme rulers of all of Sumer. Goaded by their nobles and priests, they were more and more likely to be found at the head of their troops than inside their temples. This left the machinery of civil government dependent upon the priests who came to have more power over the people. In time, the high priest and the king became rivals. Service to the gods receded into the background while personal wealth and power became more of a motivation. Subjective consciousness was establishing its place on the world stage and the "I" wanted more.

In the city of Lagash at this time, we have a clear example of conflict between the warrior and the priest mentality and also for the first time between the emerging merchant mentality as each vied for power over the state.

After the death of a previous king (name unknown), two high priests in succession ascended the throne. Under their rule, the priests began to flagrantly abuse their power of office, charging high fees for their duties. The second of these high priests was powerful enough to bequeath the kingship to his son, Lugalanda (approximately forty-four hundred years ago).[41]

Lugalanda, the Greedy King

Lugalanda demonstrated no religious pretense whatsoever. He was only interested in wealth. Immediately upon taking office, he seized the most important temples, those of the gods Ningirsu (the god of Lagash), Shulshag (the grand-daughter of Enlil and the goddess of Umma), and the goddess Bau (who was also called Gula).[42] He placed one of his henchmen over them, who was not a priest, and appointed himself and his wife, Baranamtarra, and other family members as Temple administrators. Having taken the temples, he no longer mentioned the names of the deities in temple documents and referred to the temples as his own private property. He levied taxes on the priesthood and, as a result, he and his wife became the largest landowners. Baranamtarra, who also held enormous power, managing her own estates and those of the Temple of Bau. She traded corn, cattle, timber, and jewelry with neighboring states. She also bought and sold slaves.[43]

Lugalanda, driven by the thirst for material wealth, also began to assert control over others' lands as well. Boatmen, shepherds, fishermen, and farmers all groaned under heavy taxation and the confiscation of their goods. As Lugalanda grew richer, the poor grew poorer.

Lugalanda represented something new in history. He was not a warrior, nor was he a priest. He did not rule by virtue of his own physical force, or through mental force. Rather, he ruled by virtue of controlling the physical wealth. While people with a merchant psychology had existed since the beginning of human existence, never had anyone with this psychology ruled a nation. Lugalanda had the mentality of a capitalist and once in power, he created the same conditions that are attributable to a capitalist society today.

Lugalanda, like Gilgamesh, was ahead of his time. He rejected the gods, and acted under his own volition. Unlike Gilgamesh, however, he was not driven by a quest for personal glory, but rather by the quest of possessing limitless wealth. His reign was short, however, only nine years and then a hero of the people arose.

Urukagina and Basic Legal Rights

His name was Urukagina. With the help of the people and the priest class, Urukagina overthrew Lugalanda and declared himself King (lugal). We are told:

> When Ningirus, Enlil's successor, gave the kingship to Urukagina, whose hand he had grasped from among the thirty-six thousand people in the city, this King restored freedom once more and obeyed the commands that Ningirsu gave him. He liberated the boatmen and the shepherds, the herdsmen and the fishermen from those who had seized the control of boats and herds and ponds. The unnecessary overseers were removed from the storehouses, and the tax collectors from the villages. A man who had a sheep sheared need pay no more shearing tax, even if the wool was white; whoever prepared perfumed oil and sold it need no longer pay the oil tax. When a dead man was buried, the surviving kin need pay the priest only three jugs of beer instead of seven, and only eight roles of bread instead of four hundred and twenty, and for the religious service, the payment expected would be at most a young goat, or perhaps a pig. No priest might force his way into the garden of a poor man any longer. If a poor man's ass foaled and the rich man wanted to defraud the owner by buying it for a ridiculous sum, the poor man could now say, 'I want so and so much for it!' And he would be given what seemed to him a fair price in good coin.[44]

We are also told that Urukagina returned all the fields and houses that Lugalanda had stolen from the gods and from the people. With this act, Urukagina became as a king of old, both warrior-prince and priest who governed at the god's behest.

Urukagina's reforms, proclaimed in his edicts, are the earliest documented effort to establish basic legal rights for citizens.[45]

We are told that he "established the freedom" for the citizens of Lagash. Here, for the first time in recorded history, the word *freedom* (amargi) was used. Freedom, however, did not apply to all people in Lagash. It did not apply to the slaves. Evidence suggests that all slaves at this time were women. Urukagina's wife, for example, had 150 female slaves to help with the housework. Apparently, the men had still not yet learned how to take other men captive and control them effectively.

While Urukagina was busy with internal reforms, the King of Umma, a rival city, was making his bid for emperor of all of Sumer. His name was Lugalzaggesi. He attacked Lagash, killed Urukagina, and defeated his army. Once inside the city walls, his army burned the Temple of Ningirsu and took away its gold, silver, and precious jewels.

Lugalzaggesi and Scientific Warfare

It is Lugalzaggesi's claim to fame that he had introduced the process of scientific warfare. In it, he devised a way to use male slaves for the first time in history. It was quite simple. The conquered cities were made to supply soldiers for the wars to follow. First, he took Uruk, then Ur, and in succession, Larsa, Shuruppak, Kish, Nippur, Eridu, and Mari. When he had accomplished this, he declared:

> Lugalzaggesi, inspired by the gods, chosen by Enlil for the kingship over the whole of Sumer, subdued the lands from the rising to the setting sun. He smooth the ways for the God from the lower to the upper sea. He made the people dwell in safety and he watered the land with the waters of joy.

To Anu, the god of the skies, he addressed the following prayer:

> Add life to my life and let the land of Sumer blossom. Let the breasts of heaven overflow! Let the good fate which the gods have ordained for me remain mine for ever. Let me remain always as the shepherd at the head of my flock![46]

Anu did not listen to Lugalzaggesi's prayer. The people of Sumer hated him for his ruthlessness. After twenty-five years, he was defeated by a man called Sargon. Sargon destroyed Lugalzaggesi's army, took him prisoner, and put him on display in a cage in front of the shrine of Enlil in Nippur.

Sargon was not a Sumerian. He was a Semite, an Akkadian. As such, none of the Sumerian cities were worthy to be his capital. He built himself a new city, which he called Akkad, to be his headquarters. From here he would become "Lord of the four quarters of the earth."

The Akkadians and King Sargon

In 2371 BC, after fourteen successive dynasties, the Sumerian city-states had now fallen to their northern Semitic neighbors, the Akkadians, under the leadership of King Sargon.

The region of Akkad was the northern plain of Mesopotamia in present-day Iraq. From here, the Akkadian kings established their control over all of Mesopotamia. Despite differences in race, language, and political control, Mesopotamian civilization, as created by the Sumerians, remained essentially the same. The fundamental religious ideas remained intact. The Akkadians also adopted the Sumerian style of architecture and records of law and government.

Following are the reigns of the successive Akkadian kings:

Name	Years of Reign	Date (BC)
Sargon	56	2371-2316
Rimush	9	2315-2307
Manishtushu	15	2306-2292
Naram-Sin	37	2291-2255
Sharkalisharri	25	2254-2230

The legend of Sargon, available in the New Babylonian and New Assyrian fragments, revealed that Sargon ("the legitimate king"), whose father was unknown and whose mother was a "changeling" (servant or one who was part spirit), was put in a River in a basket of rushes. Akki, the goddess of Akkad, drew him out and made him a gardener (priest). Here we see the Great Goddess in the role of "water-drawer," who brought gods to birth out of the primal deep. In such a way, the pharaoh's daughter would draw

Moses out of the Nile, and, later Acca Larentia would draw Romulus and Remus out of the water to found the city of Rome.

Sargon had served as cupbearer to Ur-Zababa, a Sumerian king of the Fourth Dynasty of Kish. Evidently he rejected this service, and then raised an army and defeated one Sumerian city-state after another. In defeating Lugalzagesi of Uruk, he established his rule over Akkad and Sumer. Then he attacked and conquered Amurru to the West, Elam to the East, and Subartu to the north. In so doing, he created the first international empire the ancient Middle East had known. Rule of a city-state, followed by rule of a nation (same people), had now expanded to include an international empire. The pattern was set for patriarchal and warrior (ksattriyan) dominance.

After Sargon's death, inscriptions revealed that "Rimush and Manishtushu, respectively the younger and older sons of Sargon, and his successors in turn, faced revolts. Rimush fought against Kaku, King of Ur, and the warriors of many cities of Sumer; Manishtushu speaks of rebellion by all the countries his father had left him."[47]

This is a unique statement, not so much because it reveals that revolts occurred against the empire, but because it speaks of the king having two sons. We know that the word *son* was used to indicate a descendant next in line for the role of sacred king, but the fact that here two sons are named seems to indicate that actual paternity was meant. Yet paternity could still have meant simply an owner of the queen's offspring, rather than actual knowledge of biological parenthood on the part of the father.

Mythological stories at this time revealed that knowledge of childbirth was going through a transition. No longer is the Goddess, or women in general, considered the sole creators of life. In *Enki and Ninmah*; for example, the oldest Sumerian record that deals with the subject of childbirth, Ninmah (the Goddess) is given credit for forming life out of clay without a male being physically involved. Yet Enki is credited with providing the *idea* of giving birth.

Again, in the *Atrahasis*, an Akkadian myth, Nintur (Ninmah) is credited with creating humans from clay and blood while Enki again is credited with having the idea of creation.

However, in the second part of *Enki and Ninmah*, apparently written during the New Sumerian period (2112 – 2004 BC), Enki is directly involved in the physical process of giving birth. It is said that he *creates* the embryo, while the goddess matures it and gives birth to it. This understanding was a revolution in thought. After one hundred and twenty-five thousand years of being homo sapiens, the connection was finally made only four thousand years ago that men played a part in the creation of human life. Men had finally made the connection between planting a seed in the earth and planting their seed in a woman's body. Semen now became a sacred substance.

By 1000 BC, with patriarchy in full force, the Babylonian myth, *Enuma elish,* was created by the Babylonian priest class. Having its roots in the Sumerian myth of Enki, we now have Marduk, the Babylonian city god, kill the Great Goddess Tiamat. Out of Tiamat's corpse, Marduk creates the heavens and the earth and appoints gods to various duties. He also takes the Tablets of Destiny, thus legitimizing his reign.[48]

Having said this, at the time of Sargon, who preceded the New Sumerian Period, it is still difficult to tell whether men actually understood biological parenthood. Yet we can certainly say they were making a bid for women's power and that the king's ability to transfer authority to his son by virtue of his own volition was a major step in this direction.

While Sargon's sons spent their lives putting down revolts and gained little glory in history, it was Sargon's grandson, Naram-Sin (2254–2218 BC) who would add significantly to the emergence of patriarchal society. Naram-Sin, the son of Manishtushu, gained a place in history by being the first Mesopotamian king to claim he personally was a god. By doing so, he challenged the bicameral consciousness head-on. From being a slave of a god, to the sacred king, to becoming a god in the afterlife, to attaining actual kingship, to Gilgamesh's attempting to become immortal, we now have a king during his own life declaring himself an immortal god. The title he assumed for himself was "The divine Naram-Sin, the mighty, the God of Akkad, king of the four quarters."[49] While being the first king in the Middle East to declare himself an immortal god, he was not the first king in the world to do so. For reference, the pharaohs of Egypt had begun to equate themselves with gods from the time of the Second Dynasty of Egypt, which began around 2890 BC. The first Egyptian king to do so was King Raneb.[50]

Naram-Sin was a great warrior and extended his grandfather's empire considerably. He marched north into Asia Minor. Along the way, he conquered the city of Ebla. This is noteworthy because, at the time, it was said that Ebla was a city of two hundred and sixty thousand inhabitants and the center of a kingdom that controlled much of Syria and Palestine. In all likelihood, this population number was a gross exaggeration, nonetheless it testifies to the importance of Elba as a city-state. Ancient texts revealed the names of six of the kings of Ebla, one of whom was Ebrum, linguistically similar to Eber, the ancient ancestor of the Hebrews (Gen 10:21).[51] In the Torah, Eber was a descendant of Noah's son Shem, the father of the Semitic people.

Yet for all his accomplishments, Naram-Sin would be damned in the history of his own people for his blasphemy. By claiming his own divinity, a result we may assume of his having gained subjective consciousness, he broke with the structure of the bicameral society over which he ruled and was judged by Akkadian priests as the one who destroyed the Akkadian people. In the *Curse of Akkad*, composed perhaps a century after Naram-Sin, it is written that originally Enlil gave Sargon rule over Akkad, while Inanna dwelt in her shrine in the city and all was prosperous. During the reign of Naram-Sin, however, the gods withdrew their favor and the city suffered. At first, we are told, Naram-Sin accepted his reversal of fortune humbly, but then defied the voice of Enlil, marched against his city Nippu, and destroyed Ekur, the sacred temple of Enlil. For this outrage, Enlil supposedly brought the Gutian tribes down from the Zagros Mountains in the northeast to destroy the Akkadian Empire. We are told that these Aryan tribes were:

> [an] uncontrollable people [who] covered the earth in vast numbers like locusts. Communications were disrupted, cities struck down, agriculture ruined, and famine and death prevailed. Finally some of the great gods uttered a curse upon Akkad, evidently that the city might suffer a worse fate than it had inflicted upon Nippur. Then would Enlil be satisfied and the rest of the land be saved. So Akkad became an uninhabitable ruin.

> On its canal boat tow-paths... no one walks among the
> wild goats and darting snakes.... Akkad is destroyed.[52]

Although the Gutian invasion did not occur in Naram-Sin's lifetime, he was held responsible for it because of his disrespect for the gods and by holding himself up to their status.

Naram-Sin's son, Sharkalisharri, tried to make amends by rebuilding Ekur, the temple precinct of Enlil and by fighting off the Gutians. He also fought a battle with the Amorites (Babylonians) in the North. Yet, what was loosed could not be taken back. The dangerous idea of personal godhood, which Naram-Sin introduced, wreaked havoc among the Akkadian hierarchy. Sharkalisharri was killed by his priests and the Empire spun into chaos.

After him, the Sumerian King List asks "Who was king? Who was not king?" Four men are named who ruled for only three years. Then two more, with longer reigns of twenty-one years and fifteen years, but of whom little is known. Then, it appears, the Sumerians regained control briefly with the Fourth Dynasty of Uruk. Five kings ruled for thirty-five years before the Gutian hordes again descended from the mountains, but this time they came to stay. Their rule lasted for nearly one hundred years. But because so little is known about them, this period is known simply as the Post-Akkadian period. It lasted from 2230 to 2112 BC.

In 2112 BC, the Sumerians, under King Utukegal of the Fifth Dynasty of Uruk, again drove out the Gutians, After King Utukegal died in the battle, King Ur-Nammu, reestablished Sumerian rule over Mesopotamia under the Third Dynasty of Ur.

Name	Years of Reign	Date (BC)
Ur-Nammu	18	2112-2095
Shulgi, son of Ur-Nammu	48	2194-2047
Amar-Sin, son of Shulgi	9	2046-2038
Shu-Sin, son of Shulgi	9	2037-2029
Ibbi-Sin, son of Shu-Sin	25	2028-2004

Ur-Nammu and the Code of Law

Ur-Nammu, the first of five kings in the Third Dynasty of Ur, chose the modest title "King of Sumer and Akkad" and spent his reign constructing great religious architecture in honor of the gods and goddesses. Building inscriptions of Ur-Nammu have been found not only at Ur, but also at Uruk, Nippur, Eridu, and Larsa.[53] At Nippur, he fully refurbished the ancient Temple of Enlil, which Naram-Sin had destroyed and Sharkalisharri had reconstructed. At Uruk, Ur-Nammu built a ziggurat to Inanna, and at Ur, his capital city, he built his mightiest known monument, the ziggurat to Nanna the moon god.

Ur-Nammu, more the intellectual than the warrior, also put forth a code of laws. This code is predated only by the law code of Ebla, the city mentioned above. Each regulation dealt with a specific case—a specific sexual offense, physical injury, property crime, etc.,—and described both the offending action and the penalty. This format became the norm for almost all ancient laws thereafter.

It is unknown how Ur-Nammu died, but he was followed by his son, Shulgi, who was followed by his son, Amar-Sin, and so forth through two more generations. It is noteworthy that, in contrast to his father's simple title, Shulgi and all succeeding generations of Sumerian kings claimed to be personally "divine" and to "rule the four quarters." Apparently, the ideological battle unleashed by Naram-Sin was lost on the Sumerians. Subjective consciousness was again making claims on power reserved for the "gods." Such a profound psychic urge changed the way the Sumerians worshiped. Shulgi completed the ziggurat of Nanna at Ur and continued his father's architectural work. According to text from several sites, however, Shulgi was "probably honored as a God with temples and offerings, both within his lifetime and afterwards."[54] At Ur, he also built a great mausoleum to his father. Later his son, Amar-Sin, would add a tomb for Shulgi, and Shu-Sin would add one for Amar-Sin.

The Royal Tombs of Ur

In the city of Ur, sacred dwelling place of the Moon Goddess Nanna, there was a great cemetery. In this cemetery, archaeologists went into the royal tombs of Ur and made a discovery that shocked the scientific world.

Upon entering the first tomb, they found the skeletons of six soldiers, their copper daggers still at their waists. As they went deeper into the tomb beyond the soldiers, they found ten women in two rows. All had headdresses of gold, lapis lazuli, and carnelian. Beyond them, they found a beautiful harp, a bull's head with eyes of gold, and then a queen's carriage, decorated in red, white, and blue mosaic with a lion's head of gold. In front of the carriage were the skeletons of the two asses that had drawn it and beside it a collection of tools, weapons, and vessels made of copper, silver, gold, marble, and volcanic glass. Also nearby lay a golden saw and the rotting remains of a wooden chest.

When archaeologists removed the chest, they found a brick vault below. A ramp led down to it with six soldiers in two rows at its foot. In front of the soldiers were two large wagons, one before the other, each drawn by three oxen.

Against the far wall, nine women lay, each wearing a headdress of gold and beads. The entire space between these woman and the wagons was crowded with men and women still draped in their jewelry. Along the side of the vault, which led to an arched doorway, more women and soldiers carrying daggers were found. Apparently, these women were musicians for they were accompanied by more harps. There were also more bulls' heads and shell plaques engraved with "grotesque scenes of animals playing the parts of men."

Behind the arched doorway, the archaeologists discovered what they called the king's burial chamber. The skeletons of several minor people were found, but the king, whose name A-bar-gi was written on a cylinder seal, was not found.

As they continued their search, archaeologists found another chamber at the end of which they found the queen's skeleton completely covered in jewelry made from gems and precious metals. On a cylinder seal they found her name, Shubad. Two women in attendance were crouched against the bier on which the queen's body had rested. Twenty-three more bodies were also found in the chamber with the queen.

What conclusion could be reached from this incredible discovery? According to Sir Leonard Woolley who made the discovery, "Clearly, when a royal person died, he or she was accompanied to the grave by all the members of the court; the king had at least three people with him in his chamber and sixty-two in the death-pit; the queen was content with some twenty-five in all."[55]

On face value, the people had apparently drunk a poison from the vessels that were found beside the carriage and, having done so, took up their respective positions. They listened to the musicians for a while and were entertained by court jesters until being overcome by the poison. Then they laid down, one by one, and went to sleep forever. Perhaps, some others then came along, straightened out the bodies, touched up their hair and clothing, and sealed the tomb, leaving the entire assembly to its eternal fate.

As astonishing as this burial site was, the grave was not unique. Archaeologists discovered another sixteen such graves at Ur in which royal personages were buried with their entire court. In none of these graves did they see any sign of panic or violence.[56] Therefore, we can assume that the willingness of the court and royal servants to follow their king and queen into death reflected their belief that they had no will of her own. They had been created for the service of their human deities and were governed by the deities' decisions. When the king or queen died, it meant that the deity had decided to leave and thus his or her servants also left to attend him or her in the next life. As Woolley concludes, "If the king, then, was a god, he did not die as men die, but was translated; and it might therefore be not a hardship but a privilege for those of his court to accompany their master and continue in his service."[57]

A question remains, however, concerning the composition of the grave we just described. That is, what happened to the king's body? Woolley does not say. Others have proposed that his body was ritually removed as part of another wedding service with the goddess. Perhaps. But perhaps there never was a king's body. Rather, what we witnessed was the burial of the queen. It was she who was the highest personage in the city of Ur. With the name A-bar-gi, there was no title found. But the cylinder in the queen's chamber gave Shubad the title Nin, the term reserved for a goddess. Other burials show the king being buried with the same treatment, however, indicating that men were of the same status as women at this time. In fact, the kings were becoming more powerful all the time. While the women maintained cultural dominance and remained active in temple and palace rituals, the men were coming to dominate political affairs, especially the defense of the city and expansion of the state. The worldview of "might makes right" had taken hold.

These kings were buried with their entire courts, as we have previously noted, as were other courts of the kings and queens at Ur who were eager to travel with their deities to a new immortality. The burial rites of Egyptian pharaohs, at the time, also included the sacrifices of servants and loyal courtiers; yet the sheer size of the burials at Ur surprised the archeologists.

While the Sumerian kings and the courts of Ur were preoccupied with their psycho-spiritual pursuits, their enemies were inexorably taking bites out of their territory. By the time of Ibbi-Sin (2028 to 2004 BC), who was the last Sumerian King, only the city-state of Ur remained, the rest were lost to local rulers who claimed to be independent rulers, or who gave up their allegiance to the divine Ibbi-Sin to become servants of local deities.

Jack Finegan, in his *Archaeological History of the Ancient Middle East,* explains:

> The final blow came with the fall of Ur. That blow was delivered by the Elamites and the Su, who stormed down out of the hills, sacked the capital city, and carried off Ibbi-Sin captive to Anshan. A long Sumerian lamentation, on more than 30 tablets and fragments found for the most part at Nippur and Ur, recalls the earlier enemies – the Gutians from the East and the Tidnum people, the Amorites, from the West – and narrates in sad detail the final downfall at the hands of the Su people and the Elamites. The deities Nanna and Ningal his wife departed from the city, and the people were so hard beset by weapons without and famine within that they flung

open the gates to the attackers. Ur was shattered like a potter's vessel, and 'in its midst there was uttered nothing but laments and dirges'. So the destruction remained in the history of local remembrance as a classical picture of national downfall. In the excavation of Ur, in fact, every building of the Third Dynasty bore the marks of violent overthrow. Later kings rebuilt many of the monuments, but Ur was never again of great importance. The Sumerians themselves gradually disappeared from the scene of military and political affairs in Mesopotamia, although their influence in literature and thought continued to be felt for a long time.[58]

Here we may note that before 2000 BC, the last Sumerian King was taken captive to Anshan. Anshan was a city in the land of the Aryan Persians. Yet, it would be another seventeen hundred years before the Persian Emperor Cyrus would sweep over Mesopotamia to create the largest Empire the world had ever known.

With the obliteration of the Sumerian empire, Mesopotamia was reduced to many small kingdoms, most no larger than the cities in which the kings lived. Yet once the mentality of patriarchy had evolved, fueled by the urge for political power, wealth, and female slaves, it could not be reversed. Male power, based on brute force and justified, either by reference to the ruthless behavior of Enlil or by one's own limitless quest for personal glory, was now in full force. War between city-states again quickly expanded into wars between nations. In this process, vast empires again emerged and fell, this time more quickly due to the implementation of "scientific" warfare. In Mesopotamia, the following empires would rise and fall in succession:

Empire	Period of Reign	Number of Years
Akkadians	2371-2230 BC	141
Gutians	2230-2112 BC	118
Sumerians	2112-2004 BC	108

Babylonians/ Amorites	2004-1595 BC	409
Hittites	1595-1115 BC	470
Assyrians	1115-612 BC	503
Chaldeans	612-539 BC	73
Persians	539-331 BC	208

The Babylonians and Marduk, the God of gods

After several years of decentralization, following the destruction of the Sumerian empire in 2004 BC, many city-states vied for control of Mesopotamia. The Amorites finally succeeded. Their capital was the city that the Akkadians called Bab-ilu (Gate of God), and thus, the Amorites came to be known in history as the Babylonians. The Babylonians, like the Akkadians, followed the great cultural tradition of the Sumerian empire. In studying Babylonian values, we can see that they were still largely in the bicameral mind-set. Yet, while they maintained the same relationship with their deities, as did the Sumerians, certain things changed to reflect their own unique culture.

In the Babylonian creation myth; for example, Marduk, a new deity, emerges to claim the highest place among the gods and goddesses. Marduk is the city god of Babylon. In *Enuma elish*, which historian's call the *Epic of Marduk* or the *Epic of Creation*, it is written how Apsu (the Sumerian Abzu, the primeval abyss of sweet water beneath the earth) and Tiamat (literally "mother goddess", the primeval ocean of saltwater) were the father and mother of all the gods and goddesses. They became annoyed with the behavior of their offspring and decided to kill them. The god Ea perceived the plan and slew Apsu. Tiamat became furious and all the more resolved in her purpose. Into the fray, stepped Marduk, son of Ea and city god of Babylon. Like other origin myths of male gods, Marduk was also a storm God. He destroyed Tiamat with lightning and hurricanes and divided her into heaven and earth. Then he placed Anu, Enlil, and Ea in their roles as guardians of the sky, the air, and the earth respectively. Marduk then established the constellations and caused the moon to wax and wane. Then, out of the blood of Kingu, leader of the hosts of Tiamat, he created humans to be the slaves of the gods. They were made to build Esagila, the great Temple complex of Marduk at Babylon, which included the ziggurat that the Bible called the "Tower of Babel (Gen 11:1-9)."

After Marduk's victory, the Babylonian priest class lauded him by telling the people how all the deities joined together in a great banquet to sing the praises of Marduk and to confer on him fifty names, which were the powers and attributes of previous deities:

> Ninurta is Marduk of the hoe,
> Nergal is Marduk of the attack,
> Zababa is Marduk of the hand to hand fight,
> Enlil is Marduk of Lordship and counsel,
> Nabu is Marduk of accounting,
> Sin is Marduk the illuminator of the night,
> Shamash is Marduk of justice,
> Adad is Marduk of rains. . . .[59]

The story concludes: "let the wise and the knowing discuss the 50 names together. Let the father recite them and impart them to his son."[60]

In this epic, we see the tendency toward the creation of the one, true God (monotheism), which Western tradition to this day tells us is the product of the Jews. We can see that this tendency toward ethnic monotheism has its origins in the attempt by the priests of ruling cities to place their chief god above all other gods and thus undergird their own supreme authority in the minds of men. In such a way, the Assyrians would have Assur, their chief god, destroy Marduk and take his supreme place, when they came into dominance later in history.

In the *Epic of Marduk,* we recognize these specific evolutionary changes: the complete overthrow of the Great Goddess; the overthrow of Enlil as the chief male deity of Mesopotamia; the making of Marduk into a supreme deity and finally, the creation of the universe by a sole male deity.

To solidify these thoughts in the minds of the people, the *Epic of Marduk* was enacted with great pomp and ceremony at the great festival of the New Year, which occurred at each spring equinox. From what historians have been able to deduce, the New Year festival, so central to Sumerian ritual, remained so for the Babylonians as well. We are told that for three days purification ceremonies took place consisting of ablutions and prayers. On the fourth day, the entire *Epic of Marduk* was enacted. On the fifth day, after further purifications, we are told that Nabu (the god of accounting) arrived from Borsippa to join in the ceremonies. This signified that business now played an important role in Babylonian culture and deserved ritual attention. By saying that Nabu arrived from Borsippa is meant that his idol, in whom the spirit resided, was carried by citizens of that city to Babylon.

Also on the fifth day, the King of Babylon made his appearance. In a ceremony based upon the ancient ritual of the sacred king, he was humiliated and slapped and made to kneel before the statue of Marduk to assure him that he has served him well in the past year. The more harshly the king was treated the better, because tears in the king's eyes were pleasing to Marduk. In the evening, a ceremony was held in which a white bull was sacrificed as a substitute for the king.

In the remaining days, a procession took place in which the king took the hand of Marduk; that is, took the idol's hand and led him from his shrine outside the city, along the Professional Way into the city. This symbolized the king's role as servant of Marduk and also the entrance of Marduk into the city for the coming year.

Finally, the Sacred Marriage was enacted between the King and the Queen as it had been since time immemorial. Now, however, Inanna and Dumuzi were called Ishtar and Tammuz. Such adherence to religious ritual by the ruling class reinforced the bicameral consciousness of the Babylonians and assured social order.

The God of My Father

The common people also followed the same tradition in their personal lives. As with the Sumerians and Akkadians, each Babylonian had his own personal god or goddess to whom he offered prayers and sacrifices, and whose duty it was to intercede for him with the other gods and to protect him against the evil spirits with which the universe was believed to be inhabited, and against whom even the gods were not immune. If something bad befell a man, it was a sure sign that he had been neglectful in worshipping his personal god. In this way, the personal gods, served as "guardian angels" to the Babylonian people.[61]

For the Babylonians, each deity resided in a statue or idol. The statues used in rituals were believed to be the embodiments of the deities themselves. Consequently, it was also believed that if the festivals were not observed and if Marduk and his divine family court were not cared for, he would leave his shrine and chaos would result. The main reason that Marduk stayed in his statue at Esagil was that his worship was maintained there. Thus, we can begin to see how the intellectuals in the role of priest caretakers began to have more power in society.

In the Babylonian society, it fell upon the priest class to care for Marduk and the court and to help interpret the deity's commands. Just as soldiering was crucial to Babylonian society, so also was the maintaining of deities.

The common people's personal deities also had to be worshiped. If they were not washed and fed and cared for, they would leave a man's home and tragedy would follow in its wake.

When a man died, he passed his gods to his son. This practice became one of the cornerstones of patriarchal society. Personal worship of a family's god, who was "the god of my father," became directed by a man's children and his children's children in successive generations."[62] In this way, religious dogma and superstition became firmly implanted in the minds of men through each successive generation. Yet, even as the age-old mentalities of warrior and priest, and their corresponding social classes, held power, another mentality was developing in the collective psychology. It behooves us to say a few words about the people who embodied this new form of power. We are talking here about the emergence of the business mind as developed by the earliest merchants, traders, bankers, accountants, and manufacturers.

Hammurabi's Code

Under the leadership of Hammurabi, the sixth king of the First Dynasty (around 1800 BC), the Babylonians consolidated their empire. In an attempt to manage the activity of his far-flung empire, he organized the laws of the land into a written form, which became known as Hammurabi's Code. From this code and from other sources, a picture of Babylonian business can be put together.

The Temple of each city owned the land, grains, slaves, animals, and jewels. It also served as a bank for the surplus production of the city. From this situation, the first bankers and businessmen emerged from the priests of the Temple. While agriculture was the base of the economy, artisans also made household items and fashioned objects from metals and precious stones. The surplus of all production was available for trade. Cities by now had come to serve the function of trading posts. Trade routes stretched from Mesopotamia to India and China in the East and to the Mediterranean in the West. Out of this extensive trade, business practices evolve which became the foundation of Western business practices in general—legal partnerships, business letters, lawsuits, interest rates, precious metals as standards of weight and measure, the designation of personal and real property, rights represented in deeds, wills, leases, and contracts, promissory notes, insurance, etc.

Hammurabi's Code was an attempt to regulate such practices. The Code regulated ownership and the leasing of land; it authorized legal partnerships; it punished dishonest practices; it permitted loans of grain and silver with interest; and it fixed prices. It also fixed the wages of apprentices and allowed for fines and other punishments for poor workmanship.

The Code also dealt with crimes against persons and property. For purposes of law, people were classified as nobles, commoners, and slaves. From the very beginning of the formulation of state laws, therefore, we witness the designation of social classes to allow special privileges for those who ruled. The law of *lex talionis* (an eye for an eye) became the first motive of law in the Middle East, but it took different forms depending upon which class member was offended. For example, if a man destroyed a noble's eye, his eye was plucked out in retaliation. If he destroyed a commoner's eye, however, he only paid a pound of silver. If he destroyed a slave's eye, he paid the price of a new slave.[63]

Hammurabi's Code also gives us an insight into the relations between men and women at the time. We have mentioned that slaves existed during Sumerian times and that men enslaved women before they learned how to enslave men. The process of turning free persons into slaves has always required physical terror and coercion. In regard to male dominance of women, this was accomplished by rape. Women were subdued physically by rape and if impregnated they became psychologically attached to their masters as well. In this manner, the institution of *concubinage* evolved and became the social institution for integrating captive women into the households of their captors. This assured their loyalty to their "master" as well as his possession of her children.[64]

For the Babylonians, a master had rights over the labor as well as the body of his female slaves. He, or any member of his family, could have sex with her without obligation. She could also be hired out as a prostitute for a fixed price with the master collecting her pay. This practice was pervasive not only in Mesopotamia but also throughout the ancient patriarchal world, and, sadly, this same practice reaches into modern society as well.

Looking at this practice closely we can see how it provided the conceptual model for the creation of slavery as an institution. Once men had discovered a means to control captive women physically and psychologically, they were eventually able to do so with men and to justify their behavior in "divinely" sanctioned law codes. These laws, in turn, institutionalized and legitimize the practice of slavery for millennia—the codes of each successive civilization building on the language of the former. While the practice of slavery exists mostly underground today, the socio-psychic imbalances of sexism, racism, and classism, which buttressed the practice of slavery for all those years, are still with us today and provide a large part of our collective social programming. Such attitudes remain the bulwark of patriarchy and inhibit the formation of a truly human society.

As Gerda Lerner points out regarding the Code:

> A man unable to satisfy a debt could pledge his wife and
> his children, his concubines and their children and his

slaves. He could do this in two ways: either by giving his dependents as a pledge for a loan he took from a merchant in order to repay his debt or by outright sale of his debt pledge. In the first case, the relative could be redeemed within a certain period of time in exchange for the money lent, but if the debtor failed to repay his debt, the pledges became ordinary slaves, liable to resale by the new owner. In the second case, the debt pledge became a slave immediately. The physical abuse of debt slaves was curtailed by Hammurabi Code #116 (HC116), which states that if a debt pledge who was a free man's son died from ill-treatment in the creditors house, and if such ill-treatment could be proven, the creditor's son was killed. But if the debt pledge was a slave and not freeborn, a money fine was to be levied, and the debt was to be extinguished. The clear implication of this law is that any man's son was expendable for his father's crime and the children enjoyed even fewer rights than did debt pledges. The fact that no mention is made of penalties in the case of the mistreatment of female debt pledges indicates that there mistreatment was regarded with greater equanimity. On the other hand, the Code of Hammurabi (HC117) actually marks an improvement in the condition of debt slaves by limiting the service of the wife and children of a debtor to three years, after which they were to go free. In earlier practice they could be held for life. HC119 specified that a man who gave his slave concubine, who had borne his sons, as a debt pledge even in outright sale had the right to redeem her from the new purchaser by repaying the purchase price. While these provisions mark a certain improvement in the lot of female debt pledges, they were enacted to protect the rights of husbands (debtors) against the rights of creditors. Two basic assumptions underlying these laws remain untouched; that male kin have the right of disposal over their female relatives and that a man's wife and children are part of his property to be disposed of as such.⁶⁵

Babylonian law, as exemplified in the Code of Hammurabi, had a profound impact on the future development of Western civilization. It laid down the foundations of patriarchal society for all subsequent Western cultures. These laws feature patrilineal descent (the family name is now traced through the father instead of the mother) and property laws that guaranteed the inheritance rights of sons. The laws guarantee male dominance in property relations, sexual relations, and in military, political, and religious bureaucracies. All these, in turn, are supported by, and constantly recreated by the patriarchal family.

Marriages are still property relations now arranged by the father of the groom and the father of the bride. A bride price continues to seal the marriage. The groom's father would pay the bride's father a betrothal gift and a bridal gift after which the couple was considered betrothed, but the bride stayed in her father's house until the marriage was completed by sexual union. After the marriage had been consummated, the father of the bride gave her a dowry. During the marriage the husband managed the dowry, but if he died, and there was something left, it reverted to his wife for her use. When she died, her sons inherited it.

The laws, however, offered a woman a measure of protection. For example, if a husband divorced his wife and married another, the first wife was entitled to stay in his house and enjoy lifelong support or to leave him and take her dowry with her.⁶⁶

In further support of women, marriage contracts could be drawn up allowing the wife certain property rights and specifying the conditions for her rights in case of separation. They could also save her from being liable to enslavement for her husband's debt incurred prior to marriage.

Such marriage laws required strict supervision of girls to assure premarital chastity. Strong family control over the selection of marriage partners strengthened the tendency for marriage between people of the same economic class.

Yet, while the wife enjoyed economic privileges similar to her husband in the interest of ruling class stability, she remained sexually subservient to her husband. Adultery was a crime that only a wife could commit against her husband, not vice versa. Adultery was only a violation against the husband's property rights. Therefore, he alone was the injured party and his wife could be subject to the death penalty.

Babylonian law gave the husband the right to put his wife and her sexual partner to death. Middle Assyrian Law (MAL15) stated these principles more graphically: "if the husband spares his wife's life and cuts off the nose of his wife, he shall turn the man into a eunuch; and they shall disfigure his whole face. But if he spares his wife, he shall also acquit the man."[67] Hittites laws (197 and 198) provided the same penalties and specified the husband's choice. Jewish law, on the other hand, required that "the adulterer and the adulteress shall surely be put to death (Lev 20:10)."

There were also laws against rape where the wife or daughter was an innocent victim. Yet, these laws also demonstrate that the wronged party was not considered to be the woman, but rather her husband or father. Assyrian law (MAL155-156) deals specifically with the rape of a virgin daughter by a married man:

> The father of the virgin shall take the wife of the ravisher of the virgin and give her to be dishonored; he shall not give her back to her husband but shall take her. The father shall give his daughter who has been ravished as a spouse to her ravisher.[68]

The law goes on to specify that if the rapist has no wife, he must pay the price of a virgin to the father, marry the girl, and never be able to divorce her. If the girl's father does not agree to this, he takes the money and gives his daughter to whomever he pleases. Nowhere do we find any mention of compensation for the woman who is the victim. In fact, a raped virgin becomes the property of the rapist!

Assyrian law, which came later, was much more brutal pertaining to women than Babylonian law. Whether this was indicative of the natural evolution of patriarchal society in the ancient Middle East, or of a more repressive Assyrians social culture, it is difficult to say. In either case, the continued degeneration of the status of women in society cannot be denied. MAL51 of the Assyrian law states that if the flogging of a man's wife has been ordered by law, it must be carried out in public. MAL58 states that all legally inflicted punishments of wives, such as tearing out of the breasts and cutting off the nose or ears, must be carried out by an official. MAL59 states that apart from those legally prescribed penalties "a man may scourge his wife, pluck her hair, may bruise and destroy her ears. There is no liability therefore."[69]

This happens to be the last law on the clay tablets on which Middle Assyrian Laws 1–59 were inscribed. It demonstrates the roots of a repressive attitude toward women from which Middle Eastern society and, in fact, Western civilization, has yet to recover. The Assyrians carried the brutal dysfunction of patriarchy to its extreme. They ruled Mesopotamia for over 500 years and their behavior, thoughts, and emotions, passed on by the sons of subsequent generations, helped form contemporary attitudes so ingrained in us that we consider them to be "natural"; that is, above question. They have become our inherited programming of what we consider to be "real." This remains especially true in Middle Eastern society today. As for Western civilization as a whole, our philosophy of *might makes right*, our attitude of male superiority, our mythology of survival of the fittest, our sexism, racism, classism, and imperialism were all given a major impetus by the Assyrian culture.

The Minoans

Before we continue our history of the Middle East and take a closer look at the role that the Assyrian empire played in history, it is necessary to interrupt our exploration of Mesopotamia and the Middle East and to divert our story to the island of Crete in the eastern Mediterranean Sea.

It was at the time, that the Minoan civilization flourished. While the Minoans are little known and little regarded by historians, we need to examine them for two reasons. Firstly, the Minoan civilization was the last great matriarchal civilization that existed well into the patriarchal period. As such, it provides us with a different model of how human beings can organize themselves, instead of the ubiquitous patriarchal warring city-states.

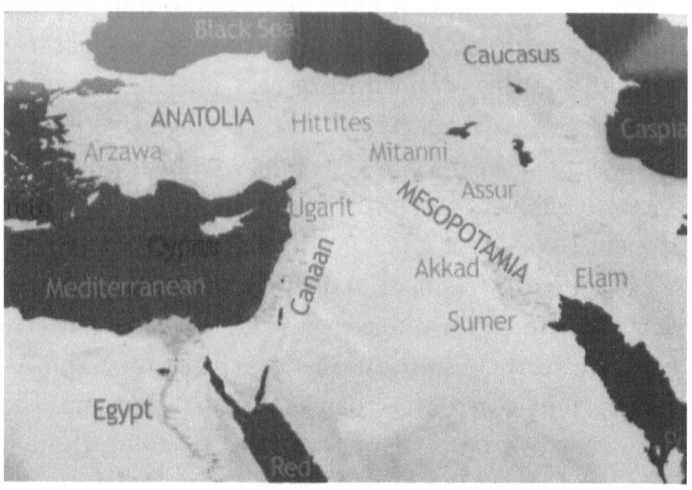

Map 2-2: Eastern Mediterranean

The second reason we want to look at the Minoan civilization, which existed on Crete and a few smaller islands nearby, was that a series of natural disasters, including the volcanic eruption on the island of Thera, occurred there between 1600 to 1200 BC that were of such magnitude that the entire eastern Mediterranean and Near East were thrown into a Dark Age. These events gave rise to a situation that comes closest to our collective nightmare of a zombie apocalypse. The civilizations and empires of Egypt, Mesopotamia, Greece, Anatolia, and the islands of the Aegean Sea were hurled into chaos as a consequence. Millions of people lost access to the basic necessities of food, water, shelter, and clothing. Survivors of the explosion turned into roving bands of scavengers moving across all borders. War parties and hostile tribes from inland regions came to pick the carcass clean. In this environment of horror and total destruction, the gods and goddesses stopped speaking to human beings. The earthquake that crashed the Zagros Mountains and brought the dark god Enlil to power was insignificant compared to this. The explosion of Thera and other natural disasters rocked the known world and the aftermath was so disruptive to human psychology that it left everyone speechless. It was an unspeakable horror. And as such the gods and goddesses stopped speaking to people. This trauma was so all-encompassing that it radically shifted the structure of human consciousness itself. The disasters ended a million years of the bicameral mind in which the gods and goddesses had spoken to human beings commanding us what to do. In its place, the child-like chirping of *I, me, mine* was given voice. The feeling of "I" and "I do," which had previously been felt by a few exceptions like Gilgamesh, was now the only option available to people. While it provided a great leap in human consciousness, it also gave rise to lies, deceptions, mistrust, murder, and chaos as far as the eye could see.

So what exactly happened? What was the Minoan civilization? And even though it altered the course of human evolution, why do we know so little about it?

The Last Great Matriarchal Civilization

The Minoan civilization inhabited the small group of islands of Thera, Crete, Santorini, and possibly Atlantis.[70] It was one of the oldest civilizations on earth. These islands had been occupied as early as 128,000 BC, when the human species was just coming into being. The Minoan civilization certainly ranks among the earliest agricultural civilizations, along with the Indus Valley, Mesopotamia, and Egypt.

As early as 3000 BC, several Minoan cities located in these Aegean islands developed into centers of commerce and trade. They traded saffron, frankincense, pepper, tin, copper, silver, and gold jewelry. They also produced beautiful crafts that were desired by the peoples of Turkey (Anatolia), Egypt, Greece, and the Middle East.

At the time, the Minoans had the most advanced society that the western world had ever seen. The Greeks were so awed by them that they copied much of their culture. The Greek myth of the *Minotaur* (half man and half bull) describes the Minoan priests who wore the heads of bulls in their religious services. The *labyrinth* was a sacred cave near the city of Knossos on the isle of Crete.

The Minoans maintained the matriarchal order thousands of years after the advent of patriarchy. It remained matriarchal longer than any other civilization and, as such, provides us with a remarkable model of what society might have looked like if matriarchy had continued to remain the dominant culture on the planet.

We know that the culture was matriarchal because of the exclusive worship of the Great Goddess and the pictures of female priestesses who led the worship services. Their religion had advanced far beyond fertility rituals. It was now a religion of a sophisticated palatial culture whose rituals addressed gender identity, rites of passage, and death. The Mother Goddess was also known as the Mistress of Animals, the protector of cities, the household, the harvest, the underworld, and more.

The symbols for males were bullhorns, the double-headed axe, the pillar, the sun, and the tree. The symbols for women and the Goddess were the serpent, birds, and the poppy flower.

There is evidence of human sacrifice that dates before 1425 BC, which was probably a manifestation of sacred king rituals. But there was no such sacrifice after this time.

Neither archeologists, anthropologists, nor historians have found evidence that the Minoans engaged in warfare—nothing before the coming of the patriarchal Greeks (Myceneans) who descended on this civilization after 1200 BC when it was already in chaos due to the volcanic eruption. In fact, after much debate among scientists about fortifications, weapons, and other articles that could be used for war, archeologist Olga Krzsykowski states, "The stark fact is that for the prehistoric Aegean, we have no direct evidence for war and warfare per se."[71]

There is no evidence of a Minoan army, nor Minoan domination of any outside people. This is significant because the Minoans also had a script that dates back to 3000 BC. As the earliest script devised by Europeans, it never was used to glorify tales of conquests of other peoples. This is another indicator that the Minoans were matriarchal rather than patriarchal in structure and policy.

Riane Eisler in her book *The Chalice and the Blade: Our History, Our Future* gives us an inside look at this ancient culture.[72] It appears that when archeologists discovered the ancient civilization of Crete sometime in the 1930s, it completely astonished them. As archeologist Nicolas Platon, who has spent over fifty years excavating the islands, stated: "Archeologists were dumbfounded. They could not understand how the very existence of such a highly developed civilization could have remained unsuspected until then." Platon writes:

> From the start, amazing discoveries were made." As work progressed, vast multi-storied palaces, villas, farmsteads, districts of populous and well-organized cities, harbor installations, networks of roads crossing the island from end to end, organized places of worship and planned burial grounds were brought to light. [73]

According to Eisler, Cretan civilization began around 6000 BC when a small group of colonists, probably from Anatolia (Turkey), settled on the shores of the islands. They brought the Great Goddess with them as well as their agrarian technology. For the next four to five thousand years, until its destruction, there was a slow and steady progress in the making of pottery, weaving, metallurgy, engraving, architecture, and other crafts, as well as the development of far flung trade routes.

Along with their industry, a "lively and joyful" artistic style evolved. In approximately 2000 BC, the Cretans began building their famous palace complexes. While war-like male gods were replacing the Great Goddess in Asia and the Middle East, she still held a place in Egypt as Hathor and Isis, in Canaan as Astarte, in Babylonia as Ishtar, and as the Goddess Arianna in Anatolia.

Even so, in these empires, she reigned as a secondary deity. In Crete, however, she remained supreme, the one Great Goddess. The worship of a loving Goddess and the existence of the matriarchal order created a prosperous economy, a vibrant culture, and a peaceful nation.

For the first and last time in human history, the world believed in and worshiped Mother Nature, the source of all creation and harmony. In this civilization, men and women stood as equal participants in life. According to Platon, the culture reflected "delight in beauty, grace and movement" in its "enjoyment of life and closeness to nature." [74]

Sir Leonard Woolley, who discovered the tombs in Sumer, describes Minoan art as "the most inspired in the ancient world." [75]

In stark contrast to the patriarchal societies of its day, one remarkable feature of Cretan society was the equitable sharing of wealth.

Fig. 2-1: Great Goddess

Platon reports that "The standard of living – even of peasants – seems to have been high, none of the homes found so far have suggested very poor living conditions."[76]

While the basis of social organization was the matriarchal clan, sometime around 2000 BC, the society became more centralized. Remarkably, this did not bring with it autocratic rule. No armies were required to keep the ruling class in place. Technology was not *owned* and hoarded by the upper class. In fact, the great palaces were not the private homes of the queens and kings, but rather great civic centers where all the organizations of society had their headquarters and places for expression. The palaces had hundreds of rooms with apartments arranged around a central courtyard. There were storehouses and vast halls for receptions, banquets, and council meetings. Gardens existed within the palace and the walls, floors, and ceiling were decorated with art. Subject matter was drawn from plants and nature, religious ceremonies, court life, and the lives of people. There were no grandiose paintings of conquest or hunting scenes.

Fig 2-2: Exterior of the Palace of Knossos

Fig. 2-3: Interior of the Palace of Knossos

And what of the men? What was life like for them? The men of the Minoan civilization lived the dream of modern men. They had good, well-paying and secure jobs in a wide selection of fields—agriculture, commerce, manufacturing, banking, urban planning, architecture, ship building, mining, construction, etc. For recreation, they watched sports, played sports and looked at women. And apparently the women did not mind being looked at because the men did not carry the attitude of predators. There are no pictures of women being dragged by their hair. Apparently, the women had a healthy sexuality if we can judge from clothing that exposed their breasts.

The men were not what Arnold Schwarzenegger called "girlie men" either. They were extremely athletic and in good shape. They strengthened themselves in martial sports like wrestling and boxing, but their favorite pastime was "bull-leaping," a sport they shared with women. See the picture below.

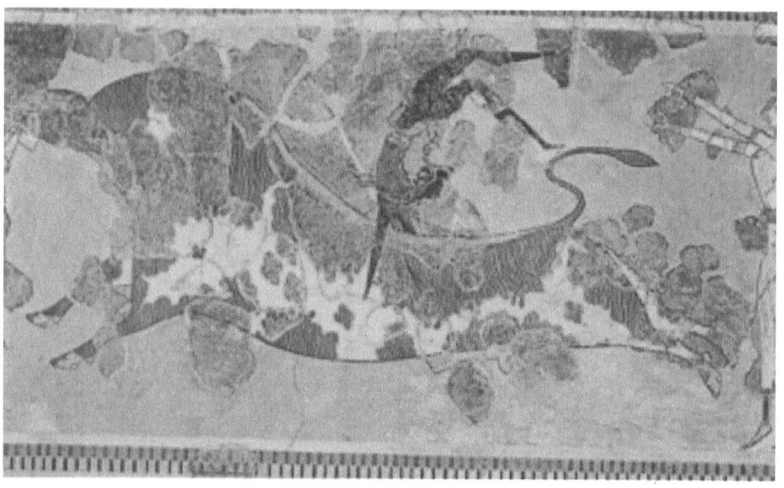

Fig. 2-4: Bull-leaping fresco, found in Knossos palace, Crete, Greece dating around 1600-1450 BCE

What we call democracy—the belief that government should represent the interests of the people—existed in Crete long before the Greeks gave expression to it. It seems safe to say that the Greeks learned their lessons from the Minoans. In Crete, the creation of a centralized bureaucracy (the state), did not depend upon warfare, hierarchy, and the subjugation of women in order to prosper.

The Cretans did not institute laws to dominate and suppress, rather they used them to improve living conditions. "All the urban centers had perfect drainage systems, sanitary installations, and domestic conveniences." There is also evidence of large-scale irrigation works with canals to distribute water to farms.

The Minoan civilization, although it existed and then disappeared over 3,000 years ago, provides us with a model of society that stands as a beacon of hope even today. No civilization before or since has reached such a pinnacle of human progress. In fact, it defies the linear logic that society is becoming more civilized as we move forward in time. The Minoans created a society of partnership and equality between men and women; a society that respected the natural world; and a society that believed in a divinity that was universal and loving.

To examine the Minoan civilization is to realize that the life we seek as human beings—one of peace and prosperity, living in harmony with nature and with each other—is not to be achieved by the patriarchal order. To recreate the virtues of Minoa, we must develop a society in which women play an equal role or perhaps even a greater role in creating a sustainable future.

Nonetheless, for all its grace and beauty, its peace and prosperity, the Minoan civilization came to an abrupt end, not by internal corruption or outside conquest but ironically by a natural disaster of unimaginable scope. Here is what happened.

The Volcano of Thera

While there were no recorded eyewitnesses to the event, geologists, exploring the evidence, conclude that a volcano exploded with such magnitude that scientists believe it was the worst natural disaster ever experienced by human beings. The eruption alone had a blast equivalent of several hundred nuclear bombs exploding simultaneously in a tiny spot in the Mediterranean Sea. This blast immediately scorched the island of Thera (Santorini), igniting buildings, forests, and farmland. While there is evidence that the people on the island evacuated before the explosion, many died on other islands and coastal settlements as well as on ships. Many more were victims of the tsunamis that followed the collapse of the volcano as it sunk below sea level.

The tsunami, with waves as high as one hundred feet, raced through the Mediterranean Sea destroying the Minoan fleet and any nearby fleets or ships unfortunate to be on the water at that time. It washed away entire settlements and cities along the coastline of the sea.

The explosion was so great that it sent an ash plume into the stratosphere. The magma and rock that was ejected from the explosion would have filled an area twenty-four cubic miles. The sound was heard thousands of miles away. When Mt Krakatoa exploded in the late nineteenth century in Indonesia, it was heard three thousand miles away while the explosion on Thera was five times as powerful. Certainly, the explosion was heard throughout Europe, Africa, the Middle East, and into South Asia. Even today you can barely put your hand on the surface of one of the islands because of the remaining heat from the volcanic eruption.

Fig 2-5: A Volcanic Explosion

Because of the massive amounts of sulfur dioxide that spouted into the atmosphere, survivors faced several years of cold, wet summers that destroyed the agriculture of the region. Famine sent millions of shocked and sunken-eyed immigrants into the unknown interiors of Anatolia, the Near East, and the Middle East seeking shelter. They became the victims of scavenging war parties and the kings who believed that they had to stop the immigrant invasion at all costs or see their empires fall.

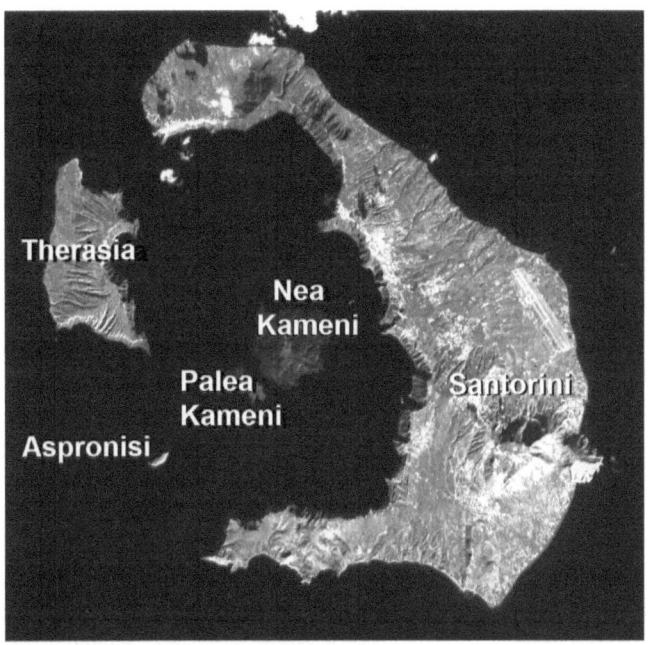

Map 2-3: Santorini: the Caldera Left From the Volcanic Explosion on Thera

The Minoan culture that had dominated the eastern Mediterranean Sea was destroyed. In less than fifty years it was completely gone. However, it was not just the Minoan civilization that fell. The mighty Hittite Empire, which controlled Anatolia and the eastern coast of the Mediterranean, including Syria and Canaan, also collapsed under the pressure of immigrants coming up through Lydia into Anatolia and further east, through Canaan and Syria.

The Mycenaean culture of ancient Greece was also destroyed. During the Dark Age that followed the explosion—because their population was dramatically reduced—the Greeks abandoned their major settlements, with the exception of Athens. Like so many others, they were turned into refugees, living in small groups constantly on the move. They became nomads and sheep herders, suspicious of strangers, and ever alert to war parties and hostile tribes. During this period, they lost their script and no longer kept records. It was not until hundreds of years later, around 750 BC, that they relearned how to write.[77] Only now they used the Phoenician alphabet, which included vowels. The Greek version of the alphabet eventually formed the base of the alphabet we use in western civilization today.

It was during this period that historians believe the Dorians, Aryan tribes who lived in the north, came down and invaded Greece. The Dorians were a war-like people who had mastered the use of iron for weapons. This invention completely changed warfare tactics from chariot wars to infantry wars and resulted in greater human casualties.

The Dorians settled in Sicily and Macedonia, and, after some time, set up sea routes in the Mediterranean to replace the destroyed routes that had existed before the volcanic explosion. From a study of language, scientists know that they also colonized Crete after the fall of the Minoan civilization. Eventually, a Dorian emperor, who came to be called *Alexander the Great*, would make his way across the Mediterranean, Middle East, and into India. In so doing, he would create the largest empire the world had ever known.

It is most likely that the natural disasters also destroyed the Egyptian Empire, which collapsed within the next fifty years. This occurred during the reign of Ramses VI. The Egyptians wrote on the Merneptah Stele, which was produced around the time of the explosion, about attacks from Libyans and other tribes called Ekwesh, Shekelesh, Lukka, Shardana, and Tursha. They spoke of a Canaanite revolt in the cities of Ashkelon. The stele even mentions the people of Israel, not as a kingdom but as a "people." This is the first historical record that references Israel.

Let us return now to the Middle East, for we have still much to learn about what happened there. Of greatest interest, perhaps, is the origin of the Jewish people, but they will come later in time. For now, at the time of the volcanic eruption, the Assyrian empire was beginning to expand.

The Gods Stop Talking

As the chaos, in the wake of the volcanic eruption, earthquakes, and droughts, swept over the land, the religious tradition based on bicameral consciousness quickly shriveled. This is clearly reflected around 1230 BC, when Tukulti-Ninurta I, king of Assyria, had a stone altar made that was dramatically different from anything previously made in history. As Julian Jaynes describes it:

> In the carving on its face, Tukulti is shown twice, first as he approaches the throne of his god, and then as he kneels before. The very double image fairly shouts aloud about this beggarly posture unheard of in a king before in history. As our eyes descend from the standing king to the kneeling king just in front of him, it is as emphatic as a moving picture, in itself a quite remarkable artistic discovery. But far more remarkable is the fact that the throne before which this first of the cruel Assyrian conquerors grovels is empty. No king before in history is ever shown kneeling. No scene before in history ever indicated an absent god. The bicameral mind had broken down.[78]

Fig. 2-6: Altar with King Tukulti-Ninurta I Showing the Absent God

The carving above described by Jaynes, is certainly symbolic of a very dramatic change in human consciousness. The belief that goddesses and gods controlled our behavior by speaking their commands in our minds had existed since the dawn of human consciousness. But now it was obliterated by the event on the island of Thera. We cannot say it was completely dead, because men and women, including the Jewish prophets, would continue to claim that they heard the voice of the gods for hundreds of years afterwards. Yet, Thera dealt this old consciousness a mortal wound.

According to Julian Jaynes, the breakdown of the bicameral mind was the psychological counterpart of the biological "involuntary inhibition of the temporal lobe areas of the right hemisphere" of the brain.[79] Jaynes proposed that in the bicameral mind there was an area on the right side of the brain that he called the "hallucinatory area" that was connected to the Wernicke's area on the left side of the brain by the "anterior commissure." The "hallucinatory area" organized admonitory experiences and coded them into "voices" that were then "heard over the anterior commissure by the left brain Wernicke's area. Because the environmental conditions caused by the volcano and its aftermath were so extreme, the right side of the brain lost its ability to process and organize admonitory warnings and thus these warning could no longer be codified into voices that could be "heard" by the left side of the brain.[80]

By this process, people no longer heard the voices of the gods and goddesses in their minds. There was only confusion and silence. This biological change was perhaps the last great event in the physical evolution of the human species. It set the stage for the development of subjective consciousness. Modern people do not have a developed "hallucinatory area" except that it still exists in the brains of schizophrenics, who still hear voices in their head telling them what to do.

The change in the brain, accelerated by the zombie holocaust of Thera, set humanity on a new course. Out of the ashes, a new life emerged so different psychologically from what preceded it that there was hardly any continuity of consciousness between the two. The explosion set in motion a three hundred year Dark Age. And out of this condition, human survival skills were raised to a new height, which honed and sharpened the sword of patriarchal rule. Not only the gods, but also the goddesses stopped speaking to men. Now the men were free to completely disrespect the feminine aspect and dominate women without restraint. And so they did. The fundamental tenets of the new mindset that emerged out of the ancient Dark Age has changed very little over the last three thousand years. Men's innate sense of superiority exists, in large part, because of this time, as misguided as it is.

The Beginning of the "I-feeling"

It is necessary to digress at this time from our march through history and look at how the consciousness of men and women split after the breakdown of the bicameral mind. The purpose of this history is not to account for events per se, but to determine how those events affected our consciousness and set the stage for our programming today.

Most men and women do not understand the difference in the way our brains tend to work. We may say "Viva la difference!" However, when this difference is not understood nor respected by men and women, we hinder our progress as human beings.

Women's consciousness tends to be embedded in the old order and derives primarily from the right side of the brain. Men's consciousness is largely a product of the left side of the brain, which came into dominance with the linear logic of patriarchy. Human consciousness, therefore, is divided most profoundly at this level and cannot be synthesized unless we are able to overcome our programming.

This can only be done by understanding how our brains work and how it came to be that women think like women and men think like men. It will not serve humanity to continually create one-sided people (i.e., "the man's man" and "the airy fairy earth mother"). Rather, both men and women must understand themselves at a deeper level than gender; that is, as human beings. If we can begin to identity with our humanity more than our gender, we will be able to synthesize both the holistic and analytical perspectives of our consciousness. We will see the whole *and* the parts, and not just one or the other. Look at the illustration below to understand this point.[81] Our institutions of learning should be obligated to teach our children how to think both ways. It is in this direction that our hope for the future lies.

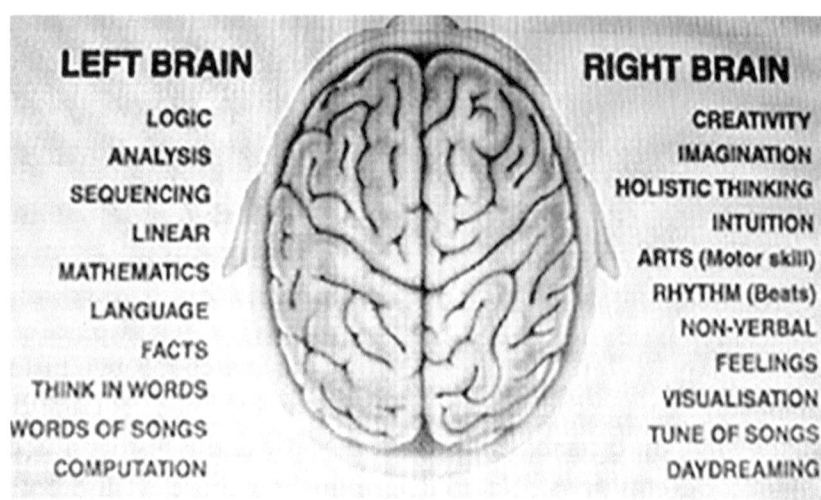

Fig. 2-7: Functions of the Left and Right Brain

When men and women could no longer hear the voices of the gods and goddesses in their mind it was very frightening. For humans to have their gods abandon them at a time when they needed them most was extremely traumatic. The literature of the period from 1300 to 1000 BC is filled with references of men being abandoned by their gods:

> One who has no god as he walks along the street,
> Headache envelops him like a garment.[82]

This condition, which began to affect all men, is best illustrated by the words on a tablet called *Ludlul bel nemegi* ("I will praise the Lord who controls misfortune"). In this story, a feudal lord named Shubshi-Meshre-Shakken complains:

> My god has forsaken me and disappeared,
> My goddess has failed me and keeps at a distance.
> The good angel who walked beside me has departed.[83]

With the departure of his deities, Shubshi describes how his god became angry with him and how he lost control over his city and became a social outcast and the target of disease and misfortune. He offered sacrifices and prayers but:

> My god has not come to the rescue in taking me by the hand,
> Nor has my goddess shown pity on me by going at my side.[84]

Finally, the angels of Marduk appeared to him in a dream with consolation and promises of prosperity. At this assurance, Shubshi goes to the Temple of Marduk to give thanks.

Here, as Jaynes points out, one of the major themes of Western religion is sounded for the first time. "Why have the gods left us? Like friends who depart from us, they must be offended. Our misfortunes are our punishments for our offenses. We go down on our knees, begging to be forgiven. And then find redemption in some return of the word of god."[85]

Thus began the mentality that dominates Western religions to this day. From its inception, the loss of god as an authority figure created a split in the Western mind. For some it meant the beginning of self-consciousness as a basis of motivation, for others it meant the creation of techniques to make the gods speak again. Such methods included the reading of omens, the casting of lots, augury, rituals, prayers, and spontaneous divination.

If the divinations proved successful, it meant that the results were caused by the gods, whose intentions were being interpreted. Such exopsychic methods of determining the will of the gods was an artifact of bicameral thinking that proliferated in the second and first millennium BC, giving rise to larger and stronger priest classes, who put themselves between man and god so that men eventually forgot the time when the gods or goddesses spoke directly to them.

In addition to the priests in the cities, certain wandering nomads also rose among Middle Eastern peoples, claiming that they still heard the word of god clearly. These were the prophets preaching fire and brimstone in a predominantly schizophrenic age.

Generally speaking, we can say that the western tradition of divination made its way into contemporary thought through the religion of the Jews, who were just beginning to make their appearance on the world stage at the time of the volcanic eruption on Thera. The Jews believed that the gods had abandoned the civilizations of their day because they had worshipped false gods. Understandably, the Jews believed that they alone worshipped the true god.

The Threshold of Subjective Thought

The threshold of subjective thought can be witnessed in the change of writing on cuneiform tablets from the time of the Babylonians to that of the Assyrians.

The skill of reading developed through the process of hallucinating the voices of idols, to hearing pictographs. Before the modern alphabet had evolved, cuneiform tablets were *heard* rather than read. Thus the Babylonian tablets were always addressed as if they had a voice of their own. The following letter of Hammurabi; for example, reads:

> Unto Sin-idinnam say: thus says Hammurabi. I wrote you telling you to send Enubi-Marduk to me. Why, then, haven't you sent him? When you see this tablet, send Enubi-Marduk into my presence. See that he travels night and day, that he may arrive swiftly.[86]

This letter is factual, concrete, behavioristic, formalistic, commanding, and without greeting. The words, "Unto Sin-idinnam say," demonstrates that it is the tablet itself that is being addressed and not the recipient (Sin-idinnam). There is no indication of a subjective relationship at this time between those involved.

About one thousand years later, however, Assyrian letters are rife with "deceit and divination, speaking of police investigations, complaints of lapsing ritual, paranoid fears, bribery, and the pathetic appeals of imprisoned officers. All these things were unknown, unmentioned, and impossible in the bicameral world of Hammurabi."[87]

In a letter from an Assyrian king to his nobles in Babylon in 670 BC, we even find sarcasm:

> Word of the king to the pseudo-Babylonians. I am well. ... You, so help you heaven, have turned yourself into Babylonians! And you keep bringing up against my servants charges – fake charges – which you and your master have concocted... The document (nothing but windy words and importunities!) Which you have sent to me, I am returning to you, after replacing it into its seals. Of course you will say, "What is he sending back to us?" From the Babylonians, my servants and my friends are writing me: when I open and read, behold, the goodness of shrines, birds of sin. . . . [88]

How far subjective consciousness had come!

Assyria and the Dark Age

While the ensuing Dark Age (1200 to 900 BC) engulfed the entire Near East, North Africa, the Caucasus, Mediterranean, and Balkan regions, spreading social upheaval and mass movements of people, Assyria was in a stronger position at this time than its potential rivals. [89]

Because they were located inland and buffered by Canaan and Syria on the Mediterranean coast and Mesopotamia to the south, the aftermath of the volcanic explosion allowed the Assyrians to expand their empire into the lands closer to them.

The Assyrians did not waste time, but took advantage of the vacuum in power that fell upon the Middle East during the Dark Age. The map below shows the expansion of their empire.

The Assyrians had a strong sense of history. They recorded their deeds and established royal libraries. Ashurbanipal, the last Emperor of Assyria, had a library of twenty-two thousand catalogued clay tablets containing records, hymns, legends, works on science, mathematics, etc.

These people are known to historians for their excessive brutality. They devised the first system of *total war*, falling like butchers upon villages and nomadic immigrants, enslaving those they could and slaughtering the rest. Bas-reliefs show entire cities of people who have been stuck alive on stakes, running up through their groin and out their shoulders. Even for their own citizens, Assyrian laws meted out the bloodiest penalties ever known in world history. Julian Jaynes attributes this excessive cruelty and rule-by-terror to the collapse of the bicameral mind that resulted from the volcanic eruption and the consequent social upheaval. At the time, when the deities stopped speaking to men, when no stranger could be trusted, when people lived in fear and chaos, and when life was cheap, it was best to just kill everyone and not be bothered. Let the slaves who lived take notice.

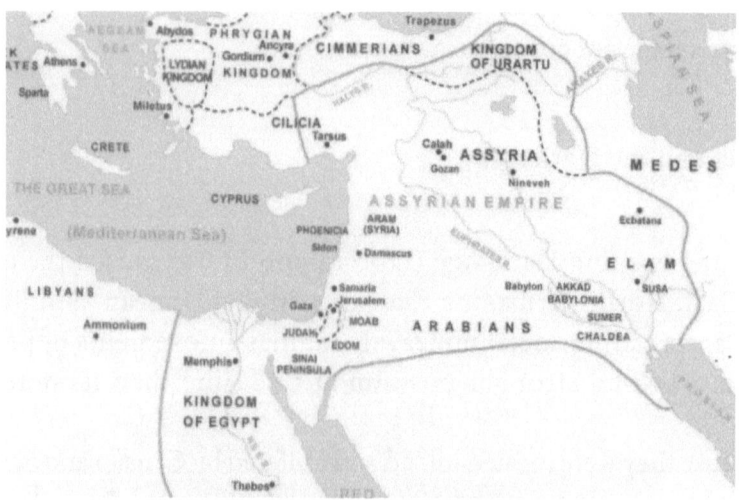

Map 2-4: Expansion of the Assyrian Empire 824 to 671 BC

Initially, the Assyrians maintained the religious tradition of Mesopotamia. Their mythology relates how their chief god, Assur, punished Marduk, Nabu, and Ishtar of Babylon. In *Marduk's Ordeal* it is written that Assur captured Marduk and took him to Assyria. This indicates that the Assyrian armies attacked Babylon and took Marduk's idol from his shrine. The *Akitu Chronicle* of the Babylonians tells us "for 20 years, Marduk stayed in Assur, and the Akitu Festival did not take place. Nabu did not come from Borsippa for the coming out of Marduk."[90]

The evolution of the "I" consciousness was forged in the fires of this chaos and its inception was expressed in daily decisions frought with fear and personal deceitfulness. No longer could men be honest with each other for everyone now had their own agenda. Deception, threats, and cruelty became the skills required to survive in the new reality. These were the means by which the heroes of the *Illiad* and *Odyssey* survived, and they are the same survival skills used by men today.

As a result of the environmental destruction that occurred, the Hittite Empire, which existed along the Aegean coast and into Lydia, completely collapsed. The Hittites were driven down into Syria with other refugees seeking a place to live. While chaos beleaguered the Hittite Empire that was inundated by refugees, the Assyrians had already begun a systematic invasion of Mesopotamia and the Middle East.

The first emperor of Assyria to begin the conquest in the wake of the volcano was Tiglath-pileser I (1115-1077 BC). Records of his conquests were written on stone tablets and kept in Ashur in the temple of Anu, the sky god, and Adad, the storm god. On these tablets, the king credits himself with conquering forty-two lands. The savagery of his conquests is reported with pride: "The corpses of their warriors I hurled down in the destructive battle like the storm god. Their blood I caused to flow in the valleys and on the high places of the mountains. I cut off their heads outside their cities, like heaps of grain, I piled them up."[91]

A dozen kings ruled after Tiglath-pileser without much note, but then around 883 BC, with the reign of Ashurnasirpal II, a series of kings brought the Assyrian empire to its height. The kings built cities and temples and recorded their exploits. They created the prototype of warrior kings, sneering at the unfortunate and boasting of their prowess in war and hunting. It was also Ashurnasirpal II who built the city of Nimrud, named after Nimrod, who, according to Genesis in the Torah, built Calah, Nineveh, and other Assyrian cities. The giant colossal winged, man-headed lions that most people equate with the Assyrians adorned the palace of Ashurnasirpal II.

The Assyrians are not known for their intellectual contribution to humanity, but for their invention of total war and ruthless imperial organization. When the Assyrians rode into battle they possessed divisions of cavalry, archers, and foot soldiers. They carried slingers, battleaxes, and daggers. Their strategy consisted of starting a pitched battle with the inhabitants of a new land and then annually returning to make inroads into their territory until their targets were exhausted and sued for peace. The Assyrians gave no quarter. Their soldiers were rewarded for carrying heads of their enemies back to camp.[92]

For centuries (1115 to 612 BC), the entire ancient Middle East was terrorized and brutalized by their rule. Even the mighty Aryan tribes to the north and east, the Medes and Persians, could not conquer them and spoke of them as devils. Because Assyrian policy included living off their victims, they engaged in mass genocide and shifted whole populations to serve them at their convenience. The effect of their rule was to create a thoroughly mixed international and interracial population that has remained essentially the same ever since.[93]

The Assyrians ruled the Middle East until an alliance of the vassal states of the Babylonians, Scythians, Chaldeans, and Cimmerians helped the Medes to capture Nineveh, the Assyrian capitol in 612 BC. Nineveh was razed and the Assyrian Empire collapsed seven years later, never again to regain the power of empire. Nevertheless, its people, culture, and religion lived on.

From the fourth century on, Christianity was an essential part of Assyrian identity and has helped preserve it to the present day despite endless persecutions and massacres, which have reduce the present-day Assyrians into dwindling minorities in their home countries. The self-designations of modern Syrians and Assyrians derive from the New-Assyrian word for "Assyrian," Assurayu/Surayu.

With the fall of the Assyrian empire, four empires vied for power in the Middle East. In Anatolia (Turkey), the Lydians ruled. Strategically located for trade, they were the first people to coin money. Their king, Croesus, became synonymous with wealth. The Median/Persian Empire now controlled all land from the Indus Valley in India to the eastern border of Turkey. The third power, the Chaldeans, were a revived Babylonian kingdom who controlled the fertile crescent of Mesopotamia. South of Mesopotamia, the Egyptians stood supreme in Africa. A stalemate between these mighty powers lasted for about fifty years.

Nebuchadnezzar and the Chaldeans

King Nebuchadnezzar II (605 to 562 BC), the greatest Chaldean king, defeated the Egyptians decisively in 605 BC to permanently eliminate them as contenders for Empire. He also spread his empire to the West, conquering Palestine and Jerusalem. He captured the Jewish king, Jehoiachin, and took him back to Babylon, while putting Zedekiah on the throne as his puppet. Yet Zedekiah proved to be no puppet. He created a rebellion against Nebuchadnezzar, which ultimately proved unsuccessful. Jerusalem was destroyed, the temple was razed, and the Jewish priest class was taken back to Babylon as slaves. This occurred in 585 BC and the event was recorded in the Jewish Torah (Old Testament) as the Babylonian Captivity.

Nebuchadnezzar had turned Babylon into a beautiful city with wide boulevards and a new Temple of Marduk, which included a seven-level ziggurat that became known in the Bible as the Tower of Babel. Our word babble comes from this reference because the slaves who built it spoke so many languages that the Jews could not understand what any other people were saying beside themselves. The king's palace was also lavish, complete with a terraced roof garden, which came to be known as the Hanging Gardens of Babylon, one of the seven wonders of the ancient world.

As the inheritors of a tradition that spanned millennia, the Chaldeans were a sophisticated people. Their engineering feats were remarkable. So also was their vast knowledge concerning medicine, law, grammar, mathematics, and astronomy. Such secular knowledge evolved to replace a religious tradition, which, by now, was decaying into meaningless superstition. Yet, for all their intellectual greatness, the Chaldeans' life was short. When Nebuchadnezzar died, the Empire disintegrated due to administrative conflicts, religious difficulties, and inattention to the armed forces, all of which are the shortcomings of a ruling intellectual class.

While Babylonia and Lydia contended for power with the Medes, this uneasy standoff did not last long. In 550 BC, Cyrus the Great of Persia moved in, conquering all the lands of the Assyrian Empire and beyond. These Aryan tribes introduced the worship of Mithra to the area. Mithra (originally called Mitra) was the ancient warrior god of the original Aryans. It was Mitra who, in the conquering of the Indus Valley, ruled along with the Aryan war-god Indra. The Median priest class was called the "Magi."[94] Aside from the worship of Mithra, on whom the mythological characteristics of Christ's life would later be built, they also introduced another religion to the area called Zoroastrianism. This religion would revolutionize man's relationship with the divine and set the stage for the western religions that followed, including Judaism, Christianity, and Islam.

The Two-God Religion and the Emergence of Free Will

The Persians Arrive

In 539 BC, the Persians, who had been biding their time, overwhelmed the weak Chaldean Empire. The Aryans now came to mix their blood and culture in the great melting pot of Mesopotamia. The Persians (the Achaemenid Empire) would consolidate their rule under the efficient administrator, Cyrus I (521 – 485 BC).

As the map below shows, Cyrus and his two successors, produced the greatest empire the world had ever known, one that extended beyond the Middle East to Greece in the West, Egypt in the South, the Caucasus in the North, and India in the East.

Cyrus I secured his Empire by borrowing the Assyrian military operations and the Chaldean medical practices. In addition, he championed the religion of Zoroaster throughout his empire. This religion caused a revolution in human thought. It was the first religion in the West based upon the principle of self-consciousness and free will. It replaced the dying polytheism, which still struggled to exist among the old ruling classes, with a simple dualism, a choice between right and wrong. In other words, the sacrificial rituals to capricious gods became subordinate to an ethical choice between good and bad behavior.

For the first time in history, humanity had an ideology that freed them from their submission to mythological deities and gave them an opportunity to control their own lives. Pessimism and hedonism surrendered to hope and principled living.

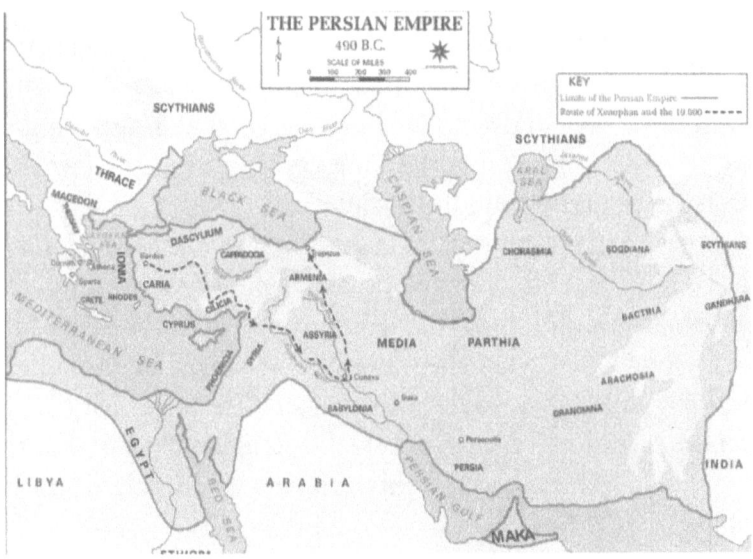

Map 2-5: Persian (Achaemenid) Empire 521 to 485 BC

Zoroastrianism would have a profound effect on the Jewish priesthood, especially the Pharisees, after Cyrus freed them from their Babylonian Captivity and allowed them to reestablish themselves in Jerusalem. Zoroastrianism advanced Jewish thinking into the age of subjective consciousness and converted Yahweh from a primitive tribal god, who was vengeful, punitive, and jealous,[95] to a humane god who now embodied the values of goodness and free will in the minds of the Hebrew people. Zoroastrianism would also become the impetus for a sect of Jewish ascetics known as the Essenes who historians believe was the sect that trained Jesus Christ and introduced him onto the world stage as a spiritual teacher.

Let us now take a look at Zoroastrianism and the impact of its thought on Western civilization. We are getting close to monotheism in the West, but we are not quite there yet. Even so, the theology of Zoroastrianism caused a great leap in human consciousness in the West, and made life much easier for the common people.

Zoroastrianism

According to archeological evidence and Zoroastrian scriptures, it seems likely that a priest/holy man named Zoroaster lived sometime between thirty-five to twenty-six hundred years ago, although his religion did not become an international force until 531 BC, when Cyrus began to spread it through the Middle East.

We are told that at the age of thirty, Zoroaster received a revelation while fetching water for a sacred ritual. He saw the shining figure of the Vohu Manah (Good Mind) who led Zoroaster to the presence of Ahura Mazda (Good God), where he was taught the cardinal principles of the Good Religion.[96] As a result of this vision, Zoroaster felt that he was chosen to spread and preach this Good Religion.[97] He stated that the source of all goodness was the only god who was worthy of the highest worship.

Zoroaster rejected the Aryan religion with its many gods and oppressive class structure. He was appalled by the *Aryan* gods, like Indra, who delighted in war and destruction. He condemned these gods as evil spirits and said they worked for Ahriman who was the destructive force who opposed the creative goodness of Ahuru Mazda. Zoroaster also opposed Aryan animal sacrifices and the use of soma, an intoxicant, in rituals.

The Zoroastrian holy book is called the *Avesta*. It includes the original words of Zoroaster preserved in a series of five hymns called the *Gathas*. The *Gathas* contain the basic beliefs of the religion. They are sacred poems directed towards the worship of the Good God (Ahuru Mazda). They address the concept of righteousness and cosmic order, and promote social justice and individual choice between good and evil. *The Gathas* provide many of the components of a universal religion and set the stage for a religion based on subjective consciousness.

At some later date (most scholars believe many centuries after the death of Zoroaster), the remaining parts of the *Avesta* were written. These new sections deal with laws of ritual and practice, along with the traditions of the faith. These were created by the Magi, the priest class of Zoroastrianism. The Zoroastrian community is sharply divided today between those who would follow exclusively the teachings of the original *Gathas* and those who believe that the later traditions are important and equally divinely inspired. We find this contradiction inherent in all religions as priests add ceremonies, myths, stories, rules, and dogmas to the teachings of the original master.

Zoroastrians believe in the God of Good (Ahuru Mazda) and the God of Evil (Ahriman). Some of the faithful believe that the battle between good and evil exists only on the Cosmic level, while others, believe that it exists only on the individual level. Some believe that the duality exists at both levels.

In the telling of our history so far, we have tried to demonstrate how the idea of god grew in human consciousness. How the gods/goddesses began as spirit voices and the ghosts of ancestors, then graduated to the forces of nature, the moon goddess, the Great Goddess, the sacred king gods, the deity of cities, the pantheon of gods and goddesses of empires and now finally the creation of a good god and a bad god. We have expanded our definition of consciousness from the idea that it existed in every form (spirits) to its present concentration in only two forms, an abstract concept of absolute good and absolute evil.

Whatever its contribution to the evolution of human consciousness, and it was considerable, this worldview saddled western civilization with a *static* and *dualist* perspective of life, which we have yet to overcome. We have been taught to believe that so long as the world exists, the forces of good must continually wage war against the forces of evil. The two remain isolated and impenetrable to the other. Good never becomes evil and evil never becomes good.

This worldview prevents our minds from conceiving a unifying principle of Oneness beyond duality. Just as the ancient Mesopotamian societies were saddled with the voices of commanding gods and goddesses to which they were enslaved, so is contemporary western society saddled with the voices of the good god and the bad god, God and the Devil. As such, we are unable to rise above this contradiction and develop an integrated, synthetic view of Absolute Consciousness. Shrii P. R. Sarkar, in propounding a universal ideology, has tried to overcome this problem. His universal ideology provides a holistic vision upon which we can view the evolution of human beings in relation to Absolute Consciousness, independent of the western religions that are limited to dualistic thinking. See *Universal Ideology: The Thought of P. R. Sakar* by Chuck and Tom Paprocki.

Without a concept of Absolute Consciousness, the minds of the people, who remain faithful to their religions, are not able to escape the laws of contradiction that govern their thoughts. God and man remain forever distinct from each other, so also does every religion remain eternally separate from all others even as they all claim to worship the one, universal God. As such, we will always require a priest class to interpret and arbitrate our understanding of the externalized good god. Given this dualistic mindset, we are unable to understand the process by which our individual consciousness is able to merge with the Absolute. We will never discover, as Jesus did, how it is possible for the "I and the Father" to be one. We cannot envision the whole and thus we remain controlled by the parts. Because we lack an understanding of our own divinity, we remain controlled by another sky god and another lord of the underworld. This thinking is the product of linear logic, the left side of the brain. Our minds can analyze and conceive of differences, but we cannot synthesize, nor envision the whole. This condition is called *moral dualism*. It is the substratum of western thought.

Zoroaster taught that the good god's gift to man was free will. Therefore, man has the choice to follow the path of evil (deceit) or the path of righteousness (truth). The path of evil leads to misery and ultimately hell. The path of righteousness leads to peace and everlasting happiness in heaven. In the mind, this dualism takes the form of a polarity between heaven and hell, happiness and sadness, truth and deception, etc.

Given this static duality, the interpenetration of opposites is not an option. We are not able to consider the possibility that good and bad are interchangeable, that good things might lead to bad, or vice versa, or that someone can contain both good and bad within him or her. This is what is meant by *static dualism*. There is no movement, no progress in thinking. This is the perfect mental state for the imposition of religious dogmas. And sadly, the priest classes have always known this and have taken advantage of people accordingly. By being able to declare fixed absolutes in a relative world, the religious authorities gain their control over the minds of men. We are told that we have a free will to choose, but we will go to hell if we choose other than what the priests tell us to choose because only they can define what is good and bad in our daily lives. This does great harm when we realize that religions are rife with sexism, groupism, and divisive dogmas and that they most often support the ruling classes at the expense of the common people. Furthermore, religions seldom respect the natural world.

A dualist religion gives rise to the question, how can a good god allow bad things to happen to us? How could a good god, take the life of a child, or kill a loved one, or destroy our beloved country, or ruin our property? How could a good god, who we have prayed to and believed in our whole life, treat us so badly? If we lose a child, we do not blame the devil. We blame the good god. We cannot understand what happened. We do not get it.

Zoroastrianism is said to promote a positive outlook because it teaches that mankind is ultimately good and that this goodness will finally triumph over evil. Unfortunately, we do not know when this mythical event will happen. In the meantime, we simply follow the dictates of our religion, hoping that the god of our priests is listening, because he does not seem to listen to us when we need him most.

Zoroastrianism presents us with the origins of a dogmatic mindset that no subsequent religion in the west has been able to transcend. Static dualism was ultimately addressed by the philosopher Friedrich Hegel in the eighteenth century, when he introduced the idea of *dialectical dualism* in which his theory of motion allowed for the interpenetration of opposites. In this philosophy, things were no longer simply static. Just as light interpenetrates darkness by degrees and just as darkness interpenetrates light in the same way, so good could interpenetrate bad and bad interpenetrate good. This gives rise to all kinds of gray areas. This theory presents us with a more rational perspective on relative reality because everything is always in motion.

Nonetheless, neither Zoroaster nor Hegel provide us with a way to transcend duality. We cannot achieve unity as long as we are immersed in duality. This riddle cannot be solved by simply using our rational faculty. It is rational to perceive duality. In our approach to life we are continually perceiving and conceiving forms to which we give names. And in so doing, we always give rise to their opposites as well. God cannot be conceived without the Devil. Neither can good be conceived without bad, light without dark, cold without hot, love without hate, etc. Therefore, we must admit that Oneness cannot be conceived by the rational mind. This is why religions always push the ultimate resolution of fundamental dualities to the "end of days." In the end, the forces of good will fight against the forces of evil and the good God will win. All the good people who followed the good God will experience the ultimate good, and all those who followed the bad god will experience the ultimate bad. This is as far as the rational mind can take us. This idea is at the base of all Western religions.

There is a difference between religions and mysticism, however, which gets to the root of this problem. The mystics may share a common belief system with the priests of their religion, but their means of knowing the Divine Oneness differs. They do not take a rational approach, they take an intuitive approach. Intuition is a more subtle faculty of consciousness than is rationality. Most human beings have had intuitive experiences of the divine, but they seem to just happen upon them. In other words, they do not know how to control their intuition. The religious practices that they perform yield little. Priests' sermons speak only to the rational mind.

While rationality is necessary to deal with relative reality, it has little value in the realm of spiritual reality. The mystics, the spiritual masters of all religions, have told us the way to develop our intuition. It is done by breaking down the duality between inside me and outside me, between what is good for me and what is bad for me. It is done by breaking down all dualities and seeing everything as an expression of the One God. To do this requires an understanding and practice of love. Only by love can I and the Father become one.

One way to practice love is by performing selfless service in this manifest world. Another important way to practice love is to develop an internal dialogue with the Divine which creates a bond between your identity and God. We will explore this theme more deeply as we look at the history of the Jews, the Essenes, and the Gnostics that follows.

The religion of Zoroastrianism and its theory of static dualism made its appearance on the world stage around 500 BC with the expansion of the Persian Empire of Cyrus I into the Middle East, Egypt, and the eastern Mediterranean. There is no denying its impact on western civilization. This Zoroastrian mindset passed to the Jews and the Christians, the Greeks and the Romans, and thus to all western society. It undergirds the perception of modern westerners to this very day. Those who hold a different point of view are still held suspect. They remain the "other." And for much of western history, under the authority of the Catholic Church, to be an "other" meant being called a heretic for whom punishment was often torture and death. Under the iron rule of the Catholic Church, free will was not allowed, nor for that matter was *free thought*, until the coming of the Protestant Revolution.

What we have been discussing is profound. By having this dualistic interpretation of reality, the western mind is prohibited from being able to understand the nature of consciousness, our human potential, or our connection to the life forms of our environment, or ultimately to Absolute Consciousness. We can act morally insofar as our group is concerned; we can use our intellect to create a roadmap to God, but knowing how to merge with Divinity is beyond our means. Just as hearing voices in the mind and interpreting them as the commanding voices of outside agents was an example of limited consciousness, so too is being locked in a static dualism an example of a limited consciousness. Yet, it remains the basis of the western mindset and explains our willingness to destroy anything else that is considered "other" and, therefore, bad or inferior. The earth itself remains an "other," worthy only of exploitation.

Having identified the limits of dualistic thinking, we must still admit that at the time Zoroastrianism was introduced into the Middle East, it was a great revolutionary step forward. It quelled the need to listen to a myriad of conflicting gods and goddesses and made things much simpler. There was a good god and there was a bad god, period. And with the dawn of subjective consciousness, a man was finally free to choose between serving one or the other. There was now an "I" consciousness, and instead of just having a feeling of doing, we also now had a sense of "I-do." How liberating it must have been when this new religion, so young and vibrant, enlightened men and women to the forces of good and evil and opened up the immeasurable possibilities of free will! What a force of good it must have been. But today, it has largely become a force of bad, casting its inertia over all possibility to solve the problems of the twenty-first century.

Zoroastrianism also introduced some level of equality to women. For example, in its creation myth, it does not blame women for the fall of mankind. Rather, evil tempts both the male and female and causes them to lose their sexual desire for each other. Their desire returns to them after fifty years and they are then able to have children. Unlike in the Vedic texts, there is no preferential treatment for male children. A male child is not necessary for parents to go to heaven. Females also share the same initiation rites as males. They represent half of the forces of good—while the sky, wind, fire, and metal are male, the earth, water, fish, and plants are female.[98] Nonetheless, after the male priest class began to warp the original message of the master, the rules of patriarchy came to dominate in the dogmas of the religion regarding male and female roles. For example, in the code of conduct for women, it says that women are especially subject to the temptation of evil and need to be closely watched. Women are ranked in a good to bad order. The best women are described in the Meno-i-Khard accordingly: "The woman who is young, who is properly disposed, who is faithful, who is respected, who is good-natured, who enlivens the house, whose modesty and awe are virtuous, a friend of her own father and elders, husband and guardian, handsome and replete with animation is chief over the women who are her associates."[99] We have to admit that there is no mention of self-expression or intelligence here. There is no respect for an older woman who is no longer sexually attractive. Men want a submissive virgin, but they do not want the mother or the crone.

Insofar as Zoroastrianism had become the state religion of the Persians and was therefore carried throughout the Middle East and beyond by the Aryan emperor Cyrus I, we know that all the people from India to the European mainland and the Aegean Sea became exposed to it. We also know that the Jews, who were beholding to Cyrus for releasing them from their Babylonian Captivity, had nothing but good words for Cyrus. They borrowed liberally from

Zoroastrianism in the creation of their own religion. We will look at this later.

When the gods and goddesses abandoned the people of the Middle East as a result of the volcano on Thera and its aftermath, people were left with no outside authority. Certainly they sought in every way to reestablish contact with their deities, but it was never again the same. The primordial trust was broken and the deities never spoke again with the same authority as they had throughout the history of the people. This breakdown led humanity in the Middle East to depend upon themselves. Feebly at first, but gradually people began to take control of their own behavior. There had been examples like Gilgamesh and other kings who had previously taken such a stand and now everyone would have to do the same. It was at this point in history when Zoroastrianism was introduced in the Middle East. It was the perfect religion for the time.

The mythological expression of the duality in Zoroastrianism is reflected in the *Millennial Doctrines*. These doctrines state that the conflict between the opposing kingdoms of goodness and evil form the history of the world, which lasts for twelve thousand years and is divided into four great ages. The first age which lasts for three thousand years is the period of spiritual existence. Ahuru Mazda knows of Ahriman's coexistence and creates the world first in a spiritual state before giving it a material form. Ahriman is ignorant of his great rival's existence, but on discovering him, he creates the hosts of demons and fiends. In the second age of three thousand years, while Ahriman is confounded by Ahura Mazda, the latter creates the world in its material form, and the world is then invaded by Ahriman. The third three thousand years is the period of conflict between the rival powers and their struggle for the souls of men. This occurs until Zoroaster comes into the world. His birth inaugurates a new era, and the fourth and last three thousand years begin. These final years are presided over by Zoroaster himself and his three posthumous sons, who are to be born in future ages in an ideal manner, the last being the Messiah called Saoshyant ("Savior").

In this struggle between good and evil, man is an important figure because the ultimate triumph of good depends upon him. Man is a free agent according to Zoroaster ("Yasna," xxx. 20, xxxi. 11), but he must ever be on his guard against the misguidance of evil. The purpose of

Zoroaster's coming into the world and the aim of his teaching are to guide man to choose the path of righteousness, in order that the world may attain ultimate perfection. This perfection will come with the establishment of the Good Kingdom. When this shall come to pass, the world will regenerate; a final battle between the powers of good and evil will take place; Ahriman and his hosts will be routed; and good shall reign supreme ("Yasht," xix. 89-93; "Bundahis," xxx. 1-33). The advent of the Messiah (Saoshyant) will be accompanied by the resurrection of the dead and the day of judgment. From thence the world will be free from evil and harm.[100]

The motto of the Zoroastrian religion is, "Good thoughts, good words, good deeds" (*Avesta*, "Humata, hūkhta, hvarshta"). Man must also take care in keeping the earth, fire, water, and air free from defilement of any kind. This might make the Zoroastrians the earliest environmentalists. Truth-speaking and honesty are the basis of every action. Kindliness and generosity are virtues to be cultivated. Agriculture and cattle raising are prescribed as religious duties. Marriage within the community of the faithful is lauded, and, according to the *Avesta* ("Vendidād," iv. 47), "he who has a wife is to be accounted far above him who has none; and he who has children is far above the childless man."

In religious matters the priesthood was supreme in authority, and the priestly order was hereditary. The Magi were a sacerdotal tribe of Medes (Aryans). In acts of worship (*Avesta*, "Yasna"), animal sacrifices were still sometimes offered, especially in the earlier days, but these immolations were eventually subordinated and gave place more and more to offerings of praise and thanksgiving.

The points of resemblance between Zoroastrianism and Judaism, and, hence, also Christianity, are striking. Ahura Mazda, the supreme lord of Zoroastrianism, is omniscient, omnipresent, and eternal and endowed with creative power, which he exercises especially through the medium of his *Spenta Mainyu* ("Holy Spirit"). As such, he presents the nearest parallel to the Jewish concept of god that is found in antiquity.

Ahuru Mazda governs the universe through angels and archangels, but his power is hampered by his adversary, Ahriman, whose dominion, like Satan's, shall be destroyed at the end of the world.

There are other striking parallels between Zoroastrianism and Judaism/Christianity, including their doctrines of a regenerate world, a perfect kingdom, the coming of a Messiah, the resurrection of the dead, the day of judgment, and life everlasting. Both Zoroastrianism and Judaism are revealed religions. Tradition holds that God revealed his teachings to both Zoroaster and Moses on the top of a mountain.[101] The six days of Creation in Genesis finds a parallel in the six periods of Creation described in the Zoroastrian scriptures. Mankind, according to each religion, is descended from a single couple. *Mashya* (man) and *Mashyana* (woman) are the Iranian Adam and Eve.

In the *Avesta,* a winter depopulates the earth except in the *Vara* ("enclosure") of the blessed *Yima*. In the Bible, a deluge destroys all people except those who are saved in the ark. In each case, the earth is peopled anew with the best two of every kind, and is afterward divided into three realms. The three sons of Yima's successor Thraetaona embody these realms. *Airya, Sairima* and *Tura* inherit the earth just as Noah's sons Shem, Ham, and Japheth do so in the Jewish story.[102] Here Shem gives rise to the Semitic peoples, Ham to the Negroid peoples and Japheth to the Caucasians. There are also likenesses in minor matters, in details of ceremony and ritual, as well as parallels between Zoroaster and Moses as sacred lawgivers.[103]

While the Jewish priests accepted Zoroastrianism as the basis of their thinking, they rejected outright the gods and goddesses of the Mesopotamian and Assyrian cultures who were their neighbors, especially those of the Babylonians who had held them in captivity. For example, Yahweh says in Isaiah 46, "Bel [Marduk] boweth down, Nebo stoopeth." In Isaiah 47 he says, "Come down, and sit in the dust, O virgin daughter of Babylon, sit on the ground: there is no throne, O daughter of the Chaldeans: for thou shalt no more be called tender and delicate."

It is interesting that in Isaiah 63, while also condemning the Edomites, Yahweh says: for I will tread upon them in mine anger, and trample them in my fury; and their blood shall be sprinkled upon my garments, and I will stain all my raiment. For the day of vengeance is in mine heart, and the year of my redeemed is come." Later in the same verse Isaiah talks about Yahweh's *loving kindnesses* to the Jews. At this point, apparently, the Israelites conception of Yahweh was still that of a tribal god, rather than a universal god. In fact, the god of Judaism remains a tribal god to this day, favoring the Jews before all others. He is called the one god, but this one god is defined only by the Jews, and the definition is not universal.

Cyrus the Great was relatively liberal. While he himself ruled according to Zoroastrian beliefs, he made no attempt to impose Zoroastrianism on the people of his subject territories. Therefore, the Jews did not incorporate the tenets of Zoroastrianism into their religion by force. More likely, they recognized a superior idea of god in Zoroastrianism than they possessed at the time. They were made more amenable to accepting the new definition of god because Cyrus had also freed them from captivity and allowed them to return to Jerusalem and rebuild their temple. This was a great boon to the Jewish priests, who desired to rebuild their nation and call in the scattered Jews from around the world.

In our original hypothesis, we stated that human beings have diminished our limitless power to *be more*, by a desire to *do more* and to *have more*. It is our conjecture that during the time of the matriarchy, the quest to do more and to have more was more sublimated than it is under patriarchy. In the matriarchy, the relationship with Divinity was developed by the need of the mothers to explain the mystery of life. While unknown quantities of physical wealth were created by the early matriarchal civilizations, it was not generally considered to be personal property. This development did not arise before the dawn of patriarchy. Wealth was collective. In time, however, as the men were given more responsibility for protection and administration of physical wealth, the desire for more wealth grew. The need for wealth and power arose, especially in the minds of men. As patriarchal tribes developed, collective property (the wealth of the goddess) gave way to the idea of property as *booty*, something which could be stolen from others. This desire for personal wealth gained even greater expression with the dawn of subjective consciousness. Patriarchal religions in the beginning were strongly tempered by the dictates of the goddess, but as she lost her influence over time and women became subjugated to a form of personal property, the male religions began to serve as the means by which wealth and power could be legally appropriated. The Aryan Vedas present a clear picture of this development. So also do the dictates of the city gods as interpreted by the male priests of the religions of the Middle Eastern empires. It is believed that, in the beginning, Zoroastrianism provided a refreshing example of equal opportunity for men and women, yet, as the male priest class gained ascendency, the role of women was again diminished and opportunities curtailed.

Alexander the Great: The Greeks Enter the Middle East

It has been said that the pen is mightier than the sword. Certainly, the impact of the pen on the mental arena is greater than the sword, as we have seen in the influence of Zoroastrian, which has lasted down through millennia into modern times. The impact of Zoroaster on humanity was much greater than that of Cyrus I whose empire lasted only several hundred years. Nonetheless, it also must be said that when it comes to power in the immediate physical arena, it is the sword, and not the pen, that determines the outcome.

We have no greater example of this than the wars of kings in the Middle East, who built great empires and ruled by physical might. But all these empires, even the great empire of Persia, would pale in comparison to the empire of Alexander the Great.

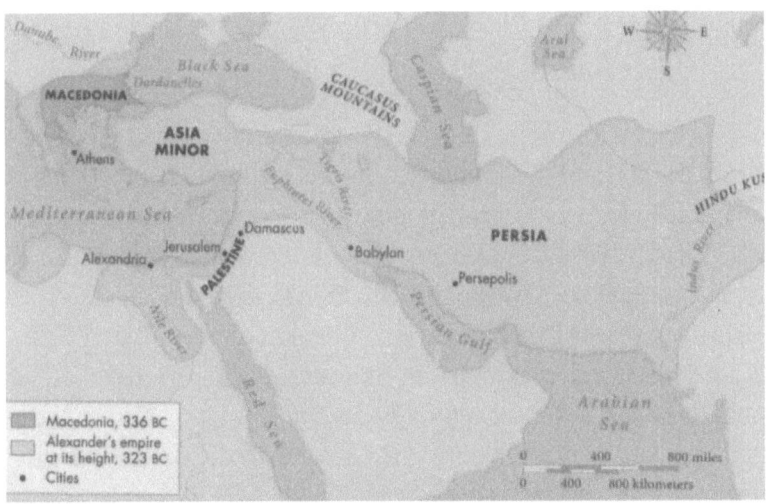

Map 2-6: Alexander the Great's Empire 323 BC

Alexander the Great was a Greek king of Macedonia. Descended from Dorian stock, he was born in 356 BC and died in 323 BC. He was tutored by Aristotle until he was sixteen years old. At the age of twenty-two, he invaded the Middle East and destroyed the Persian Empire. When he died at the age of thirty-three, he had created the largest empire of the world. It was his dream to reach the "ends of the world and the Great Outer Sea." Alexander was never defeated in battle and is considered even today to be the world's most successful military commander.[104]

Alexander died in Babylon. In the years following his death, a series of civil wars tore his empire apart, resulting in several states being ruled by Alexander's surviving generals and heirs.

Alexander's legacy was the introduction of the West to the East and the East to the West. The colonies that were set up in his wake spread Greek culture in a process historians call Hellenization. It was characterized by a secular and rational approach to reality. The Greeks, such as Socrates, Aristotle, and Plato, played a dominant role in initiating secular thought, replacing religion with philosophy and blind faith with reason. This, along with Greek art and letters, was a great contribution to western thought.

The Seleucid (Greek) Empire

The Seleucid Greek Empire controlled the Middle East from 312 BC to 63 BC, following the division of Alexander's empire, including Babylon, the place of Alexander's death. At the height of its power, the Greek Seleucid Empire included central Anatolia, Persia, the Levant, Mesopotamia, and what is now Kuwait, Afghanistan, Pakistan, Turkmenistan, and northwest parts of India.[105] The Seleucid Empire was the major center of Greek culture in the Middle East. It maintained the Greek customs and political rule. When it tried to expand into Anatolia, however, it was abruptly halted by the Roman army that had by then entered its expansive phase. Ultimately, it was overthrown by the Roman general Pompey.[106]

During the decline of the Seleucids, the Parthians (Iranians) conquered much of their eastern empire. Frequent civil wars between Parthian contenders to the throne, however, destabilized their empire and led to their destruction by the Sassanid Empire (Persians) in AD 224. The Sassanid Empire remained in place until the Muslim conquests of the seventh century.

Chapter Two: Jews and the Rise of Monotheism

Who is a Jew?

WITH THE JEWISH PEOPLE, we start to move into ancient history as generally covered by western education. Everyone has some idea of Jewish history and knows something about the Jews as a people, both from a religious and from a political-economic perspective. For all intents and purposes, the Christians believe the Jewish Torah to be the Old Testament of the Bible. Christians accept this iconic scripture as the history of the Jews prior to the coming of Jesus Christ, whose story forms the New Testament. The Bible is both the Old and the New Testament.

Most of the world is familiar with the treatment of the Jews in European history during the twentieth century. We know something about the impact they had, and continue to have, on European and American cultures, and we know about their impact in the Middle East, given the modern state of Israel. The Jews have had a long history as a people, and if we want to understand what it means to be a human being, we must look at how the Jews helped define us, particularly in the West.

Unfortunately, much of what we accept as Jewish history is attributable to the Old Testament. The Old Testament, however, is more of a myth, similar to the myths of other people we have read about. Its purpose was not to preserve historical accuracy, as we understand it, but to provide a story about external deities and convey the rules by which to serve those deities and, in so doing, solidify the Jewish people's beliefs and build a common socio-sentiment. The Torah/Old Testament is primarily myth with a sprinkling of historical accuracies.

Like the myths of the peoples who established other cities and empires in the Middle East before the Jews came along, the Jewish myth is rooted in a bicameral consciousness, but much of it was also written within the dawn of subjective consciousness. As such, the Torah provides us with an excellent, perhaps the best example, that humanity has, of the transition in thinking that occurred in the first and second centuries BC between bicameral and subjective consciousness. The Jewish god, Yahweh, was born in a fashion similar to the birth of Enlil who arose out of the earthquake that shattered a nine mile stretch of the Zagros Mountains. Yahweh was born out of the volcanic eruption that caused the destruction of Thera, the eastern Mediterranean, and the Levant. A myth is not rational, nor is it historical. Rather it was a story told by a priest class that was primarily a product of a bicameral mind that served to explain the behavior of natural forces (deities) and to build a common socio-sentiment of a people who were bound together by their subservience to these forces. Yahweh, when he was born, like Enlil, was a blood thirsty, fickle, vengeful, and jealous god.

If we want to understand the revolutionary significance of the shift from a bicameral to a subjective consciousness that took place at this time, we must understand the difference between subjective and objective consciousness. A *subject* is the source of identity and authority. It is the entity that perceives and conceives. It is the subject that has the sense of *I am, I do*, and the mental screen on which to project its observations. An *object*, on the other hand, is that which is perceived, conceived, and identified by the subject.

Today scientists define subjective consciousness as a Subject-Object relationship. This means that our internal sense of "I" (subject) establishes a relationship with mental or physical forms (objects) according to its volition (sense of *I do*). Up until the Thera catastrophe, human beings attributed subjectivity to the spirits and the gods, who were external forces that controlled us. They were the knowers (subjects) and we were the known (objects). The mythologies of ancient men confirm this universal predicament. The gods controlled us because we perceived these powerful external forces as being superior to us.

They could change their shape at will; they lived longer than us (i.e., possessed immortality); and they would hurt us if we disobeyed their wishes. At worst, we were their slaves. At best, we were at their mercy. In either case, our own sense of self was either latent or in a primitive stage of development at this time and was unable to contest their authority, which manifested in the voices in our minds.

This situation existed because the two halves of our brain were linked by a bridge (anterior commissure) over which the right side of the brain, which was responsible for comprehension, sent its messages to the left side of the brain, which heard these messages as verbal commands. All human beings were continually "hearing voices" in their head and we attributed the source of these voices to external spirits or gods. They told us what to do.

From a philosophical perspective, therefore, we can say that our bicameral consciousness was based on an objective-subjective relationship. The authority was in the object rather than in us. Once subjective consciousness emerged, however, and our I-feeling became the source of our identity and authority, all this changed. Now human consciousness was inverted. We have subjective-objective relationships. The source of authority went from an external force (the gods) to an internal force (our selves).

But as always, things are more complicated. Even with our evolved sense of "I" as an internal authority, the fact remains that there will always be conscious forces that remain superior to our limited definition of "I am." For example, most people still give authority to their idea of God and to the priests and to the religious institution that represents this authority on earth. So now the question becomes, "What is my relationship with the Divine" and "Is my faith in God based upon personal experience or simply faith in another man's words"? In the former case, we have an opportunity to experience a *subjective–subjective* consciousness where both the individual and God are in mutual communication. In the latter, if we simply have faith in another man's word, we have reverted to the previous state of having an objective-subjective relationship in which an external force still controls our self. We will address these distinctions in our study of the early history of the Jews, for it was at this revolutionary time in history when the possibility of having a *subjective-subjective* consciousness first arose in Western Civilization. We will observe how the idea of Yahweh, as an external authority, changed over time and how the minds of some Jews began to solve the riddle of merging one's limited self-identity with the cosmic consciousness, the Supreme Oneness we call God.

When we speak of the Jews, we must get our terms right. Do Hebrew, Jew, Israelite, and Zionist mean the same thing? No. A *Jew* is someone who practices the Jewish religion. A *Hebrew* is someone who spoke or speaks the Hebrew language. The Jews emerged from a much greater pool of Hebrews. An *Israelite* is a citizen of Israel. A *Zionist* is a nationalist that supports the re-establishment of a Jewish homeland in the territory defined as the biblical land of Israel. You can be one or all of these things. An Israelite need not be a Jew, and a Hebrew need not be a Jew. A Jew need not be a Zionist. Having said this, there is a loose historical progression from Hebrew to Jew to Israelite to Zionist. Zionists did not come about however until the twentieth century with the movement to create a modern homeland for the Jews.

Another term that gets thrown into the mix is *Semite*. Contemporary Jews speak as if they are the only Semites in the world and that to criticize the Jews is to be *anti-Semitic*.

Actually, the word "Semite" refers to those who speak a family of languages native to the Middle East. The languages include the ancient and modern forms of Ahlamu, Akkadian (including Assyrian and Babylonian dialects), Amharic; Amalekite, Ammonite, Amorite, Arabic, Aramaic/Syriac, the Canaanite languages (Phoenician, Punic and Hebrew), Assyrian, Chaldean, Eblaite, Edomite, Ge'ez; Old South Arabian, Modern South Arabian languages, Maltese, Mandaic, Moabite, Proto-Sinaitic, Sutean, Syriac, Tigre and Tigrinya, and Ugaritic, among others.[107] Today the Arabs, Lebanese, Jordanians, Iraqis, etc., are as much Semites as the Jews.

Yahweh the Volcano God

When it comes to real people and real events, the Jews in Israel arose out of the Hebrews who consisted of local nomadic tribes as well as refugees from the destruction of the volcanic explosion on Thera. We first hear about the Jews around 1200 BC from the Egyptians.

There is an inscription on the Merneptah stele (praising the Pharaoh Merneptah for his martial victories) that mentions a people living in Canaan called the Israelites.[108] The bulk of the inscription deals with Merneptah's victory over the Libyans, but the last lines shift to Canaan:

> The princes are prostrate, saying, "Peace!"
> Not one is raising his head among the Nine Bows.
> Now that Tehenu (Libya) has come to ruin,
> Hatti is pacified;
> The Canaan has been plundered into every sort of woe:
> Ashkelon has been overcome;
> Gezer has been captured;
> Yano'am is made non-existent.
> Israel is laid waste and his seed is not;
> Hurru is become a widow because of Egypt.

The "nine bows" is a term the Egyptians used to refer to their enemies. Ashkelon, Gezer, and Yano'am were Canaanite cities in present day Israel. Israel at the time was not a city-state, nor a nation, so the Israelites, while they had a tribal identity, were still a people without a land base. They were probably a loosely affiliated tribal confederation. It is worth noting that they were not living or enslaved in Egypt. Rather, they were identified as a people living in Canaan.

This contradicts the story of the Exodus that was written by the Jewish priests after the Babylonian Captivity and introduced into the Torah or Old Testament. This will need a later discussion.

During the 1970s, Israeli archeologists began to find small hilltop villages in the central hill country north and south of Jerusalem and in lower Galilee. These villages seem to be the original habitat of the Hebrew Jews as they began to settle after years of being nomads.[109] These villages are called "proto-Israelite" sites. They emerge in great numbers after 1200 BC. Scientists call the emergence of these sites "colonization from below"; that is, they were not created by a central policy but by the clans and small tribes of people, some indigenous and some refugees from

Thera. These villages were agro-pastoral, and their economies were based on cereals, sheep, and goats. As we would expect from an area reeling with refugees in the aftermath of the volcanic explosion, these villages increased in number and population in the highlands and decreased along the coastlines. Likewise, the population of cities along the coast decreased and the population in the villages increased.[110]

Fig. 2-8: Egyptian Stele Placing the Israelites in Caanan ca 1200 BC

At this time, like so many other tribes who were refugees of the great catastrophe and the resultant Dark Age, the Hebrews were primarily nomads "wandering in the desert." Constantly on the move, they shepherded their goats, wary of strangers. We are told that they wandered in the desert for forty years, which is a symbolic number to define a change in epochs or generations. Whether the Hebrew were refugees from Thera or indigenous herdsmen, or both, a group of them, who self-identified as Jews, began to settle out after 1200 BC. However, it was not until a hundred and seventy years later, around 1030 BC, that they were successful in conquering enough land in Canaan to establish Saul as their first king. Before this, they were a loose confederation of peoples, ruled by their tribal chieftains (the *Judges*) and by their *prophets* (the *Nabi*) who still claimed to hear the "Word of God" in their minds. During this time, the land of Canaan was ruled by the Egyptians.

The time of the Thera volcano and its aftermath is the time period described in the Old Testament's Book of Joshua and Book of Judges.[111] While Jewish scribes would later claim that its tribal leaders were faithful servants of Yahweh, this seems unlikely. What is more likely is that the priests of a nomadic or dispossessed people, existing on the edge of the destruction, and attributed the catastrophe of Thera to a "volcano god" whom they called Yahweh. Yahweh evolved into simply being called the "Lord," and further evolution of the idea, turned Yahweh, or the Lord, into the One God.

Historians know that the Jews were polytheistic for centuries; they did not become monotheistic until much later after being introduced to Zoroastrianism. Now they were finally able to establish Yahweh as the *one true god* and replace all the other gods and goddesses worshiped by the Jewish people. Even though this had been a long term mission of the priests (Levites), the people did not immediately subscribe to it. The struggle of the priests to enthrone Yahweh lasted from around 1200 BC to 500 BC. Polytheism existed among the Jews through their years as nomads and refugees, through their years of settlement and kingship, and through their destruction by the empires of the Assyrians and Babylonians. The people remained polytheistic even after the Babylonian Captivity. The Bible mentions deities who competed with Yahweh for the people's attention. These included Asherah, Baal, Anath, El, Dagon, and many others. They were worshipped alongside Yahweh. The Great Goddess Asherah was also considered Yahweh's consort for centuries.

Apparently, Yahweh was introduced to the Hebrew tribes by the Levite tribe. The Levites were a hereditary priest class, who instructed the people on how to worship. The Book of Leviticus reveals their teachings and instructions.

The Levites worshiped a fierce and violent god. According to the book of Exodus, the Hebrews could not worship Yahweh in Egypt, because they could not see him from there. The people, we are told: "... took their journey from Succoth and encamped at Etham, in the edge of the wilderness. The Lord Yahweh went before them by day in a pillar of a cloud, to lead them the way; and by night in a pillar of fire, to give them light; to go by day and night (Exodus 13:21)." This is a clear description of an active volcano—smoke seen by day, fire by night.

Then the Levites told the people, "Take heed to yourselves, that ye go not up into the mount, or touch the border of it: whosoever toucheth the mount shall be surely put to death (Exod 19:12)." The passage continues: "And Mount Sinai[112] was altogether on a smoke, because the Lord Yahweh descended upon it in fire: and the smoke thereof ascended as the smoke of a furnace, and the whole mount quaked greatly." Another clear description of an active volcano.[113]

According to the Torah, in acknowledging the volcano god, Moses, the people's leader, gave them instructions on how to worship this god (Code of Law) and in so doing made an agreement (covenant) with Yahweh that for his protection the people would worship him as their chief god.

While the Levites called their new god Yahweh, the people did not worship Yahweh with any firm commitment. They liked their old gods. As did their neighbors, they worshiped El and Asherah, the Canaanite chief god and great goddess.[114] They also worshiped the Canaanite god and goddess Baal and Anat.

Yahweh, as was typical of deities in the Middle East, was paired with other gods and goddesses. Prior to the Babylonian Captivity, Yahweh is often paired with Asherah (Astarte), the Great Goddess of the Akkadians, Babylonians, and Assyrians. Although the Hebrew priests and prophets felt it necessary to denigrate the Mother Goddess, Asherah was widely venerated among the Hebrew people. Many female figurines unearthed in ancient Israel show Asherah the Goddess as the "Queen of Heaven" and a consort of Yahweh. In II Kings 23, which describes the reforms of King Josiah in the late seventh century, it talks about how Josiah purged the Temple of all the cult paraphernalia of Asherah. As soon as Solomon built the first Temple in Jerusalem, other gods beside Yahweh were moved in.[115] The Hebrews also worshipped the Great Goddess under the names of Anath, Astarte, and Ashima.[116] Small figurines of the Goddess have been found in Israel by the thousands indicating that she was worshipped in the majority of Hebrew households at the time.

This polytheism, so typical at the time, could not be denied or covered up by later Jewish scribes. In Exodus, the Hebrews create a "molten calf" and "the people declare: "These be thy gods, O Israel, which brought thee up out of the land of Egypt" (Exod 32:4). Aaron then built an altar before the calf and proclaimed the next day to be a feast to the new gods. So they rose up early the next day and "offered burnt-offerings, and brought peace-offerings; and the people sat down to eat and to drink, and rose up to play" (Exod 32:6). The golden calf was associated with the Canaanite god, El.

Fig. 2-9 - Small Figurine of a Goddess Worshiped by the Hebrews

Like other tribes in the Middle East, who were still within the bicameral consciousness, the Hebrews needed the "voices of gods" in their minds in order to feel safe. They needed the Great Goddess to bless their crops and their families. The Jews worshiped the *golden calf* as an idol, because, like their neighbors, they believed that the gods lived in their idols and spoke through their idols. It was necessary for the Levite priests to stop this practice if they were going to institute Yahweh as the only god and gain the people's obedience. Later, after the Babylonian Captivity, when the Torah/Old Testament was written, the first and second commandments were put into the mouth of Moses: (1) You shall not have any other gods before me and (2) You shall not make idols.

Thus, the idea of monotheism came later in Jewish history. In fact, after centuries of non-acceptance, the idea finally gathered steam after the Jews were freed from their Babylonian Captivity and introduced to Zoroastrianism by their liberator, the Persian king Cyrus the Great. The Jewish prophet Isaiah, although he is proposed to have lived around 750 to 725 BC, now had words put in his mouth by the priests, which extoled the accomplishments of Cyrus promising Yahweh's support for his campaign. Isaiah was the *first prophet to speak of monotheism* and he did so while praising Cyrus and revealing how the Jewish god would help Cyrus in his conquests:

> 1. Thus saith the Lord to his anointed, to Cyrus, whose right hand I have holden, to subdue nations before him; and I will loose the loins of kings, to open before him the two-leaved gates; and the gates shall not be shut.
>
> 2. I will go before thee, and make the crooked places straight: I will break in pieces the gates of brass, and cut in sunder the bars of iron:
>
> 3. And I will give thee the treasures of darkness, and hidden riches of secret places, that thou mayest know that I, the Lord, which call thee by name, am the God of Israel.
>
> 4. For Jacob my servant's sake, and Israel mine elect, I have even called thee by thy name: I have surnamed thee, though thou hast not known me:
>
> 5. I am the Lord, and there is none else, there is no God beside me: I girded thee, though thou hast not known me:
>
> 6. That they may know from the rising of the sun, and from the west, that there is none beside me. I am the Lord, and there is none else.
>
> 7. I form the light, and create darkness: I make peace, and create evil: I the Lord do all these things (Isaiah 45:1-7).

This is a very interesting passage because it presents an idea of one God (monotheism) who *forms the light, and creates darkness: who makes peace, and creates evil.* It seems that for an instant the priests might have made the leap from Zoroastrian dualism to Jewish monotheism. Unfortunately, it was only a passing reference because as we know, the Jews and their Christian descendants fell into the same trap of dualism. There may be a god in heaven, but the devil rules on earth.

Isaiah also introduced the idea of false gods—a basic requirement for monotheism. A universal god demands that only He is to be worshiped. If the god of the Jews were simply a tribal god, this would imply polytheism, because other tribes also had their gods.

Before the Babylonian Captivity, the Hebrew god was a vengeful, bloodthirsty, and jealous anthropomorphic volcano god who ruled by fear,[117] much like Enlil who was worshiped and feared throughout Mesopotamia (Chaldea) and the Jews would surely have been aware of him. When Cyrus liberated the Jewish priests, however, at least seven hundred years after the volcano, the Jewish god became a better-tempered god, more identical to Ahura-Mazda the good god of Zoroastrianism.

Who Are the Hebrews and From Where Did They Come?

If, as historians and scientists tell us, the Jews did not originate in Egypt, where did they come from? We do not know. Probably they were tribes indigenous to Canaan or refugees from the volcano. Perhaps they were a mixture of both. As we have said, the earliest known reference to them is on an Egyptian stele that places them in Canaan in 1200 BC. The land area of Canaan roughly corresponds to present day Israel, Palestine, Lebanon, western Jordan, and southwestern Syria. So the odds are that the Jews were indigenous to Canaan, while their ranks may have swelled with refugees.

Canaan was of significant economic and geopolitical importance at the time and the Egyptians, Hittites, and Assyrians all wanted to control it. Canaanite culture was developed locally from nomadic tribes, farmers, merchants, and traders. The ancient Greeks would later refer to the Canaanites as Phoenicians.[118]

From 1500 BC to around 1000 BC, within the time of Thera and the writings of the Judges, Canaan was a colony of the Egyptians. Around 1350 BC, we have the Amarna letters written by Canaanite governors and princes to the Pharaoh Amenhotep IV regarding political matters. At this time, no mention is made of the Hebrews by any sources. They might have been a small loose confederation of nomadic tribes in the area, without any power or stature. Most assuredly they were not in Egypt. And regardless of Jewish mythology, they did not build the pyramids under the lash of Egyptian masters. Evidence suggests that they were instead conscripted to work on farms in Canaan and were "enslaved" by Egyptian masters there.

At the time, when other more settled nations in the Middle East were vying with each other for conquest, building their cities, imposing their gods and creating their empires, the Hebrews were not players in the game. Jerusalem was a city built by the Canaanites that now paid tribute to Egypt.

The Hebrew Vagrants

During the time period we are discussing, there were no Jews or Zionists. There were only Hebrews and other Semitic tribes. Some Hebrew tribes would eventually be united under a religion promoted by the Levite priest class, which would in time be called Judaism, and those who ascribed to this religion would eventually be called Jews.

Julian Jaynes, who developed the theory of the breakdown of the bicameral mind and the origin of subjective consciousness, paints a picture of the Middle East after the Thera disaster. In this picture we find that the Hebrews were a locus of small tribes within a large landscape of nomadic people spread across the eastern shore of the Mediterranean, to the central region of Mesopotamia and northward into the land of the Assyrians.

Jaynes tells us that during the time of 2000 to 1000 BC, amorphous masses of half-nomadic peoples moved about with no fixed grazing grounds. Some of these people were refugees from the Thera eruption; some were from the Dorian invasion that followed in its wake; and some were indigenous nomadic tribes. In this period of zombie apocalypse, the mixture of strange, savage, and wary men were continually separating out and coming together in an attempt to organize themselves into larger groups for security reasons. Life was cheap and dying was a daily occurrence. Some men created raiding parties or fought over water holes; some were caught and enslaved; and some bartered control over their lives for food and seed. Some clung to the edges of settled lands still trying to hear the voices of their gods, fearing to move out or take action without direction. This period of terror, lawlessness, slavery, hunger, and death must still lurk in our collective subconscious as the zombie apocalypse. There must still be a collective karma remembrance of a time when we lost our contact with god and the earth turned into an arid landscape of death and destruction.[119]

The people of the great city-states like Babylon and Nineveh survived the great upheaval because they were well inland. To them, the migratory hordes of refugees and nomads were social outcasts who were barely given a human status. They were the robbers and the vagrants, the squatters and the insane. These people stole whatever they could and menaced the surrounding countryside. The word for *vagrant* in Akkad, the universal language at the time, is *khabiru*. These khabiru are referenced on cuneiform tablets. It is very possible that *khabiru*, in time, softened into *hebrew*. Apparently, from among the discordant collection of landless and nomadic masses, a group emerged that took on a unique identity. In time this group of Hebrews, perhaps calling themselves Israelites, ransacked Jericho and later Jerusalem in the land of Canaan. Hundreds of years later, they would call themselves Jews, the people who lived in the land of Judah that had once been called Canaan.

The Kingship of David

According to the biblical timeline, the first kingdom of the Hebrews lasted about a hundred years during the reigns of Saul, David, and

Solomon. Saul lived around 1030 BC, David around 1010 BC, and Solomon, who built the first Jewish temple, around 970 BC. Jerusalem was the city chosen by King David to be the capital of the conquered territory, mainly because the city was not tied specifically to any of the twelve tribes.[120]

This enabled David to conquer the city with royal forces and retain it as royal property beyond the reach of any one tribe. David used Jerusalem as the symbol to unite the tribes. In order to emphasize the uniqueness and importance of Jerusalem, David brought the Ark of the Covenant there and turned the city into the religious center of the people of Israel. He built an altar there to the Lord (2 Sam 24:21-25). He also designated Solomon, his son and heir, to build the Temple after his passing. David was a visionary as the Psalms of the Bible, attributed to him, attest.

An inscription found on a stele in Tel Dan, a town in northern Israel near Damascus, mentions the kingship of David providing textual evidence for his existence outside the Bible.[121]

Certain tribes among the Hebrews called their captured territory Israel after Jacob was given this new name by god according to Levite scribes. According to the Book of Genesis, Jacob is the son of Isaac and Rebecca and the grandson of Abraham and Sarah. Jacob and his wife Leah had thirty-three sons and daughters including the twelve sons who, as the story goes, originated the "Tribes of Israel." One daughter, Dinah, was also mentioned to have "gone out to see the daughters of the land," but was raped by a prince named Shechem.

The reign of Solomon, David's son, is considered the Golden Age of the Jewish people. The story relates now the Hebrews were wealthy, powerful, numerous, and united. They controlled Israel and dominated many lands beyond. Solomon had personally amassed a great fortune and had married women from other tribes. Yet, according to the priests, these actions were expressly prohibited by the Torah. The priests accused his wives of reintroducing the Canaanite gods and goddesses into Jewish society. This was not likely, however, because the Jewish people had been worshiping these deities since their beginning. Despite this tension, Solomon built the Temple that his father wanted. The books of Proverbs, Ecclesiastes, and Song of Songs are attributed to Solomon.

While it was important for later biblical scribes to idealize David and Solomon as kings chosen by Yahweh, most archeologists, including

Jewish archeologists, argue that the *United Monarchy* was not much more than a small-scale hill-country chiefdom.[122]

After Solomon, his son Rehoboam, who historians acknowledge was a bad ruler, heavily taxed the people. In response, the people revolted against Rehoboam and chose Jeroboam, of a different tribe, as their ruler. This caused a split between the two monarchies (ca. 920 BC). As a result, the Northern Kingdom of *Israel*, composed of ten tribes, and the Southern Kingdom of Judah, composed of the tribes of Judah, Benjamin, and Levi, became different states. While Israel controlled the fertile lands in the north, Judah controlled the spiritual center of Jerusalem in the south.[123]

The Kingdom Splits into Israel and Judah

The story of the split into two kingdoms is significant for two reasons. Firstly, it can be verified by the historical writings of different peoples; secondly, it established the time period and the reason why the mythology of the Pentateuch was created.

In his article, S. David Sperling, a professor of Bible studies at Hebrew Union College–Jewish Institute of Religion in New York, raises the question, "Were the Jews slaves in Egypt?"[124] He argues that while the Torah devotes more than four books to the proposition that the Hebrews came to Canaan after generations of subjugation in Egypt, there is absolutely no evidence that this occurred—no cuneiform tablets, nor steles, no unearthed Hebrew encampments, no records from the construction of the pyramids; in fact, not a single pottery shard like those found in early Hebrew settlements in Canaan. In short, the enslavement in Egypt appears to be a complete fabrication. But why?

Sperling believes that the story is an allegory invented "to obscure the fact that the Israelites were native to Canaan." But why should Israelite scribes invent a story that only undercut their claims to the land in which they lived?

Biblical historian Robert Carroll tells us that the Exodus myth originated in the northern tradition (Israel) and was virtually unknown in the south (Judah).

During the period after the United Monarchy, the division into two kingdoms (ca. 920 BC–720 BC) occurred. In 720 BC, the kingdom of Israel fell to the Assyrians, resulting in the "ten lost tribes." When this happened, many members of these tribes became slaves and were taken out of the area and sold by slave traders. Others, however, found refuge in Judah bringing with them their literature and traditions, among them the story of the Exodus, which depicted the Israelites as foreign invaders from Egypt.

Map 2-7: Kingdoms of Israel and Judah ca 921 BC

Why did this tradition of foreignness arise in Israel? Why does the Torah tell us that the priesthood, the sacrificial cult, the tabernacle, the festivals, the covenant traditions to serve Yahweh exclusively, and the laws governing most of life's activities originated outside Israel? Why does it say in Leviticus 18:1-5: "Yahweh spoke to Moses, saying, Speak to the Israelite people and say to them: I am Yahweh your god. You shall not emulate the practices of the land of Egypt where you dwelled, nor shall you emulate the practices of the land of Canaan where I am taking you. Not their statutes shall you follow but my norms you shall observe and you shall take care to follow my statutes. I am Yahweh, your god."

The reason, according to Sperling, is that it enabled the Israelites to assert their distinctiveness in a land still in chaos and confusion, having a great mixture of peoples all trying to survive and gain a foothold in an environment in which the strong vied for limited land and power.

During this period, the people were still largely in the bicameral mind, searching for direction from their silent deities. The biblical scribes of the day developed the strategy of claiming "foreignness" as a means to foster Israelite religious, social, and political solidarity. As long as the Israelites were conscious of their foreignness, they would be able to maintain their alleged religious and moral superiority to the masses around them. As foreigners having no roots in Canaan, they would find it easier to heed the admonitions of the authors of the Torah to reject Canaanite and Egyptian practices.

Under such conditions, the myth of slavery in Egypt served another important function. If Yahweh freed the Israelites from slavery, then their god was entitled to exclusive worship by them. As written in Exodus 20:2-3, "I am the Lord thy God, which have brought thee out of the land of Egypt, out of the house of bondage. Thou shalt have no other gods before me."

We must also remember that at the time of Thera, Canaan was under Egyptian rule and we know that the Egyptians required of their Canaanite governors that they use the displaced masses as forced labor to cultivate food for them.

It seems, therefore, according to Sperling, that, "the biblical writers invented the idea that the Israelites lived in Egypt in order to impel them to maintain their distinctiveness in Canaan. And the story of servitude *in* Egypt is an allegory of servitude *to* Egypt." The Jews, among other tribes in Canaan were likely subjected to forced labor by Egyptian taskmasters, but they were never slaves in Egypt.

The Babylonian Captivity

Since we last discussed the situation of the Hebrews' mighty neighbors to the east, things have changed. The Babylonians in 612 BC overran Nineveh, the Assyrian capitol, and drove the Assyrians to Carchemish on the Euphrates River. The Assyrians allied with the Egyptians to try to defeat the Babylonians. A battle took place at Carchemish in 609 BC where the Babylonians massacred the combined forces of the Egyptians and Assyrians. Assyria was so hated by people that it never appeared again as a nation and not a single Egyptian soldier made it out alive.

The Bible tells a story about how the Egyptian army of Pharaoh Necho II was delayed at Megiddo by the forces of King Josiah of Judah. The Battle of Megiddo is recorded as having taken place in 609 BC, the same year as the battle at Carchemish. According to the story, the Egyptians had to pass through the territory controlled by the Kingdom of Judah to get to Carchemish. Necho requested permission from its king, but Josiah refused to let the Egyptians pass. A battle took place in which Josiah was killed and his army defeated. The reason for Josiah's refusal to let the Egyptians pass is attributed to a command by Yahweh that, "A sword shall not pass through your land" (Lev 26:6). The battle with the Egyptians is recorded in the Torah in II Kings 23:29-30 and in II Chronicles 35:20-25.[125]

After the Battle of Carchemish in 605 BC, Nebuchadnezzar, the Babylonian king, besieged Jerusalem and the new king of Judah, Jehoiakim, was forced to pay a tribute to Babylon. After four years of this, Jehoiakim stopped paying and Nebuchadnezzar attacked Jerusalem. He put the prophet Zedekiah on the throne as his puppet, but Zedekiah also rebelled. The Babylonians then attacked Jerusalem again in 587 BC, burned the temple, and took the ruling class priests and nobility into captivity in Babylon.[126]

The Jewish leadership remained slaves of the Babylonians until the Persian king Cyrus the Great conquered Babylon in 539 BC and allowed the exiled Jews to return to the land of Judah. The return of the exiles was a gradual process rather than a single event, and many of the freed slaves or their descendants never returned.

According to the biblical Book of Ezra, construction of a second temple in Jerusalem began at this time. All these events are considered significant in Jewish history and culture, and had a far-reaching impact on the development of Judaism.

When the Assyrians sacked Samaria, the capital of Israel, in 722 BC, they deported the Hebrews-Jews and replaced them with settlers from other areas. This was an established part of Assyrian policy because it destroyed the old power structures of the areas.[127] Israel never again became an independent nation until after World War II during the twentieth century.

For its part, Judah managed to survive as an Assyrian vassal state until 587 BC but after Assyria's collapse, the Babylonians destroyed Jerusalem, the temple, and the kingdom of Judah. The religious ideology of the Jewish priests that Yahweh, the god of Israel, had chosen Jerusalem for his dwelling place and that the kingship begun by David would last forever, was now shattered. The fall of Jerusalem and the end of Jewish kingship was a crushing blow that forced the Jewish leaders who had been exiled to Babylon to completely rethink their ideas. It was in Babylon, therefore, that the major sections of the Torah (Old Testament) began to be rewritten or written anew. These books included Deuteronomy to II Kings[128] as well as Isaiah 40–55, Ezekiel, the final version of Jeremiah, and the priestly source in the Pentateuch. After the Jews were liberated from the Babylonians, they also incorporated the doctrines of one god and individual responsibility into their liturgy. Like Zoroastrianism, Judaism began to emphasize personal purity and holiness.

The trauma of the exile experience did not destroy the Jews, but gave rise to a strong sense of unity among those who had been previously dispersed and who now lived in Israel, Judah, and Babylonia. This trauma resulted in the development of a myth of common origins that kept the worshippers of Yahweh together and distinguished them from other peoples. The priests also differentiated the Jews from their neighbors by prohibiting intermarriage and by instituting the ritual of circumcision[129] and the observance of the Sabbath. The Jewish priests were also now fortified by a powerful new religious ideology, Zoroastrianism. All these things combined to make the Jews feel that they were once again, the "chosen people" of god.[130]

To recap, a few tribes of nomadic Hebrews (vagrants) organized themselves over a couple of centuries to take control over the cities of Jericho and Jerusalem. In doing so, they chose their own kings, fought battles with their neighbors, got obliterated by the Assyrian and Babylonian empires, were freed by the Persians, and then the Jewish priests pieced together a story of common origins out of historical fragments which served to unite the Jews as a people chosen by Yahweh. Because their homeland was Judah, they now called themselves Jews, meaning the people of Judah. The people once again had a common religious identity and a homeland of their own. In all likelihood, however, their identity, unlike the Babylonians, Akkadians, Assyrians, etc., did not derive solely from common tribal ancestry, but rather from the experience of a common trial by fire and the acceptance of a common religious identity. This is why, today, the term "Jew" refers, not to a people, but to those who practice Judaism.

The Jews returned slowly to Judah and from there formed a new nucleus, inviting those who had been displaced or who had abandoned the original group of Hebrews. Among them were many of the Israelites who were dispersed by the Assyrians, those who escaped into Israel territory during the Babylonian conquest, those that remained in Judah, and also those who remained in Babylon after their liberation by Cyrus.

When Babylon fell to Cyrus the Great in 539BC, Judah became an administrative division of the Persian Empire. Cyrus was succeeded by Cambyses, who added Egypt to the empire. After his death, in 522 BC, his successor Darius introduced administrative reforms including the collection, codification, and administration of local law codes. It is reasonable to suppose that this policy impacted the rewrite of the Torah at this time.

After 404 BC, the Persians lost control of Egypt, causing them to tighten their administrative control over Judah and the rest of the Levant in order to strengthen their defenses. Egypt was eventually reconquered, but soon afterward Persia fell to the Macedonian king, Alexander the Great, which ushered in the Hellenistic period in the Levant.

Judah's population over the entire period was probably never more than thirty thousand and that of Jerusalem no more than three thousand.[131] Most of the people were connected in some way to the Temple.

The Persians may have experimented with ruling Judah as a client-kingdom, but by the mid–fifth century BC, Judah had become a theocracy, ruled by a hereditary priest class,[132] with a Persian-appointed governor, often Jewish, who was charged with keeping order and collecting taxes.[133]

According to biblical history, the prophets Ezra and Nehemiah arrived in Jerusalem at this time (450 BC). Nehemiah was given the status of governor and a commission to rebuild the temple. Apparently, in this regard, there developed a clash between the Jews who had remained in Judah and the aristocracy returning from Babylon who had now developed an attitude of exclusivism. The problem originated over disputes of property. Much of the property of the exiles had been bought up by the Jews who had remained in Judah. Ezra and Nehemiah attempted to reintegrate the rival factions into a united society, inspired by the prophecies of Ezekiel and his followers.[134]

Ezekiel was a Jewish prophet, born around 622 BC. His visions included four angels with four wheels that he describes in great detail. He also incessantly prophesied the destruction of Jerusalem and its temple, which came true when Jerusalem was finally sacked by the Babylonians. Later, he began to have visions of a new Temple. It was this vision that inspired Ezra and Nehemiah in their attempts to reconcile the Jews in Judah.

There is no question that the Persian era, especially the period between 538 and 400 BC, congealed the Jewish religion and laid the foundations for their scriptural canon and that of the Christian religions that followed. The renewed religion of the Jews acted as a magnet to draw Jews back to Judah that had been scattered from the time of the Assyrian invasion.

Greek Gods in Jerusalem

Judah (Judea) remained under the governorship of the Persians from 539 BC to 332 BC until it was conquered by Alexander the Great, who set up his capitol in Babylon. After Alexander's death in 323 BC, his empire was divided by two of his generals. Ptolemy took control of

Egypt and Seleucus I Nicator took control of the Near East. Through the Seleucid line, the Greeks remained in control of Judah until the revolt of Judas Maccabeus in 167 BC.

The Seleucid king Antiochus IV, who ruled between 175 BC to 164 BC, sought total control over the Middle East and beyond. He even entered Egypt and destroyed the rule of Ptolemy. Afterwards, he captured the city of Jerusalem. He had help from the Jewish ruling class in this endeavor. A man named Joshua was brother to the Jewish high priest. He bribed the Greek king Antiochus IV into deposing his brother and appointing him as high priest. As compensation, Joshua changed the name of Jerusalem to Antiochia and erected a gymnasium in the capital, where Greek culture was promoted. Josephus, the Jewish historian at the time, reports that Joshua "at once shifted his countrymen over to the Greek way of life."[135]

Antiochus, however, was not content with this. He issued a decree to suppress public observance of Jewish laws and all forms of worship under pain of death. He used the Temple for pagan rituals that included sacrificing unclean animals on the altar in the Holy of Holies. Antiochus also forbade circumcision, the possession of Jewish scriptures, and observance of the Sabbath. In a final insult to the Jewish faithful, he required Jewish leaders to sacrifice to the Greek gods.[136] Apparently many of the Jewish ruling class happily complied. Their elaborate tombs and elegant mansions have been discovered in Jerusalem with their beautifully paved ritual baths, fancy dinnerware, and costly furniture.

In place of Yahweh, Antiochus promoted the pantheon of Greek gods and goddesses, who represent archetypes of human experience.[137] These anthropomorphic deities look like humans and are subject to the same feelings, desires, virtues, and foibles as humans. These deities no longer represent natural forces, but now represent social forces. They have advanced from concepts of raw physical powers to include psychological powers, including abstract thought.

The Greek gods and goddesses are still external and as such must be worshipped because they can do harm to people, but they are not the voices of god in the mind that existed for the bicameral societies. Nonetheless, these deities controlled every aspect of Greek society, and if they were not placated by the meticulous practice of rituals, the entire city could suffer.

Like all religions, the Greek religion was composed of myths, which were stories and tales of the deities that had nothing to do with falsehood or truth. There were many stories, often contradictory, told about the same gods and goddesses because priests invented their attributes as a means to discuss more subtle abstract concepts.

If the priests of Greek society introduced a new god that was relevant to another people, the priests would adopt the new god into their own pantheon.

The Greeks believed that they were introducing the civilized deities of the empire to the rustic Jews of the Middle East. These included: Aphrodite, the goddess of love, beauty, desire, sex, and pleasure; Apollo, the god of music, arts, knowledge, healing, prophecy, poetry, manly beauty, etc.; Ares, the god of war, bloodshed, and violence; Artemis, the virgin goddess of the hunt, wilderness, animals, young girls, childbirth, plague, and the moon; Athena, the goddess of intelligence, skill, peace, warfare, battle strategy, handicrafts, and wisdom; as well as many more deities like Demeter, Dionysus, Hades, Hephaestus, Hermes, Hera, and Zeus.[138] For a more extensive review of the Greek gods, see Appendix A.

Later, when the Church of Rome began to destroy the Greek and Roman deities in favor of Christian monotheism, they destroyed a great reservoir of imagination and art, human emotions and earthiness.

When the Catholic Church seized control, their monotheistic god became a completely abstract concept, the highest abstraction possible. The fight between the church and its heretics, including the Gnostics, was a fight between knowing God as Jesus taught versus defining the perfect thought of God and the perfect order of men to God. Unfortunately God is not attained in this manner. God is attained through love, selflessness, and the development of the intuition. But we are getting ahead of ourselves.

The Jewish Revolts

The Jews resented the forced imposition of the Greek pantheon on their religious and social life. The attempt to destroy Jewish culture split the Judeans. While the rich may have benefitted by making deals with their oppressors, the middle class and poor had no such opportunity. After some time, a rural Jewish priest named Mattathias called upon loyal Jews to oppose the Greek invaders and the Jewish Hellenizers. With his sons, he began a guerrilla campaign against them that became known in history as the Maccabean Revolt. In 165 BC, the revolutionaries freed the Temple from Greek control and consecrated it so that Jewish services could begin again. The festival of Hanukkah was instituted by Judas Maccabeus and his brothers to celebrate this event (1 Macc. 4:59). Today Hanukkah is an eight-day Jewish celebration that occurs around the time of Christmas.

Judas Maccabee's brother Simon was named the prince of Israel and the high priest. Simon and his successors formed the Hasmonean Dynasty, which was a Jewish kingship.[139] Simon led the people through a deceitful and turbulent period, until the Greeks murdered him in 135 BC. Nonetheless, the Hasmonean kingship lasted—and even expanded—in part, because the Greek empire had begun to disintegrate due to pressure on all sides. During this expansion, the Hasmoneans, just as the Greeks had done, forcibly converted the tribes in their area, (Moabites, Edomites, and Ammonites) to Judaism.

In 63 BC, the Roman general Pompey conquered Jerusalem and made the Jewish kingdom a colony of Rome. In 40 BC, the Roman Senate appointed Herod to be King of the Jews and by 6 CE, Judea was placed under direct Roman administration. The area was henceforth called Syria Palestinia (Syria-Palestine). The Jewish kingdom had, nonetheless, survived for 103 years.

In AD 66, the Jews revolted against Roman rule, but were brutally put down. The Romans besieged Jerusalem in AD 70, killing most of the population and enslaving the survivors. This horrific oppression created the great migration that the Jews call the Diaspora. It was the last of the Diasporas, which had begun with the Assyrians, then the Babylonians, and now the Romans. Israel would cease to exist as a homeland for the Jews for the next two millennia, until it was created again in 1948, when David Ben-Gurion, the head of the Jewish Agency, proclaimed the establishment of the State of Israel soon after the end of World War II.

The Torah / Old Testament

Now that we have provided a brief summary of Jewish history, let us take a closer look at the Torah/Old Testament of the Bible. The Bible arguably has had a greater impact on western civilization than any other book. It is the source of western religious ideas and both Jews and Christians embrace it as the "word of god." It undergirds their faith in Divinity and helps them through times of suffering and confusion. It gives them hope and the promise of a better tomorrow. Unfortunately, mixed in with these blessings, are harmful myths, which go unquestioned and have become the source of much of our debilitating unconscious programming. When people mistake myths and stories for historical fact, they prevent their minds from growing and expanding. Myth becomes dogma to which the mind becomes enslaved and people lose their rationality. This is why it is important to determine what is myth and what is history in the books of the Bible.

The historical study of the Bible began when early scientists noticed discrepancies in the Book of Genesis. The first big question that arose was, "Why did god have two names, Elohim and Yahweh?" Other questions quickly followed: Why does Genesis contain two creation myths? Why is sacrifice mentioned at the dawn of time? Why does it play such a big role with Cain and Abel? If Adam and Eve were the first humans, from where did Cain get his wife and how can he be afraid of other people retaliating for murdering his brother? Why is the flood story so choppy and repetitive? Why are there two stories of the dispersing of the nations? Who is Melchizedek and how can he be a priest of Israel's God as far back as Abraham's day? Why are there two covenant making stories with Abraham? (Gen 15 and 17)? How is it that Abraham is described as a law keeper long before the law was given? These problems led to a rational analysis of the writings of Genesis and the other books of the Pentateuch.

In Deuteronomy; for example, which Moses was supposed to have written under the guiding hand of Yahweh, he is discussed as a historical figure in the third person. We are told in verse 6 "to this day no one knows where his grave is." In verse 10, it says, "Since then no prophet has risen in Israel like Moses." If Moses wrote this he would have been bragging about himself and writing about his future death in the third person as if it had already occurred. Unlikely. It is also unlikely that Moses would have stated that no one knew where he was buried.

Rather, it is clear that another writer is telling us about a man called Moses. But if Moses did not write Deuteronomy, who did?

Rather than focusing on the "history" of Moses, Noah, or Abraham, biblical scholars began to focus on the historical circumstances that gave rise to the writers who produced the books of the Bible. This approach differs from those who read the bible as fact and then make projections as to the meaning of these facts. From the perspective of modern biblical scholarship, we learn that the Bible does not accurately recount events in neutral fashion, but rather it tells us what the writers (priests) believed or wanted the reader to believe about those events at the time they were being written. If there is any historical truth in the Bible, and there is, the writings are corroborated by outside textual and archaeological sources.

Apparently, there were three significant periods in Jewish history when the raw materials of Hebrew-Jewish myth and history were consolidated and enlarged upon by the priest class. The first was during the rule of King Josiah around 621 BC; the second was during the time of the Babylonian Captivity; and the third was after the exiles returned to Judea during the period of the Second Temple.

Some of the oldest materials of the Torah/ Old Testament were found in the Temple of Jerusalem by the Hebrew priests under the rule of King Josiah, twenty-six hundred years ago. The king had ordered the temple cleaned and cleared of all the remnant bicameral scrolls. When the priests found the scrolls, however, they did not discard them but used them instead as a base upon which to create their scripture going forward. With certain modifications, they created an imaginary ancestry with an imaginary past—one that united the people, but also established the priests' legitimacy and position in society.[140] Their intention was never to create an accurate history of the Jews, it was to tell a story to unite the people under their authority. The old materials, creatively manipulated, became known as the Pentateuch, the first five books of the Torah/Old Testament. Also created at this time were the Book of Joshua, Judges, Ruth, Samuel, and Kings. Later, after the Babylonian Captivity, the books of the Prophets, Psalms, Proverbs, Ecclesiastes, and the Chronicles were added to the Torah materials.

Because most people in the West believe that the Torah/Old Testament provides historical fact, we must begin with a clarification. According to rabbinical interpretation (Midrash), the Pentateuch was created prior to the creation of the world and was used as the blueprint for Creation. The Pentateuch is the first five books of the Bible, which include Genesis, Exodus, Leviticus, Numbers, and Deuteronomy. The priests say that these books were given by God to Moses, who was the first Jewish prophet and savior. This interpretation of the origins of the Pentateuch is obvious dogma. It is an idea that constricts the mind because it is something that can never be questioned simply because the priests say so.

Scientists and historians have proven that the books of the Pentateuch had been written and reworked by at least four different scribes (priests) at four different times in Jewish history. The Pentateuch, as well as other books in the Old Testament, went through several drafts, each to serve the agenda of the priests who created the revisions. The majority of Biblical scholars believe that the Pentateuch and most books of the Torah were written by priests around the time of the Babylonian Captivity (ca. 600 BC) and were completed around 400 BC.[141] This is fourteen hundred years after Abraham and Moses purportedly existed.

The creation of the Pentateuch was not an exceedingly difficult job for the priests at the time of Josiah. The Book of Genesis consists primarily of a composite of the creation myths of previous civilizations with the adjustment that now the goddess became Yahweh a god. Exodus is a fabricated story about the Hebrews enslavement in Egypt, which was written at the time of Josiah, but improved upon by later priests after the Babylonian exile. The story gave the Hebrew tribes a common, yet unique, heritage among the immigrants and nomadic populations of their day. Leviticus consists of rules of worship as demanded by the Levite priest class. Numbers consists of the story of the tribes in their nomadic state. They are largely powerless and preyed upon at this time. They take a census of their numbers, and the priests tell them that god continues to punish them for their unfaithfulness but, if they worship him exclusively, he will forgive them. Moses, we read, is not allowed to enter the "promised land," probably because it would have been too difficult for the priests to account for his behavior in such recent history. The Book of Deuteronomy, the fifth book of the Pentateuch, is clearly a creation of the Deuteronomist, actually a group of post-exile priests writing over a period of three hundred years with the intention of enforcing their rule on the people. It reveals new laws that the people must follow. The term itself means "second law."

In 1878, the German Old Testament scholar, Julius Wellhausen, published his Prolegomena to the History of Israel, still considered the most influential book on Old Testament scholarship ever published. Wellhausen argued that there was an editor (a priest or priests) who compiled biblical source material at the time of the return from the Babylonian Captivity. In his essay, Peter Enns tells us that the editor: "made no effort to respect the integrity of the originals or their chronological order. In fact, he cut and pasted the sources together driven by a striking - for some even disturbing - theological agenda."[142]

According to Wellhausen's analysis, the Pentateuch obscures Israel's real history. He sought to untangle the original documents and put them back into a chronological order.

Wellhausen identified four distinct writers of the Old Testament that he called: J, E, D, and P, in that order. J stands for "Yahwist" (spelled with a J in German). He is writing in the ninth century BC, during the period of the split between Israel and Judah. The Yahwist text itself is most likely a compilation of stories, traditions, and archival material that was shaped into a continuous narrative by southern Judean scribes who were attempting to promote the politics of Judah. Many of the Yahwist's stories display knowledge of the geopolitical world as it was in the ninth to eighth centuries BC. The final form of the Yahwist text was probably fixed sometime in the seventh century BC and continued to be revised into the exilic and post-exilic periods (sixth to fifth centuries BC).[143] The Yahwist is so called because of his use of the word "Yahweh" to refer to god. This writer is closest in time to the Thera explosion when Yahweh was the new volcano god.

The Elohist source (E), named on account of its use of the Hebrew *elohim* to designate the deity instead of Yahweh, orients itself around the traditions, cultic sites, and patriarchs of the northern kingdom of Israel. E's date of composition has also been assigned to the ninth century BC. It supported the reign of Jeroboam in Israel, as a counter narrative to the pro-Solomonic Judean narrative of the Yahwist. It is the shortest in length of the Pentateuchal sources, making its first appearance midway through the book of Genesis (20:1) and extending itself into the book of Exodus where it has its strongest showing. In both the books of Genesis and Exodus, E is often presented as narrating the same story as J, however, with contrasting narrative details and theological emphases.[144]

The Jahwist and the Elohist wrote most of the material of Genesis. Next in time is D, the Deuteronomist, who wrote in the early seventh century BC when the Judean king, Josiah, was trying to institute reforms, just prior to the Babylonian conquest.

The book of Deuteronomy, like the other sources, was composed in stages and by different authors living in different historical periods. Despite this fact, Deuteronomy displays a remarkable unity in its style, theology, and message, largely because the various revisions and additions of the book were written by a specific school of scribes. This group of priests was active from the late monarchal period of the seventh century BC, through the exilic period of the sixth century BC, and into the Persian period of the fifth century BC. The making of the book of Deuteronomy was an accumulative process of several drafts that transpired over three centuries. Because these three centuries witnessed such radically different historical crises, the Deuteronomic scribes freely amended the text in various ways so that it reflected the current concerns, beliefs, and needs of the communities for which they wrote. The later scribes had to explain to the Jews why Jerusalem was destroyed, the land of Judah was no longer their possession, and its people were living in exile.

The book of Deuteronomy was composed around a core text which now makes up the prescribed rules of worship that are expounded in chapters 12-26. This text, called "the scroll of the covenant," was allegedly found during renovations to the temple under the reign of Josiah, Judah's king from 640-609 BC. As we shall see, this text has striking affinities with the religious and political policies implemented by Josiah as depicted in II Kings chapters 22-23, and was most likely used and/or written to legitimize and endorse those policies.[145]

Essentially, the Deuteronomist sets the stage for Jewish dogma that was created and carefully guarded by the priest class. Worship was now controlled by the clergy and performed in only one place, the Temple. At this time, during the reign of King Josiah, the rich were also becoming jealous of this priestly power and wanted a part of it. Religion was not an isolated matter as it is today. Religion at the time was politics. It defined society, the universe, nature, social power, and the status of human beings. The rich bought their way into priestly office. Now we have the Sadducees. Stories were then constructed to empower and justify the need for the new ruling class. The myths of the Pentateuch were created to give the people a deeper sense of belonging and ensure obeisance. The myths and stories now became dogma (i.e., articles of faith that no one can question under pain of ostracism or penalty for blasphemy and heresy). The priests now owned the ancient knowledge and controlled the rituals of service to god. The original source materials for the Pentateuch are basically stories and rules pieced together from the myths of the older civilizations that surrounded the Jews.

The final source, P, was writing after the Babylonian exile and much of the writing is concerned with ritualism and the law. These are subjects that a priest class would produce.

The legal and ritualistic material (P), which was purportedly given to Moses on Mt. Sinai to begin the exodus of the Jews was therefore written last, about one millennium after Moses was said to have existed. The priests had an agenda—they wanted to put Jewish law at the very beginning of Israel's history and thereby empower their rule by establishing the longevity of the law and the fact that it was handed to the Jews by god himself in the mists of the hoary past. The editing job was only partially successful. Anachronisms and theological contradictions permeated the effort.

The Priestly literature makes up the largest portion of the Pentateuch and it provides the main voice and framework for the first four books of the Torah/Old Testament. Its creation account opens the book of Genesis, and inserts genealogies, dates, land settlements, and marriage records to provide a chronological framework to the Jahwist/Elohist material throughout Genesis and into the book of Exodus. In Exodus, there are large blocks of Priestly material. Exodus chapters 25-31 and 35-40 are entirely from the Priestly writer. The book of Leviticus is likewise from the Priestly pen, and approximately seventy-five percent of the book of Numbers as well. In fact, excluding Exodus 32-34, which is a compilation of J/E material, the literature spanning Exodus 25:1 to

Numbers 10:28, including the entire book of Leviticus, is all from P. In other words, a total of 50 consecutive chapters of Priestly material now occupy the central position of the Pentateuch, and the following texts make up an additional seventy percent of Priestly material. The Priestly writers' central purpose in Genesis was to establish Abraham as the original founder of the faith and to show that Yahweh made a covenant with him in which he promised Abraham and his lineage the land of Canaan.

The book of Exodus presents a fuller picture of the Priestly writer's agenda. The Priests' insertion, found in Exodus 1:7, harkens back to the Priestly blessing in the opening creation account of the book of Genesis: "be fruitful and multiply." Here we are informed that this blessing has come to pass and that there has been a marked transition from the seventy male persons, the children of Jacob that came down to Egypt to the over six hundred thousand males that embarked on the exodus. In Exodus, the largest additions to the J/E material was the instructions for building the tabernacle (Exod 25-31) and its construction (Exod 35-40), which introduces us to the ritualistic and legal dogmas of the priest class that are now consecrated as the sole officiating authority over the people's relationship to their god. The tabernacle, symbolic for the temple itself, was erected on New Year's Day and the keeping of sacrificial and other rituals safeguarded the covenantal promises that God established with Abraham's descendants.

The book of Numbers continues with many of these same Priestly concerns, but additionally includes more settlement records, this time associated with the tribal organization of the camp; a census of all males over the age of twenty; and the establishment of a working itinerary for the scattered J/E material in the larger wilderness narrative. The latter half of the book of Numbers provides evidence of Priestly legislation written at a later period, which amended previous laws found in the book of Leviticus.

The central element of the Priestly theology is the Tabernacle and its altar. These provide support for the Priestly position that Yahweh dwells among the people. Just as previous nations built their temples to their gods and created their idols and icons, so now the Jewish priests did the same. The temple became the home of god and the tabernacle the holy of holies. The people were to observe strict regulations of ethical and ritual purity. The commandments and sacrificial observances were there in order to preserve the purity and holiness of the community. Thus Yahweh's foes, the other gods, were claimed to be false gods, impure and unholy. In this Priestly conception, there are no demonic forces or a Satan figure yet.[146] Such ideas emerged in later literature after Zoroastrianism was more fully absorbed by the priest class and the bad god (Ahriman) became the prototype for Satan.

Another expression, unique to the Priestly work, was the emphasis on eternal covenants and eternal laws. This dogma established the rules and laws that can never be changed or violated by the Jewish people under any circumstances. The covenant of circumcision (Gen 17:1-14), the covenant of the Sabbath (Exod 31:16), and the covenant of the eternal priest class (Num 25:10-13) became fixed in Jewish religion eternally. The observance of Passover and the Festival of Unleavened Bread and Feast of Booths (Exod 12:14, 17; Lev 23:14, 41) and certain rules for the priests were also decreed as eternal laws. Other examples include the lamp that must always be kept lit (Exod 27:21; Lev 24:4) and the priests' portion of any animal sacrifice (Exod 29:28; Lev 6:11; 7:34; 10:15; 24:9). These eternal covenants assured the religious tenure of the priest class over the people who now stood firmly between the belief of the faithful and their deity.

There are also laws that cut people off from the community if they are bad. These include the neglect and non-observance of: "circumcision (Gen 17:14); the festival of unleavened bread (Exod 12:15, 19); Passover (Num 9:13); the Day of Atonement (Lev 23:29, 40); Sabbath violations (Exod 31:14); contact with the dead (Num 19:13, 20); bootlegging holy oil or incense (Exod 30:33, 38); eating a sacrificial meal in a state of impurity (Lev 7:20, 21); eating fat or blood (Lev 7:25, 27), slaughtering or sacrificing outside the temple (Lev 17:4, 9); a blemished priest near the temple (Lev 22:3); various sexual offences (Lev 18:29; 20:17-18); necromancy (Lev 20:6); child sacrifice (Lev 20:2-5); and any intentional sin (Num 15:30-31)."[147]

Jewish mythology transitioned now from freedom of expression to increased legalistic control by the priest class after the Babylonian Captivity. For example, the J and E earlier sources reflect a simpler, unencumbered relationship with God, devoid of ritual. When Abraham built altars at Shechem and Bethel (Gen 12:6-8), services were devoid of priestly ritual. Formalized ritual, which began with D and reached its apex in canon law with P, was a later imposition.

While there are problems with Wellhausen's theory, it has generally held up well over the centuries of modern history. There is general consensus, and little room for debate, that the Pentateuch, as we know it, was not authored by a second millennium Moses, but is the end product of a complex literary process, both written and oral, that did not come to a close until sometimes after the Jewish priest class returned from the Babylonian exile around 426 BC.

Apart from the apocalypse of Thera, the Babylonian Captivity was the most traumatic event in Jewish history. The priests had promised the people a special covenant with god. They were promised the land of Canaan for all times by their god. Their kings would rule forever in this land. They saw themselves as the favorite people of god. In a short time, however, the pillars of their faith were shattered—now they had no land, no temple, no priests to offer sacrifices, and no king. And to make matters painfully evident, the nations of the world did not come to acknowledge their god as the supreme god. Rather the Jews were now humiliated and enslaved by these other nations. They faced the same consequences that all their neighbors had, the destruction of their city-state and the destruction of their gods and goddesses.

In captivity, the Jewish priests were estranged from their god. Now they had nothing to hold on to. There was only one thing to do; they created a glorious mythological past. They invented a story to reinforce the greatness of the Jewish people. More than any other event, the Babylonian Captivity was the driving force behind the collection and editing of writings that has since become known as the Torah[148] or the Old Testament of the Bible. As Walter Brueggemann summarizes the scholarly consensus:

> It is now increasingly agreed that the Old Testament in its final form is a product of and response to the Babylonian Exile. This premise needs to be stated more precisely. The Torah (Pentateuch) was likely completed

in response to the exile, and the subsequent formation of the prophetic corpus and the "writings" i.e., poetic and wisdom texts as bodies of religious literature (canon) is to be understood as a product of Second Temple Judaism [postexilic period]. This suggests that by their intention, these materials are . . . an intentional and coherent response to a particular circumstance of crisis. . . . Whatever older materials may have been utilized (and the use of old materials can hardly be doubted), the exilic and/or postexilic location of the final form of the text suggests that the Old Testament materials, understood normatively, are to be taken precisely in an acute crisis of displacement, when old certitudes—sociopolitical as well as theological—had failed.[149]

The Creation Myth and the Curse of Women

The Pentateuch, which is the first five books of the Torah and which is sometimes referred to as the entire Torah, begins with the Book of Genesis. This book is probably better known than any other book in the Torah/Old Testament. Like the myths of other peoples that try to explain the origins of life, the Book of Genesis attempts to explain how the world came into existence and how human beings came to inhabit the earth. The creation myth of Adam and Eve in the Garden of Eden is accepted by Jews, Christians, and Muslims alike to explain the origin of human existence. Having said this, no myth has done more damage to the relationship between men and women in modern society more than this myth.

Belief in this myth, as if it really occurred, is irrational and has been an impediment to individual and social progress. Yet, it lies deep within western programming and people unconsciously accept it as the primary reason to believe that women are inferior to men. Most people do not understand its origins. The creation myth in the Bible is based upon the myths of older civilizations, which were composed by male priests attempting to justify their authority over women in the early centuries of patriarchy. Let's begin by looking at the idea of *Eve*.

In northern Babylonia, Eve was known as "the Divine Lady of Eden," or "Goddess of the Tree of Life."[150] The Assyrians called her Nin-Eveh, "Holy Lady Eve." Eve was the Great Goddess of the Semitic tribes prior to the development of patriarchy in the Middle East. In fact, the Assyrian capitol, Nineveh, founded around 6000 BC was named for her.[151]

In the myth of the Great Goddess, we, therefore, have the origins of the biblical Eve. As the Great Goddess, she was the giver of life to the Assyrian people, the very people who had suppressed the Jews and destroyed Israel. The Bible's creation myth is largely taken from the Assyrian creation myth, with the "correction" that the goddess of creation had now transformed into the god of creation.[152] In the creation myth of the Torah, Eve, the female of the species, is not just stripped of her role as the creator of life, but she is reduced to a sinful woman responsible for the "fall of man." Women have since been viewed from the perspective of this destructive falsehood.

As we know from our look at matriarchy in Volume 1, the consort of the Goddess was the serpent, believed to be immortal because it could shed its skin. People during the matriarchy regarded the Goddess and the serpent as their parents. As late as the first century BC, some Jewish traditions still identified Yahweh with the serpent deity who accompanied the Goddess in her garden.[153]

The name *Adam* means clay. The ancient idea was that human beings were made from a mixture of blood and clay. In direct contrast to rational experience, in the Jewish creation myth, a wombless god makes his male offspring with his hands and then Eve is created from Adam's rib. The priests who created the myth were determined to separate the concepts of *deity* from *mother* as much as possible. To do so, they eliminated completely the reality of giving birth.

In the Jewish creation myth, we now have an Eve that no longer represents *life* but has come to represent *death*. Under the "teachings" of the Jewish priests, every living thing is now doomed to die because of Eve, the woman. Instead of blaming their vengeful god for evicting Adam from paradise, they blame the woman, Eve, because she sought to share knowledge with Adam. As Jewish scholar, Jesus ben Sirach, (ca. 180–175 BC) expounds, evil began with woman (Eve). "Because of her, we all die."[154]

The patriarchs that followed, in their roles as theologians, philosophers, and spokesmen for Judaism, Christianity, and Islam embraced this idea without question. The Book of Enoch said god created death to punish all humanity for Eve's sin. St Paul, a pillar of Christianity, blamed Eve but absolved Adam from any sin. He tells us, Adam was not deceived, but the woman being deceived was in the transgression" (I Tim 2:14).

St John Chrysostom, one of the early Catholic Church patriarchs, declared that since the seed of all women already existed in Eve, in her sin "the whole female race transgressed." Tertullian, another church father, speaking to all women, said: "And do you not know that you are an Eve? The sentence of God on this sex of yours lives in the age; the guilt must of necessity live too. You are the devil's gateway . . . the first deserter of the divine law; you are she who persuaded him whom the devil was not valiant enough to attack. You destroyed so easily God's image, man. On account of your desert—that is, death, even the Son of God had to die."[155]

And even Saint Augustine, who converted to Christianity and became one of the most influential of all "Fathers" of the Roman Catholic Church—a man who had intercourse with concubines and wrestled with lust his whole life—blames women for his own lack of self-control. He writes that a man's erection is sinful, but it is involuntary because it is not under a man's conscious control. His solution for resolving this male sin was to control women and ensure that they are limited in their ability to influence men.[156]

Augustine opined that the serpent (now Satan) approached Eve because she was less rational and lacked self-control. On the other hand, he argued that Adam's choice to eat the forbidden fruit was an act of kindness so that Eve would not be left alone.[157] Augustine believed that sin entered the world because man did not exercise enough control over woman.

The authority of the *Decretum Gratiani*, a collection of Roman Catholic *canon law* compiled in the twelfth century, set the prohibition against women leading, teaching, or being a witness. It was compiled largely on the views of Augustine, the Bishop of Hippo, and other Church Fathers. The laws and traditions, founded upon the early patriarchs' view of sexuality and women, continue to dominate Christian dogma today. In western civilization, women are not allowed to be priests in the Jewish, Catholic, or Islamic religions, nor are they allowed to have any role in leading or teaching men. There are exceptions, but these are few in number. It is not surprising to know that Augustine also had a profound impact on the thinking of Martin Luther and John Calvin, the architects of Christian Protestantism. Here too it is dogma that men should not be under the leadership of women.

There is a strong case to be made that Christianity would not even exist if it were not for the dogmatic victimization of Eve and the female gender. As Mary Daly, in *Beyond God the Father*, states: "Take the snake, the fruit tree, and the woman from the tableau, and we have no fall, no frowning Judge, no Inferno, no everlasting punishment—hence no need for a Savior. Thus the bottom falls out of the whole Christian theology."[158]

The denigration of woman in the canon of the Jewish patriarchs, and subsequently in the canon of the Christians and Muslims, has allowed generations of priests (rabbis and imams as well) to cement their rule over the minds of the people. The Jewish priests cursed the Great Goddess, whom the majority of Jews still lovingly worshiped in their households. So long as the Jewish people worshiped the Goddess, the power of the priests was limited. To fight the people's sentimental attachment to the Goddess, they accused her daughters of originating sin and causing the downfall of humanity.

So disrespected were women by the Jewish priests that they did not even give women credit for childbirth! Instead, they had a male god break off a piece of a man's rib to make Eve. Jews, Christians, and Muslims accept this myth without question. Many men still believe, because it is the "word of god," that women are the cause of all life's problems and therefore no man should be under the authority of women.

We must realize that all creation myths are fantasies, just made-up stories told to explain how reality came into existence. The Jewish creation myth is no exception. It was composed at a time that we no longer remember or understand, by a male priest class whose ambition was to undergird their power over Jewish people at a time when women were still respected and the Goddess still worshipped by the common people. This myth was not written to establish the truth of reality, nor does it reflect the intentions of Divinity.

Most educated Christians and Jews no longer believe the creation myth,[159] however, the priests continue to propagate this destructive story, and in so doing, provide the rationale for holding women inferior to men.

There is a second, perhaps even more harmful, aspect of the creation myth of Adam and Eve. In this myth, we are told that Eve offers Adam the fruit of divine knowledge, but the jealous Jewish god considers this a great affront. He tells Adam that it is a sin for people to achieve divine knowledge. In reality, however, the whole purpose of living is to try to achieve divine knowledge. The creation myth views human existence as a fall from grace, instead of recognizing that human existence is the greatest gift that Divine Consciousness can give to us, for it is in having a human body that one achieves the ability to be great and to achieve limitlessness. To discourage people from striving for limitlessness, which is inherent in our nature, is to sin against the purpose of creation. The Judea-Christian creation myth says to people if you try to know God on your own, without the intervention of priests, you will be a sinner. In the perpetration of this dogma, men as well as women are spiritually disempowered. The Jewish priests, sadly, were no exception to religious male authorities attempting to disempower their followers during the rule of patriarchy. We shall see this same pattern express itself in the rule of Christianity and Islam as well. It is repeatedly supported because it keeps women and therefore humanity as a whole, subservient to the priests. Unlike priests dispensing dogma to their followers, a true spiritual teacher provides the means to expand one's consciousness and achieve divinity. To suppress the mind with dogma is the typical want of the priest; whereas, to expand the mind is the approach of the mystic or the spiritual teacher.

The Jewish Prophets

We have discussed how the Jews came about as a people—how they were a loose confederation of small tribes that coalesced out of nomadic tribes and immigrants displaced by the aftermath of the Thera volcanic explosion. For a more detailed timeline of Jewish history see Appendix B.

Before the volcanic explosion on Thera, everyone thought like a prophet, (i.e., they all heard the voices of their gods and goddesses in their heads). The prophets of the Jews that we know from the Bible were the devotees of Yahweh who still heard the voice of their god in their mind even at a time when most people were transitioning into subjective consciousness. The graph below gives a timeline of when the major prophets lived.

In analyzing the pronouncements of the Prophets in the Torah/Old Testament over the course of a few centuries, we can witness the evolution of human beings from a bicameral to a subjective consciousness.

According to Jewish legend, the prophets were chosen by their god Yahweh to speak on his behalf. The prophets are presented as models for holiness, wisdom, and closeness to god. They set the standard for teaching the people how to act. The Talmud talks about there being hundreds of thousands of prophets, yet, the scripture only recognizes fifty-five. The Jews called their prophets the Nabi. The Nabi were transitional human beings partly bicameral and partly subjective. They thought subjectively, but they still heard voices, which they attributed to a deity, as had all human beings since the time we emerged out of animality. The transition from the bicameral mind to the subjective mind occurred largely between thirty-two hundred to two thousand years ago, or in Biblical terms 1,200 BC to 1 BC. Since there was a written language at the time, the messages of certain prophets were written down.

These prophets, mostly men, but some women, expressed the "voice of god" to the tribal peoples as they wandered as nomads in the desert, ruled by their Judges (chieftains). The authority of the prophets lasted into the period of the kings and, in some cases, as late as the post-exilic period (after 500 BC).

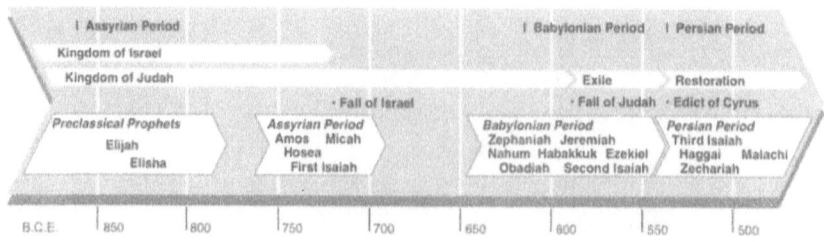

Fig. 2-10: Timeline of the Major Hebrew Prophets

It is difficult to know how much of the books of Samuel I and II were rewritten or created by later priests. We do know that as subjective consciousness became more commonplace, later prophets were not as sure of "the voice of god" as Samuel. Apparently, when they heard the "voice of god", it was not a pleasant experience. The prophets often distrusted themselves in their role. Amos said, "I was no prophet, neither was I a prophet's son; but I was a herdsman, and a gatherer of sycamore fruit" (Amos 7:14-15). Jeremiah said, "Oh Lord, thou hast deceived me, and I was deceived: thou art stronger than I, and hast prevailed: I am in derision daily, everyone mocketh me" (Jer 20:7). The prophets felt unworthy. Jeremiah says, "Then said I, Ah, Lord God! Behold, I cannot speak: for I am a child" (Jer 1:6). Isaiah says, "From the sole of the foot even unto the head there is no soundness in it" (Isa 1:6).

The Nabi were torn; they knew with their subjective consciousness what was "normal," but the voices in their heads would not give them peace. It made them crazy. Isaiah said it was like having a red-hot coal put on his lips (Isa 6:7). Jeremiah compared it to a raging fire shut up in his bones that could not be contained (Jer (20:9). Later Muhammed, who is considered the last of the prophets by Muslims, said that it was as though an angel had enveloped him in a terrifying embrace so that his breath was being forced from his body.

The movement from Samuel in the twelfth century BC to Zechariah in the fifth century BC reflects the change in Jewish consciousness from the bicameral to the subjective mind. As such, it also reflects a change in their idea of god. At the dawn of subjective consciousness, the Nabi were still feared and revered. During the wandering in the desert (1200 to 1000 BC), the people, as was also true of their contemporaries, followed those who announced the "voice of god" in their minds. At this time, the Hebrew Jews were led by tribal chieftains, who are called the Judges in the Torah. During the period of the kingdoms (1000 to 500 BC), the prophets were still allowed a voice, but they did not rule. They were given an audience by the kings, but their voices were discordant and at odds with each other. The prophets (seers) said different things, making the "voice of authority" difficult to determine. While they were still consulted by nervous kings, they could not be trusted.

The ambiguity as to the authority of the prophets is clearly on display by the ninth century BC. Now we have Jezebel, the wife of the Jewish king Ahab, ordering a massacre of the Nabi for speaking out against her. This event is referred to in I Kings 18:4. At this time, Obadiah, another Nabi, hid a hundred of his companions in a cave bringing them food and water until the massacre was over. However, a few years later, Elijah, a Nabi, organized an event to prove that he was the true Nabi and that the Nabi who worshiped Baal were false prophets. When Elijah's god won the event, he ordered a massacre of the Nabi of Baal (I Kings 18:40).

After this, we no longer hear about groups of Nabi in the Torah/OT. What remains were a few individuals whose voices are reported in the Old Testament.

At the time of Jeremiah, around 650 BC, the prophets were no longer respected and could be imprisoned for making prophesies. The people, to whom Jeremiah, spoke threatened to report him. In time, we know that the Nabis were rounded up and killed wherever they were found.

By the post-exilic period (500 BC to 100 BC), the prophets had become pariah, rejected and hated by the Jews. No one listened to the Nabi any longer. "The nabiim shall be ashamed every one of his vision." (Zech 13:4). We are told that if parents caught their children saying that they hear the voice of god in their mind, they were ordered to kill their children on the spot (Zech 13:1-4).

The prophets were put to death by the Jews. Only Daniel and Malachi escaped this fate. The book of Daniel, not accepted in the prophetic books of the Torah, is composed of stories, most likely written by a priest about his life during the Babylonian Captivity and how the Lord saved him. He concludes that the god of the Jews would also save others who believed in him. While not in the Torah, the Book of Daniel is considered a part of the Old Testament.

As for the prophet Malachi, it is difficult to see how he made the cut because his book presents a lengthy diatribe against the corruption and hypocrisy of the priest class. His book is the last book in the Torah. Malachi is noted for prophesizing that the Lord would send Elijah back to the Jews, "Behold, I will send you Elijah the prophet before the coming of the great and dreadful day of the Lord; And he shall turn the heart of the fathers to the children, and the heart of the children to their fathers, lest I come and smite the earth with a curse" (Mal 4:5-6).

Elijah is equated with Jesus by the Jewish and later Christian mystics. Scholars place the writings of Daniel and Malachi during the post-exilic period.

The Story of Samuel the Prophet and Saul the King

The first book of the Prophets is 1 Samuel. It includes the story of the prophet Samuel in which he anoints the first two Jewish kings, Saul and David. The story of Samuel and Saul is a perfect tale to demonstrate the transition from the bicameral to the subjective mind. Samuel is the first major prophet discussed in the Torah. Saul is the first king of the Jews whom Samuel anoints.

Samuel is the last of the tribal leaders during the period of the Judges. We are told that he was born of a barren woman who prayed to the Lord for a son. She promised, if granted a son, she would give him to the service of god. Samuel was sent at a young age to serve the judge Eli who controlled the place of worship at Shiloh. Eli had two bad sons who took advantage of the people who came to offer sacrifice. They also raped the women who came. Samuel's first account of hearing "the voice of god" was when he heard a voice tell him that Eli and his lineage would be destroyed for their sins. Although Eli had not sinned directly, he was guilty of closing his eyes to the sins of his sons.

Samuel's reputation spread after the Philistines killed Eli's sons and Eli had a heart attack on hearing the bad news. Thereafter, it is said that his name became known throughout all of Israel. During Samuel's day, the greatest enemies of the Hebrew Jews were the Philistines. The Philistines lived in five city-states: Gaza, Ashdod, Ashkelon, Gath and Ekron along the eastern Mediterranean coast. The Philistines too were refugees in the Levant. Some believe that they were the Sea People who emigrated from the coastlands of the Mediterranean and Aegean Seas in the wake of Thera. Just as the Hebrew Jews arose out of the ashes of Thera, so also did the Philistines.[160]

The Egyptians called these people "Peleshet" (Philistines) which meant "invader." It seems unlikely that the peaceful Minoans led the fighting forces of the Sea People, but as we know many peoples were uprooted by Thera and became refugees within a great horde of migratory people.

The Jews and the Canaanites called these invaders "Peleshtim" and both fought battles with them. At the time of Samuel, the Philistines dominated the Hebrew/Jews. They did not colonize the Hebrew Jews, nor did they turn them into a vassal state. The Jews had no state at this time, nor did the Philistines. The Philistines would simply conduct raids into the Hebrew-Jews territory to kill, terrorize, and steal from them.

In Samuel I, we read of a battle between the Hebrew Jews and the Philistines in which the Philistines killed over four thousand of the Jews (1 Sam 4:1-2). In preparation for the battle, the Jews were frightened by the Philistines' greater army and asked that the Ark of the Covenant, kept at Shiloh, be brought to the battlefield. Eli agreed and sent his sons to accompany the Ark. When it arrived at the Jewish camp, a great cheer went up among the fighters. The Philistines heard this and were then hesitant to fight, but their generals aroused them to battle ("Quit yourself as men and fight"[161]). The Philistines then destroyed the Jewish fighting force, killed Eli's sons, and took the Ark back to their city Ashdod. They put the Ark in the temple of their god Dagon. We are told that the statue of Dagon fell over twice in the presence of the Ark and broke. The Philistines were also stricken with Bubonic plague, which they blamed on the god of the Jews. Eventually they sent the Ark back to the Hebrew Jews. When the Ark was returned, being pulled in a cart by two cows, it entered a rural land where the people were harvesting wheat. We are told that the Hebrew people looked into the Tabernacle and god killed over fifty thousand of them for this blasphemy (1 Samuel 6:19). Apparently, only the priests could go near the Ark.

Presumably, the Ark was not returned to Shiloh because of the sins of Eli and his sons. Instead it was taken to Kirjath-jearim on the border between the tribes of Israel and Benjamin. It remained there until King David had it brought to Jerusalem after his conquest of that city.

After twenty years at Kirjath-jearim, Samuel addressed the Hebrew Jews (now called Israelites in the Bible, although Israel did not yet exist), and told them that if they wanted their god to return to them, they must give up their worship of other gods and the Great Goddess Asherah. At this time, the Hebrew-Jews, as was common among all people in the Middle East, worshiped many gods. Among these, the Great Goddess was the most sacred to them.

Samuel had called all the tribes together at a place called Mizpeh to fast and pray. The Philistines hearing of this gathering organized a fighting force to destroy them. We are told that god (no longer referred to as Yahweh, but only as "the Lord") "thundered with a great thunder" and the Philistines panicked, allowing the Jews to defeat them. Afterward, the Philistines never again returned to the land of the Hebrew Jews.

Flush with their victory, the Jews now wanted to have their own kingdom. The Lord, we are told, did not like this because he was jealous that the people would worship their king and not him. Samuel told the people that the Lord had told him to tell them that they would end up working for the king and having their wealth taken from them. Nevertheless the people insisted on having a king. Apparently the Lord changed his mind because he then told Samuel to listen to the people and find them a king. Samuel chose Saul, a village boy and the son of a Benjamite, who "from his shoulders and upward he was higher than any of the people" (1 Sam 9:2).

Samuel anointed Saul in his house and as part of his instruction to the boy, told him to rendezvous with "a company of prophets" and to prophesy with them for seven days. The prophets put themselves in a trance with a zither and other musical instruments. Saul began to prophesy and the people were confused by this. When the seven days were over, the prophets stopped their prophesying and Saul went home. He was not well received in his village, but messengers were sent throughout the land to tell people that Saul was now their king. Saul killed a group of doubters from Jabesh with the yoke of an oxen team and then took a census of his people. We are told there were three hundred thousand from Israel and thirty thousand from Judah. This appears to be quite an exaggeration, as are most numbers provided in the Torah. It is also anachronistic to talk about Israel and Judah, which did not yet exist for a hundred years.

Samuel was a bicameral prophet with little self-identity. He expressed no subjective emotion or thought. Saul, on the other hand, had a subjective consciousness but was still subservient to the voice of god in others. He tried to figure things out and did his best to serve "the Lord." For all his good intentions, however, Saul was constantly upbraided by Samuel for sinning against "the Lord." At the onset of a great battle with the Philistines, Saul was at Gilgal waiting for seven days to rendezvous with Samuel. During this wait, his soldiers continued to desert in the face of a superior Philistine army. When Samuel did not show during the agreed seven days, Saul offered his own sacrifice to god. Samuel showed up afterwards and told Saul he acted foolishly and, in doing so, violated god's will. He told Saul that "the Lord" had renounced his kingship and he left Saul alone on the battlefield. We are told that only six hundred men remained with Saul. That night, however, Saul's son Jonathan, against his father's knowledge, attacked a Philistine garrison and thinking themselves surrounded by the Jews, the entire army of Philistines awoke and fled in panic. The Israelites were saved despite Samuel's pronouncement and Saul's fears. Jonathan was now a hero to the Jews, but because he violated a pre-battle fast imposed by Saul, he was condemned to death according to custom. Saul, in agony, was still willing to kill his own son to appease "the Lord," but his soldiers would not let him. This resistance could only happen in a post-bicameral time.

After the defeat of the Philistines, Saul went on a campaign and attacked all the neighboring cities, killing Moabites, Ammonites, Edomites, Zobahites, and Amalekites. Prior to the fight with the Amalekites, Samuel again returned to meet Saul and told him: "Thus saith the Lord . . . Now go and smite Amalek, and utterly destroy all that they have, and spare them not; but slay both man and woman, infant and suckling, ox and sheep, camel and ass" (1 Sam 15:2-3).

Here we have "the voice of the Lord" at its most savage. Samuel ordered Saul to kill the common people, including their toddlers and infants. We can see that the idea of a "loving god" had not yet made his appearance in Jewish history. The Jewish god was still a savage, vengeful, and immoral god demanding animal as well as human sacrifices by his "chosen people."

Saul could not abide the total massacre that Samuel demanded. He actually told some of the enemy to leave the area. He did not slay Agag, the Amelite king, as Samuel had commanded. We are told that Saul's army did not destroy "all that was good, but everything that was vile and refuse, that they destroyed utterly" (1 Sam 15:9). Saul thought that by showing mercy and taking the animals for later sacrifice to the Lord that he was doing his god's bidding. Not so.

The Torah tells us that when Samuel heard that Saul violated his order, "the Lord" went to Samuel and told him that he was grieved that he had made Saul king, even though the Lord had approved anointing Saul as king of the Jews. Hearing this from his lord, Samuel wept all night. The next morning, he confronted Saul and accused him of disobeying the word of god, adding that, as a consequence, god had rejected his kingship. Saul was not strong enough to stand up to Samuel and asked his forgiveness. Samuel forgave Saul because he had humbled himself, but in doing so, he had Agag brought to him and "Samuel hewed Agag in pieces before the Lord in Gilgal" (1 Sam 15:33).

The remainder of 1 Samuel accounts the downfall of Saul, his loss of sanity and the rise of David who as a child became Saul's armor bearer. It is David, we are told, who slew the Philistine giant Goliath and became the hero of the Hebrew Jews. As David's star ascended, "an evil spirit from God" came over Saul and he became jealous of David. After several attempts at prophesying, dream interpretation, casting lots, and even consulting a witch, Saul remained unable to "hear the voice of god." In his obsession with David, Saul made several attempts to assassinate him; he then felt guilty and apologized to David. The young David refused to take retribution on Saul because he believed that Saul was appointed by god to be king. Finally, in an epic battle with the Philistines, Saul's sons were killed and he himself was wounded. Rather than be captured by the enemy, Saul committed suicide by falling on his sword. This is the first suicide recorded in history. It is clearly an act of a subjective mind.

Thus, ends the tragic life of a man who having possessed a subjective consciousness still believed in and still tried to please an anonymous bicameral voice as represented by Samuel and his bands of prophets, who still existed in apparent numbers at the time and who still commanded the people's attention. For his part, the Torah tells us, Samuel died an old man and was buried and revered by the people.

As the priests, under the rule of Joshea (early seventh century BC), began to piece together the bicameral scrolls, they found whole pieces of material intact. The Book of Amos; for example, was probably one of the oldest of all biblical documents and was written around 800 BC. It provides another good example of the bicameral mind. Amos was an illiterate desert herdsman. We find no signs of subjective consciousness in him. He does not think, reflect, or feel anything as a human being. He does not think before he speaks. When the voice in his mind began, he overrode everyone with "Thus saith the Lord!" He then would follow that with a disconnected and incoherent rant that he himself probably did not understand.

Here is an example of Amos venting the angry "word of god":

> "The Lord will roar from Zion, and utter his voice from Jerusalem; and the habitations of the shepherds shall mourn, and the top of Carmel shall wither.
>
> Thus saith the Lord; For three transgressions of Damascus, and for four, I will not turn away the punishment thereof; because they have threshed Gilead with threshing instruments of iron:
>
> But I will send a fire into the house of Hazael, which shall devour the palaces of Ben-hadad.
>
> I will break also the bar of Damascus, and cut off the inhabitant from the plain of Aven, and him that holdeth the scepter from the house of Eden: and the people of Syria shall go into captivity unto Kir, saith the Lord.
>
> Thus saith the Lord; For three transgressions of Gaza, and for four, I will not turn away the punishment thereof; because they carried away captive the whole captivity, to deliver them up to Edom.
>
> But I will send a fire on the wall of Gaza, which shall devour the palaces thereof.
>
> And I will cut off the inhabitant from Ashdod, and him that holdeth the scepter from Ashkelon, and I will turn mine hand against Ekron: and the remnant of the Philistines shall perish, saith the Lord God" (Amos: 1-8).

Amos continued his rant, citing how god will also punish the cities, peoples, and nations of Tyrus, Edom, Teman, the Ammonites, Rabbah, Moab, Judah, and Israel for their "three transgressions or four" and then he continued in an angry and incoherent blast against everything in his environment. This is pure bicameral consciousness.

The books of the prophets, like the Pentateuch, hold little historical value. They reflect a later period in which the priests were setting up their theological scheme by which to judge the obedience of their followers to the teachings and laws they had set down in Deuteronomy.[162]

Chapter Three: A Revolution in Human Consciousness

Ecclesiastes

Before we leave the Torah and our discussion of the prophets, it is instructive to look at the Book of Ecclesiastes in the Torah/Old Testament to get an idea of how far subjective consciousness had evolved from the times of Samuel and Amos to the post exilic period. The "post exilic period" refers to the time after the Jewish priest class were freed from their Babylonian Captivity by the Persians in 538 BC. Ecclesiastes was written by someone who called himself "The Preacher." Purportedly, King Solomon wrote it, but such a subjective outlook is beyond Solomon and the book is written anonymously probably around the third century BC.[163]

The book is in the form of an autobiography in which the "Preacher" (not prophet) tells us of his investigation into the meaning of life and the best way to live. The Preacher proclaims all the actions of man to be inherently "vain," "futile," "empty," "meaningless," "temporary," "transitory," "fleeting," or "mere breath." As proof, he offers that the lives of wise or foolish people, rich or poor, end in death. While the Preacher endorses wisdom as a means to live a good earthly life, he is unable to ascribe any spiritual meaning to it. In light of this cosmic senselessness, he concludes that one should enjoy the simple pleasures of daily life, such as eating, drinking, and taking enjoyment in one's work, which are gifts from the hand of God. The book concludes with a priestly injunction: "Fear God, and keep his commandments; for that is the whole duty of everyone" (12:13).

Here is a passage from Ecclesiastes:

> And I gave my heart to seek and search out by wisdom concerning all things that are done under heaven: this sore travail hath God given to the sons of man to be exercised therewith.
>
> I have seen all the works that are done under the sun; and, behold, all is vanity and vexation of spirit.
>
> That which is crooked cannot be made straight: and that which is wanting cannot be numbered.
>
> I communed with mine own heart, saying, Lo, I am come to great estate, and have gotten more wisdom than all they that have been before me in Jerusalem: yea, my heart had great experience of wisdom and knowledge.
>
> And I gave my heart to know wisdom, and to know madness and folly: I perceived that this also is vexation of spirit.
>
> For in much wisdom is much grief: and he that increaseth knowledge increaseth sorrow.(Eccles 1:13-18).

Here is the subjective mind in its full glory. The "I feeling" has not only taken responsibility for its own thoughts, but it actually accounts for its own limitations. Nonetheless, it still leaves us spiritually wanting. The mind has not yet discovered the idea of the soul, much less realize that the soul is the source of the "I-feeling" in the mind. Even so, the Western world is now getting closer to uncovering the fundamental mystery of the nature of consciousness. In the remainder of our look at the Jews, we will explore their attempts to discover the source of self-consciousness through the teachings of a Jewish mystical community called the Essenes and through them, the teachings of Jesus Christ.

The Jewish Mysticism of the Essenes

The Essenes lived in Judah from approximately 200 BC to AD 50, which includes the time of Jesus Christ. They wrote much of what has come to be called the *Dead Sea Scrolls*. These scrolls were discovered in a cave near the Sea by an Arab shepherd in 1947.

In 1961, John M. Allegro, an expert in Near Eastern and Old Testament studies, was appointed by King Hussein to advise the Jordanian government as to the significance of the scrolls. Allegro subsequently became one of the original publishers of the scroll materials. This was unusual because the publication team was largely composed of Catholic priests. There were no Jews on the team. To their discredit the Catholic priests refused to release the texts of the unpublished fragmentary scrolls. This decision produced what Geza Vermes, a distinguished commentator on the scrolls, called "the academic scandal par excellence of the twentieth century." It is in this environment that Allegro, continually at odds with the Catholic publication team, wrote his book *The Dead Sea Scrolls and the Christian Myth*.[164] In doing so, he provides us with a unique picture of the Essenes, a Jewish mystical cult through whom we are able to glimpse the link between traditional Jewish writings and the story of Jesus Christ. While considered an "outlaw" by the "official team" of experts, we believe that Allegro has provided a great service by offering an alternative to orthodox Christian dogma. His link between Jewish texts and the story of Jesus, more than any other historical or scientific interpretation to date, describes the transition from self-consciousness to God-consciousness within the Jewish tradition.[165]

Of the scrolls that have been found to date: about forty percent of them are copies of texts from the Jewish Bible. The scrolls contain the oldest version of the Old Testament, with the exception of the Book of Esther, which was not found among the scrolls. Approximately another thirty percent of the scrolls are texts from the post-exile period that were not included in the Torah, including the Book of Enoch, Jubilees, the Book of Tobit, the Wisdom of Sirach, Psalms 152–155, etc. The remaining thirty percent of the scrolls are previously unknown documents that shed light on the rules and beliefs of the Essene ascetic community, who were the keepers of the scrolls. These documents include the Community Rule, the War Scroll, the Commentary on Habakkuk, and The Rule of the Blessing.[166] Allegro tells us how these texts relate to other extant religious texts and the history of the Jews at the time. The following story of the Essenes is largely taken from Allegro's interpretation of the Dead Sea Scrolls.

The Essenes lived in communal settlements loosely attached to towns and villages throughout Judea, but as ascetics they kept themselves apart from the mainstream while practicing a primitive form of communism in which they shared their worldly wealth and cared for the sick and aged from a common fund. Their mother community, called Qumran, was where the scrolls were found. Subsequent to the first discovery of scrolls in a nearby cave, archeologists also found several buildings at this settlement, which included a library. In time, over eight hundred scrolls were discovered. Qumran was located on the banks of the Dead Sea and thus the scrolls came to be called the "Dead Sea Scrolls."

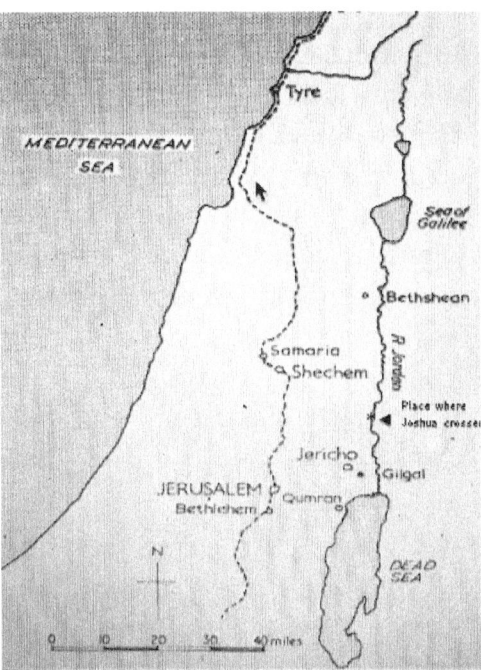

Map 2-8: Location of Qumran

The Essenes were the mystics of the Jews. This is not to say that they were the only mystics within Judaism, but at the time they were the only large organized movement of Jewish mystics. Another mystical path within Judaism, which found its fullest expressing centuries later, is the Kabbalah movement.

More than the Sadducees (the elite) or the Pharisees (the main stream), the Essenes dedicated themselves to understanding the will of God. They lived simple, disciplined, and ascetic lives. Their main occupation was to immerse themselves in the study of the scriptures, looking for clues to interpret the events of their day so that they might be able to predict the coming of the Messiah, who would lead the Jews out of captivity, prove to the world that they were the chosen people, and bring humanity to the realization of the one true Jewish God. The Essenes practiced herbal medicine and people considered them to be "physicians." They were also believed to have the power to exorcise demons (i.e., negative voices in the mind). The Essenes wore simple white clothing and baptized their initiates.

At the time of the Essenes, the land was rife with political intrigue, purges, and assassinations. They had lived through the period of Hellenization and had witnessed the treason and treachery of the Jewish leaders. If we are to understand Jesus Christ as more than a mythological figure, having more in common with the Roman god Mithra than a Jewish rabbi, we must understand how the Essenes thought and how Jesus actually lived prior to his thirtieth birthday when he magically appears on the scene according to the Christian gospels of the New Testament.

God's Master Plan and the Role of the Chosen People

The Essenes believed that the entire history of the Jews was part of God's master plan for humanity and that they were the people chosen by God to fulfill this plan. In the beginning, the world lived in harmony, but then the disobedience of Adam and Eve introduced sin and suffering into the world. This corruption became worse in time with the murder of Abel, and eventually got so bad that God entirely destroyed humanity except for Noah and the population of his ark.[167] Then the world again fell into sin and God created Abraham to found a lineage of the faithful. Thereafter, he nurtured the Jews by sending prophets to them to reveal his plan. While wandering in the desert, after their captivity in Egypt, the people achieved a national identity and were allowed to know the secret name of God. They were also given the Torah.[168]

According to their reading of the scriptures, the Essenes believed that the history of the Jews was cyclic in nature. In this cycle, certain events continually reoccurred:

1. The Jews were confirmed by Yahweh, the Lord, as his chosen people.
2. The people forgot their agreement with the Lord and fell into sin.
3. They were warned by their prophets but failed to listen.
4. God chastised the people for their sins.
5. The people repented.
6. Their status as the chosen people was reconfirmed.
7. In every age the people would go astray and in every age God would send a charismatic leaders, king, priest, or prophet to bring them back to their responsibility as the chosen people.

Ultimately, in the "end of days," a great battle would be fought between the forces of good and evil. The Jews would be saved and paradise would come down to earth.

According to the Essenes, the record of this cycle was revealed in the events of the scriptures and in the words of the prophets. The Essenes paid more attention to the prophets than the more orthodox Jews as they searched for clues and signs of the "end of days" when the Messiah (Savior) would appear. The long history of death and humiliation that they had suffered at the hands of the Assyrians, Babylonians, Greeks, their own corrupt leaders, and now the Romans led them to believe that the "end of days" was soon approaching. The "end of days," according to prophecy, would be preceded by a Messiah who would save the Jews and usher in the new age.

The art of divining the future lay in determining which part of the cycle they were at in the present. This required analyzing the clues from the past, especially the words of the prophets, to see the quality of the Jews' previous response to god's commands and comparing them to the Jews current response to the signs of god.

For the Essenes, it was not enough to simply understand the "signs of the times," they must follow god's commands to the letter. They needed to become perfect instruments of god. The Essenes were the mystical elite of the chosen people. In their own minds, they were the true believers in the story of the Jews and their god. They dedicated their lives to their god.

By understanding this characteristic of the Essenes, we can begin to understand why they chose to live in the desert on the banks of the Dead Sea. The choosing of Qumran as their base was not an accident. It was a highly significant act because just north of their compound was the place where, according to scripture, Joshua had crossed the River Jordan and brought the Jews into the "promised land." Just as their god had parted the waters of the Red Sea to allow Moses to lead the Jews out of Egypt, so the Jewish god parted the waters of the Jordan River to allow Joshua to lead the people into Canaan.

In this repetition of history, the Essenes saw a clear sign of Joshua's prophetic office and of their own master's messianic role in the future of Israel. It was also significant that at this place, Joshua had led the people in a renewal of their covenant with god in preparation for the trials and tribulations to come. In the "promised land," the Jews would not only have to fight for their lives, endure the oppression of foreign conquerors, and face betrayal from within, they would also have to face the allure of the cults of different gods and goddesses to which many had already fallen prey. The Essenes believed that the New Age would be characterized by a restoration of the harmony of nature. As a sign of this, the desert itself would bloom again into a new Garden of Eden, and they would be sitting right in the middle of it.

Isaiah had said, "The wolf shall dwell with the lamb, and the leopard shall lie down with the kid, and the calf and the lion and the fatling together, and a little child shall lead them (Isaiah 11: 6). Isaiah had also said:

> When the poor and the needy seek water,
> and there is none,
> and their tongue is parched with thirst,
> I, the Lord, will answer them,
> I, the God of Israel, will not forsake them.
> I will open up rivers on the bare heights,
> and fountains in the midst of the valleys;
> I will make the wilderness a pool of water,
> and the dry land springs of water.
> I will put in the wilderness the cedar,
> the acacia, the myrtle, and the olive;
> I will set in the desert the cypress,
> the plane and the pine together;
> that men may see and know,
> may consider and understand together,
> that the hand of the Lord has done this,
> the Holy One of Israel has created it (Isa 41:17-20).

Zechariah, who was prophesying at the time of the exile in Babylon, also made a revelation about the "new age" that must have had great significance for the Essenes. He prophesied that on the judgment day:

> ... living waters shall flow out from Jerusalem, half of them to the eastern Sea (i.e., the Dead Sea) and half of them to the western Sea (i.e., the Mediterranean); it shall continue in summer as in winter (Zech 14:8).

Enoch, a prophet, whose words were not included in the canonical Torah, also spoke of a miraculous stream running eastward from the Temple that would change the desert into a plantation of "aromatic trees, exhaling the fragrance of frankincense and myrrh" (Enoch 29:1).

Thus, the Essenes saw their desert monastery, due east of Jerusalem on the Dead Sea, as the place wherein god would recreate the Garden of Eden in the new age. To feed their fantasy, a small stream, the "ain Feshkha" ran from Jerusalem to the Dead Sea just a little south of the monastery. It was this stream that the Essenes believed god would change into the promised river.

The Essene's preoccupation with water was steeped in spiritual symbolism. It stood for divine knowledge (gnosis). All the great transformations in Jewish history were presaged on an event concerning water—Moses on the Red Sea, followed by Joshua and then Elijah at the exact same place on the River Jordan.

The sanctity of water as a bringer of life was translated into scripture as the sacred river of divine knowledge. This interpretation of the meaning of water gave rise to the Essene's rite of baptism in which they immersed their initiates in the flow of this sacred knowledge. The Essenes were the first Judeo-Chrisian sect to baptize their initiates. John would baptize Jesus in the Jordan River at the place where Joshua parted the river to take the Jews into the promised land of Canaan. It was also at this place that Elijah and his disciple Elisha parted the Jordan River. Jesus would later instruct his apostles to baptize all the faithful in the manner in which John baptized him. According to scriptures:

> Jesus answered, "Truly, truly, I say to you, Except a man be born of water and of the Spirit, he cannot enter into the kingdom of God" (John 3:5).

> "For John truly baptized with water; but you shall be baptized with the Holy Ghost not many days hence" (Acts 1:5).

> Then Peter said to them, "Repent, and be baptized every one of you in the name of Jesus Christ for the remission of sins, and you shall receive the gift of the Holy Ghost" (Acts 2:38).

Following this command, all Christians were baptized as an initiation into the Christian faith by which they would gain the forgiveness of their sins and access to heaven.

So, at the site of their monastery at Qumran, where the Teacher of Righteousness had led the Essenes, the New Covenant had its beginning, and the new world as promised by their god would begin. This transformation would not occur, however, until an epic battle between the sons of light and the sons of darkness would be fought. The idea for such a battle was introduced to the Jews by Zoroaster who had visualized a pitched battle between the forces of good and evil during the "end of days." For the Essenes, this idea was given greater poignancy because Zechariah had also prophesied such a battle (Zech 14:2). In this battle, Israel would fight all of its foes under the leadership of the Messiah, and in their victory all the nations would come to recognize the god of Israel. The survivors would live in peace and prosperity and paradise would return to earth.

The Qumran monastery was probably built before the coming of the Greeks, perhaps around 200 BC, but certainly before the rule of the king/high priest Alexander Jannaeus, who was the second Hasmonean king of Judea from 103 to 76 BC.

While the Essenes opposed king Jannaeus and the Sadducee ruling class on religious grounds, they also despised them for their deal-making with the Greek and Roman invaders. They believed that their own Teacher of Righteousness was the Messiah who the Jewish people had anxiously been awaiting. While not violent, like the Zealots, the Essene's War Scroll shows that they were expecting a great battle and were preparing for it in their own way. As such, they were also considered dangerous opponents by the Jewish, Greek, and Roman ruling classes.

The Traitor King and Wicked Priest

It will serve our story to go back a few years before the coming of the Romans to Judea (Judah) wherein, about 90 BC, the Jewish king, Alexander Jannaeus (103 BC to 76 BC), was king and high priest of Judea.

Jannaeus was a member of the ruling class and supported by the Sadducees. As a warrior king, he had secured his position within the Hasmonean dynasty by military conquest at a time when internal problems consumed the Greeks and Romans and kept them from their mission of colonial expansion.

The relations between Jannaeus and the Pharisees were probably never very cordial. Jannaeus abused his religious responsibilities as the High

Priest, a position which had been taken over by the Jewish monarchy since the Maccabean Revolt.

One year, during the Jewish Feast of Tabernacles, Jannaeus, while officiating as the High Priest at the Temple in Jerusalem, intentionally poured the sacred libation of water on the ground instead of on the altar. The crowd was shocked at this mockery of Jewish law and began to pelt him with the lemons they were holding as part of the ritual. Jannaeus had secretly intended to incite the people to riot and when the lemons were loosed, he ordered his soldiers to fall upon the crowd. Six thousand people were reportedly slaughtered in the Temple courtyard that day.[169]

This incident, during the Feast of Tabernacles, led to a Judean civil war between the middle class Pharisees and the ruling nobility and priest class under Jannaeus. In *A Jeremiah Apcryphon,* one of the tracts of the Dead Sea scrolls, it speaks of a civil war and the need to remove the king and the Hasmonean priesthood.[170]

The problem was long standing. In 175 BC, as discussed above, a contender for the Jewish throne named Jason—who had Hellenized his Hebrew name, Joshua—bribed the Seleucid (Greek) monarch, Antiochus IV, to depose his brother and in his place appoint Jason to the office of High Priest in Jerusalem. Later Antiochus would issue a decree banning Judaism in which he outlawed circumcision, religious study, the observance of festivals, and worship on the Sabbath. Instead, he forced Jews to worship Greek gods and to eat foods that could no longer be sanctified by ritual on the temple altar.

Such punitive measures, as well as the forced imposition of Greek culture, brought on the Maccabean Revolt, which gave birth to the Hasmonean dynasty of Jewish kings and high priests (142-137 BC). What began as an anti-Hellenistic revolt, however, soon turned into a pro-Hellenistic dynasty. Political intrigue was rife among the Hasmoneans, and the highest political authority (the King) was soon combined with the highest religious authority (the High Priest). Religious schisms widened and antagonistic religious parties vied with one another. It was in this milieu that the sacrilege on the Feast of Tabernacles took place.

After Jannaeus defiled the Feast of Tabernacles, which was among the holiest of holy days, and then massacred the people who expressed their outrage, the faithful scattered. Jannaeus, however, would not let the matter drop. Seeing an opportunity to destroy his enemies, he ordered his army to seek out those faithful to the Jewish religion and kill them. In his campaign to destroy Judaism, his men searched the towns as well as the wilderness, especially the caves in the plateau above the Dead Sea, where it was possible to hide. Josephus, the Jewish historian, tells us that the fugitives took refuge in the caves (the House of Shade) around the monastery. It was from these caves that Jannaeus' army dragged many fugitives back to Jerusalem to be killed. On another Jewish high holy day, the Day of Atonement (Yom Kippur), he made an increased assault on the followers of Judaism to discourage and humiliate them. At this time, he sought out and captured many of the faithful. He knew they would be fasting and praying and according to Jewish law, avoiding any form of movement.

On a day soon after this mass arrest, Jannaeus crucified eight hundred people in front of the doors of the Temple. Crucifixion had never before been commanded by any Jewish leader and must have been especially horrific for those who witnessed it. We are told that Jannaeus also slaughtered the families of those he crucified before their eyes. As for the king, he observed the massacre from the shade of the Temple columns, eating fruit, and amusing himself with harlots. Among the victims to die that day was the Teacher of Righteousness, the spiritual master of the Essenes. The year of his crucifixion was 88 BC.

The Teacher of Righteousness

In the *Damascus Document*,[171] which was written by Essenes in exile after the Roman diaspora, there is a reference to their "Teacher of Righteousness." This Teacher was also referred to as "the unique teacher," or "the teacher of the One," or "the Lawgiver." In this document, it says: "And God observed their deeds, that they sought Him with a whole heart, and He raised for them a Teacher of Righteousness to guide them in the way of His heart." The Teacher is also mentioned in several other documents found among the Dead Sea scrolls.

Josephus, the Jewish historian at the time of the Roman conquest, tells us that next to God, the Essenes worshipped their "Lawgiver" before any other. The Damascus Document describes the Essenes as having been leaderless for twenty years before the Teacher of Righteousness established his rule over the group. Usually historians date the Teacher to around 150 BC, since the document states that he arrived three hundred and ninety years after the Babylonian Exile.[172] This date is probably a little early in time for when the Teacher actually lived.

In the Dead Sea scrolls there are many references to the battle between the Wicked Priest and the Teacher of Righteousness. The Wicked Priest rejected the words of the Teacher of Righteousness who spoke from the mouth of God.

We know that Jannaeus held the title of King and High Priest. As such, it is most likely that Jannaeus is the Wicked Priest in the writings of the Essenes. From a reading of the Dead Scrolls we can discern a scenario in which the Teacher of Righteousness, who was living in Jerusalem at the time, consistently challenged the authority of Jannaeus, accusing him of sinning against God's covenant. As a consequence, Jannaeus and his ruling elite developed a bitter hatred for this so called "holy man," and retaliated by mocking him, criticizing him, spreading scandalous rumors about him, scourging him, threatening his life, and driving away his disciples who feared for their own lives. Ultimately, Jannaeus crucified the Teacher of Righteousness.

One of the great discoveries among the Dead Sea scrolls is a collection of poems or hymns attributed to the Teacher of Righteousness. Scholars who discovered them call them the Thanksgiving Hymns because each hymn begins with the phrase "I give thanks to You, O Lord." There are about fifty of these hymns. They are intensely personal and stand in sharp contrast to the other scrolls. Michael Wise, one of the interpreters of The Dead Sea Scrolls,[173] says:

> The author speaks of himself in the first person and recounts an agonizing history of persecution at the hands of those opposed to his ministry. In addition, the writer describes having received an empowering spirit granting him special insight into God's will, opening his ears to wonderful divine mysteries, using him as a channel

of God's works, and fashioning him as a mouthpiece for God's words.

The unique personal presentation of the work and the self-conscious divine mission of the author have led many researchers to conclude that the Psalms were written by the Teacher of Righteousness himself.[174]

These hymns present us with something new in the evolution of the idea of God as it developed in the Middle East. We have now graduated from hearing "the voice of god" in the bicameral mind, to musing about God from the perspective of a subjective consciousness, to now having an interpersonal relationship with the Divine. In philosophical terms, we have moved from an object-subject relationship (authority is external), to a subject-object relationship (authority is internal), and now to a subject-subject relationship in which both the individual and the Divinity possess a subjective consciousness (authority exists externally and internally). This spiritual insight is the building block on which the merging of the individual consciousness and Divine consciousness is made possible. It calls forth a response of both parties and this response is called love. It is the love of which Jesus Christ spoke and of which he dedicated his life.

At the time, for an individual to speak of such an intimate relationship with Divinity was fraught with danger because it confronted head-on the dominant social consciousness as established and maintained by the ruling elite. The elite always wants to be seen as the authority or the only ones having access to divine authority. Therefore, one who follows his own conscience or says that he speaks directly to the Divine is a great threat to the established order for it disavows the need for the intervening authority of the priest class. In the subjective-subjective relationship, we are finally talking about true spirituality, the link between Universal Consciousness that transcends all religions, and the self-consciousness that resides at the subtlest core of each human being.

The Teacher realizes that he has a unique relationship with God because he has had spiritual experiences that other men have not had:

> I give thanks to You, O Lord, for You have redeemed my soul from the pit. From Sheol and Abaddon You

> have raised me up to an eternal height, so that I might walk about on a limitless plane, and know that there is hope for him whom you created from the dust for the eternal council. The perverse spirit You have cleansed from great transgression, that he might take his stand with the host of the holy ones, and enter together with the congregation of the sons of heaven. And for man, you have allotted an eternal destiny with the spirits of knowledge, to praise Your name together with shouts of joy, and to recount Your wonders before all Your creatures (Hymn 13).[175]

The Teacher knows what impact his spiritual knowledge has on his disciples and on others:

> But by me You have illumined the face of many and have strengthened them uncountable times. For You have given me understanding of the mysteries of Your wonder, and in Your wondrous counsel You have confirmed me; doing wonders before many for the sake of Your glory, and making known Your mighty deeds to all living.[176]

Yet, in his effort to share his divine experiences with men, the Teacher is faced with detractors on all sides:

> > But the wicked of the people rush against me with their afflictions, and all the day long they crush my soul (Hymn 17.)
> >
> > But You, oh my God, have opened a wide space in my heart, but they continue to press in, and they shut me up in deep darkness, so that I eat the bread of groaning, and my drink is tears without end. For my eyes have become weak from anger and my soul by daily bitterness. Grief and misery surround me, and shame is upon my face. (Hymn 18).[177]

The Teacher is not just being overwhelmed with hatred and derision; he also faces death threats from the king, the ruling class, and the priests:

> Ruthless men seek my life, while I hold fast to Your covenant. They are the fraudulent council for the congregation of Belial; they do not know that my appointment is from You. By Your mercies You save my life, for my very steps are from You. Their attack on my life is from You that You might be honored by the judgment of the wicked, and that You might display Your might through me against the children of men, for I stand in Your mercy (Hymn 11).[178]

The Teacher speaks to the deception in the hearts of the priests:

> But they are mediators of a lie and seers of deceit. They have plotted wickedness against me, so as to exchange Your law, which You spoke distinctly in my heart, flattering words directed to Your people. They hold back the drink of knowledge from those who thirst, and for their thirst they give them vinegar to drink, that they might observe their error, behaving badly at their festivals and getting caught in their nets (Hymn 16).[179]

Under this constant assault on the Teacher of Righteousness, many of his own students abandoned him, which proved to be the greatest sadness to the Teacher:

> But I myself have become strife and contentions for my fellows, jealousy and anger to those who have entered into my covenant, a grumbling and a complaining to all who are my companions. Even those who share my bread have lifted up their heel against me, and all those who have committed themselves to my counsel speak perversely against me with unjust lips. The men of my counsel rebel and grumble round about. And concerning the mystery which You hid in me, they go about as slanderers to the children of destruction (Hymn 18).[180]

As his battle with the exploiters, traitors and violent men continued, and as his own camp abandoned him to his enemies, the Teacher confessed his weakness of will, but then remembered what made firm his great resolve:

> I know that man has no righteousness, nor does the son of man walk in the perfect way. All the works of righteousness belong to God Most High. The way of man does not last except by the spirit which God created for him, to perfect a way for humankind so that they may know all His works by His mighty power and the abundance of His mercies upon all those who do His will.
>
> But as for me, fear and trembling have taken hold of me and all my bones break apart. My heart melts as wax over the fire, and my knees become as water which is poured down over a slope. For I remember my guilt together with the unfaithfulness of my fathers, when the wicked rise against Your covenant and the scoundrels against Your word. I said in my transgression, I am abandoned by Your covenant. But when I remembered the power of Your hand together with the abundance of Your mercies, I stood upright and firm and my spirit grew strong to stand against affliction (Hymn 185).

Eventually, the Teacher of Righteousness was captured by the soldiers of King Jannaeus and taken to Jerusalem where he, along with others, was hanged from a tree. This knowledge comes from the Essene documents and from a statement by Josephus about the crucifixion that was ordered by the king.

The acknowledgment of the Teacher's death in the scrolls is not immediately apparent because the writers of the scrolls spoke in code. This was necessary because any mention of real people could have meant a death sentence for those in possession of the scrolls. For example, the Teacher's name was never used, although we will find out later through the texts of the Gnostics that the Essenes equated him with Joshua ("Jesus" in the Greek language). Neither is Jannaeus mentioned in the Dead Sea Scrolls, although there is no other who fits the role of the Wicked Priest.

The evidence for determining the timeline of the Teacher of Righteousness and the Wicked Priest is gleaned from several indirect references to Jannaeus, whom we know of through other sources.

In the *Commentary on Habakkuk*, found in the translation of the Dead Sea Scrolls, there is a reference to the Wicked Priest Jannaeus:

> And indeed, riches betray the arrogant man and he will not last; he who has made his throat as wide as Hades, and who, like Death, is never satisfied. All the Gentiles will flock to him and all the peoples will gather to him. Look, all of them take up a taunt against him, and invent sayings about him, saying, 'Ho, one who grows large on what is not his, how long will he burden himself down with debts?'"

The editors of the Dead Sea Scrolls tell us that this refers to the Wicked Priest, who had a reputation for reliability at the beginning of his term of service; but when he became ruler over Israel, he became proud and forsook God and betrayed the commandments for the sake of riches. He amassed by force the riches of the lawless who had rebelled against God, seizing the riches of the peoples, thus adding to the guilt of his crimes, and he committed abhorrent deeds in every defiling impurity.[181]

This statement reveals that the Wicked Priest is both a ruler over Israel and a priest who used his power to exploit the people's wealth. This can only refer to Jannaeus, who was guilty of suppressing the Jewish people, especially the Pharisees and the Essenes. This passage also makes special reference to the fact that the "Gentiles will flock to him." As we have seen, Jannaeus defended the Greeks against the faithful Jews.

Jannaeus also had a reputation for reliability in the beginning because he was a descendant of the Maccabees who had actually saved the Jews from Greek conquest.

In another passage from the *Commentary on Habakkuk* it states:

> Look, suddenly your creditors will appear, your enemies will rouse themselves and you will become booty

> for them. Yes, you yourself have plundered many nations, now the rest of the peoples will plunder you for the murder of a man and injustice in the land, the city and all who live in it.

Jannaeus did plunder many nations after becoming king. This was a unique act that no Jewish king had engaged in since the time of Solomon almost nine hundred years in the past. This passage also mentions the murder of a man. While Jannaeus obviously murdered many men, this reference in the Dead Sea Scrolls must specifically refer to the Essene's spiritual master, the Teacher of Righteousness.

One more reference places the Wicked Priest and the Teacher of Righteousness at the same time in history. In one of the scrolls, *A Commentary on Nahum*, it mentions an identifiable historical figure, Demetrius III Eukairos, the king of Seleucid Syria, who invaded Judah in 88 BC.[182] As we said earlier, the rule of Jannaeus set off a civil war in Judah between the Hellenizers and those that wanted to remain pure in their devotion to Judaism. The civil war became so intense that the Pharisees formed a pact with Demetrius, inviting him to invade Judah and depose the king. Demetrius complied and put Jannaeus to flight in a battle. Now, however, the Pharisees, not wanting Greek rule to be reestablished in Judah, went over to the side of Jannaeus, forcing Demetrius to withdraw. Jannaeus was furious at the subterfuge of his Jewish enemies and crucified them in Jerusalem. Because of these many references in the Dead Sea Scrolls, scholars believe that the Wicked Priest was Jannaeus.

As far as the Essenes were concerned, Jannaeus was the most wicked of kings. He demonstrated this wickedness by ordering his soldiers to take the Teacher of Righteousness prisoner on the highest of Jewish holidays, Yom Kippur. This day even today is called the "Sabbath of Sabbaths." It says in the Commentary on Habakkuk:

> Woe to the one who gets his friend drunk, pouring out his anger, making him drink, just to get a look at their holy days.[183]

This refers to the Wicked Priest, who pursued the Teacher of Righteousness in anger to destroy him at his place of exile. At the time set aside for the repose of the Day of Atonement, the Wicked Priest appeared to the Teacher of Righteousness to destroy him and to bring him to ruin on the fast day, the Sabbath intended for repose.[184]

According to Jewish tradition, God inscribes each person's fate for the coming year into the Book of Life on Rosh Hashanah and waits until Yom Kippur eight days later to "seal" the verdict. During the intervening days, a Jew tries to amend his or her behavior and seek forgiveness for wrongs done against God and other human beings.[185] He fasts and does not travel. Because of this, Jannaeus knew exactly where the Teacher of Righteousness would be in order to seize him.

The Teacher of Righteousness and Jesus Christ

Now the tantalizing question arises, was the Teacher of Righteousness the real Jesus Christ of history? Certainly there is enough evidence to suggest this. Of the synoptic gospels (Matthew, Mark, Luke, and John) agreement rests on several overlapping descriptions of the Son of God. His name is Jesus. He was born in Bethlehem, performed miracles, gave a Sermon on the Mound in which he introduced the Beatitudes (Blessed is he who. . . .), convened a Last Supper, and was crucified and rose again from the dead. He also gave instructions to his followers to baptize in his name, which became known as the Great Commission.

Except for explicit references to being born in Bethlehem, all the other things attributed to Jesus were attributed to the Teacher of Righteousness. The Teacher in his hymns speaks not specifically of performing miracles but he says:

> For You have given me understanding of the mysteries of Your wonder, and in Your wondrous counsel You have confirmed me; doing wonders before many for the sake of Your glory in making known Your mighty deeds to all living (Hymn 16).[186]

Or

> Neither did they esteem me; even when You displayed Your might through me (Hymn 16).

The Sermon on the Mount finds its prototype in an Essene scroll that is called *Secrets of the Way Things Are*, which served as their catechism for new initiates. In their commentary on The Secrets, the interpreters of the Dead Sea Scrolls report:

> Again and again the teacher returns to the theme of poverty and the importance of being satisfied with what God has provided. "Blessed are the poor (Luke 6:20). The Secret seeks to motivate by appeal to the judgment to come and the eternal damnation of the wicked – another new theme that foreshadows the importance of the Last Days for early Christianity. The nearest analog once again is in early Christianity: the collection of sayings called the Sermon on the Mount (Matt. 5-7) is the same type of genre, that is, ethical instruction under threat of impending judgment.[187]

In the "Messianic Banquet" of the Essenes, we have the prototype of the Last Supper:

> And then the Messiah of Israel shall [take his place] and the chiefs of the [clans] shall sit before him, each in the order of his dignity.

> And when they are gathered together at the common table to eat and to drink new wine mixed for drinking, let no man extend his hand over the first-fruits of bread and wine before the Priest (ie the Priestly Messiah); for he will bless the first-fruits of bread and wine, and will [stretch forth] his hand over the bread first. . . .

> It is according to this prescription that they shall proceed at every ritual Meal at which at least ten men are gathered together.[188]

Such a meal was a holy event for the Essenes. It instilled in them their connection to the Messiah and to the "end of days." Here is mentioned the bread and wine, which in later scripture would become the body and blood of Jesus.

Another link between the Teacher of Righteousness and Jesus Christ is the concept of redemption and resurrection. In the Dead Sea Scrolls we find reference to these ideas in a tract called *Redemption and Resurrection*. The translators in their introduction to this tract tell us:

> The Gospel of Matthew tells us of an occasion on which John the Baptist sent word to Jesus, asking, "are you the one who is coming, or are we to look for another?" Jesus answered John's followers, "go and report to John what you hear and see: the blind have regained their sight, the lame walk, lepers are cleansed, the deaf hear, the dead are raised, and the poor have the good news preached to them" (Matt 11:2-5).
>
> This account of Jesus' response to John the Baptist parallels the Dead Sea Scrolls Redemption and Resurrection in a remarkable way. Both the Gospels and this scroll presuppose that during the age of the Messiah, the dead would be resurrected, either by God himself or through his messianic agent. Yet nowhere in the Old Testament do we clearly read of this belief. This fact suggests that the gospel writers may have known Redemption and Resurrection – or at least been familiar with the traditions it contained. Thus Jesus's response to John's disciples was "yes, I am he." His works reflected the messianic expectation.[189]

The Scroll itself reads:

> ... for the heavens and the earth shall listen to His Messiah and all which is in them shall not turn away from the commandments of the holy ones. Strengthen yourselves, Oh you who seek the Lord, in His service.
> Will you not find the Lord in this, all those who hope in their heart? For the Lord attends to the pious and calls the righteous by name. Over the humble His spirit hovers, and He renews the faithful in His strength. For he will honor the pious upon the throne of His eternal kingdom, setting prisoners free, opening the eyes of the blind, raising up those who are bowed down. (Psalms 146:7-8) And forever I shall hold fast to those who hope. And in His faithfulness shall . . . and the fruit of good deeds shall not be delayed for anyone and the Lord shall do glorious things which have not been done, just as He said. For He shall heal the critically wounded, He shall revive the dead, He shall send good news to the afflicted (Isaiah 61:1), He shall satisfy the poor, He shall guide the uprooted, he shall make the hungry rich. . . .[190]

In another fragment of this tract, although badly damaged, we again find words evident of the resurrection of the dead:

> ... as those who curse. They shall be destined to die when the Reviver raises the dead of His people.

> Then we shall give thanks and relate to you the righteous acts of the Lord which . . . those destined to die. And He shall open [the graves...] and open a valley of death . . . and a bridge of deep . . . the accursed shall languish. . . and the heavens shall advance ... and all the angels. . . . .[191]

There is also no doubt that the Teacher of Righteousness saw himself as a chosen one who would draw the line between good and evil and establish God's new covenant with humanity. In one of his hymns, he clearly states:

> And You, my God, have appointed me as a holy counsel to the weary. You have taught me Your covenant and my tongue is as one of Your disciples.... For all who attack me You will condemn to judgment, so that in me You might divide between the righteous and the ungodly. You have established my heart in accordance with Your teaching and Your truth, setting my steps straight in the paths of righteousness, so that I may walk in Your presence in the domain of the righteous ones in paths of glory and life and peace without turning and never ceasing (Hymn 20).[192]

The Suffering Servant and the New Covenant

The theme of the suffering servant is a long one in Jewish history. In fact, it is at the very core of Jewish mysticism and religion. For nearly a thousand years, the prophets and the priests had reiterated this theme as a means of explaining to the Jewish people that, in their suffering, they were fulfilling the will of God. Their suffering was essential so that all mankind might eventually know His glory. Through suffering, God tested his peoples' determination and obedience. And through their sacrifice, they became purified and able to achieve eternal life. The god of the Jews, as had all previous gods, demanded blood sacrifice. In this way, the gods had always achieved their purpose by permitting the persecution of their servants. As in previous civilizations, the Jewish Messiah would redeem the world through his sacrifice.

There is, however, a new element to this theme that is revealed in the life of the Teacher of Righteousness. The suffering servant of the Jews is now no longer a nation but an individual. The arena is no longer the external world of national conquest but an internal world in which the human soul battles with evil to achieve the companionship of God. The idea of the Messiah/Savior is no longer one who simply fructifies the earth with his blood. Nor is he the one who will lead Israel to the Promised Land. The blood sacrifice of the new covenant meant something much more profound in the life of the individual. It meant the forgiveness of his personal sins and the attainment of eternal life. Divinity was now within the grasp of the common man. He or she could reside among the angelic hosts in the presence of the Absolute Loving God. This was a revolution in human thought.

With the coming of the Teacher of Righteousness, we have the dawning of mystical consciousness in the Western world. With this new consciousness, the impulse of a new era of humanity is triggered. The stage is set for the transformation of consciousness out of the warrior age and into the age of the intellectual. The Teacher is not a priest but an individual intellectual who achieves a high level of spiritual consciousness by virtue of his own mystical experiences. The ideas set forth by Zoroaster have borne fruit in the Teacher of Righteousness. We now have a universal God who is personal and accessible through one's individual eperience.

Was the Teacher of Righteousness the Messiah? It appears that he and his followers believed that he was. Was he, in fact, the real Jesus Christ or was Jesus another Teacher who followed in his footsteps a hundred years later? Did it take a hundred and seventy years for the story of the Teacher of Righteousness to reach the mainstream of the Greek and Roman civilizations where he was presented with a new identity to give him greater mass appeal? Was his new identity somehow more palatable to a larger population, many of whom were Gentiles (i.e., not Jews)? Unfortunately, it is impossible to say. The similarities between the life of the Teacher of Righteousness and Jesus the Christ are uncanny. Yet, there is contradictory testimony that a man named Jesus did exist and that he was put to death by the Romans and not the Jewish king Jannaeus. It also must be said that the words that Jesus spoke on the nature of love transcended anything that the Teacher of Righteousness had to say on the subject. The truth is that evidence both supports and detracts from the theory that the Teacher of Righteousness and Jesus are the same man. While it seems we may never know for sure, the evidence for two distinct spiritual masters is greater. It seems that Jesus, as an Essene rabbi, followed in the footsteps of the Teacher of Righteousness and even surpassed him in wisdom.

What we can say, unequivocally, is that the mystical teachings of the Teacher of Righteousness and Jesus Christ that assert a human being can have a personal and loving relationship with the Absolute Divinity was new in the West, and that this idea caused a revolution in human consciousness, the waves of which we continue to swim in today.

It is certain that the mystical experience of the Teacher of Righteousness was slow to dawn on his followers. In their immediate grief and confusion, the death of the Master probably was interpreted as a profound spiritual failure. Many other Jews before them had watched their brothers and sisters enslaved or killed and had been disillusioned in their interpretation of the "covenant." In like manner, the Essenes now faced their own personal tragedy. As Allegro says:

> The first reaction of the monastery's survivors must have been one of numbed shock. . . . Crucifixion of the Master was not a matter for mystical speculation, but rather of hushed and fearful whispers, in the sense of disillusionment that God should have allowed such a tragedy to overtake His servant, the spiritual mentor and guide of His Elect.[193]

Even before the Teacher died, we know from the Dead Sea Scrolls and from later Gnostic writings that many of his disciples had jumped ship under the pressure. The remaining faithful found themselves hiding in caves, hounded by soldiers dispatched to hunt them down. And then, when the Romans came, it was the final straw. The Romans destroyed the Jewish community, seized control over Jerusalem, burned their temple to the ground (70 AD), and drove many of the faithful out of Judea. The result was the great Diaspora that sent the Jews in all directions. They would remain homeless for the next two thousand years.

There is evidence that the Romans also attacked Qumran and set fire to it. The Essenes, then, can be counted among the refugees who fled in fear of death, dispersed to many lands where they formed small quiet communities. In time, they tried to re-establish contact with each other. Over the years, different groups became attached to different aspects of the master's teachings and inevitably different sects emerged. Among these can be counted the Ebionites, Carpocratians, the Cerinthians, the Elcesaites, the Naassenes, the Nazarenes, and the Sampsaeans.[194] These groups were spread throughout the Middle East, Egypt, and the Mediterranean. In time, they would come to be called Gnostics from the word gnosis, which means spiritual knowledge. They preached an intuitive experience of Divinity beyond religious law or reason.

Before we approach the subject of the Gnostics and the next stage of western mysticism, let us briefly summarize what we have discovered about the Essenes.

We know that the Essenes transmitted the idea of a New Covenant to early Christians along with many of its core ideas. As Allegro tells us, the Essenes "called themselves the 'men of the New Covenant, or New Testament', and prepared themselves under their Teacher, another Joshua (Jesus in Greek), to enter the Promised Land of the new era."[195]

In the Dead Sea Scrolls, the Essenes call this covenant the "Covenant of Mercy"[196] or the "Covenant of the Eternal Yahad" (Community).[197] This is the same covenant that Jesus would bring to his disciples and to "those who have ears to hear."

Were the Essenes the first Jewish Christians? In so far as Jesus was an Essene master, this was more likely. Certainly, the life of the Teacher of Righteousness profoundly influenced the teachings of Jesus and colored the interpretation of his life in both the Gnostic writings and in the writings of the early Church of Rome patriarchs. It seems likely, therefore, that the largest group of early converts to "Christianity" was the Essene community. This is supported by the passage in the Acts of the Apostles:

> "And the word of God increased; and the number of the disciples multiplied in Jerusalem greatly; and a great company of the priests were obedient to the faith" (Acts 6:7 7)."

This mention of "priests" likely referred to rebel Pharisees, because in a passage right above it (Acts 5:40), the apostles of Jesus are still being beaten by the Pharisees for preaching in his name.[198]

The Essenes built their Qumran community on a site that linked them with the messianic figure of Joshua who made the second covenant with the Jewish god that allowed them to enter the Promised Land. Joshua when translated in Greek becomes Jesus. We also know that the Essenes believed that their master was the new Messiah, who brought a new covenant to the Jews that would "renew the faithful in His strength." In the *Redemption and Resurrection* tract found among the Dead Sea Scrolls, we know that through this new covenant, God would open the eyes of the blind, raise up the poor, and no longer postpone access to Divinity. We are also told that the Messiah would do glorious things that had not been done before, including healing the sick, reviving the dead, satisfying the poor, guiding the uprooted, sending the good news (gospels) to the afflicted, and making the rich suffer for the injuries they have caused others.

The new covenant, it was believed, would carry the Jews through to the "end of days" when an epic battle between good and evil would occur and the good would ultimately triumph.[199] God would then judge the living and the dead, and the righteous Jews would live forever in an earthly paradise located in the area of Qumran.[200]

We know that the Essenes, like the Pharisees,[201] were heavily dependent upon Zoroastrianism for this dualistic interpretation of the world and their understanding of how this earthly conflict would eventually be resolved during the "end of days," just prior to the Day of Judgment.

While this belief can easily be attributed to the history of the suffering Jews and to the conditions prevalent at the time of the existence of the Essenes, it is given deeper meaning by the proclivity of the Essenes to view every mundane condition as a cosmic event within their eschatology.

In the last analysis, the information gleaned from the Dead Sea Scrolls indicates that it was neither Jewish scripture nor Jewish law that provided the core beliefs of the Essenes. Neither was it Zoroastrianism, at least not at the deepest level. Rather, the Essenes added something new to the idea of God. They attributed their deepest intuitive insight to their Teacher of Righteousness, who suffered greatly in his mission to bring the word of Divine union to the common people and whose personal relationship with Divinity gave him the sustenance to continue his work, even to the point of crucifixion and death.

The Teacher of Righteousness was more than a teacher, more than a priest, or even more than a prophet. Like Joshua, he was the one chosen by God to revitalize the covenant and his stature could be recognized by his revelations and his miracles. The crucified teacher was linked to Joshua and perhaps was even considered a reincarnation of Joshua.[202] In a similar vein, the Naassene Gnostics would consider Jesus Christ the reincarnation of Elijah. All four of these men were anointed Messiahs and each performed their miracle at the Jordan River.

The documents of the Essenes also give us the prototypes, if not a record of actual events, concerning the teachings of Jesus Christ. These include the ritual of baptism as an initiation into divine knowledge, the miracles performed by the Teacher, the idea of a New Covenant, the Sermon on the Mount, The Last Supper, access to mystical knowledge, the crucifixion, and resurrection of the dead.

When their Master was killed, the Essenes were in crisis. They were being hunted and killed just as their Master had been. The period of continual harassment under the Jewish ruling class, the Greeks, and the Romans created a protracted exodus out of Judea.

The Essenes began their exodus out of Judah during the lifetime of the Teacher of Righteousness and continued for the next hundred years. The Essenes show up again in history, thanks to the books uncovered in the small village of Nag Hammadi in Egypt. Here the Essenes appear as Jewish Christians whom the Gentile patriarchs of the Church of Rome called Gnostics.

During their exodus, the Essenes spread throughout the Middle East, Egypt, and the Mediterranean. Many went north to Damascus while others went south into Egypt where they congregated in Alexandria and also in the small farming town called Nag Hammadi on the Nile River. It was here, in 1945, that local farmers found a sealed earthenware jar containing thirteen leather-bound papyrus books. These books, another rare discovery in the history of Judeo-Christianity, contain additional information on the life of Christ, including the writings of many other early Christians. It is in these documents that we find the earliest Jewish reference to "Jesus Christ."

It seems fitting that it was on the Nile River that these documents were uncovered because as we have seen, the Essenes' main symbol for mystical knowledge (gnosis) was water. Qumran was to be converted into a Garden of Eden because of the river (gnosis) that would flow from Jerusalem to the Dead Sea at the "end of days." Likewise, every covenant between the Jews and their god was made by crossing a body of water. This included the covenants of Moses, Joshua, Elijah, the Teacher of Righteousness, and Jesus Christ. Baptism by water was also the rite of initiation that brought one into contact with this spiritual knowledge (gnosis).

In Egypt, the link between the symbolism of water and gnosis (divine knowledge), as revealed in the books found at Nag Hammadi, took on even greater significance. While the tragedy of the Teacher's death eliminated the vision of a sacred spring giving birth to a new Garden of Eden at Qumran, the interpretation of the Messiah, as the bringer of the sacred flow, came to be understood as an even greater miracle that would fructify the Garden of Eden in one's own heart. Now any individual who had "ears to hear" became eligible to achieve God-realization.

While this had indeed been the message of the Teacher all along, the Essenes had continued to view him as a Messiah who had been prophesied as the one to end the suffering of the Jews as a nation. Now, in exile from Qumran, they began to realize that their Master's covenant was not one between God and a people, but between God and the individual human heart. It applied to Jews and Gentiles alike, anyone, in fact, who desired spiritual knowledge and served the poor.

Of all the Jewish groups, it was the Essenes who were best trained to accept such a vision. They were; for example, not dependent upon temple doctrine and laws as were the Sadducees, nor were they mired in political subversion and extremism like the Pharisees and Zealots. The Essenes, therefore, were the first Jewish sect to grasp the idea of the Kingdom of God as an internal reality rather than as a theological-political event that required the direct intervention of God to remove the evil-doers among humanity by brute force.[203] "The Kingdom of God is within you," Jesus said. In realizing this, one became an heir to this great kingdom.

While the Essenes agreed with the Pharisees and the Zealots that Jannaeus and the Greeks had to be stopped, they came to take a more introspective approach. As Allegro tells us, "Essenism itself continued and developed along more quietist lines, renouncing the corrupt world altogether and seeking individual salvation through mysticism and the occult."[204]

The Essenes did not reject violence outright, however, for they did envision an epic battle between good and evil, as did the Pharisees and Zealots who also were deeply influenced by Zoroastrianism. The Essene *War Scroll*, which is one of the Dead Sea Scrolls, paints a vivid picture of how this war would play out on the battlefield. Nonetheless, the Essenes, more than any other Jews, were open to the idea of personal salvation as opposed to the idea of salvation of the Jewish nation.

This idea of personal salvation or the "New Covenant" was to revolutionize western consciousness and set the stage for the onset of the Intellectual Age in which a priest class would seize power from the warrior class and establish an all-powerful Christian church-state. With the idea of personal salvation, the intellectuals in the West had finally developed the highest principle of unity (i.e., One God accessible to all humanity, irrespective of tribe, nation, city, region, or empire). This idea, still in its nascent phase, would eventually crystallize into the formation of a complete institutional authority at the hands of intellectuals, in the guise of a priest class, who would rule the western world, beyond the power of kings, for the next seventeen centuries, and who would continue to do so until the end of the Middle Ages.

Before we leave the story of the Essenes, there are two large issues that we still need to address. The first is the evolution of the idea of *love* as it is expressed in the gospels of Jesus Christ. The second is the idea that Jesus was resurrected from the dead and visited his apostles before he bodily ascended into heaven. These issues of faith require our attention. They will become clearer as we begin to understand the concept of divine love and the link between the Essene Teacher of Righteousness, the Gnostic Christ, and the Christian Jesus, as he appears in the teaching of the Church of Rome. Fortunately, we have the treasure trove of Gnostic scriptures discovered at Nag Hammadi to help us in this exploration. These documents provide us with the missing link between the Essenes and the evolution of Jewish and Gentile Christianity.

During the period from the first century BC to the third century AD, a revolution in human consciousness created a social upheaval. It was not just that people were going through a political transformation, they were also going through a spiritual one. In the East, thanks to the spiritual jumpstart provided by Lord Shiva, people already had five hundred years with which to ponder the teachings of Lao Tzu, Lord Krishna, and Buddha. In the West, where thinking was more secular, the ideas of Zoroaster, Aristotle, and Plato had been shaping human consciousness. These individual intellectuals, along with their peers, were giving birth to a new Western civilization. They had already invented theatre, literature, philosophy, history, and science. But now, something new was being added to the mix. Thinking men and women were now caught up in the greatest mystery of all. They were beginning to delve deeply into the same questions presented by a Universal Ideology. Such questions include: What is human nature? What is the Cosmic Entity? What is this World? Who am I and What am I? What is my relationship with the universe and the Cosmic Entity? How should human beings live in this world? What is the aim of humanity? In the attempt to answer these profound questions, mysticism, or spirituality, was born in the West. The reality of Oneness had now begun to take root in the minds of men and women. Oneness of consciousness was now accessable through the merger of individual and God consciousness.

It was during these days that the Teacher of Righteousness and Jesus Christ walked the earth, and the time when the Essenes and the Gnostics were born. It was a time when every variety of philosopher and sect proliferated and intermingled throughout India, the Middle East, Egypt, Turkey, Syria, Greece, and Rome.

Human beings now began to explore the idea of God from a purely subjective perspective. In so doing, the Teacher of Righteousness and Jesus Christ introduced human beings in the West to the highest understanding of God. Their intuitive understanding of the Divine surpassed all religious dogma and religious law and minimized the theologizing and philosophizing of the rational mind. Their intuitive understanding was achievable, they claimed, only through acts of love and selfless service. Jesus taught that only through love was a human being able to "experience" God within as an interpersonal relationship.

Jesus did not speak as a priest or from an ego perspective when he said, "I am the way, the truth, and the light." He was not speaking figuratively when he said, "I and my Father are one." He was speaking from personal experience.

Early Jewish Christians and the Gnostics

In our study of early Jewish Christians and the Gnostics, we will see how the mystical seed, planted by the Essene Teacher of Righteousness, grew into a full understanding of God-consciousness. With the Gnostics, the I-feeling had finally identified its highest state of achievement, a state that transcended the mind and resolved itself in the merging of the soul with Absolute Consciousness. In this revolutionary understanding, as is generally believed, another Essene master followed the Teacher of Righteousness and advanced the idea of personal identity with Divinity. This man was Jesus of Nazareth, who came to be known as Jesus Christ.

When Zoroastrianism was incorporated into the Jewish religion during the time of the Babylonian Captivity, the Pharisees and the Essenes accepted the good god—bad god theory. They accepted the sons of light (the Jews) fighting with the sons of darkness (the Gentiles). They accepted the idea of the "end of days" when the good god would defeat the bad god. They accepted the idea of Judgment Day and the resurrection of souls. The Pharisees, however, were too preoccupied with the rules and rituals of Judaism to explore the idea of having a personal relationship with God. While the idea of Yahweh did evolve into a more humane god under the Pharisees in order to fit the requirements of the "good god," his purpose was still to lead his "chosen people" through the "end of days." The role of Yahweh was not to encourage self-realization. The break with the orthodox Jewish religion and the onset of western mysticism, therefore, actually began with the Teacher of Righteousness of the Essenes. He introduced the "new covenant" to the Jews, one that was based upon love and mercy; one in which an individual could become a "son of God" and have a personal relationship with the Father, regardless of religion.

As the Essenes began to appreciate this new covenant as revealed by their Teacher, they set the groundwork for the coming of Jesus Christ. The Essene master's legacy was the message that it was possible to commune directly with God. One could now merge with the Divine in this lifetime and not, according to prevailing religious dogma, have to wait until after Judgment Day.

The term "Christian" comes from the idea of being anointed with sacred knowledge. In the diaspora of the Essenes, which continued from the time of Jannaeus to the Roman conquest, they carried their message of the new covenant. With the coming of another Essene master, Jesus Christ, they became known as Jewish Christians and then as "Gnostics," so designated by their Gentile overlords in the Church of Rome. The Roman Church scoffed at the mystics with their secret knowledge (gnosis in Greek), for if the spiritual knowledge of the mystics were to spread among the people, the people would have no use for a religious institution or for a priest class to tell them what to do. As such, the Gnostics were always a threat to the Gentile priests in Rome who were working to convert the story of Jesus into an institutionalized religion. From their perspective, they had a legitimate concern. The ideas about the Savior were proliferating, and in this proliferation he took on various identities. This development could not continue. As the Christian Jews and Gnostics abandoned the dictates of the Jewish religion, they also came to challenge the legitimacy of Yahweh and, in fact, the entire cosmology of the Jewish priest class.

These concerns of the patriarchs of the Church of Rome, nonetheless, had little to do with the reality of mystical knowledge. Rather the patriarchs were concerned with the political questions of who would represent the authority of God on earth. Who would declare right (the orthodox view) from wrong (the view of heretics). Who would establish the rules; who would rule over the population; and who would punish the false prophets and false believers. These were their concerns. While the Gnostics exulted over their secret mysteries and were content in their mystical knowledge, the patriarchs of the Church of Rome were pouring over the Gnostic scriptures looking for ways to discredit them. It did not take long for the religious institution to become politically superior to the spiritualists and in so doing systematically eliminate them by calling them heretics and blasphemers. Once the emperor Constantine accepted the Church of Rome as the official religious institution of the Roman Empire and provided the church with an army, the Gnostics did not stand a chance. They were killed or driven underground. Their scriptures were sought out and destroyed. In this way, the sacred scriptures that threatened the patriarchs of the Church of Rome were discarded and those that agreed with their approach remained, although most in a redacted form.

In a process similar to the creation of the Torah or Old Testament so also was the New Testament created. It was not a complete revelation, but a careful selection of existing stories and written materials, produced in a manner to serve the ambitions of the early leaders of the Church of Rome. Let us now take a look at how this process unfolded.

The Gospel of the Nazarenes

The earliest Christian gospel is probably the Gospel of the Nazarenes. It was written in Hebrew and emphasizes Jesus's adherence to Mosaic Law. The Nazarene was a term applied to Jesus of Nazareth. According to Matthew (2:23), Jesus "came and dwelt in a city called Nazareth; that it might be fulfilled which was spoken by the prophets. He shall be called a Nazarene."

The original term for Christians, which appears in the New Testament, is "Nazarenes." It was used derisively by the Jewish lawyer Tertullus against Paul when he called him "a ringleader of the sect of the Nazarenes" (Acts 24:5). Around AD 331, Eusebius recorded that Christ was called a Nazarene from the name Nazareth, and that in earlier centuries "Christians," were once called "Nazarenes."[205] The modern Israeli Jew term for Christian is still Nazarene.

It is interesting that historical proof of a first century town called Nazareth has never been found. The town does not show up in the Jewish Talmud or in any of the thirty-nine books of the Old Testament. Neither does it show up in any Jewish apocrypha. Josephus, who himself lived in Galilee, lists towns throughout the province as well, but never mentions

Nazareth. Furthermore, none of the prophets ever mentioned Nazareth. So what are we to make of this? The Gospel of Luke says the village was located on the precipice of a mountain. The Gnostic Gospel of Thomas says that the name is symbolic for "Truth." It is most likely, then that Jesus of Nazareth meant Jesus of the Truth. This seems most likely because today's city of Nazareth is not on a mountain peak but in a depression surrounded by small hills. Archaeological digs in contemporary Nazareth have unearthed first century funerary equipment that would have made the area ritually unclean to Jews.[206]

The term Nazarene was also applied to those Jews who believed that Jesus Christ was the long-awaited Messiah. When this sect began to move into the Gentile world, they became known as Christians.[207]

Thus, at the time of Jesus, the term Nazarene was applied to himself and his followers. The Nazarenes were therefore the first Christians. They were Jewish, and they were led by James, who was the brother of Jesus. As such, James became the first Bishop of Jerusalem. We will discover the significance of James's thought by later looking at the teachings of the Naassenes, the oldest Jewish Christian Gnostic sect that claimed to have received higher teachings from James through an intermediary, a female teacher named Mariamne.[208]

The name of the *Gospel of the Nazarenes* is hypothetical. Only a few quotes and commentaries from an original document come to us in writings from the Church patriarchs, Hegesippus, Origen, Eusebius, and Jerome.

Most modern historians believe that the Gospel of the Nazarenes was actually the original Gospel of Matthew. What has come down to us as the Gospel of Matthew was largely redacted by priests within the Church of Rome. Jerome, a church patriarch of the fourth century tells us:

> Matthew, also called Levi,[209] apostle and aforetime publican, composed a gospel of Christ at first published in Judea in Hebrew for the sake of those of the circumcision who believed, but this was afterwards translated into Greek, though by what author is uncertain.[210]

So now we have discovered the oldest Christian sect and the source for the Gospel of Matthew. Most scholars today agree that the Gospel of Matthew found in the Bible was composed after his death. Whether the Gospel of the Nazarenes was the original manuscript of Matthew is still being debated. If it is, it probably would have been called the Gospel of Levi.

Another gospel written by early Jewish Christians was the *Gospel of the Ebionites*. It also survives only in fragments, as referenced by the Church patriarchs in their writings. This gospel poses some variation to the canonical gospels. There is no mention of the virgin birth or a discussion of Jesus's family. Jesus is not considered to be exceptional until the moment of his baptism when he is initiated into spiritual knowledge. The gospel also paints Jesus as being a vegetarian and one who speaks out strongly against animal sacrifice.

This perspective is similar to that of the Essenes as we have seen. The interpretation of baptism here suggests that Jesus is a mortal man who, by virtue of his righteousness, achieves God-realization and as such is able to carry out his prophetic task. This is the mystical interpretation of Jesus.

There is a third Jewish gospel, called the *Gospel of the Hebrews*. Like the other early gospels, it survives only as quoted material in the writings of the Church patriarchs. The fragments, however, contain information concerning Jesus's pre-existence, his incarnation, his baptism, and some of his sayings. In this Gospel, the Holy Spirit is envisioned as Jesus's Divine Mother. The gospel also says that Jesus first appeared to James after his resurrection. This has more validity than the belief that he first appeared to Peter, who was less of a mystic than James, but whom the Church of Rome was noted to vigorously promote as the means to establish their claim as the reigning authority of orthodox Christianity. We will discuss this more in the next chapter.

The Gospel of the Hebrews is the only Jewish–Christian gospel that the Church patriarchs referred to by name. Passages from the gospel were quoted by Clement, Origen, and Didymus the Blind. They were also quoted by Jerome. The gospel was originally used by early Gentile Christians as a supplement to their canonical gospels to provide source material for their commentaries on scripture. The gospel was no longer referenced after the fourth century when the Church of Rome put out their final version of the New Testament. At that time, the Church expunged the Jews Christians and other mystics from their definition of true Christians.

"Love and mercy" is the primary message of the Jewish spiritual master Jesus Christ. According to the synoptic gospels (Matthew, Mark, and Luke), Jesus specifically conveys this message on more than one occasion to the Pharisees who pester him concerning his disregard for Jewish law. In one scene; for example, the Pharisees see Jesus eating in a house with non-Jews, including Roman tax collectors and other street people. They ask his apostles, "Why eateth your master with publicans and sinners?" Their inference is that, as a rabbi, Jesus should know that according to Jewish law, a pious person must never associate with lower beings so as to maintain his personal purity. When Jesus overhears this, he tells the Pharisees, "They that be whole need not a physician, but they that are sick. But go ye and learn what that meaneth, *I will have mercy, and not sacrifice*: for I am not come to call the righteous, but sinners to repentance" (Matt 6:12-13).

The New Covenant is not dependent upon rules, rituals, or animal sacrifices. Neither is it a covenant to express a people's nationalistic dependence on a partisan god. Rather it is through mercy and love that the Father and the Son are known to each other. All who have "ears to hear" can be united with them.

Like the Essenes, the Gnostics also believed that they were custodians of the secret spiritual knowledge inherited from Jesus Christ. Just as agnostic means "not knowing," the term Gnostic means "knowing," Here knowing does not refer to rational knowledge but to spiritual knowledge. This kind of knowledge is not derived from the rational mind of science, but rather derives from the intuition and refers to the process of knowing oneself as an expression of God.[211]

It is revealing that the Gnostics held to this mystical belief while the Orthodox Jews and the patriarchs of the Church of Rome held to the myth that God is external to the mind of human beings. In their religious dogma, God is always "other," personally unknowable and unapproachable. The best that a believer in this orthodox god could hope for would be to exist in his presence after death or after judgment day.

Much information concerning this revolutionary period of spirituality is now available through the spiritual tracts discovered at Nag Hammadi, Egypt. These tracts, now called the Nag Hammadi scriptures, provide a treasure trove of information about early Christianity similar to the trove of information about the Essenes discovered at the Qumran settlement on the Dead Sea that provide information about mystical Judaism.

The scriptures at Nag Hammadi contain nearly fifty texts that were read as sacred literature. The texts include "The Prayer of the Apostle Paul," "The Secret Book of James," "The Gospel of Truth," "On the Origin of the World," the gospels of Thomas, Mary Magdelene, Philip, and Judas, "The Wisdom of Jesus Christ," "The Acts of Peter and the Twelve Apostles," and many more. These texts present various viewpoints of early Christians concerning the nature of Divinity, Jesus, the Creation Theory, the role of humankind, etc. The Gnostics were not a single organization, as were the Essenes; rather the Gnostics were composed of many individuals and groups of early Christians, each holding different beliefs. They received the name "Gnostics" from Irenaeus, the Church patriarch who condemned them all as heretics for their claim to possess mystical knowledge (gnosis). The gnostic groups included Hermetics, Sethians, Valentinians, Manichaens, and Naassenes among many others. The Gnostics also included powerful individuals, some of whom were apostles or great mystics themselves including Thomas, Philip, Mary Magdelene, and others who wrote their own gospels or had revelations written in their name. What the Gnostics held in common was a belief in personal transcendence and unity with a loving God. The Gnostics who began as Jewish Christians now included Gentile Christian mystics among them. They differed from orthodox Gentile Christians whose primary concern was not mysticism but the politics of creating a church based upon Jesus Christ and his teachings.

According to the Gnostic teacher Theodotus, who wrote around AD 140 to AD 160, the Gnostic is one who has come to understand:

> "who we were, and what we have become; where we were, whither we are hastening; from what we are being released; what birth is, and what is rebirth."[212]

Another Gnostic teacher, Monoimus said:

> Abandon the search for God and the creation and other matters of a similar sort. Look for him by taking yourself as the starting point. Learn who it is within you who makes everything his own and says, "My God, my mind, my thought, my soul, my body."[213]

This is the fundamental perspective of mysticism. To know oneself at the deepest level is to know God. Self-realization *is* God-realization. This was the secret knowledge of which the Gnostics spoke. It is the core message of Jesus Christ. "I and my Father are one" admits of no distinction between one's self and God.

In the Gnostic gospels, Jesus speaks of illusion and enlightenment and not of sin and repentance as does the Jesus of the New Testament. As Elaine Pagles tells us:

> Instead of coming to save us from sin, he comes as a guide who opens access to spiritual understanding. But when the disciples attain enlightenment, Jesus no longer serves as the spiritual master: the two have become equal – even identical.[214]

While the Church of Rome holds that Jesus is the "only begotten Son of God" and therefore also God, the Gnostics see Jesus as one who makes all human beings the sons and daughters of God. According to the Gnostic Gospel of Thomas, which is older than any of the other gospels, we find Jesus saying:

> I am not your master. Because you have drunk, you have become drunk from the bubbling stream which I have measured out. . . . He who will drink from my mouth will become as I am: I myself shall become he, and the things that are hidden will be revealed to him.[215]

The Naassenes

The gnostic group most similar to the Essenes and the Nazarenes were the Naassenes. If we assume that the Teacher of Righteousness was followed by another Essene master, whom history calls Jesus the Nazarene, the Naassenes were among the earliest Jewish Christians. Their roots were in Jerusalem and their writings were produced in the original Hebrew, not as most documents which were produced in Coptic (Egyptian) or Greek. In other words, the Essenes, Nazarenes, and Naassenes provide a single continuum of mystical thought that remains identical regardless of label.

The Naassene Sermon comes to us only through the criticism of Hippolytus, one of the most virulent of the anti-heresy patriarchs. He cites this Sermon in his *Refutation of all Heresies*, calling the Naassene ideas, "the root error from which all other heresies had sprung." [216]

Needless to say, the mystical understanding of the Naassenes was not grasped by Hippolytus. The Naassene Sermon is about devotion and spiritual enlightenment. Like the writings of the Essenes, it is filled with symbolism and parables.

While the Nazarenes were the original small community led by James the Just, the Naassenes also claimed to have been taught by James. Perhaps, Naassene was no more than a linguistic distortion of Nazarene. In the Gospel of Thomas, which predates the Catholic Church's official canonical gospels and was not later redacted (rewritten by priests), there is a passage in which the disciples of Jesus asked him who would lead them when he is gone. Jesus replies, "No matter where you have come from, you are to go to James the Just, for whose sake heaven and earth came into being (Thomas NHC II, 2, 12 [2]). We are essentially talking about the same community of people here.

The Naassenes also regarded Mary Magdelene as Jesus's most spiritually advanced student and the disciple whom he most loved. Mary was not the prostitute that the Church of Rome would later create. According to most Gnostics, Mary possessed great devotion and wisdom and was thus an example for all. Many also regarded her as the lover of Jesus. Both Mark and John say she was the first person to see Jesus in a vision after his death.

According to Irenaeus, another patriarch of the Church of Rome, who wrote *Against Heresies*, the Naassenes were "Gnostics" because they believed that they were the custodians of a revolutionary mystical knowledge. The Naassenes interpreted their knowledge within the Jewish religious tradition, as did the Essenes who preceded them. They used the same symbolism. For example, they inherited their interpretation of *water* as a symbol for the spiritual flow. Just as the Essenes spoke about the River Jordan as a symbol of spiritual knowledge and a place in which the Jews made their covenants with God, so also did the Naassenes.

They built on the Essene story of the Jordan River by adding to it the mysterious event that occurred on its banks between the prophets Elijah and his disciple Elisha sometime during the ninth century BC. To get a flavor of the mystical thinking of the early Christians, it is worth looking at this story.

Elijah is one of the most human and most romanticized prophets that Judaism ever produced. He was known for his fearless opposition to King Ahab and his wife Jezebel, who had attempted to destroy Judaism in Israel and replace it with the worship of Baal and other Canaanite gods. Jezebel, the "wicked" queen, was a Phoenician (Canaanite) by birth and a powerful woman who was able to impose her will on the Jewish king.

According to legend, Elijah performed many miracles, including raising the dead, bringing fire down from the sky, and having himself taken up "by a whirlwind."[217] He was expected to return to earth at the "end of days" to announce the coming of the Messiah. In Malachi 3:24 in the Old Testament it says, "I will send Elijah before the coming of the Lord."

Toward the end of Elijah's rich and colorful life, an event occurred that included his disciple Elisha, whom Yahweh instructed Elijah to "anoint" as a prophet.[218] This story of Elijah and Elisha detailed a third "parting of the waters." It occurred as Elijah, now an old man, was returning to his hometown of Gilead across the Jordan River from Jerusalem. During this crossing, Elijah was accompanied by his disciple Elisha and fifty members of the "brotherhood of the prophets." This story is told to us by the Deuteronomist priests, who also told us about the parting of the waters with Moses and Joshua. The presence of the fifty prophets indicates that the story is extremely sacred and is to be understood as real history and not just as legend.[219] In this story, Elijah parts the Jordan

River and after Elijah is taken metaphorically into heaven, Elisha parts it again. This demonstrates that Elisha assumed the mantle of his master. According to II Kings:

> And they went on together. Fifty of the brotherhood of prophets followed them, halting some distance away as the two of them stood beside the Jordan. Elijah took his cloak, rolled it up and struck the water; and the water divided to left and right, and the two of them crossed over dry-shod. When they had crossed, Elijah said to Elisha "Make your request. What can I do for you before I am taken from you?" Elisha answered, "Let me inherit a double-share of your spirit." "Your request is a difficult one," Elijah said. "If you see me while I am being taken from you, it shall be as you ask; if not, it will not be so." Now, as they walked on, talking as they went, a chariot of fire appeared and horses of fire, coming between the two of them, and Elijah went up to heaven in the whirlwind (II Kings 2:7-11).

This extraordinary image does not end here, for we are then told:

> Elisha saw the chariot and shouted "My father! My father! Chariot of Israel and its chargers!" Then he lost sight of Elijah and taking hold of his clothes he tore them in half. He picked up the cloak of Elijah, which had fallen, and went back and stood on the bank of the Jordan. He took the cloak of Elijah and struck the water. "Where is Yahweh the God of Elijah?" he cried. He struck the water, and it divided to right and left, and Elisha crossed over. And when the fifty prophets saw this they said that the spirit of Elijah now rests on Elisha. And they came to him and bowed to the ground before him (II Kings 2:12-15).

This story of Elijah and Elisha presents a spiritual lesson without parallel in the Old Testament. The event involved the third parting of the waters, but it is also linked to spiritual ascension, spiritual initiation, and the sacred relationship of teacher and disciple. It was made more extraordinary by the fact that it presaged the meeting of John the Baptist and Jesus Christ when Jesus went to be baptized by John in the Jordan River. After his baptism, the Spirit descended on Jesus as a sign that he also became an anointed prophet of Yahweh. In this scene, Yahweh called out from heaven that Jesus was his beloved son in whom he was well pleased. While this ended the scene of the baptismal rite in the gospels of Matthew, Mark, and Luke (John does not describe the baptism), it is not so for the Naassenes. In fact, according to the Sermon of the Naassenes, Jesus, following in the footsteps of Elijah and Elisha, also commanded the waters. The Sermon reads, "This . . . the great Jordan. . But Jesus drove it back, and made it flow upwards."[220]

The symbolism here no longer refers to just a physical phenomenon, but primarily to a spiritual one. By making the water "flow upward," the spiritual knowledge now returns to its source. This act of Jesus expresses an evolution in the meaning of baptism. No longer does mastery over the waters simply indicate mystical control over physical elements, now the language is symbolic of an interior process of spiritual attainment. As Mark Gaffney tells us:

> By making the river reverse its flow, Jesus achieves the absolute; supreme union with the Godhead – and he does it while still part of this world, which distinguishes him from Enoch, Noah, and Elijah, all of whom represent previous cases of heavenly ascent. In the process of reaffirming the old theme of mastery over the waters, the Savior announces a new mystery that is even more profound, involving a new series of cosmic lessons on a higher level.[221]

According to Hippolytus,[222] the symbol of water for the Naassene had to do with the act of generation. Jewish history, to the Naassenes, was symbolic of an internal spiritual process. The Jews had to leave Egypt, Egypt being the body. To do so they had to cross over the Red Sea, which symbolized physical generation through sex. In doing so, they passed into a "wilderness" where spiritual work had been forsaken. When they arrived at the Jordan River, they came to a place where mortal men had been born and lived for generations. Now, however, through the miracle of Jesus, who rolled the river upward to its source, men gained the ability to enter the divine realm. With the new spiritual covenant of Jesus, human beings can now become one with God. As it says in Psalms 82:6, "I have said Ye are gods; and all of you are children of the most High."

For the first time in Western history, a man can be made a god through spiritual initiation. This is the symbolism of the baptism of Jesus Christ. And it is through baptism that one is initiated into mystical knowledge. If people then remain in a spiritual intercourse with Divinity, they will experience the divine bliss that remains hidden to most, yet can be revealed to those who have eyes to see. This is what is meant by the statement that the kingdom of heaven is to be sought from within. On the other hand, if the people return to Egypt (the body), through carnal intercourse, "they shall die like men."[223]

At the time of John the Baptist, many Jews were expecting the coming of the Messiah who would signal the "end of days." Many were greatly inspired by John the Baptist and came to believe that he was the returned Elijah that was prophesied.[224] John even looked like Elijah. "John wore a garment of camel skin, and he lived on locusts and wild honey" (Mark 1:6). In II Kings 1:8, Elijah is described as wearing a "hair cloak … and a leather loincloth."

Notwithstanding John's denials that he was the reincarnated Elijah, the gospels of Matthew, Mark, and Luke substantiate the fact that he was Elijah. In Matthew 11:10-15, Jesus tells John's disciples point blank that their master was a reincarnation of Elijah who was prophesized by Malachi to return and announce the coming of the Lord. Malachi had said, "Behold, I will send Elijah the prophet before the coming of the great and dreadful day of the Lord." (Mal 4:5). Jesus's words to John's disciples were, "And if ye will receive it, this is Elijah, which was for to come. He that has ears to hear, let him hear" (Matt 11:14-15).

If John was Elijah, then who was Jesus? He must have been the reincarnation of Elisha, who, in his last lifetime, had asked for a "double share of spirit." Apparently Elisha now had surpassed his old teacher in wisdom. Mark Gaffney, an expert on the Naassenes, who sought a quantification of this "double share," observed that the Deuteronomist attributed seven miracles to Elijah, while Jesus had fourteen miracles attributed to him.

This spiritual inversion may be the reason for the verse in the Gospel of Thomas, in which Jesus states: "The man old in days will not hesitate to ask a small child seven days old about the place of life. For many who are first will become last, and they will become one and the same...."

The same message appears in Matthew 19:30, "Many who are first will be last, and the last first."

In the mystical tradition, the role of the teacher is to awaken the spiritual energy of the disciple. According to Gaffney, "The moment when the disciple experiences the full flowering of his innate divinity, disciple and teacher become "one and the same."[225]

There is additional evidence to support the link between the Old Testament pair and John and Jesus in the New Testament. In Matthew 3:14-15, we are told that when Jesus came to be baptized, John demured. Gaffney explains it this way:

> When Jesus insists upon it, John says, "It is I who need baptism from you. And yet you come to me!" Jesus then gives a reply so cryptic that it has never been explained by scholars: "Leave it like this for the time being; it is fitting that we should, in this way, do all that righteousness demands," at which point John acquiesces. Based on everything we have discovered, the meaning of this puzzling exchange becomes clear. Although the spiritual attainment of Jesus (Elisha) has far surpassed that of his former teacher (Elijah), out of love and respect, Jesus deems it fitting to be baptized by him.[226]

Later, we are told that Jesus also baptized John in the River Jordan (John 3:22-23).

The Gnostic Gospels

The Gnostics were not a homogenous group, nor were they a religion. Rather, they were mystics and groups of mystics, identified by the Church of Rome as "heretics" and by other mystics as their brethren because of their quest for union with the Absolute. The Gnostics, like the Essenes, tended to be disciplined spiritualists, even ascetics.

Some major groups or movements within the Syrian/Egyptian Gnostic world were the Sethians, Valentinians, and the Ophites (including the Naassenes). In the Persian world were the Manichaens (dualist followers of Jesus) and the Mandaeans (followers of John the Baptist).

While Gnostics shared a common understanding of mystical reality, their language and understanding of theological concepts were highly diverse. Even so, they held beliefs in common which merited their being called "heretics" by the Church of Rome.

The Gnostics emphasized personal spiritual experience as the key to unity with God. In so doing, they rejected the Church's dogma that in order to achieve salvation one had to have faith in the Church and its sacraments. They also rejected the bodily resurrection of Jesus, believing this event was purely spiritual in nature. Some went so far as to state that Jesus only appeared to possess a physical body.

By the mid-second century, Christian Gnostics often believed that the God of the Jews (Yahweh) was a different, lower being from the true God. They called this lower god "the Demiurge," and believed that the true God is androgynous (beyond the duality of gender), and is not a trinity but a unity. Those who did believe in a triune god characterized God as Father, Mother, and Son.

The Gnostics also believed that Thomas and Mary Magdalene received special knowledge from Jesus, which was withheld from less enlightened disciples such as Peter. They also held that women could administer baptism and act as priests.[227]

Some Gnostics, in common with such Neoplatonic philosophers as Plotinus, held matter to be inherently evil. However, others believed that matter was not evil in and of itself. Rather, it was a person's identification with matter rather than spirit that led one astray. Gnostics often referred to the "bridal chamber, as a symbol for union of the human soul with God.

In the Nag Hammadi library of gnostic texts, we find gospels other than those of Matthew, Mark, Luke, and John. We find, for example, the gospels of other apostles— Thomas, Philip, and Judas. We also find the gospel of Mary Magdelene, who was the companion of Jesus. Among the texts are also other documents attributed to Peter, John, James, and Paul. It is worth taking a look at some of these gospels because they give us a flavor of early Christianity before the Church of Rome destroyed most mystical teachings. We will later explore why the Church felt it necessary to do this.

The Gospel of Thomas

While the canonical gospels (i.e., those accepted as orthodox by the Church of Rome) contained the gospels of Matthew and John, who were both disciples of Jesus, they also included the gospels of Mark and Luke, who were not disciples. Rather, Mark and Luke were followers of Paul and wrote from his perspective. In a letter Paul tells Timothy, who was his disciple and assistant, "Only Luke is with me. Take Mark, and bring him with thee: for he is profitable to me for the ministry" (Second Epistle to Timothy 4:11).

Aside from the Jewish-Christian gospels cited earlier, the earliest gospel written by an apostle appears to be the *Gospel of Thomas*. This gospel does not tell a narrative story of Jesus's life as do Matthew, Mark, and Luke (synoptic gospels), but is a collection of 114 sayings and stories that Thomas attributes to Jesus. It is noteworthy that the Gospel of Thomas does not focus on the crucifixion and resurrection as do the synoptic gospels. Thomas does not portray Jesus as someone who dies for peoples' sins on the cross or who bodily ascends from the dead. In Thomas's gospel, Jesus only refers to himself once and he calls himself a son of man. This is certainly modest because he was a realized master. In Thomas's gospel, neither is Jesus presented as the "only begotten Son of God," which was a later creation of the Church. Thomas was thought by many, especially the Christians in Syria, to be the twin brother of

Jesus and, as such, one whose gospel could be trusted as real. We know, there was a large community of Essenes who lived in Damascus.

According to the Gospel of Thomas, Jesus is a rare spiritual master, the likes of whom the western world had never seen before. He was Thomas's and the other apostles' spiritual master, and Thomas recorded some of his teachings that were compiled into his gospel. The significance of Jesus in this gospel is that he was united with God and that he could teach others how to also be united with God. By his sayings and parables, Jesus attempted to trigger the mind into an intuitive understanding of reality, one in which duality could be consciously transcended by one's intuition. In his introduction to the Gospel of Thomas, Marvin W. Meyer, the editor of the *The Nag Hammadi Scriptures,* in which the complete gospel was found, tells us:

> In the Gospel of Thomas, the sayings of Jesus are open to interpretation, so that disciples and readers are encouraged to search for the meaning of the sayings of Jesus and complete his thoughts after him. The Gospel of Thomas is an interactive gospel, and wisdom and knowledge come when readers creatively encounter sayings of Jesus and respond to the sayings in an insightful manner.[228]

The Gospel of Thomas opens with a prologue:

> "These are the hidden sayings that the living Jesus spoke and Judas Thomas the Twin recorded. And he said, "Whoever discovers the interpretation of these sayings will not taste death." Several of these sayings follow:
>
> 2. Jesus said, "Let one who seeks, not stop seeking until one finds. When one finds, one will be troubled. When one is troubled, one will marvel and will reign over all."
>
> 3. Jesus said, "If your leaders say to you, "Look, the kingdom is in heaven," then the birds of heaven will precede you. If they say to you, "it is in the sea," then the fish will precede you. Rather, the kingdom is inside you and it is outside

you. When you know yourselves, then you will be known, and you will be understood that you are children of the living Father. But if you do not know yourselves, then you dwell in poverty, and you are poverty."

5. Jesus said, "Know what is in front of your face, and what is hidden from you will be disclosed to you. For there is nothing hidden that will not be revealed."

13. Jesus said to his disciples, "Compare me to something and tell me what I am like." Simon Peter said to him, "You are like a just messenger." Matthew said to him, "You are like a wise philosopher." Thomas said to him, "Teacher, my mouth is utterly unable to say what you are like." Jesus said, "I am not your teacher. Because you have drunk you have become intoxicated from the bubbling spring that I have tended."

108. Jesus said, "Whoever drinks from my mouth will become like me; I myself shall become that person, and the hidden things will be revealed to that person."

What is Jesus telling Thomas and his other disciples here? In essence, he is saying that God-realization occurs when the mind, which is only able to perceive duality, merges with the spirit and therein one's individual consciousness merges with the Absolute Consciousness. This intuitive experience occurs because the "I-feeling" of the mind, which accounts for one's limited identity, is transcended. Now there is only one identity, (i.e., Infinite Oneness). All persons, places, and things are finite. We give a name to everything we perceive and conceive. This preoccupation of the mind, keeps it from seeing everything as only a form of God, a form of Oneness.

Even one's "definition" of God is limited by the very fact that it "defines" and thus separates *what is* from *what is not*. When the unit consciousness is able to overcome its identification with relative reality, then it is able to merge into Absolute Reality and become One. This is why Jesus says that the kingdom is within and without. It is beyond form. This is why he says if you know what is in front of your face you will know what has been hidden from you. Thomas most accurately "defines" Jesus because he says he cannot define him. He has grasped the spiritual knowledge that Jesus was transmitting through his parables.

Jesus gave instructions to his apostles on how to teach people about the unfathomable:

> 14. "When you go into any region and walk through the countryside, when people receive you, eat what they serve you and heal the sick among them. For what goes into your mouth will not defile you; rather, it is what comes out of your mouth that will defile you."

Because the disciples were so engrossed in their myth about the "end of days" and the possibility that Jesus was the Messiah who was promised by the Jewish prophets, they said to him:

> 18. "Tell us how your end will be." Jesus said, "Have you discovered the beginning, then, so that you are seeking the end? For where the beginning is the end will be. Blessed is one who stands at the beginning: that one will know the end and will not taste death."

Again Jesus speaks about Oneness, the spiritual reality that absorbs the duality of the mind. The beginning and the end are the same. Life and death are the same. In the Oneness, neither the beginning nor the end has meaning, nor do life and death. They are only temporary forms of consciousness, not the eternal Consciousness itself.

Again, the same lesson:

> 22. Jesus saw some babies nursing. He said to his disciples, "These nursing babies are like those who enter the kingdom." They said to him, "Then shall we enter the kingdom as babies?" Jesus said to them, "When you make the two into one, and when you make the inner like the outer and the outer like the inner, and the upper like the lower, and when you make male and female into

a single one, so that the male will not be male nor the female be female, when you make eyes in place of an eye a hand in place of a hand, a foot in place of a foot, an image in place of an image, then you will enter the kingdom."

Jesus rejected the idea that the body gives birth to the soul:

> 29. Jesus said, "If the flesh came into being because of spirit, it is a marvel, but if spirit came into being because of the body, it is a marvel of marvels. Yet I marvel at how this great wealth has come to dwell in this poverty."

Jesus was always at odds with the established church of his day as represented by the Sadducees and Pharisees. They were not interested in spiritual realization; rather they were only interested in creating dogmas, rituals, and laws that kept human beings bound to them in poverty and ignorance:

> 39. Jesus said, "The Pharisees and the scholars have taken the keys of knowledge and have hidden them. They have not entered, nor have they allowed those who want to enter to do so. As for you, be as shrewd as snakes and as innocent as doves."

> 102 Jesus said, "Woe to the Pharisees, for they are like a dog sleeping in the cattle manger, for it does not eat or let the cattle eat."

Regarding the prophets and his previous master Elijah, who reincarnated as John the Baptist, Jesus had this to say:

> 46. Jesus said, "from Adam to John the Baptizer, among those born of women, there is no one greater than John the Baptizer, so that his eyes should not be averted. But I have said that whoever among you becomes a child will know the kingdom and will become greater than John."

> 106. Jesus said, "when you make the two into one, you will become children of humanity, and when you say, "mountain, move from here," it will move."

To become a child means to adopt the mind of a child because it does not as yet make distinctions between this and that. A child has not yet created a duality between "inside me and outside me."

To know the Father, (i.e., Absolute Consciousness), one has to extract the mind from all attachment to distinctions of thought and thereby merge into Oneness. This is the meaning of the next saying as well.

> 72. A person said to him [Jesus], "Tell my brothers to divide my father's possessions with me." He said to the person, "Mister, who made me a divider?" He turned to his disciples and said to them, "I am not a divider, am I?"

Just as Jesus and the mystics used water to symbolize spiritual knowledge, so they also used the symbol of "light." Neither water nor light can be divided.

> 77. Jesus said, "I am the light that is over all things. I am all: from me all this has come forth, and to me all has reached. Split a piece of wood; I am there. Lift up the stone, and you will find me there."

Jesus tells his disciples:

> 50. "If they say to you, "Where have you come from?" Say to them, "We have come from the light, from the place where the light came into being by itself, established itself, and appeared in their image." If they say to you, "Is it you?" Say, "We are his children, and we are the chosen of the living Father." If they ask you, "What is the evidence of your Father in you?" Say to them, "It is motion and rest."

> 51. His disciples said to him, "When will the rest for the dead take place, and when will the new world come?" He said to them, "What you look for has come, but you do not know it."
>
> 52. His disciples said to him, "Twenty four prophets have spoken in Israel, and they all spoke of you." He said to them, "You have disregarded the living one who is in your presence and have spoken of the dead."

Still bound by the duality of good and evil, the good god and the bad god, the present and the "end of days," etc., his apostles asked Jesus:

> 113. "When will the kingdom come?" Yeshua said, "It will not come by watching for it. It will not be said, 'Look, here it is,' or 'Look, there it is.' Rather, the Father's kingdom is spread out upon the earth, the people do not see it."

The Gospel of Thomas closes with an intriguing scene:

> 114. "Simon Peter said to them, Mary should leave us, for females are not worthy of life." Jesus said, "Look, I shall guide her to make her male, so that she too may become a living spirit resembling you males. For every female who makes herself a male will enter heaven's kingdom."

Here Jesus is addressing the belief of his contemporaries that women are bound to the earth and are thus spiritually dead. He is telling his disciples that women too have the capacity to become "living spirits" and achieve God-realization.

The earliest surviving written references to the Gospel of Thomas are found in the writings of the Church patriarchs, Hippolytus of Rome (ca. 222–235) and Origen of Alexandria (ca. 233). Hippolytus wrote in his *Refutation of All Heresies* (5.7.20):

> [The Naassenes] speak of a nature which is both hidden and revealed at the same time and which they call the thought-for kingdom of heaven which is in a human being. They transmit a tradition concerning this in the Gospel entitled "According to Thomas," which states expressly, "The one who seeks me will find me in children of seven years and older, for there, hidden in the fourteenth aeon, I am revealed."

While Hippolytus misinterpreted the meaning of seven and fourteen, as we now know and have previously discussed, the fact remains that he associated the Naassenes with the Gospel of Thomas and therefore, by implication, considered Thomas the apostle to be a Gnostic.

Richard Valantasis and other scholars argue that it is difficult to date Thomas because, as a collection of *parables* without a narrative framework, individual sayings could have been added to it gradually over time. Valantasis dates Thomas to AD 100 – 110, with some of the material certainly coming from the first stratum which is dated to AD 30 – 60.[229]

Other Gnostic gospels, believed to be written by the apostles but rejected by the Church of Rome, also present Jesus in a mystical way similar to Thomas.

The Gospel of Mary Magdalene

The Gospel of Mary[230] is the only Christian gospel ascribed to a woman. Yet, as with most of the gospels, it is unlikely that Mary wrote the gospel herself. Because of its language, scholars date the piece to the second century, most likely composed in Egypt.[231]

The language is more Gentile in its terminology than Jewish. Therefore, scholars attribute it to a community that she taught or that appealed to her for apostolic authority, just as others had appealed to James, Thomas, Paul, and Peter.[232] It is also possible that material originally written by Mary was discovered by someone who later changed the language to appeal to a wider audience.

The Gospel of Mary reveals a scene in which Jesus discusses the questions of matter and sin. Regarding the nature of matter, Jesus says:

> "Every nature, every modeled form, every creature exists in and with each other. They will dissolve again into their own proper root. For the nature of matter is dissolved into what belongs to its nature. Whoever has ears to hear should hear" (7,1-9).

When Peter asks about the "sin of the world," Jesus replies:

> "There is no such thing as sin; rather, you yourselves are what produces sin when you act in accordance with the nature of adultery,[233] which is called 'sin.' For this reason, the Good came among you, pursuing the good that belongs to every nature. It will set it within its root."

> He continued: "This is why you get sick and die: because you love what deceives you. Anyone who thinks should consider these matters" (7,10-8,11).

When Jesus departs he tells his apostles to "Acquire my peace within yourselves" (8, 11-9, 5). He cautions them about listening to people who will tell them to look outside themselves for God, "For the Child of Humanity exists within you. Follow it" (8, 11-9, 5).

His last words to the apostles were, "Do not lay down any rule beyond what I determined for you, nor promulgate the law like the law giver, or else you might be dominated by it" (8, 11-9, 5).

Despite the instructive and consoling words Jesus gave to his apostles, they are distraught and fearful at his departure. Mary consoles them and they ask her to impart the secret knowledge that she received from Jesus because he had loved her beyond all women (10.1-10).

Mary responds by telling them about the soul's ascent past the attachments of desire, ignorance, and wrath, and why it is necessary to overcome these dark forces in order to "rest"; that is, achieve enlightenment (15, 1-17, 9).

Peter and Andrew then dispute Mary's words. Andrew says that these teachings are strange ideas. Peter questions why Jesus would speak to a woman in private. "Are we to turn around and listen to her? Did he choose her over us?" Mary begins to weep and asks Peter whether he thinks she has made up what she said, or that she is telling lies about the Savior (17, 10-19, 5).

Then Levi (Matthew) steps in and accuses Peter of always being a wrathful person and now making Mary the enemy. He says:

> "For if the Savior made her worthy, who are you then for your part to reject her? Assuredly the Savior's knowledge of her is completely reliable. That is why he loved her more than us. Rather we should be ashamed. We should clothe ourselves with the perfect human, acquire it for ourselves as he commanded us, and announce the good news, not laying down any other rule or law that differs from what the Savior said" (17, 10-19, 5).

Scholars have suggested that this dialogue probably represents the brewing controversy between the Church of Rome (i.e., the rule givers) and the mystical communities. It is a position that makes sense. Yet, be that as it may, the core issue here is who is best qualified to go out and teach. Mary presents a heartfelt and sober character, while Peter cannot get past Mary's gender to see her spiritual nature. What ultimately matters is the state of one's soul. Leadership must be based on heartfelt sobriety, not sexism and anger.

The Gospel of Mary is completely gender neutral. She calls God, the "Good," and Jesus, the "Savior." When Jesus departs from the apostles, they are distraught and Mary consoles them with the words: "Rather, we should praise his greatness, for he has prepared us and made us human beings."

It is a principle of mysticism that gender is not an issue in spirituality. Both male and female are human beings and both are capable of self-realization. Gender only becomes an issue in a religion that seeks to control women for political ends.

The gospel ends with the apostles going out to teach (17, 10-19, 5).

The Gospel of Philip

Perhaps the most interesting gospel, from a mystical perspective, is the one attributed to the apostle Philip. Like the Gospel of Thomas, it is not a narrative of the life of Jesus but a collection of his sayings and ideas, as well as an attempt to interpret them from a spiritual perspective. This gospel contains information that is found within the New Testament as well as within Jewish scriptures. It also contains sayings of Jesus that do not appear elsewhere. The gospel is quite long and scholars are uncertain how to qualify it. Some refer to it as a "notebook" because it contains many themes that present themselves without order. Yet the central theme appears to be the distinction between relative reality and spiritual Oneness and how the mind must understand the difference in order to make spiritual progress. Many of the sayings, attributed to Jesus, refer to our use of words to describe a reality that is beyond words. Words create duality. By defining something, we establish what it is and what it is not. Therefore, words cannot help the mind escape duality. They can never enlighten us as to spiritual reality.

In the sayings below, Philip reveals the problem of trying to describe the indescribable, of trying to use forms (words and images) to reveal the formless. This is an important mystical concept because when people use words to describe a mental concept, they think they have actually grasped its reality but, in fact, they have only grasped a mental image. In the spiritual world, all forms merge into One because all forms are simply emanations of the One. Only in the psycho-physical world do they remain distinct. This is why there are so many gods whom religions claim to be the One God. Each religion has its own One God, while denying the others. This is important to remember when we speak of God. Our idea of God is only a mental concept, not the Absolute Reality. To achieve the absolute, we must go beyond thought and definition. What follows are quotes from the Gospel of Philip as they pertain to this predicament:

> The names of worldly things are utterly deceptive, for they turn the heart from what is real to what is unreal. Whoever hears the word "god" thinks not of what is

> real but rather of what is unreal. So also with the words "father," "son," "holy spirit," "life," "light," "resurrection," "church," and all the rest, people do not think of what is real but of what is unreal, though the words refer to what is real. The words that are heard belong to this world. Do not be deceived. If words belong to the eternal realm, they would never be pronounced in this world, nor would they designate worldly things. They would refer to what is in the eternal realm (53, 23-24, 5).
>
> Here in the world you see everything but do not see yourself, but there in that realm you see yourself, and you will become what you see (61, 20-35).
>
> Light and darkness, life and death, and right and left are siblings of one another, and inseparable. For this reason the good are not good, the bad are not bad, life is not life, and death is not death. Each will dissolve into its original nature, but what is superior to the world cannot be dissolved, for it is eternal (53, 14-23).

The sayings below refer to the forces that control our minds. As a mystic, it is important to remember that having "faith" is only believing what another man believes. Unless one has a direct relationship with a master, physically incarnate or not, one cannot make spiritual progress. Spiritual reality is personal; it is not a religious belief. Regarding the political powers, whether of church or state, Philip informs us:

> The rulers wanted to fool people, since they saw that people have a kinship with what is truly good. They took the names of the good and assigned them to what is not good, to fool people with names and link the names to what is not good. So, as if they are doing people a favor, they take names from what is not good and transfer them to the good, in their own way of thinking. For they wish to take free people and enslave them forever (54, 18-31).

> There are forces that do favors for people. They do not want people to come to salvation, but they want their own existence to continue (54, 31-55, 5).

What causes human beings to remain in darkness or ignorance? The statements below are profound. They echo Mary Magdelene's gospel in which Jesus says, "There is no such thing as sin." For the mystic, there is no Devil, nor are there "forces of evil" who scheme for control of our souls. Rather there is only immaturity and ignorance that keep us from understanding our divine nature:

> Ignorance is the mother of all evil. Ignorance leads to death, because those who come from ignorance neither were, nor are, nor will be. But those in the truth will be perfect when all truth is revealed. For truth is like ignorance. While hidden, truth rests in itself, but when revealed and recognized, truth is praised in that it is stronger than ignorance in error. It gives freedom.
>
> The word says, "If you know the truth, the truth will make you free." Ignorance is a slave, knowledge is freedom. If we know the truth, we shall find the fruit of truth within us. If we join with it, it will bring us fulfillment (83, 30-84, 14).

Baptism is another central theme that runs through this gospel, for it is through baptism that one is initiated into divine knowledge. This belief carries through all Jewish mysticism since the time of the Teacher of Righteousness:

> Anyone who goes down into the water and comes up without receiving anything and says, "I am a Christian," has borrowed the name. But one who receives the Holy Spirit has the name as a gift. A gift does not have to be paid back, but what is borrowed must be paid. This is

> how it is with us, when one of us experiences a mystery (64, 22-31).
>
> We are born again through the Holy Spirit, and we are conceived through Christ in baptism with two elements. We are anointed through the Spirit, and when we were conceived, we were united.
>
> No one can see oneself in the water or in a mirror without light, nor can you see yourself in the light without water or a mirror. So it is necessary to baptize with two elements, light and water, and light is chrism (69, 4-14).
>
> Jesus revealed himself at the Jordan River as the fullness of heaven's kingdom. The one conceived before all was conceived again; the one anointed before all was anointed again; the one redeemed redeemed others (70, 34-71, 3).
>
> Chrism is superior to baptism. We are called Christians from the word "chrism," not from the word "baptism." Christ also has his name from chrism, for the Father anointed the Son, the Son anointed the apostles, and the apostles anointed us. Whoever is anointed has everything: resurrection, light, cross, Holy Spirit. The Father gave all this to the person in the bridal chamber, and the person accepted it. The Father was in the Son and the Son was in the Father. This is heaven's kingdom (74, 12-24).

Philip's interpretation of the resurrection is also a mystical one. As such, it is in keeping with the laws of nature:

> People who say they will first die and then arise are wrong. If they do not receive the resurrection first,

while they are alive, they will receive nothing when they die. So it is said of baptism, "Great is baptism," for if people receive it, they will live (73, 1-8).

Those who say that the master first died and then arose are wrong, for he first arose and then died. If someone is not first resurrected, wouldn't that person die? As God lives, that one would die (56, 15-20).

In the following sayings, Philip reveals a practical and yet transcendent understanding of Jesus. Jesus here is not a mythical creation, a Yahweh or Son of Yahweh, a Zeus or Son of Zeus; rather he is the "perfect human." He is a real man, who, by virtue of his human nature, proves that other humans can also become divine. It is in the nature of human beings to desire limitlessness. Therefore, the goal of personal evolution is to achieve Divinity. Jesus shows the western world how a person can become God-realized:

Before Christ came there was no bread in the world, just as paradise, where Adam lived, had many trees for animal food but no wheat for human food, and people ate like animals. But when Christ, the perfect human, came, he brought bread from heaven, that humans might be fed with human food (55, 6-14).

Jesus tricked everyone, for he did not appear as he was, but he appeared so that he could be seen. He appeared to everyone. He appeared to the great as great, he appeared to the small as small, he appeared to the angels as an angel, to humans as a human. For this reason his word was hidden from everyone. Some looked at him and thought they saw themselves. But when he appeared to his disciples in glory upon the mountain, he was not small. He became great. Or rather, he made the disciples great, so they could see him in his greatness (57, 28-58, 10).

Philip revered Mary, the mother of Jesus, as one born without sin. In other words, Mary too was born self-realized. The Gnostics believed that the Holy Spirit was the Divine Mother, thus making the Holy Trinity, God the Father, God the Mother, and God the Son.

> Some said Mary became pregnant by the Holy Spirit. They are wrong and do not know what they are saying. When did a woman ever get pregnant by a woman?[234] Mary is the virgin whom none of the powers defiled. This is greatly repugnant to the Hebrews, who are the apostles and apostolic persons. This virgin whom none of the powers defiled wishes that the powers would defile themselves (55, 23-33).

Philip also reveals another Gnostic belief concerning Mary Magdalene:

> The companion of the Savior is Mary of Magdala. The Savior loved her more than all the disciples, and he kissed her often on her mouth. The other disciples said to him, "Why do you love her more than all of us?"
>
> The Savior answered and said to them, "Why don't I love you like her? If a blind person and one who can see are both in darkness, they are the same. When the light comes, one who can see will see the light, and the blind person will stay in darkness (63, 30-64, 9).

Philip indicates that Jesus was born like any other man, with a father and a mother. Thus he had an earthly father and a spiritual Father.

> The master would not have said, "My Father who is in heaven," if he did not also have another father. He would simply have said, "My Father" (55, 33-36).

The gospel of Philip concludes with these words:

> Those who received the light cannot be seen or grasped. Nothing can trouble such people even while they are living in this world. And when they leave this world, they have already received truth through images, and the world has become the eternal realm. To these people the eternal realm is Fullness.
>
> This is the way it is. It is revealed to such a person alone, hidden not in darkness and night but hidden in perfect day and holy light. (85, 32-86, 19).

The above quotes from the gospels of Thomas, Mary, and Philip provide a look at the mystical core of the teachings of Jesus Christ. In these gospels, Jesus is not some other-worldly being who eternally and single-handedly removes the sins of those who believe in him. Rather he is a spiritual master who teaches human beings how to enter the "eternal realm of Fullness." Sin is not overcome by a single event perpetrated by an outside mythical god but by one's effort to overcome ignorance and purify one's self through selfless service. No one can take away another's sins because we must all face the consequences of our own actions. To believe other than this is to violate the laws of nature.

It is by giving humanity the model of his life and his eternal spiritual knowledge that Jesus shared with humanity the greatest treasure known to man.

This view was shared by most early Christians before the dogma of the Church of Rome was institutionalized at the end of the fourth century. This Church dogma paints Jesus as an other-worldly mythical divinity, approachable only through following the leadership of the church bishops and those whom they appoint. By such practice, politics takes control and the mystical knowledge shared by Jesus is suppressed and for the most part eliminated. Why the Church of Rome suppressed mysticism within its structure and why it fought desperately to portray Jesus as an exception to the natural order and as the "only-begotten Son of God," is a question of politics rather than the reality of God-realization. Before we look into this phenomenon, however, let us now examine more closely the canonical gospels of Matthew, Mark, Luke, and John and the letters of Paul from which we obtain our present religious view of Jesus.

Canonical Gospels

The *canonical gospels* refer to those gospels that were approved by the Church of Rome. They have come down to us as the *only* gospels acceptable to the Roman Catholic Church and the Protestant religions. There are four canonical gospels: Matthew, Mark, Luke, and John.

The *synoptic gospels* refer to the gospels of Matthew, Mark, and Luke, because they are very similar in their construction and content and were probably created by the same priests after the death of the apostles. The synoptic gospels share the following features: (1) they have a similar length; (2) they are all composed in Koine Greek; (3) they were completed within a century after Jesus's death; and (4) the majority of Mark and almost half of Matthew and Luke coincide in content and sequence, often in nearly verbatim language.[235]

As we have seen, Matthew, also called Levi, was considered a Nazarene (man of Truth) and most likely Matthew was a writer of one of the first gospel, along with Thomas. The fragments of Matthew's gospel are today called the Gospel of the Nazarenes. What passes today as the Gospel of Matthew is a redaction published by the Church long after his death. Even though the Gospel of Matthew is the first entry to appear in the New Testament, modern scholars believe that Matthew's gospel of the Church and Luke's gospel both drew upon the Gospel of Mark as the major source for their works.[236]

John was the last gospel written. It is from the perspective of a different tradition, perhaps that of the Gnostics. During the following centuries, each canonical gospel was attributed to an apostle (Matthew and John) or to the close associate of an apostle (Mark and Luke).[237]

Almost all scholars of antiquity agree that Jesus existed, but they differ radically on the historicity of specific episodes described in the synoptic accounts of Jesus. The only two events subject to "almost universal assent" are that Jesus was baptized by John the Baptist and was crucified by the order of the Roman Prefect Pontius Pilate. Scholars reject the historical authenticity of the nativity of Jesus, his miracles, certain details of his crucifixion, his bodily resurrection, and bodily ascension into heaven. If such claims about the life of Christ are false, how did such claims originate and why did they originate?

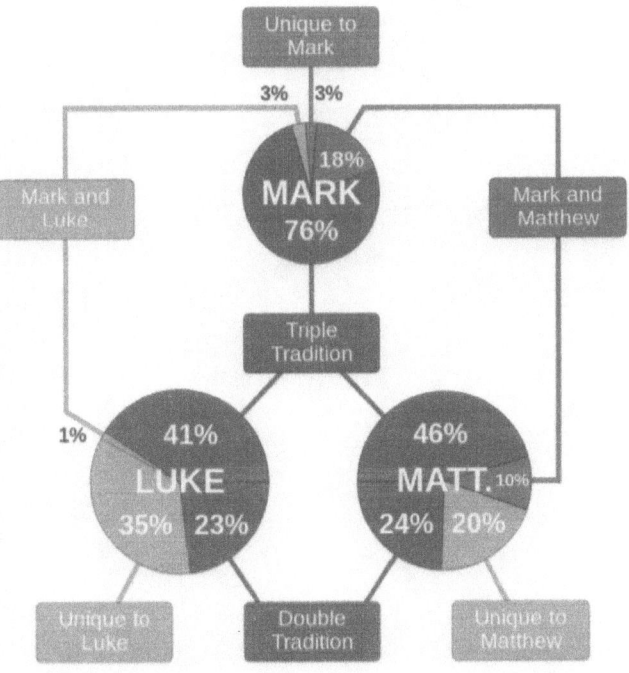

Fig. 2-11 Relationship Between Synoptic Gospels

Mithra

The Church of Rome's greatest assault on reason and spiritual knowledge is the imposition within the synoptic gospels of a common narrative about the life of Christ that is not based on historical fact. Rather, much of it is a virtual plagiarism of the myth of the god Mithra, who at the time was the chief god of the Roman ruling class as well as the Roman army that was in control of the Near East and Europe during the time that Paul was spreading his interpretation of the meaning of Christ and Christianity.[238]

Mitra, if you remember, was one of the original gods of the Aryans. He was one of the good gods who oversaw fair covenants. In fact, his name came to mean "covenant or promise."[239] In Sanskrit and modern Indo-Aryan languages, mitra also means "friend."

Fig 2-12: Mithraic Alterpiece Found Near Fiano Romano, Near Rome, Now in the Louvre

Mitra of the Vedas became Mithra to the Persian Aryans, and this myth made its way into Zoroastrianism and ultimately into the Roman army as a god of a mystery religion. In addition to being the divinity of covenants, Mithra was viewed as the judge and the all-seeing Protector of Truth. Mithra was also worshipped as the Sun God, not the sun personified, but rather as Light.[240]

The narrative of the life of Christ, as painted in the synoptic gospels, is largely based upon the story of Mithra. For example, Mithra was regarded as having these qualities:

1. Mithra was born on December 25th (on the winter solstice)[241] of a virgin Goddess;

2. He was born in a cave;

3. He was wrapped in swaddling clothes, placed in a manger and attended by shepherds;

4. His birth was witnessed by the Magi (priests of Zoroastrianism);

5. He was considered a teacher and master;

6. He had 12 companions (the zodiac);[242]

7. He performed miracles;

8. Mithra sacrificed himself for world peace;

9. He ascended to heaven;

10. Mithra was viewed as the Good Shepherd, the "Way, the Truth, and the Light," the Redeemer, the Savior, the Messiah;

11. Mithra is omniscient, as he "hears all, sees all, knows all: none can deceive him";

12. He was identified with both the Lion and the Lamb;

13. His sacred day was Sunday, "the Lord's Day," hundreds of years before the appearance of Christ;

14. His religion had a Eucharist or "Lord's Supper";[243]

15. Mithra "sets his mark on the foreheads of his soldiers." (Christian sacrament of Confirmation); and

16. Petra, the sacred rock of Mithraism, became Peter, the foundation of the Catholic Church.

In the Jesus myth, the three wise men or "kings" from the east who followed the Star of Bethlehem in order to pay homage to the infant are Magi priests of Zoroastrianism. Their attendance in the Jesus nativity story honors the tradition of Mithra and thereby legitimized the story in the eyes of the Roman populace.

The Mithraic myth also included a last supper, celebrated with his twelve companions, in which bread was a sacrament. It was called *mizd*, or in Latin, *missa*, and in English the *mass*.[244] Mithra performed miracles including raising the dead, healing the sick, and making the blind see and the lame walk. He also cast out devils. After his death he was buried in a rock tomb and was withdrawn from it and was said to have lived again.[245]

The fact that so much of the mythology of Mithra was incorporated into the story of Jesus's life, led St Augustine, the most renowned of early Church theologians, to declare that the priests of Mithra worshipped the same deity that he did.[246]

The fact that the Mithraic myth is common across all three synoptic gospels (Matthew, Mark, and Luke) and is used to describe the life of Jesus, suggests that these gospels were composed by the early Church to make the image of Jesus acceptable to the people of the Roman empire. When critics began to deride this obvious falsehood, the Church fathers tried desperately to explain the similarity between Mithra and Jesus. Their chief argument was that the Devil had anticipated the true faith and *imitated it before Christ's birth*. This is an obvious example of the limited value of possessing faith without reason.

Mithraism, as a rival to early Christianity in Rome, was eliminated by the Church once Constantine, the first Christian Emperor, put the weight of the Roman army behind the Church.

Yet, when all is said and done, the legend of Jesus resembles the stories of a god that preceded Jesus, having originated with the Aryan Persians. As has previously been said, it is not the purpose of religious myth to present a historically accurate truth. Myths are written by a priest or priests to communicate the story of a god, an authority figure, so that the faithful would share a common, unifying idea of wherein power existed. Just as the story of Yahweh and the early history of the Jews was fabricated by the Jewish priest class, so also was the story of Jesus as told to us in the canonical gospels of the New Testament. Because we cannot really know the historical truth from Church mythology, our approach will be to ascribe stories of the mystical teachings of Jesus to the original gospels, while ascribing stories that create the rationale for the Church of Rome authority to the redacted gospels. We must remember, the apologists or the ruling class, or aspiring ruling class, have always revised history to justify their authority. Historical revisionism is how the kings and priests have always justified their rule. We have concrete examples of how the Pharaohs and the Assyrian kings rewrote history on their steles. We have seen how the Jewish scribes, during the time of Josiah and during the Babylonian Captivity, rewrote history and created legends to justify their right to rule over the Jewish people. So also historical scholarship leads us to conclude that the priests of the Christian faith adapted the same methods of rewriting history.

Jesus Christ

This understanding of the canonical gospels, has led scholars to the question "Did a man called Jesus actually exist and if so, what was he like?" Because of the obvious manipulation of his identity by the early Church of Rome and the dearth of hard evidence as to his physical existence, many believe that Jesus Christ never existed. Surprisingly, however, most scholars believe that he did.

The "hard evidence" for the existence of Jesus Christ comes from two references in the *Antiquities of the Jews*, written around AD 93 by the Jewish historian Josephus and by a single reference to Christus and his execution by Pontius Pilate in the *Annals* of the Roman historian Tacitus around AD 116.

Let us look at these references more closely because the entire structure of Christianity and the consequent moral base of Western civilization is built upon these three short statements.

First, let us consider who Josephus was. He is unquestionably the best-known historian of ancient Jewish society. He was born in AD 37 as a member of the Jewish ruling class and educated in biblical law and history. On his mother's side he was a descendent of the Hasmonean Kings, and on his father's side, his family was composed of priests of the Temple. In 66 AD, when the Jews in Palestine revolted against Roman rule, Josephus was given command of the Jewish forces in Galilee. He was utterly defeated by the Romans but survived, and because of his skills and malleability, he became an advisor to the Roman general Vespasian. When Vespasian became Emperor of Rome in AD 69, he moved to Rome and sent his son Titus back to Judea to finish the war against the Jews. Titus took Josephus with him as an interpreter and spokesman to the Jews in Jerusalem. Josephus's repeated calls for his countrymen to surrender understandably created much hatred against him. In AD 70, the Romans crushed the Jewish revolt and destroyed Jerusalem.

Josephus returned to Rome with Titus, where he was rewarded for his efforts with a house and a life-time pension. In his leisure, Josephus turned to writing history. In the 70s, he wrote Jewish Wars, which provided a chronicle of the wars of the Jewish people. Thereafter in the 90s, he wrote a much broader history of the Jewish people called Jewish Antiquities.[247] In this chronicle, Josephus discusses John the Baptist, Jesus's brother James, Pontius Pilate, the Sadducees, the Sanhedrin, the High Priests, and the Pharisees. As for Jesus Christ, there are two references to him in Antiquities. In a section dealing with various actions of Pilate (Book 18), in a passage called "Testimonium Flavianum," Josephus says:

> Now there was about this time Jesus, a wise man, if it be lawful to call him a man, for he was a doer of wonderful works, a teacher of such men as receive the truth with pleasure. He drew over to him both many of the Jews, and many of the Gentiles. He was the Christ, and when Pilate, at the suggestion of the principal men among us, had condemned him to the cross, those that loved

him at the first did not forsake him; for he appeared to them alive again the third day; as the divine prophets had foretold these and ten thousand other wonderful things concerning him. And the tribe of Christians so named from him are not extinct at this day.[248]

It is generally believed that while there may be a core of truth to this statement, the fingerprints of the Church patriarchs are all over this passage.[249] Scholars hold that no Jew would have written that "he was the Christ" and "he appeared to them alive again the third day."

At best, scholars speak of "partial authenticity" regarding this statement. Most believe without Christian redaction, the original text of Josephus would read something like this:

> At this time there appeared Jesus, a wise man. For he was a doer of startling deeds, a teacher of people who receive the truth with pleasure. And he gained a following among many Jews and among many of Gentile origin. And when Pilate, because of an accusation made by the leading men among us, condemned him to the cross, those who had loved him previously did not cease to do so. And up until this very day the tribe of Christians (named after him) had not died out.[250]

The second reference to Jesus Christ appears in a paragraph in Book 20 where he describes the stoning of Jesus's brother, James, at the hands of Ananus, the High Priest:

> But the younger Ananus who, as we said, received the high priesthood, was of a bold disposition and exceptionally daring; he followed the party of the Sadducees, who are severe in judgment above all the Jews, as we have already shown. As therefore Ananus was of such a disposition, he thought he had now a good opportunity, as Festus was now dead, and Albinus was still on the road; so he assembled a council of judges, and brought before it the brother

> of Jesus the so-called Christ, whose name was James, together with some others, and having accused them as lawbreakers, he delivered them over to be stoned.

Josephus scholar, Louis H. Feldman, has stated that, "few have doubted the genuineness" of this reference.[251] Regarding Tacitus, the Roman historian, his reference to Christus occurs in his description of Nero's persecution of the Christians after a large fire burned half of Rome in AD 64:

> But all human efforts, all the lavish gifts of the emperor, and the propitiations of the gods, did not banish the sinister belief that the conflagration was the result of an order. Consequently, to get rid of the report, Nero fastened the guilt and inflicted the most exquisite tortures on a class hated for their abominations, called *Christians* by the populace. Christus, from whom the name had its origin, suffered the extreme penalty during the reign of Tiberius at the hands of one of our procurators, Pontius Pilatus, and a most mischievous superstition, thus checked for the moment, again broke out not only in Judæa, the first source of the evil, but even in Rome, where all things hideous and shameful from every part of the world find their center and become popular. Accordingly, an arrest was first made of all who pleaded guilty; then, upon their information, an immense multitude was convicted, not so much of the crime of firing the city, as of hatred against mankind. Mockery of every sort was added to their deaths. Covered with the skins of beasts, they were torn by dogs and perished, or were nailed to crosses, or were doomed to the flames and burnt, to serve as a nightly illumination, when daylight had expired.[252]

Scholars believe that the negative tone of Tacitus' comments about Christians makes it unlikely that the passage was later forged by a Christian scribe. Therefore, the Tacitus reference is now widely accepted as an independent confirmation of Christ's crucifixion.

Chapter Four: Religion and the Attack on Mysticism

The Church of Rome

HAVING SAID THIS, LET us now return to our discussion of the canonical gospels with the understanding that, in all likelihood, there was a real Jesus, and aside from the secular views of Josephus and Tacitus, we also have a great body of literature from the Essenes, Jewish Christians, Gnostics, and early Gentile Christians that testify to a revolution in consciousness that was occurring in the period from 100 BC to AD 100. Because a man named Jesus Christ was at the nucleus of this revolution, we study the reports of his contemporaries, whether fabricated or not, to see how such a revolution occurred. Now let us turn our attention to the gospels which are the only ones recognized and approved by the Gentile Church of Rome.

The Gospel of Matthew

While Mark is credited with being the oldest redacted gospel, it is more interesting to look at the gospel of Matthew because it is the most Jewish of the gospels and provides more sayings of Jesus as incorporated from the Q source. The Q source is a hypothetical written collection of Jesus's sayings that scholars believe influenced the gospels of Matthew and Luke but not the gospel of Mark.

Most scholars believe that the revised or edited Gospel of Matthew was composed between AD 80 and AD 90 with a range of possibility between AD 70 to AD 110. The author takes pains to put Jesus firmly within the Jewish tradition. The gospel begins by tracing the lineage of Jesus back to Abraham. After the customary "begats," the author concludes:

> So all the generations from Abraham to David are fourteen generations; and from David until the carrying away into Babylon are fourteen generations; and from the carrying away into Babylon unto Christ are fourteen generations (Verse 1:17).

Having established this lineage, the gospel devotes twenty-five verses to the story of Jesus's birth in a cave in Bethlehem. This can only be a major fabrication as we have seen. The Gospel of Mark never speaks about it, while Luke gives greater attention to the birth of John the Baptist than he does of Jesus. Thus, it appears that the priests of the Church of Rome did not find it essential to incorporate the story of Mithra in the earliest gospel of Mark, but felt compelled to do so in the later redacted gospel of Matthew.

After the revised story of the nativity of Jesus in the gospel of Matthew, we are then introduced to his baptism at the hands of John the Baptist. This story is accepted as true by most scholars because it is so widely held as truth across so many religious scriptures. What follows Christ's baptism is the Sermon on the Mount. Now we have something akin to the Gnostic gospels that recount stories and parables attributed to Jesus that contain mystical content. The Sermon, many have argued, constitutes the spiritual core of Christ's teachings across all Christian denominations. It is certainly the most widely quoted story of the canonical gospels.

In Chapter 5, Jesus speaks about those who are blessed by the Father:

> Blessed are the poor in spirit: for theirs is the kingdom of heaven.
> Blessed are they that mourn: for they shall be comforted.
> Blessed are the meek: for they shall inherit the earth.
> Blessed are they which do hunger and thirst after righteousness: for they shall be filled.
> Blessed are the merciful: for they shall obtain mercy.
> Blessed are the pure in heart: for they shall see God.
> Blessed are the peacemakers: for they shall be called the children of God.
> Blessed are they which are persecuted for righteousness' sake: for theirs is the kingdom of heaven.
> Blessed are ye, when men shall revile you, and persecute you, and shall say all manner of evil against you falsely, for my sake.
> Rejoice, and be exceeding glad: for great is your reward in heaven for so persecuted they the prophets which were before you.

These "blessings" are not mentioned in Mark and only four are mentioned in Luke. We can say, therefore, that this material is original to Matthew and as such has not been redacted. It contains an original mystical revelation from Jesus the Christ.

Contrary to our daily experience, Jesus tells people that the poor, the mournful, the meek, the pure in heart, the peacemakers, and those who are reviled for speaking the truth are the successful ones in this world. Our experience tells us such people are rather the outcasts of society. Yet these are the same people whom Jesus says will inherit the kingdom of heaven. The reason being that they are willing to sacrifice themselves and to suffer hardship for union with God. In order to make such a sacrifice, these people must know something that others do not know. They must carry something in their hearts that other men do not feel. The people that Jesus blesses are the ones who willingly suffer in the service of the Lord. Why would they do this? Surely, there is a personal reward that most men have never known.

Those who are "blessed," according to Jesus, are those who take up the cross of personal sacrifice because, by virtue of their endeavor, they come to know the "infinite." They come to experience the love of the Divine Consciousness, or in the words of Jesus, "the love of the Father." Together, the "Beatitudes" present a new set of ideals, not only for the Jews, but for all of humanity. They present a new covenant that is focused on love, selfless service, and humility rather than on obedience to the law and the exaction of punishment for those who violate it. The *Sermon on the Mount* presents the highest ideals of Jesus's teachings on spirituality and compassion within the canonical gospels.

Those who honor this teaching will achieve spiritual enlightenment just as assuredly as a person in any other religion will achieve enlightenment by doing the same. This is what makes this teaching universal and beyond the confines of a religious institution. This is why spiritual masters always tell us that such teachings are for the good of all human beings. We may give preference to our religion over others because it agrees with our lifestyle, but the core message is the same and should be respected as such. It is a flaw of human nature to condemn another for his religion and to think one's own superior. Not only does one wound another's spiritual sentiment by such criticism, but it also reduces one's own religion to a mere socio-sentiment, because it no longer respects a universal God. In the fifth century, Saint Augustine began his book, *Our Lord's Sermon on the Mount*, by stating:

> If anyone will piously and soberly consider the sermon, which our Lord Jesus Christ spoke on the mount, as we read it in the Gospel according to Matthew, I think that he will find in it, so far as regards the highest morals, a perfect standard of the Christian life.

He should have said a perfect standard of the *human* life, but Augustine's mental outlook was limited to his religion.

Jesus was unquestionably a mystic. He did not preach as a Jew or as a Gentile. Rather his message of love was available to all human beings, "all nations". The Sermon on the Mount, in Matthew, ends with Jesus saying:

> You have heard that it was said, 'Love your neighbor and hate your enemy.' But I tell you: Love your enemies and pray for those who persecute you, that you may be sons of your Father in heaven. He causes his sun to rise on the evil and the good, and sends rain on the righteous and the unrighteous. If you love those who love you, what reward will you get? Are not even the tax collectors doing that? And if you greet only your brothers, what are you doing more than others? Do not even pagans do that? Be perfect, therefore, as your heavenly Father is perfect (Matt 5:43-48).

Perfection can only be defined here as "universal love" (loving across all man-made barriers). Later, in the Gospel of Matthew, when Jesus is asked by a Pharisee what is his greatest commandment, he says:

> Thou shalt love the Lord thy God with all thy heart, and with all thy soul, and with all thy mind. This is the first and great commandment. And second is like unto it, Thou shalt love thy neighbor as thyself. On these two commandments hang all the law and the prophets (Matt 22:37-40).

"Love" was such an important message for Jesus because he knew the spiritual significance of love. Love is not of this world. It is a spiritual force that originates in the heart of God and is experienced as a great joy whenever one, by serving others, comes to see God hidden in everything. Love is the fruit of coming together. It is the fruit of divine unity. It is the fruit of serving each other. Jesus knew that the people in his day did not understand this truth and that they would kill him for his message. He died a horrible death to bring us a simple message: If you do not understand love, if you do not practice love, you will never understand God nor get closer to God. You will never understand the purpose of your existence nor your destiny as a human being.

To seek a link with the Father, (i.e., Absolute Consciousness) is to be engaged in a love affair in which each party tests the other to determine the depth of their love. Love God or love your neighbor; they are the same. Both get the ego out of the way and lead to enlightenment. Neither demands religion.

Jesus went so far as to tell his disciples not to worry about meeting their own basic needs:

> So do not worry, saying, 'What shall we eat?' or 'What shall we drink?' or 'What shall we wear?' For the pagans run after all these things, and your heavenly Father knows that you need them. But seek first his kingdom and his righteousness, and all these things will be given to you as well. Therefore do not worry about tomorrow, for tomorrow will worry about itself. Each day has enough trouble of its own (Matt 6:31-34).

Most people do not believe it is possible to follow such advice. They worry continuously about meeting their basic needs and this puts them in competition and conflict with others for available resources. Yet, for those who are disciplined enough to make this leap of faith, they discover the profound truth hidden within this advice. The true disciple knows, regardless of religion, that when one takes up the burden of the Lord, the Lord takes up his or her burden in turn. The relationship between Divinity and the individual is a subjective one. Acting in a selfless manner is the same as giving yourself to God. When you do this, Divinity becomes yours and it is well within the capacity of Divinity to take care of the needs of the spiritual seeker.

This then constitutes the mystical core of the teachings of Jesus Christ. It emphasizes purity of heart and defines Christian righteousness. Christians who try to follow these teachings are the true disciples of Christ. Those who do not are merely "Christian" in name only.

The mystical teachings of Jesus Christ, found in Matthew, are also cited, although to a lesser degree, in the other canonical gospels.

In summary, much of the canonical gospels were redacted. Nonetheless, we have seen that most scholars believe that Jesus Christ was a real human being. We have reviewed his mystical teachings and judged them to be universal in scope. We have also seen how the Church of Rome dressed

Jesus in the robes of Mithra, an Aryan god, to give credence to the story of Jesus insofar as the Romans and other Gentiles were concerned.

There is more to be said about the elements in the life of Jesus, but for now let us take a look at the apostle Paul, for it was he who designated himself the "apostle to the Gentiles," and it is his interpretation of the meaning of Jesus's life and death that has formed the core of the Catholic Church and Protestant religious dogma and the essential belief of western Christianity to date.

Paul the Apostle and the Church of Rome

Paul the Apostle was originally known as Saul of Tarsus because he was a Jew. In fact, he was a zealous Pharisee, who took it upon himself to punish the disciples of Christ for their sins against the Mosaic law and the Jewish community. Upon one of his journeys to Damascus, to return captured "Christians" to Jerusalem, he reported that Jesus appeared to him in a blinding light and converted him. After this event, Paul began to preach about Jesus with the same zealousness that he had previously persecuted his followers.

About half of the Book of Acts of the Apostles is dedicated to Paul's life and works. This amounts to fourteen of the twenty-seven books in the New Testament. Seven of his letters (epistles) are undisputed by scholars as being authentic, with varying degrees of argument about the remainder. The Pauline authorship of the "Epistle to the Hebrews," was doubted in the second and third centuries, but almost unquestioningly accepted from the fifth to the sixteenth centuries. It is now almost universally rejected by scholars. Who wrote this epistle is uncertain, but it is a letter directed to Jews to convince them that Jesus was the promised Messiah.[253]

Paul is credited with founding several Christian communities in Asia Minor and Europe. He spoke Greek, the principle language in the Middle East, Turkey, and Egypt. He also inherited Roman citizenship from his father. Paul excelled at communication and fundraising, and wherever he went to preach, he also raised money. Although, not among the original apostles of Jesus, Paul considered himself an apostle by virtue of his mystical experience of Jesus, his relentless work, and the suffering he endured at the hands of non-believers.

Paul's initial mystical experience changed the course of his life. In a single instant, he grasped intuitively the meaning of Christ's life and message. He knew the meaning of the "New Covenant," which meant the possibility of spiritual enlightenment for all. The phenomenal repercussion of this understanding was almost unspeakable. For the first time in the known world, the way to Divinity was opened to the individual. The eternal gulf between man and God was now erased. God had always been a god of a specific people. The Canaanites had Baal, the Assyrians had Enlil, the Babylonians had Marduk, and the Jews had Yahweh. The gods belonged to the nations of people who worshiped them. Now, Jesus introduced a completely revolutionary understanding of the meaning of God. The God of Jesus was loving and universal. He was everyone's "Father." The Father was personally approachable; not through meaningless animal sacrifices, but through returning the love that he shared with you. And how did one return this love?—through simple acts of prayer and selfless service to the less fortunate. Finally, western man had penetrated the deepest understanding of the Cosmic Consciousness, a universal God the Father. The mind had reached its penultimate achievement. It now knew how to fulfill its thirst for limitlessness. Now it was only a matter of spiritual practice.

This realization was so profound that Paul immediately became a true believer and now risked life and limb to defend and spread the message of Christ. We know this by virtue of the Acts of the Apostles and his letters (epistles), which, aside from the gospels of Matthew, Mark, Luke and John, constitute the majority of the New Testament of the Bible.

Being an ardent Jew, Paul knew the scriptures very well. Jesus was born a Jew and as a spiritual teacher, he also spoke in terms of the law. He had challenged the Pharisees because the Jewish priests had placed the law above love and mercy. Paul immediately recognized Jesus as the Messiah who was promised by the Jewish prophets to bring a new covenant to the Jews. This new covenant meant the forgiveness of sin, not just for Jews, but for all who "had ears to hear." Paul held that God sent his own Son to be crucified for the sins of humanity and that he arose from the dead after three days, thus defeating death itself and thereby proving his divinity. Jesus would soon return to judge the living and the dead and create the new era of righteousness. Those who believed in the miracle of Jesus Christ, the Lord, would gain eternal life with him and the Father in heaven. To "believe" meant that one also had to live an exemplary life of prayer and service.

Jesus had performed the ritual *blood sacrifice*, but now it was not simply the sacrifice of a burnt animal, nor a chosen *sacred king*. Paul believed that Jesus had sacrificed his own life for the redemption of humanity (Romans 3:24). Such a man could only be the Messiah! A heady tale such as this was never before contrived. Following Paul's lead, most of those within the Christian church were not disposed to portray Jesus as a God-realized master who taught wisdom and performed miracles. No, in order to cement their leadership, they needed something truly astonishing to grab public attention. The fact that Jesus's teachings spoke to the ability to conquer death and experience eternal life, and the fact that the apostles and others had mystical visions of him after his crucifixion, somehow got translated into Jesus "bodily" resurrecting from the dead (Romans 1:30). Paul, himself said opposing things about this bodily resurrection, or more likely, had words put into his mouth by later redaction of his letters, but we will look at this subject later. In Matthew 22:23-32, we have a clear statement by Jesus to the Sadducees that resurrection of the body is impossible. Rather resurrection means the soul has achieved God realization either before or after the death of the body. Resurrection to Jesus was not the same as reincarnation. Rather it was the achievement of a spiritual state in which reincarnation was no longer necessary. In this state, Jesus tells the Pharisees that resurrected souls are "as the angels of God in heaven." To be clear, Jesus never preached physical resurrection from the dead. In fact he denied it.

Paul, in believing that Jesus was the Messiah or Christ, not just of the Jews but of any human being with ears to hear, also believed that Jesus's appearance on earth signaled the "end of days." Jesus would soon come again to judge the living and the dead and usher in a new age of righteousness (Rom 13:11-12). This was the belief that had been passed by Zoroaster to the Pharisees and the Essenes.

Having intuited this incredible vision, Paul went out with great zeal to take this message to the world. Unfortunately for Paul, having a powerful spiritual vision and the skills to communicate it was not enough to be accepted by the Christian leadership in Jerusalem. He found himself consistently at odds with the "pillars of the church" who were the actual apostles Peter, James, and John. These apostles looked at Paul as an outsider, a rebel who acted without authority. There were many among the Jewish Christians in Jerusalem and later in Antioch and Damascus, who held that for any Gentile to become a Christian, they first had to become Jews. In other words, they had to also follow the Mosaic Law, which included being circumcised and observing the Sabbath and Passover.[254] Paul found himself in a constant battle with these "Judaizers," who still viewed Gentiles as the enemy and who strenuously opposed any attempts to water down Jewish laws. They disrespected Paul and even came to hate him for his cavalier approach to the law. Paul, on the other hand, believed his sole mission was to bring the word of Jesus to the Gentiles. He, in fact, considered himself to be the "apostle of the Gentiles" (Rom 15:16). He viewed the Judaizers as small-minded people who completely missed the point of Jesus's message. The New Covenant was for all mankind, not just Jews.

Paul told the Gentiles that they did not have to be circumcised to be a Christian. Neither did he hold them accountable for following the Jewish dietary laws. Paul got into trouble with the Jewish Christians on both of these counts, but the big battle was fought over the issue of circumcision. Circumcision was the sacred sign of the covenant between the Jews and Yahweh as directed by Moses and then Joshua, when he led the Jews into the "promised land" of Canaan. Circumcision had been a requirement of being a male Jew since the beginning of the Jews as a people. To violate this commandment was to completely reject one of the cornerstones of Judaism.

Paul's position was that circumcision was a matter of the old law and that the New Covenant trumped the old law. Faith, love, and mercy were greater than the law. Had not Jesus, himself, violated the law by healing the sick on the Sabbath (Matt 12:10-14). Had he not also violated the law by consorting with women and Gentiles? Paul saw himself in the same situation as Jesus, but ironically he was called a blasphemer, not only by the Pharisees but also by his own Christian brethren.

Paul's argument in defense of the Gentiles was that "faith" trumped the law. If the Gentiles believed in Jesus and lived according to his mission, they would be saved and could call themselves Christians.

On face value, Paul's argument, "by faith alone," certainly weakened the mystical teachings of Jesus. As we know, faith without action is virtually worthless, just as theory is worthless without practice. Union with God does not happen instantaneously, but rather is earned by self-sacrifice, as all love is earned. Can we say that one who faces dangers and hardships for his faith or for his neighbor's security is valued the same as one who sits back and does nothing? Paul himself, as did many other early Christians, gave his life for his faith. Martin Luther also risked his life for his faith. Would it have been of equal value if they just sat back and said, "I believe"? It does not measure up to the scrutiny of rational thought; nor does it do justice to Paul's meaning when he made the argument in defense of faith alone.

In fairness, Paul was not saying that faith alone is enough to realize God. Rather, he was opposing "faith in Jesus" to the Mosaic Law, particularly as it pertained to the need of non-Jewish men to be circumcised in order to be considered Christians. Paul was taking a groundbreaking position that flew in the face of Jewish tradition. Jesus and all the apostles, even Paul, were Jews and it was the Mosaic Law that every Jewish male must be circumcised as part of their covenant with God as established by Moses and Joshua. In the face of this inviolable Jewish tradition, Paul argued that it was "faith" and not the law that made one a disciple of Christ. This blasphemous position, coupled with the fact that he disrespected apostolic authority by doing whatever he wanted, made Paul many enemies in Jerusalem where the Christian church, now established by Peter and James, had already created thousands of Jewish converts.

Yet, Paul had a valid point. In this case, "faith" in the power of love was certainly more righteous than mere rites and ritual as ordained by law. Finally, after a bitter and rancorous struggle regarding this matter, the apostolic Church called a Council in Jerusalem to address the issue of circumcision. Peter and James ultimately supported Paul's position as long as the Gentiles kept the other covenants of the law. Peter consented (Acts 15:7–11) and James submitted a proposal, which was accepted by the Church leaders and became known as the Apostolic Decree:

> It is my judgment, therefore, that we should not make it difficult for the Gentiles who are turning to God. Instead we should write to them, telling them to abstain from food polluted by idols, from sexual immorality, from the meat of strangled animals and from blood. (Acts 15:19–21).[255]

This pronouncement gave Paul the apostolic authority to continue his work with the Gentiles free of internal conflict. In granting this "license" to Paul, the Christians in Jerusalem were quick to tell him that it was also necessary for the Gentiles to remember the poor. This was, in fact, a reminder to Paul that the Gentiles should be sending money back to Jerusalem. Paul immediately agreed. Raising funds was not a problem for him. He had overcome a big hurdle, but it had been costly and anger against Paul still simmered within many of the Jewish converts.

This victory was arguably Paul's most significant accomplishment because it allowed him to take a small, mystical Jewish religion and introduce it to the Roman Empire and the great cities of the Gentile world. In Paul's defense, this was the spoken desire of Jesus and following his own mystical experience, Paul was on fire. He wanted to tell the world about Jesus. As such, as he went from city to city, it was not his top priority to confer with the apostles in Jerusalem to get their permission. He simply went out and started preaching to the world and in doing so legitimized his claim to be the "apostle of the Gentiles" (Rom 15:16).

As Paul traveled, he stopped at many of the major cities moving west from Judea into the heart of the Roman Empire. He traveled to Damascus, Antioch, Galatia, Ephesus, Corinth, Philippi, Achaea, and eventually Rome itself. His base seems to have been in Ephesus, a coastal city on the Aegean Sea, which was centrally located for his travels. He could take boats from there to many cities in the region.

At the time of Paul, Ephesus was the capital city of Ionia and had a population of more than 250,000 people, making it the second largest city in the Roman Empire and also the second largest city in the world. Strabo, a Greek geographer, philosopher, and historian said, "The city in all other respects, owing to the favorable situation, is increasing daily, for it is the greatest place of trade of all the cities of Asia west of the Taurus."[256]

The city was an ancient city, even in the days of Paul. It was most likely built by the matriarchal Amazons and still contained a beautiful temple that housed an ancient statue of Artemis (The Goddess Diana). People came from all over the world to worship the Great Goddess there, and when it was decided to build a new temple for her, famous artists and craftsmen from throughout the empire donated time and work to build her new home.[257]

When Paul was in Ephesus for a couple of years (Acts 19:10), there was an uprising against him led by a silversmith named Demetrius, who earned his money making silver shrines for Diana. He accused Paul of preaching against the Great Goddess, thus not only jeopardizing the craftsmen's income, but also insulting the Goddess who was the patroness of the city. There was a raucous demonstration against Paul, which was finally quelled by the town clerk who pronounced that Paul had broken no laws of the city and that Ephesus would get a bad reputation if the protestors kept up this uproar. Paul and the Christians were spared from any further confrontation. Nonetheless, Paul left Ephesus soon after the dispute.

The early Christians co-existed for some time with the worshipers of the Goddess (whom the Christians called pagans), but as the Church of Rome became established, Christians made raids against her Temple. The Temple was completely destroyed under the Christian Emperor Theodosius (346-395) and its columns and stone distributed throughout the realm. The immense dome of Hagia Sophia in Constantinople (Istanbul) now rests upon columns of green jasper that were originally from the Temple of Artemis.[258]

As Paul traveled from city to city, he created a network of Christian communities that kept in contact with each other as their members travelled the realm. Paul also wrote letters to these communities to instruct them.[259] These letters, called epistles, were, in turn, circulated to other communities. The letters now form a part of the New Testament.

The content of these letters basically contain words of encouragement and exhortations to avoid conflict with each other. As Paul's initiates began to pass away as a matter of course, his message regarding the imminence of the "kingdom of God" began to be questioned. Paul struggled to assure community members that Jesus was still going to return from his ascension into heaven as the Messiah. His Gentile communities also faced continued criticism from traveling Jewish Christians that unnerved his students. The Jewish Christians looked down on the Gentiles, questioned their spiritual practices, and humiliated them for their lack of understanding and disregard of Jewish law.

The strain of this constant undermining of his work by fellow Christians incited Paul to challenge Jewish religious law and the worthiness of the Jews themselves. He became angry in his communications. In a letter to the Romans he said, "by the deeds of the law shall no flesh be justified in his sight; for by the law is the knowledge of sin" (Romans 3:20). This was like throwing a lit torch through the window of the Temple. He had explicitly stated that the law was completely without merit and that the only thing the law was good for was creating sinners. He gave himself as an example of this. He told the Philippians in a letter to them that he had been an exemplar Pharisee upholding the law without question, and yet the law did not stop him or anyone from killing the righteous or persecuting the Christians (Phil. 3:6).

In his anger, Paul even began to attack the Jews themselves. He charged them with a history of disobeying God's law and killing his prophets. He condemned them for killing Jesus and then went so far as to charge Jewish Christians with forbidding him to preach to the Gentiles to selfishly save themselves according to their law. He accused them of storing up sins by doing so and said they would face the wrath of God accordingly (Thess 2:15-16). As to the value of the law, Paul said it was love that was the fulfillment of the law. Anything else was of little or no value. He held that the Ten Commandments were simply an amplification of love your neighbor (Rom 13:10).

After an intense life of continual travel and relentless opposition from within the church and without, Paul, toward the end of his mission, wrote a letter to the Christians in Rome, expressing his frustration and telling them that he intended to visit them. But first he said he had to make a trip back to Jerusalem. In preparation for this trip, he began to collect donations as a peace offering.

The trip back to Jerusalem was a disaster for Paul. In his letter to the Romans, Paul had ripped into the Judaizers and spoken disgustedly of their position. He was expecting tensions to be high, but the situation was even worse than he thought. Upon arriving at the church in Jerusalem, he was greeted by James, the brother of Jesus, who also was the bishop of Jerusalem, as well as by other elders who thanked him for his donation and his good news about all of the Gentile converts. Immediately thereafter, however, they told him that he had better go to the Temple and purify himself, for he had made many enemies who were willing to bring him before the Sanhedrin (court of the Jews) or even do him bodily harm. Paul assented. His history of conflict with the Jerusalem church was now at a boil.

The Jews, whether they were Sadducees, Pharisees, or Christians all wanted his scalp. To the Sadducees and Pharisees, Paul was a charlatan, a blasphemer, and a heretic and subject to be put to death. To the Jewish Christians, he was an uncontrollable rebel who had created his own concept of the church outside the teachings of Jesus and Jewish law.

As soon as Paul stepped outside the door of the Temple, after performing his ritual purification, he was surrounded by an angry mob that began to kick and punch him. They intended to beat him to death. He was saved fortuitously by Roman soldiers and taken into custody. Knowing that if he were tried in a Jewish court he would be put to death, Paul appealed to the Romans that they should try him according to Roman law and not that of the Jews. Because he was a Roman citizen, the army colonel acquiesced. Paul was arrested, made a prisoner and transferred to Caesarea. In Caesarea, he was tried not as a religious offender, but as a rebel and potential threat to the Roman Empire. He stood in judgment before the Roman procurator Felix. The Sanhedrin traveled to Caesarea to make their case against Paul. Felix listened to their caustic arguments and to Paul's defense and said that he would consider the matter. He kept Paul in custody for over two years, hoping that Paul could arrange a bribe, but it never happened.

When the Sanhedrin again approached Felix for settlement of the case, not wanting to be in the bad graces of the Jewish leaders and not having received any money from Paul, Felix said that he would transfer the case back to Jerusalem. When Paul heard this, he requested, as was his right as a Roman citizen, to stand trial in Rome before the emperor himself. Paul was then taken to Rome where he was allowed to rent a house pending judgment. He carried on his missionary work for two years and then we have no more information about him. The Acts of the Apostles ends with Paul awaiting his trial before the emperor.

Although no proof of this exists,[260] Christian tradition holds that Paul was beheaded in Rome during the reign of Nero in the mid-60s. Tertullian in his Prescription Against Heretics (AD 200) writes that Paul had a similar death to that of John the Baptist, who had been beheaded. Eusebius of Caesarea in his Church History (AD 320) testified that Paul was beheaded in Rome while Peter was crucified. He wrote that the tombs of these two apostles, with their inscriptions, were extant in his time and quotes as his authority a holy man by the name of Caius.[261]

Paul's legacy proved more enduring than any other Christian sect. His Gentile communities gave birth to the official Christian church of the Gentiles whose authority was centralized in the Church of Rome, which later became the Roman Catholic Church. The reason for this legacy is well known. In AD 62, the Jewish High Priest Ananus condemned James, the Bishop of Jerusalem and the leader of the Jewish Christian community, "on the charge of breaking the law." The Jews executed James by stoning.[262] In the mid-60s, Nero executed Peter. The loss of the Jewish Christian leadership was followed by the destruction of Judea and the Temple in AD 70. This massacre of the Jews ended both Jewish and Christian religious activity in Jerusalem. What remained of orthodox Christianity were the communities that were established throughout the empire, some by Peter, but most by Paul. While the Gnostic mystics still held a strong base in Syria, Egypt, and Greece, the Gentile churches established within the Roman Empire would continue independently of official Judaism, which had regrouped under the Pharisaic priests (rabbis) in their synagogues. Therefore, it was Paul's version of Jesus Christ and his nurturance of Gentile Christianity that prevailed in the empire and survives to this day.[263]

What can we say about Paul? Like his spiritual master, Jesus Christ, he was a mystic. He shared this in common with the Gnostics and other mystical Christians. The Church of Jerusalem certainly considered him a heretic, although this word was never used. Did the Gnostics, who also later came to be called heretics by the Church of Rome, also consider Paul to be a heretic? It is impossible to say. But it is unlikely that a mystic would criticize another mystic based on noncompliance with the law and religious dogma.

As regards Christian orthodoxy, Augustine, the Bishop of Hippo (AD 354-430) built on Paul's ideas of "faith alone" as well as his idea of the gospels being a gift of God. He also adopted Paul's definition of morality as living life in the Spirit, as well as his ideas of predestination and original sin. These "Christian" ideas, then, derive from Paul, not Jesus.

Because an orthodoxy was created by the Church of Rome, a schism between Christian spirituality and religious law resulted. Let us look now at how this schism unfolded with the establishment of the Church of Rome and how the definition of the "faithful" ironically came to mean those who followed the law, while the true mystics would be defined as heretics.

The Gentile Church of Rome

In the development of Christianity, one encounters the same process by which any new ideology becomes institutionalized, be it religious or secular. In the beginning, a new idea is propounded. In the next phase, those who believe in the idea develop it so as to increase its influence and understanding. At this stage, the new idea stands in contradiction to established beliefs and lifestyles. The contradictory perspectives often lead to conflict and in some cases violence and death as perpetrated by the established order. In the third phase, internal conflicts arise regarding what is true and what is not true within the emerging ideology and institution. In time, the strongest faction overrides its weaker opponents and creates the "orthodox" dogmas and laws. These are thereafter imposed on the people from above.

As the ideology becomes institutionalized, (i.e., given a governing structure) whether it be a church, state, army, or corporation, the internal views that challenge the orthodoxy of the strongest political faction are deemed heretical and crushed. Any gaping holes in the original idea are plastered over by new rationalizations based on reason or faith. Finally, those who were active in the creation of the new orthodoxy become the new ruling class and their ideas now become the ruling ideas that are used to dominate the masses for purposes of gaining wealth and power. The forming of an institution provides the new ruling class with the continued ability to establish new rules and punish offenders. The people are now told what to believe and what not to believe. In religions, this is what passes for "faith."

Dogmas form the connective tissue that hold the edifice together and cannot be challenged lest the entire edifice become weakened. Therefore, the need arises to punish the nonbelievers, to spy on them, discredit them, torture them, and even put them to death through physical force. This process we have witnessed in our historical survey to date. But now, with the coming of the Christian ideology and the institution of the Catholic Church, this process became extremely sophisticated and all encompassing. From the fourth century until the seventeen century, the Catholic Church spread its domination throughout the Western world, killing and torturing all who challenged the "Holy Mother Church." It prevented all "believers" from speaking a single word of opposition, or even questioning the decision of a local priest. During the Middle Ages, the spiritual roots of Christianity were completely cut off because of the church hierarchy's unquenchable desire for wealth and power.

In the history of Christianity, it was not Jesus, but the Catholic Church, that formed its orthodoxy. Jesus, as we have seen, could not have cared less about rules and regulations. He made this clear to the Pharisees, to his disciples, and to the people to whom he preached. Rather, the Catholic orthodoxy was formed by men who needed to create an ideology by which to take over a state apparatus, in this case, the Roman Empire. It was imperative that they had an idea that could easily be sold to the masses and that bore no contention. It was this imperative that led to the destruction of all those who challenged the orthodox point of view. The Jewish Christians, the Gnostics, and any others who veered from the new ideology were accused of heresy and punished for their "sins." We are told that "It may truly be said that the blackest and bloodiest records that history can show us are the attacks of the Orthodox Church upon the Gnostic mystics."[264]

In this way, the faithful Christians lost their spiritual inspiration due to enforced dogma. In time, it was not even important that the faithful have spiritual experiences. They simply had to know the catechism that the leaders had imposed on previous generations. They simply had to "have faith" in what the priests told them. It became sinful to have thoughts independent of Church dogma. This insistence upon blind faith lies at the root of religious socio-sentiment in which reason loses all meaning and thus its value.

We have seen this pattern in the creation of religious socio-sentiment throughout our survey of history. We have seen it in the creation of religions in the Middle East. We have seen it in the creation of Judaism. And now we will see it in the creation of Christianity. This is the reason why religion and spirituality can never be equated. The former is based on the politics of domination, the latter on individual liberation.

By the end of the first century, Christianity began to be recognized internally and externally as a separate religion from Judaism.

The success of Paul's efforts, as "Apostle to the Gentiles," had accelerated the split between Christianity and Orthodox Judaism.[265] If it had not been for Paul, the Christians, in all likelihood, would have remained a small dissenting sect within Judaism, as the Essenes had always been. The difference was that, as Jewish mystics, the Essenes accepted the Mosaic Law, whereas the Gentiles who became Christians did not.

This led to Orthodox Jews condemning Jewish Christians as "apostates," which meant those who defected to another religion. At first, they were just banned from the synagogues. But soon the price for the sin of apostasy became grave. As it says in the Torah/Old Testament:

> If your very own brother, or your son or daughter, or the wife you love, or your closest friend secretly entices you, saying, "Let us go and worship other gods" (gods that neither you nor your fathers have known, gods of the peoples around you, whether near or far, from one end of the land to the other), do not yield to him or listen to him. Show him no pity. Do not spare him or shield him. You must certainly put him to death. Your hand must be the first in putting him to death, and then the hands of all the people. Stone him to death, because he tried to turn you away from the LORD your God, who brought you out of Egypt, out of the land of slavery. Then all Israel will hear and be afraid, and no one among you will do such an evil thing again (Deut 13:6-11).

The early Christians were cast out of Judaism under penalty of death. John the Baptist, Jesus, James, Steven, and others were killed by the Orthodox Jews for being defectors.

The early Christians were also persecuted by other faiths, particularly those who worshipped the Roman pantheon, within the Gentile world. Such events tended to be sporadic and initiated by local people whose faith or livelihoods were threatened by the Christians. We previously presented the incident when Paul was run out of Ephesus for jeopardizing the jobs of the silversmiths and disrespecting the Goddess.

The Roman government had little motivation to persecute local Christians unless they "disturbed the peace." This meant that the people themselves were getting riled up about the Christians and creating a public disturbance. There were many reasons that caused the people to attack the Christians. Christians worshipped in their homes and this "secrecy" frequently aroused suspicion among the pagan population accustomed to religion as a public event. So also, the Christians refused to participate in public worship. Rumors developed that Christians committed "outrageous crimes" like cannibalism and incest because of their practices of eating the "blood and body" of Christ and of referring to each other as "brothers" and "sisters."[266] The people sensed that bad things would happen if the established gods were not respected and worshiped properly. Edward Gibbon wrote:

> By embracing the faith of the Gospel, the Christians incurred the supposed guilt of an unnatural and unpardonable offence. They dissolved the sacred ties of custom and education, violated the religious institutions of their country, and presumptuously despised whatever their fathers had believed as true, or had reverenced as sacred.[267]

Gibbon also argued that the seeming willingness of Christians to renounce their family and country and their frequent predictions of impending disasters instilled a feeling of apprehension in their neighbors. As Christianity became more widespread and better understood, these suspicions faded away. Yet this took time.

The first "official" persecution of Christians organized by the Roman government took place under the emperor Nero in AD 64 when he needed a scapegoat on which to pin the Great Fire of Rome. We are told that the people gladly accepted Nero's persecution of the Christians because, according to Tacitus, they were despised for "hating humanity."

According to historical documents, persecution under the Roman emperors, prior to the Edict of Milan (313), was sporadic and usually a result of local disturbances. Historians question whether any persecution existed under Domitian (89-96). The emperor Trajan (109-111) ordered persecutions only on a case by case basis according to the discretion of the local governor. Under Hadrian (117-138) there were no known persecutions. Under Marcus Aurelius (161-180) only local persecutions were reported. One incident is documented during his reign as having occurred in France at Lugdunum (present-day Lyons) in 177. The same conditions characterized the reign of Septinus Severus (193-211).

With the emperor Decius (249-251), however, things began to turn ugly. In AD 250, the emperor issued an edict requiring everyone in the Empire (except Jews, who were exempted) to perform a sacrifice to the Roman gods in the presence of a magistrate and obtain a signed and witnessed certificate. The decree was part of Decius's drive to restore traditional Roman values. While there is no evidence that Christians were specifically targeted, this was the first time that Christians had been forced by imperial edict to choose between their religion and their lives. Some church leaders died as a result of their refusal to abide by the edict. Many other Christians, however, denied their faith and performed the sacrifices. The edict was only enforced for eighteen months, but it sent a cold chill down the Christian community and left bitter memories between those who held to their faith and those who had capitulated. It also raised important issues about the nature of forgiveness and the value of martyrdom within the Church. Many Christians refused to welcome back those who had become apostates under threat of death.

The emperor Valerian (253-260) was away in Antioch fighting the Persians who had taken over the city. He was killed in the war but not before he had written two letters back to Rome regarding the Christians. The first (257) said that they must publicly worship the Roman gods as had Decius required. The second letter (258) went further. He ordered that bishops and other high ranking church officials be put to death, and that senators who were Christians lose their titles and property. If they would not perform sacrifices to the gods, they were to be executed.[268]

The fact that there were Christians in high ranking positions within Rome indicates that the Christians had generally prospered within the empire. But now, with the empire in serious decline and feeling threatened by any group that challenged the status quo, there were serious grounds for concern. The ruling class itself was being split apart and the Roman gods were being directly challenged.

Among those executed under Valerian was Cyprian, the Bishop of Carthage. The examination of Cyprian by the proconsul Galerius Maximus, on September 14, 258, has been preserved:

> Galerius Maximus:"Are you Thascius Cyprianus?"
> Cyprian: "I am."
> Galerius: "The most sacred Emperors have commanded you to conform to the Roman rites."
> Cyprian: "I refuse."
> Galerius: "Take heed for yourself."
> Cyprian: "Do as you are bid; in so clear a case I may not take heed."
> Galerius: (after briefly conferring with his judicial council, with much reluctance pronounced the following sentence) "You have long lived an irreligious life, and have drawn together a number of men bound by an unlawful association, and professed yourself an open enemy to the gods and the religion of Rome; and the pious, most sacred and august Emperors ... have endeavored in vain to bring you back to conformity with their religious observances; - whereas therefore you have been apprehended as Principal and ringleader in these infamous crimes, you shall be made an example to those whom you have wickedly associated with you; the authority of law shall be ratified in your blood." He then read

> the sentence of the court from a written tablet: "It is the sentence of this court that Thascius Cyprianus be executed with the sword."
>
> Cyprian: "Thanks be to God."

Cyprian was beheaded for his faith.

When the dictator Diocletian (284-305) took the throne, the tide against Christians crested. He spent the first fifteen years of his reign campaigning to restore the glory of Rome. This meant, in large part, getting rid of Christians. Diocletian was faced with an empire that was falling apart. He was desperately trying to bring contesting generals and rulers together. He accomplished this by appointing Galerius as his co-emperor, and appointing Constantius I and Maximinus as co-junior emperors. He could not tolerate the Christians who challenged Roman tradition and were obedient only to another "Lord" and to his "kingdom of heaven." In brief, they could not be trusted. Diocletian purged Christians from the army and put anti-Christians in leadership positions. He also condemned some Christians (the Manicheans) to death. In the winter of 302, he was urged by Galerius (305 to 311), his co-emperor, to begin a general persecution of all Christians in the empire. Diocletian consulted the oracle of Apollo for guidance and announced a general purge on February 24, 303.

During the "Great Persecution," which lasted from AD 303 to AD 313, local Roman governors were given direct edicts from the emperors to destroy Christian churches and texts. Christian worship was banned and all inhabitants of Rome were required to sacrifice to the Roman gods. Christian clergy were to be arrested and tried for treason. Persecution varied in intensity across the empire. While Galerius and Diocletian were avid persecutors, Constantius I, the father of Constantine the Great and founder of the Constantinian dynasty, was sanguine about the issue. He did not require Christians to sacrifice to the Roman gods within his domain, nor did he punish them in any respect.

It was during this period, however, that Christians in Rome were fed to lions for public entertainment. The period, which came to be known as the "Great Persecution," lasted for about ten years. Perhaps it would have lasted longer but during this time, Diocletian abdicated the throne

(305) due to poor health and Constantinius I died in 306. Maximian was forced out of office in 308. This left the empire in the hands of Galerius and Constantine (306-337). Galerius ended his persecution in 311 and Constantine brokered the Edict of Milan in 313. This edict restored Christians to full legal equality within the empire while returning their confiscated property.

Provincial governors in the Roman Empire had a great deal of personal discretion to make decisions concerning Christians. Although there were local and sporadic incidents of persecution and mob violence against them, for most of the first three hundred years of Christian history, they were able to live in peace, practice professions, and rise to positions of authority. Only for approximately ten out of the first three hundred years of the church's history were Christians executed due to orders from a Roman emperor.

Obviously, the persecution failed to destroy Christianity. By 324, Constantine was sole ruler of the empire, and the Christian church, under his governance, began to build a base of power that has lasted until this day.

Religion vs Mysticism

As we have said, Jesus was born during a time of profound intellectual revolution when the individual mind (as opposed to the bicameral mind) was coming to grips with its ultimate potential; that is, the merger of self-identity with Divinity. This was a time in the West when the idea of God was reaching its highest definition. Two distinct paths opened up by which this idea gained expression. The first was the mystical path, in which the idea of Absolute Consciousness became available to each individual, not as an external abstraction of the Greatest Good, but as an internal living reality. Any individual, by performing selfless service and internal communication with God, could achieve self-realization or God realization, the summum bonum of individual life. This was the message of Jesus Christ and the path pursued by the mystics among the Christian Gnostics, the Desert Fathers, and others.

The other path was the religious path, in which, the idea of the Absolute Consciousness was still conceived as an external Deity. As in the past, a priest class was able to define the myth and build a religion upon it. Here the best religious idea of God served as a principle of social unity and the means by which the Church of Rome could gain authority over society in a manner never envisioned by humanity up until that point. One God led to one Pope, which led to one Church, which led to one Law, which led to the punishment of all those who challenged the law.

In order to accomplish such a staggering feat, the Church of Rome needed a blockbuster story line. Most of the powers and characteristics attributed to Jesus were nothing new. Other gods had been born of a Virgin, spoke of an immortal soul, fought the greatest evil, identified the greatest good, brought a message from the true god, performed miracles, were crucified as a blood sacrifice, resurrected from the dead, ascended into heaven, saved humanity, became a god, was called the son of god, would come again to judge the living and the dead, etc. These accomplishments had been attributed to other gods and were known by people throughout the empire. The gods of the Persians, Jews, Greeks, Romans, Egyptians, the mystery religions, and even the gods going back to the matriarchy reflected some of these characteristics. And each had added to the idea of the Absolute Divinity. The Church of Rome had to come up with something new, something truly unbelievable, in order to make people take notice. Logic did not matter, neither did mysticism. They needed a myth, a story that people could believe in, a story in which they could have faith that was under their exclusive control. They finally came up with the super idea. They packaged all of the above powers and characteristics and then added the pièce de résistance —Jesus was a unique superhero god because he bodily resurrected from the dead and bodily ascended into heaven! This was truly something new! Prior to Jesus Christ, other sacred kings and emperors were said to have resurrected from the dead, but their resurrection referred to the spirit, not the body of a man, which, if truth be told, clearly contradicts the laws of nature. But, the Church dismissed criticism of their outlandish myth. As Tertullian, "the father of Latin Christianity" and "the founder of Western theology," insists, "it must be believed, because it is absurd."[269] As we shall see, it was upon this "absurdity" that the Church of Rome was truly built.

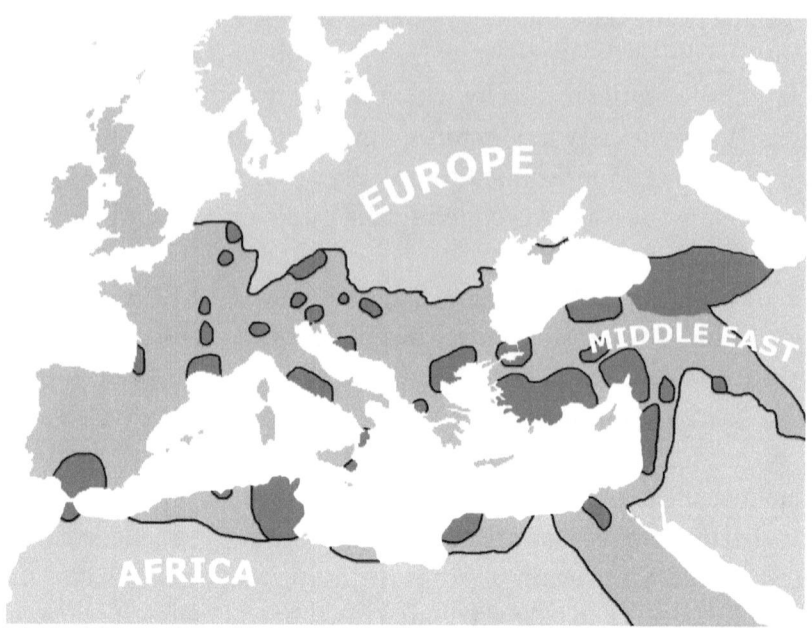

Map 2-9: Spread of Christianity in Europe, Southwest Asia, and North Africa to the year AD 600 (by AD 325 in dark spots; by 600 in gray areas within border lines; water in white)

It is estimated that the number of Christians grew by approximately forty percent each decade during the first and second centuries.[270] As their population grew, the Christian communities became larger, more numerous, and spread to other regions. This required a greater attention to organization.

The church had originally begun with small communities that had formed in cities where the apostles traveled. Aside from Jerusalem, notable cities included Antioch, Damascus, Alexandria, Ephesus, and Corinth.

In these days, there was no set definition of leadership beyond moral competence. Local communities would choose their own leaders and call them what they wanted. There were bishops, presbyters, deacons, overseers, elders, as well as other names for those who oversaw Church functions.

The oldest Christian treatise dealing with the question of leadership is the Didache or The Teaching of the Twelve Apostles dated from the mid to late first century. It was basically written by Jewish Christians to inform themselves how to work with Gentile Christians. It is part catechism, part ethical teaching, and part rules for rituals (specifically baptism and the Eucharist). The fourth part deals with Church organization. In this section it speaks of "appointing for yourself bishops and deacons."[271] Bishops oversaw an area, perhaps a city, and the deacon was his assistant.

An established Church hierarchy began to form in the late first century and early second century and was certainly formalized before Constantine "legalized" Christianity with the Edict of Milan in 313. It was not an easy effort to bring various local leaders under the control of the Church of Rome or to define standard roles. Disputes lasted for years and earned many the name of "heretic" for their opinions that challenged what became the "official Church" under Constantine. Certainly, the Greek Eastern Church and the Roman Western Church never saw eye to eye on this matter. This difference of opinion became a permanent schism when the Church of Rome declared its bishop to be the supreme bishop of the realm (i.e., the Pope).

Important *bishops* of the time included Polycarp of Smyrna, Ignatius of Antioch, and Clement of Rome. These men reportedly knew and studied under the apostles or their immediate students and are therefore called *Apostolic Fathers*.

As Christian communities grew, they added more layers of administration. *Presbyters* were created and ordained by the bishop to assist him. As Christianity spread, especially in rural areas, the presbyters exercised more responsibilities and took distinctive shape as *priests*. The *deacons*, who were not ordained, took care of the poor and sick and served other local needs. The official designation of church offices and roles were defined at the First Council of Nicaea in 325. About fifty years later, under emperor Theodosius I, the Church of Rome would become the "official Church" of the entire Roman Empire. From an organizational standpoint, its claim to religious supremacy was based on the concept of apostolic succession. This concept held that each bishop was successor to a previous bishop who could be traced back in a line of authority to the apostles themselves.[272] The supreme authority rested with the bishop of Rome because it was Peter who founded the Christian community in Rome and the Church leaders in Rome made sure that the canonical gospels had clearly stated that Peter was appointed by Jesus himself to be the supreme authority of his Church.

This claim, by which the Church of Rome established its total authority over early Christianity, is worth an investigation. In doing so, we will look at the claim that Jesus arose physically from the dead and that Peter was the first to whom he spoke. In doing so, we will leave our practical discussion about Church organization and look at the myth upon which the Church authority is based.

Peter the First Pope

The religious supremacy claimed by the Roman Catholic Church is based upon the Petrine Primacy and the Primacy of the Bishop of Rome. The former states that Peter is preeminent among the twelve apostles. The latter claims that the Bishop of Rome is preeminent among all the bishops of the Church.

It is argued by the Roman Catholic Church that since Peter was stationed in Rome, he was the first Bishop of Rome. And his authority in this position leads to the Primacy of the Bishop of Rome over all other bishops in the realm. So also, each successive Bishop of Rome (Pope) continues to have primacy over all bishops from other cities. This dogma had come to be called "apostolic succession." It also justified the supremacy of the clergy over the laity. No member of the faithful had the authority or the right to question a clergyman under penalty of sanction, including death and eternal damnation. The entire structure of Church authority, therefore, is based on Peter.

Of course, this was the Roman Gentile perspective. Most Christians at the time actually looked to James, the brother of Jesus and the Bishop of Jerusalem, as the supreme authority. Certainly the Jewish Christians looked to James for leadership, as did other Christian groups whom the Roman Church derisively called "Gnostics."

The Roman hierarchy claimed that Peter was the leader of the apostles, chosen by Jesus, according to scripture. They point to Matthew 16:18 in which Jesus said to Peter, "And I say also unto thee, that thou art Peter, and upon this rock I will build my church; and the gates of hell shall not prevail against it."

The Church also points to the Acts of the Apostles in which Peter steps forward to take a leadership role. The Acts, written by the writer of Luke, is dedicated to extolling the accomplishments of Peter and Paul.

The passages in Matthew and the Book of Acts are suspect, however, because, as we have seen, both Matthew and Luke/Acts were rewritten (redacted) by priests after the fact.

In Thomas and Mark, the two oldest gospels, Peter is not considered the greatest among the apostles. He is rather a somewhat loutish character. In Thomas, as we have seen, his criticism of Mary Magdelene for being a woman displayed complete ignorance of the mystical message of Jesus. In Mark, we find no mention of Peter having any leadership position. The verse that is found in Matthew simply does not exist in Mark. In fact, Peter is presented as a bumbler, unable to make sense of what Jesus is telling the apostles. When Jesus tells the apostles that he will be rejected by the elders and the chief priests and that he will suffer for his teaching, Peter openly rebukes Jesus for saying such things. Jesus, frustrated by Peter, replies angrily, "Get thee behind me, Satan: for thou savorest not the things that be of God, but the things that be of men" (Mark 8:31-33).

In another instance, when Peter, James, and John witnessed Jesus change into a bright light (the Transfiguration) and stood with Moses and Elijah, the only thing that Peter could say was that they should build a tabernacle for each of them. Jesus did not respond to this, but told his apostles not to mention this to anyone (Mark 9:2–8).

In a third instance in which Peter is mentioned, Jesus is telling the apostles that it is nearly impossible for the rich to enter heaven (i.e., have a mystical experience). They wanted to know then, who could be saved. Peter immediately felt it necessary to justify himself by telling Jesus that the apostles had given up everything to follow him. Jesus responded that those who suffer hardships on his account will have eternal life, but quickly warned, "many that are first shall be last; and the last first" (Mark 10:24:31).

The final time that Mark records an action of Peter is when he denies knowing Jesus three times after Jesus was seized by the Jewish "high priests and the scribes and the elders" (Mark 14:29-72). It is interesting that Mark does not mention that it was Peter who cut off the ear of the high priest's servant in defense of Jesus.

Thus, Peter does not have a great track record with those who had interactions with him, namely Thomas, Levi, Mary Magdalene, Paul, and Mark. In his gospel, John mentions Peter on three occasions. In the first occasion, Jesus is teaching a lesson of selfless service to his disciples by washing their feet. Peter tells Jesus he will never let him wash his feet. Jesus responds that if he does not let him, their relationship is over: "If I wash thee not, thou hast no part with me."

Jesus tells him that if he has bathed (been made spiritually clean) he does not have to worry about his feet being clean because he is completely clean. But he says that "while you are clean, you are not all clean" (John 13:5-20).

In the second mention of Peter, he is denying Jesus before the Pharisees. In the third incident, Jesus asks Peter three times in a row if Peter loved him more than the other apostles. When Peter said he did, Jesus replied each time, "Feed my lambs." The Church holds that this incident proves that Jesus chose Peter above all the other apostles to serve his Church. However, a case can certainly be made that Peter's lack of understanding of Jesus's message induced him to compel Peter to repeat three times that he must perform selfless service (John 2:15-17).

John makes no mention of Peter being the Rock on which Jesus builds his Church. In fact, Jesus gives all the apostles the same authority to forgive sin as well as determine the sins of others (John 20:23). Paul certainly never mentions Peter as an authority. In his only recorded interaction with Peter, he rebukes him for duplicity. In Galatians 2:11–13 Paul says: "When Peter came to Antioch, I opposed him to his face, because he was clearly in the wrong. Before certain men came from James, he used to eat with the Gentiles. But when they arrived, he began to draw back and separate himself from the Gentiles because he was afraid of those who belonged to the circumcision group." The issue of contention here refers to the Gentiles not following the dietary laws of the Jews.

In his letters to his students, Paul refers to Peter as Cephas, which means Peter in Aramaic, the language that Jesus spoke. Catholic theologian Rudolf Pesch argues that the Aramaic *cepha* means "stone, ball, clump, clew" and that *petros*, in Greek, does not mean "Rock," rather it means "small stone, firestone, sling stone, moving boulder."²⁷³ Thus the symbol of Peter as being the "rock" on which Jesus would build his Church is dubious at best.

These observations are made, not to belittle Peter, who obviously loved Jesus very much and who spent his life in service to him. Rather these observations are intended to question the Church's claim to absolute authority, which is solely based upon a false presentation of Peter that they themselves created. The Church Fathers, we may conclude, had little understanding of the mystical message of Jesus Christ. As such they found themselves, despite whatever good intentions they may have had, trapped solely in the realm of sentimental power politics, determined to snuff out any opinion that countered their official proclamations.

Nonetheless, by virtue of the process of "institutionalizing an ideology" that we mentioned above, the Petrine Primacy and the Primacy of the Bishop of Rome became the law of the land, supported in turn by Irenaeus, Ignatius, Cyprian, John Chrysostom, and Augustine.

The Bodily Resurrection of Jesus

Once the justification for their authority was set in stone, no pun intended, the next ruse of the Church authorities became easier to promote. Now they completely abandoned any pretense to natural law, human rationality and intuition. Now the faithful are commanded to believe in Jesus as the "only begotten Son of God," who was born of a virgin and when put to death, physically arose from the dead to offer his disciples additional information before they saw him ascend bodily into heaven to sit at the right hand of God.

The Church now demanded complete and utter "blind faith" in a myth that has no greater credibility than any other myths created about gods throughout the history of the Middle East.

The first statement of this new *faith* was converted into law when Emperor Constantine called all the bishops of the empire together for a meeting in AD 325. This meeting, called the First Council of Nicaea, was the first ecumenical council of the Church. At this council, the first official Roman Catholic doctrine, the *Nicene Creed*, was established. With the creation of this creed (statement of faith), a precedent was established for subsequent local and regional councils of Bishops to create other statements of orthodox belief and law.[274]

The Nicene Creed reads:

> We believe in one God, the Father Almighty, Maker of heaven and earth, and of all things visible and invisible. And in one Lord Jesus Christ, the only-begotten Son of God, begotten of the Father before all worlds (æons), Light of Light, very God of very God, begotten, not made, being of one substance with the Father; by whom all things were made; who for us men, and for our salvation, came down from heaven, and was incarnate by the Holy Ghost of the Virgin Mary, and was made man; he was crucified for us under Pontius Pilate, and suffered, and was buried, and the third day he rose again, according to the Scriptures, and ascended into heaven, and sitteth on the right hand of the Father; from thence he shall come again, with glory, to judge the quick and the dead; whose kingdom shall have no end. And in the Holy Ghost, the Lord and Giver of life, who proceedeth from the Father, who with the Father and the Son together is worshiped and glorified, who spake by the prophets. In one holy catholic and apostolic Church; we acknowledge one baptism for the remission of sins; we look for the resurrection of the dead, and the life of the world to come. Amen.[275]

Most Christians today repeat these words without giving them any thought, not realizing how illogical they are. The tragedy now, however, lies in the fact that for the first time in Western history, human beings, thanks to a spiritual master like Jesus Christ, were taught how to experience the deepest mystery of Divinity and to know that through the performance of certain spiritual practices, we could actually merge with Divinity into eternal bliss. But the big lie, promoted by the political institution of the Church, took all that away. The spiritual message was obliterated. People could no longer be the same as Jesus, (i.e., become one with the Father). What remained was a tepid shell of truth made available only through the intermediary of the priests of the Church. Once again, myth was promoted as truth, and spirituality was superseded by politics.

Let us look at this idea of bodily resurrection from the dead that is the cornerstone of Catholic ideology. In the Dead Sea Scrolls there is a text called *Redemption and Resurrection*. This Essene text holds that during the time of the Messiah, either God or the Messiah would resurrect the dead ("He shall open the graves"). The Messiah would then judge the souls of the dead and, if worthy, they would go to heaven ("heaven will advance"); if unworthy, they would die eternally ("the accursed shall languish"). This Judgment would signal the "end of days."

In the New Testament, John the Baptist sends a messenger to Jesus asking if he is the one who is coming, (i.e., the Messiah). Jesus confirms that he is the Messiah by telling John to witness the signs: "the blind have regained their sight; the lame walk, lepers are cleansed; the deaf hear; the dead are raised. . . ." (Matt 11:2-5). Here the reference to the dead refers to Jesus raising Lazarus from the dead. But this too is a spiritual event. For Jesus tells us later, "It is the spirit that quickeneth; the flesh profiteth nothing: the words that I speak unto you, they are spirit, and they are life" (John 6:63).

The apostles and early Christians expected Judgment Day to occur in their lifetime because they believed that Jesus was the Messiah. John has Jesus saying:

> "For as the Father hath life in himself, so hath he given to the Son to have life in himself; And hath given him authority to execute judgment also, because he is the Son of man. Marvel not at this: for the hour is coming, in which all that are in the graves shall hear his voice, And shall come forth, they that have done good, unto the resurrection of life; and they that have done evil, unto the resurrection of damnation. I can of mine own self do nothing: as I hear I judge: and my judgment is just; because I seek not mine own will but the will of the Father which hath sent me" (John 5:26-30).

The reference to life and death in this statement by Jesus refers to spiritual life and death. Resurrection is a spiritual phenomenon. Most Christians at the time regarded the resurrection of Jesus as a spiritual phenomenon. Jesus, they said, rose from the dead because he was the son of God, (i.e., spiritually alive). The example of Jesus' resurrection held out the promise that all mankind could be resurrected into life. All could become the sons and daughters of the divine. How did one become spiritually enlightened? Jesus had given the answer. First, one had to believe in him as the Way, the Truth, and the Light (John 3:15-19). Second, one had to be in a human body (John 3:13). Third, one had to be baptized (initiated) into the sacred mystery of God (John 1:33). Fourth, one had to be spiritually awakened, (i.e., "born again") (John 3:3). Fifth, he or she had to love others and serve them. In doing this, they would be resurrected from the dead (John 5:25).

It was not surprising to the Gnostics that after the death and resurrection of Jesus that his disciples would see him again. What is alive spiritually can never die. But they believed that those who loved Jesus experienced him in the intuitional realm, through trances, visions, dreams, and intuitional illuminations. These were real experiences common to all advanced mystics. But the Church of Rome fabricated a story of Christ rising bodily from the dead and thereafter visiting with his closest followers.

As we have seen, Tertullian, one of the earliest church patriarchs, claimed that if you do not believe in the resurrection of the flesh, you are a heretic, even though it is absurd to believe such a thing.

This is the essence of "blind faith"—a faith without rationality or understanding. Why is it better for a religious elite to have its followers believe in the absurd rather than have true spiritual understanding? Elaine Pagels, in "The Gnostic Gospels" answers this question for us:

> When we examine its practical effect on the Christian movement, we can see that the doctrine of bodily resurrection serves an essential political function. It legitimizes the authority of certain men who claim to exercise exclusive leadership over the churches as the successors of the apostle Peter.[276]

We know that in the first two centuries of early Christianity there were many diverse forms of practice and belief that created contrary claims. This became a problem for the Church of Rome under Constantine, who wanted to establish a political hierarchy under his control. This required a set of orthodox beliefs.

We know that such a matter was not important to Jesus who, as a mystic, rejected the entire idea of authority and hierarchy. He had told the Pharisees on more than one occasion that love was more important than the law. He held this same principle within his own circle. For example, when John and James came to him and asked to be elevated to the highest position beside him in heaven, Jesus rebuked them for their desires to place themselves above others. He told them that Christian leaders would be judged by their selfless service to the people; those of the highest rank would be the slaves of all (Mark 10:42-44). This position is absolutely consistent with the spiritual commandment to love one's neighbor as God.

But for a political organization, a mystical injunction would not work. Rather, Church authorities required a different principle. They needed a strategy to establish law and order, regardless if it diverged from the teachings of Christ and human reason. The Church unquestionably developed one of the most ingenious methods by which to skirt the spiritual definition of leadership while at the same time making it appear that it was their spiritual understanding that justified their authority. Their method was simple. The first step was to claim that Jesus rose bodily from the dead. It did not matter that this was against reason and against the teachings of Jesus. The second step was to sell the point that Peter was the first witness of the bodily resurrection. Thirdly, in the resurrected state, the gospel redactors had Jesus telling the apostles that, "All authority on heaven and earth has been given to me" (Matt 28:16–20). After this, Jesus delegated this absolute authority to Peter before ascending bodily into heaven. Through this myth, the Church of Rome established a small, elite circle that were granted "all authority on heaven and earth." By redacting the gospels and putting words in the mouth of Jesus and the apostles, the Church established the rationale for its absolute authority. After all, no one would ever again experience Jesus like the apostles had. All other believers would only receive less direct forms of interaction from Jesus. No one could compare to the twelve apostles and among these, Peter was made the undisputed leader.

Church authority derived exclusively from the apostles' supposed experience of a bodily-resurrected Christ, an experience now closed forever to the rest of humanity. Because Peter was the leader of the apostles and he was also the Bishop of Rome, it followed that the Church of Rome deserved leadership over the Christian world. Again Pagels points out the implication of this myth for the Christian community:

> First it restricts the circle of leadership to a small band of persons whose members stand in a position of incontestable authority. Second, it suggests that only the apostles had the right to ordain future leaders as their successors.

The Church of Rome used this argument to establish the restricted chain of command for itself and for all future generations of Christians even onto this day. Unfortunately, the successors could never verify for themselves the mystical experience of Jesus. They could only believe in the system, rule according to the system, and hand down their authority to future generations. It was a bald trade-off. Mystical experience was rejected for political power. In the next volume of this history, we shall see where this abuse of political power led humanity through the Church's crusades, inquisitions, and witch hunts during the Middle Ages when it reigned supreme in Western Europe.

Pope Clement I was considered to be the first Apostolic Father of the Church. He was listed by Irenaeus and Tertullian as the Bishop of Rome from AD 92 to 99. Clement said that God delegated his "authority to reign" to "rulers and leaders on earth." Who were these leaders? They were the bishops, priests, and deacons. According to Clement, whoever refused to "bow the neck" and obey these church leaders was guilty of subordination against Jesus himself. Clement warned that whoever disobeyed the divinely ordained authorities "receives the death penalty!"[277]

Hereafter, the Church edicts applied to all who considered themselves Christians. It was a major turning point in early Christianity. We now had the Church of Rome claiming dominance over all of Christendom. Those who did not accept its authority were to receive the death penalty.

This dictatorial statement by Clement also placed the laity, (i.e., family people), completely under the yoke of the priest class. The political ingenuity, that had introduced the idea of a bodily resurrected Jesus Christ, had now led to the practice of draconian edicts that put to death all those who refused to "bow the neck" to the authority of the Church of Rome. Absolute power was now in the hands of a small elite priest class. In this way, the Church smothered independent thought for the next seventeen centuries.

Irenaeus, the Bishop of Lyon in France, who was the greatest of the heretic-hunters, immediately set about to discredit the mystical writings of the Gnostics. He chose four gospels that he said were the only real gospels. These were the gospels of Matthew, Mark, Luke, and John. He condemned the other gospels as presenting false doctrines concerning Jesus. Of course, scholars do not hold his statement as truth.

Irenaeus's justification for choosing the canonical gospels was as irrational as Tertullian's statement about why a Christian must accept an "absurd" bodily resurrection. Irenaeus proclaimed:

> The heretics boast that they have many more gospels than there really are. But really they don't have any gospels that aren't full of blasphemy. There actually are only four authentic gospels. And this is obviously true because there are four corners of the universe and there are four principal winds, and therefore there can be only four gospels that are authentic. These, besides, are written by Jesus' true followers.[278]

The Church patriarchs set about to systematically discredit the Gnostics who responded that the Church claimed authority but knew nothing about true mysticism. The Church, they argued, only relied on surface teachings and not the secret teachings of Jesus. They held that Jesus gave secret teachings to some of his apostles, particularly Mary Magdalene, James, and John, who transferred these teachings to their more advanced students. These teachings revealed specific practices to allow one to know

God directly through intuitive understanding. It was this understanding that they called "gnosis." It was also why the Church of Rome derisively referred to the early Christian mystics as "Gnostics."

What about Paul? Should we consider him a mystic or a political operative? Most Christians believe that Paul supported the party line by virtue of his first letter to the Corinthians:

> For I delivered to you as of first importance what I also received: that Christ died for our sins in accordance with the Scriptures, that he was buried, that he was raised on the third day in accordance with the Scriptures, and that he appeared to Cephas, then to the twelve. Then he appeared to more than five hundred brothers at one time, most of whom are still alive, though some have fallen asleep. Then he appeared to James, then to all the apostles. Last of all, as to one untimely born, he appeared also to me. For I am the least of the apostles, unworthy to be called an apostle, because I persecuted the church of God (1 Cor 15:3-9).

There is nothing to support Paul's claim in any of the gospels or the epistles that Jesus actually appeared to Paul in his resurrected body, so it is difficult to say why Paul wrote this. He must have been speaking of his intuitive vision. What we do know is that Paul did not believe in Christ's physical ascension into heaven. In the same letter to the Corinthians, a few verses later, he states:

> Now this I say, brethren, that flesh and blood cannot inherit the kingdom of God; neither doth corruption inherit incorruption. Behold, I show you a mystery; We shall not all sleep, but we shall all be changed (1 Cor 15:50-51).

To Paul, therefore, the physical body somehow transmutes into a spiritual body in order for souls to enter heaven.

In another letter to the Corinthians, Paul admits his experiences of Jesus were intuitive. Paul speaks of one such occasion:

> This same person (Paul) whether in or out of the body I do not know; God knows – was caught up into paradise and heard things which must not and cannot be put into human language (2 Cor 12:2).

Paul was reticent to speak about such experiences because he thought they would glorify him in the eyes of his students. He preferred to express a more humble nature.

Valentinus, who led perhaps the largest school of Gnostics, claimed that Jesus taught Paul through these mystical experiences. He, himself, was taught the higher mysteries by Thaddeus, who was a student of Paul.[279] As we have seen in our previous look at the Gnostic gospels, they spoke of revelations that came from personal experiences.

The Gnostic writings are intentionally written to share the writers' revelations and mystical experiences. Just as the priests of Rome put their agenda into the mouths of the apostles, so too did the Gnostics. Yet, their intentions were markedly different from the priests in Rome. While the gospel of Thomas appears to actually have been written by one of the apostles, the gospels of Mary Magdalene, Philip, Judas, and the other writings attributed to the apostles, were not so. Rather, they were most likely written by their students who used the names of their personal teachers to share their insights about Jesus and his teachings.

If our goal is to achieve historical accuracy, we must admit that there is great room for error in the study of the Gnostic writing. No more so, however, than what is found in the canonical gospels. Is one camp worse than the other in terms of the consequences of their actions? While the intention of the mystics was to teach others about the mystery of God, the Church's intention was to dominate others. If the Gnostics had not been declared heretics and killed and their writings burned, the worse that could have happened was that we would have had a proliferation of mystical stories about Jesus. We do not have to speculate about what would have happened if the Church's attempt to dominate others had succeeded. We can witness the result with our own eyes. The history of the Church of Rome is a largely a legacy of dominance and persecution that lasted for seventeen centuries before it was challenged by the Protestant Reformation.

The Church covered over Jesus's message and in its place created a fantastical myth by which they could use the name of Jesus to control ordinary people. This myth was not created out of thin air, however. Many previous gods, as mentioned above, possessed the powers and attributes of Jesus. Regarding, Jesus's crucifixion, however, it was a continuation and fulfillment of the ancient rite of the Sacred King (the Messiah or Savior). The Sacred King had always lived as a human god, a successor to the previous sacred king whom he called his father. He was always sacrificed for the good of the people, died, and was resurrected as an immortal god, often as a star in the sky. The rite of the sacred king had been the central ritual of all matriarchal cultures, whose religious events were based on the mystery of the annual cycle. Sacred kings existed well into the age of patriarchy, and still existed within the cultures that were coterminous with the early Christian period. Dionysus, Adonis, and Tammuz were still worshiped as sacred kings by local people in Greece, Egypt, and the Middle East during the time of Jesus.[280]

The sacred king was the "blood sacrifice" by whose death the people were saved. But, under the Church of Rome, this ancient story that lived within the conscious and subconscious of the people was taken to its highest fabrication. Jesus was not an ordinary sacred king who died to save his people; rather he died to save all mankind. He did not just save people for another annual cycle but for all eternity. He did not just ensure their finite, physical needs, but their infinite spiritual needs. Jesus was not just the son of a God; he was the only begotten Son of the Absolute God. He was not just spiritually resurrected from the dead to become immortal; rather he was bodily resurrected from the dead and bodily ascended into heaven. The myth created about Jesus Christ, despite the fact that it was irrational and preposterous, captured the minds and hearts of the people. They loved this myth because it brought the hope of eternal salvation and happiness to a life of suffering. The most unimaginative or lazy person could become immortal by simply believing in the myth of Jesus created by the Church. No one had ever proposed such a thing. Divinity had never been within reach of the average person. Jesus was now a Caucasian superhero who saved the planet.

The true mystical reality of Jesus was even more astonishing than the myth but, having been lied to, few pursued it. In any case to "believe" in the Church of Rome's mythology about Jesus was a thousand times easier and safer than to follow his example. Very few cared to discover what it actually meant to love their neighbor or to relinquish their attachment to physical pleasure. Very few cared to live simply, serve others, or endure hardships to sanctify their belief. Only a few, no more than a handful, actually "got it." They carried within themselves a personal relationship with God that made wealth and power no more appealing to them than cheap plastic children's toys. These people were more than intellectuals, more than priests. They were the *spiritual warriors*. They embodied the psychology of both the warrior and the intellectual, which made them qualitatively different from the average man. Such people possessed spiritual intuition, the "subtle intellect." They were the ones who, in gaining enlightenment, were willing to lay down their lives for the welfare of humanity and the world.

The spiritual warriors were committed to a spiritual reality far above institutions and their laws. During the early days of Christianity, such warriors could be found among the established Church and among the heretics. They could be found among the Jews and the Gentiles. Neither a physical institution, nor a mythology, could contain them. They were not interested in belonging to a group or following its rules or regulations, unless; of course, such rules quickened their spiritual experience. One group of these warrior-mystics, who managed to survive the purge of the heretics, were the ascetic Christians who came to be known as the Desert Fathers and Desert Mothers.

Desert Fathers and Desert Mothers

The Desert Fathers and Desert Mothers were Christian ascetics, monks and nuns who lived mainly in the deserts of Egypt beginning around the third century AD. The most well-known was Anthony the Great, the purported founder of desert monasticism. By the time Anthony died in AD 356, thousands of monks and nuns had been drawn to the desert to follow his example. More than any other force within orthodox Christianity, the ascetics kept a small flame of mysticism alive within the church. Their communities would later become the model for Roman Catholic monasticism and an inspiration for Protestant groups such as Pietism and the Methodist Revival as late as the eighteenth century.[281]

Much of Eastern Orthodox mysticism, including the Hesychast movement,[282] also had its roots in the practices of the Desert Fathers.

Sometime around AD 270, Anthony, a relatively wealthy person, heard a sermon stating that perfection could be achieved by selling all of one's possessions, giving the proceeds to the poor, and following Christ (Matt: 19.21). He took up this challenge and moved into the desert seeking complete solitude.

Anthony lived at the time when there was a growing persecution of Christians in the Roman Empire. While many of his contemporaries in the Gentile Church viewed martyrdom as the highest form of sacrifice, Anthony believed that spiritual transformation through solitude and austerity was more important. The challenge for Anthony was to rid the mind of material attachments and thereby purify the spirit. During his years alone in the desert, Anthony spoke of combating the Devil and his demons on many occasions.

Anthony gained followers who understood the mystical teachings of Jesus and sought a way to separate themselves from the material world. The *Apophthegmata Patrum*[283] is a collection of the writings of some of the early desert monks accounting their stories and their Divine revelations. It is still in print as *Sayings of the Desert Fathers*.[284]

These sayings of the monks (called Abba or father) express the need to live a simple life. For their sacrifice, they received mystical knowledge that they called "special privileges from God," such as the ability to perform miracles, heal the sick, and even converse directly with God.[285]

The central focus of the ascetic life is to attain stillness or quiet. This allows the senses to be detachment from the physical world. As the senses are withdrawn, the mind is also freed of attachments. This allows the I-feeling in the mind to go more deeply within. Previously held captive in the mind, it is now able to identify itself directly with the soul, which is the nucleus of individual consciousness. The identification of the I-feeling with the soul is experienced as stillness. Just as the reflection of the full moon can be seen when a turbulent pond is quieted, so also the full reflection of God can be seen when the mind is quieted. In reality, the soul and God are one, having been distinguished only by the waves of the mind. It is from this state that miracles are generated, as are all things generated.

The monks lived in cells or one-room huts out of ear shot from each other. In their cells they battled with their attachments—their thoughts and feelings that they called "their demons."

As Shiva had introduced the practice of sense withdrawal and mantra meditation to the East, so the monks introduced these spiritual practices to the West. We are told that, "The meditation practices and rules for living of these earliest Christian monks bear strong similarity to those of their Hindu and Buddhist renunciate brethren several kingdoms to the East. The meditative techniques they adopted for finding their God suggest either a borrowing from the East or a spontaneous rediscovery."[286]

Here are a few stories told of Anthony the Great or Abba Anthony.[287] More stories can be found in Appendix C.

> *On correct behavior:*
> Pambo asked Abba Anthony, "What ought I to do?" The old man said to him "Do not trust in your own righteousness do not worry about the past, but control your tongue and your stomach."
>
> *On loving your neighbor*
> Abba Anthony said, "Our life and our death is with our neighbor. If we gain our brother, we have gained God, but if we scandalize our brother, we have sinned against Christ."
>
> *On lack of self-control*
> Some brothers were coming from Scetis[288] to see Abba Anthony. When they were getting into a boat to go there, they found an old man who also wanted to go there. The brothers did not know him. They sat in the boat, occupied by turns with the words of the Fathers, Scripture, and their manual work. As for the old man, he remained silent. When they arrived on shore they found that the old man was going to the cell of Abba Anthony too. When they reached

the place, Anthony said to them, "You found this old man a good companion for the journey?" Then he said to the old man, "You have brought many good brethren with you, father." The old man said, 'No doubt they are good, but they do not have a door to their house and anyone who wishes can enter the stable and loose the ass.' He meant that the brethren said whatever came into their mouths.

On conflict
The brethren came to Abba Anthony and said to him, "Speak a word; how are we to be saved?" The old man said to them, "You have heard the Scriptures. That should teach you how." But they said, "We want to hear from you too, Father." Then the old man said to them, "The Gospel says, 'if anyone strikes you on one cheek, turn to him the other also.'" (Matt. 5.39) They said, "We cannot do that." The old man said, "If you cannot offer the other cheek, at least allow one cheek to be struck." "We cannot do that either," they said. So he said, "If you are not able to do that, do not return evil for evil," and they said, "We cannot do that either." Then the old man said to his disciple, "Prepare a little brew of corn for these invalids. If you cannot do this, or that, what can I do for you? What you need is prayers."

The Desert Mothers also had words of wisdom for those on the mystical path:

> Amma Sarah said, "If I prayed God that all people should approve of my conduct, I should find myself a penitent at the door of each one, but I shall rather pray that my heart may be pure toward all."
>
> Amma Syncletica said, "There are many who live in the mountains and behave as if they were in the town; they are wasting their time. It is possible to be a solitary

in one's mind while living in a crowd; and it is possible for those who are solitaries to live in the crowd of their own thoughts."

Amma Theodora said that neither asceticism, nor vigils, nor any kind of suffering are able to save. Only true humility can do that. There was a hermit who was able to banish the demons. And he asked them: "What makes you go away? Is it fasting?" They replied: "We do not eat or drink." "Is it vigils?" They said: "We do not sleep." "Then what power sends you away?" They replied: "Nothing can overcome us except humility alone." Amma Theodora said: "Do you see how humility is victorious over the demons?"[289]

Such examples of enlightenment by ordinary men and women testify to the ability of all human beings to achieve this same state. They confirm the message of Jesus Christ that one need not be an other-worldly, one-of-a-kind super-hero in order to receive God's Grace and become spiritually enlightened.[290] Jesus Christ was a son of man who taught us that we are moving out of animality and into Divinity and that the method to do so was to practice love. By doing so, one merges with Divinity. It has nothing to do with religious laws, rituals, or dogmas. It has to do with enlightenment.

As ascetic mystics, the Desert Fathers and Mothers were not persecuted as heretics by the orthodox Church because they did not challenge the Church on any political or ideological grounds. Rather, they simply renounced physical pleasures and focused on the basic spiritual principles—praying, fasting, giving selflessly to those in need, and preserving love and harmony with one another.

This is not to say that the ascetics were politically unconscious. When the Orthodox Church began working with the Roman state, the Desert Fathers saw this as a compromise between "the things of God and the things of Caesar." They doubted that religion and politics could ever produce a Christian society. For them, the only Christian society was spiritual and not mundane.

Thousands joined the ascetics in the desert, mostly men but also women. Religious seekers also began going to the desert seeking advice and counsel from the early Desert Fathers and Mothers. By the time of Anthony's death, there were so many men and women living in the desert that it was described as "a city" by Anthony's biographer.[291]

In time, the influence of these desert ascetics spread to the West. The Church approved Monastic orders as long as they did not engage in heresy. The Rule of Saint Benedict was strongly influenced by the Desert Fathers and the *Sayings of the Desert Fathers* was widely read in the early Benedictine monasteries.[292]

It was possible for the ascetics to avoid conflict with social evils by living in the desert, but what about those of us who live in society? Certainly, spiritual practices are accessible to us just as they were to the hermits. But each day that we live in society, we are reminded of the exploitation all around us. If we acquiesce to it, we become a part of it. As our families, our neighbors, and our environment are destroyed by institutional greed, is it Christian to turn the other cheek to this, or is it necessary to fight for what is right? When we see the lies and fabrications on which religious and secular institutions have built their empires, are we to simply let it go? Is the past so inconsequential that history is simply a story that we read and write about, but from which we remain uninspired to change our behavior for the better? We have seen how our "faith" is not based on true spirituality, but rather on a belief of what those in power have told us to believe. Does this matter?

Apparently, it does not matter in our day-to-day lives, or the world of politics. We do not have time to discern the truth from the lies and if we do, so what. What can we do about it? Vote every four years and go to church on the Sabbath? We live under a barrage of information, in which truth and falsehood may only be matters of perception. Politicians lie to get elected. Businessmen exploit us to become wealthy. It is perfectly acceptable. Who can blame us if we do not care about the truth?

In an Essene text called the "Book of Secrets," it says: "It is true that all the peoples reject evil, yet it advances in all of them. It is true that truth is esteemed in the utterances of all the nations—yet is there any tongue or language that grasps it?"

If one's goal is to simply provide for one's physical welfare, then truth is inconsequential. It is "relative," meaning that it is only useful when it furthers one's end. Yet, from a spiritual perspective, truth remains vital. It means absolutely everything to us because it is impossible to make spiritual progress without it. Truth is the bread; it is the wine; it is the water; it is the chrism; and it is the Light.

People were given the spiritual truth by Jesus. Some understood it; other squandered it on politics. Such has always been the case when religions are built in the wake of a spiritual master. This is still the way with people today. The average person seldom takes the time to understand the spiritual mystery and a good many of the priests (intellectuals) will always be there to prey on their sentiments and live off their contributions.

Jesus shared the way, the truth, and the light of God. Other masters have also come to salve the heartache of humanity and reveal to us how to achieve our highest potential as human beings. This is God's grace. Without it, there would be no human evolution. There would be no thirst for limitlessness. When the master comes, so do his soldiers to reconfirm the value of truth. And because the Spirit of the masters is always with us, there is always an opportunity for human beings to become spiritual warriors. Is there any among us who would argue that Jesus Christ was not a spiritual warrior? Is there any who would say that he refused to challenge the institutions of his day? Jesus fought and died to bring humanity the message of God-realization and he remained conscious of his mission every day of his life.

Let us now pick up our historical narrative at the time of Emperor Constantine. It is at this time, when the Church of Rome, freed from persecution throughout the empire, began to constitute itself into what would become the greatest power the world has ever seen—an absolute dictatorship that lasted for seventeen centuries and even today exerts tremendous power across the planet.

Constantine and the Pax Deorum

Emperors had always assumed the role of High Priest of the state religion in Rome. Under the title of Pontifex Maximus, it was his duty to ensure that the gods were worshipped with proper deference so that the nation might prosper under their protection. He was charged with maintaining the pax deorum ("peace of the gods"), which depended on the correct practice of prayer, ritual, and sacrifice. Similar to the religion of the Jews, as well as the Greeks, religion was supposed to be a covenant by which humans and gods existed in harmony. Religious error or negligence led to divine disharmony and ira deorum ("anger of the gods").[293] We are told:

> Roman ideologies claimed that the empire's existence was so closely interwoven into the beneficent deity's plans for bringing humankind to its fullest possible potential that it was actually providential divine power which had first brought it into existence, and supported it subsequently.[294]

The Pontifex, as the administrator of divine law (*jus divinum*), oversaw all religious ceremonies, including the consecration of temples and sacred places, the regulation of the religious calendar (which determined state functions), burials and the worship of the dead, marriages, the succession of priestly offices, and the regulation of public morals, including punishing offending parties.[295] He was also head of the College of Pontiffs.[296]

Following this tradition, the reign of Constantine established a precedent by which the emperor assumed the position of supreme authority in the Catholic Church as well. He was, in essence, the first official Pope and the bishops became his College of Pontiffs. Constantine understood the need for prayer, ritual, and sacrifice, but he did not understand what true mysticism or spirituality was. Nor did he concern himself much with the Christian priest class's concepts of *faith* and *dogma*. The understanding that existed between Constantine and the bishops of the Church of Rome was that the bishops would define religious doctrine (dogma), while the emperor would enforce the dogma as well as help root our heretics in order to uphold the strength and unity of the Church in its service to God.

Neither Constantine, nor the emperors who followed, understood that they had set in motion the process by which they would eventually be replaced by a rising priest class.

It is difficult to say how deep Constantine's personal religious fervor ran, but we do know that he understood his sacred duty as Pontifex Maximus and believed that he and the nation needed the support of the gods in their endeavors.

Constantine came to power as an army general. When his father Constantius Chlorus died, his father's troops declared Constantine to be the new emperor.[297] Eusebius, a bishop in the Church of Rome and a distant relative of Constantine, wrote that Constantius was secretly a Christian as was his first wife Helena.[298] This claim cannot be substantiated, but we do know that Constantine's father Constantius did not persecute Christians in the areas of the empire that he controlled during the time of the Diocletian persecution.

As the new emperor, it was imperative for Constantine to align himself with the most powerful gods or god and learn how to appease them/him. In the army, many of his men were followers of the god Mithra. In the bureaucracy, many were Christians. Constantine was looking for a sign as to whom he should pay obeisance.

Eusebius tells us that Maxentius, a rival of Constantine for control of the western empire, engaged in magical enchantments, and that Constantine felt the need to find a more powerful god on whom he could rely for protection and help.

Thus, Constantine's disposition at the time he became emperor was to seek a god whom he could depend upon. In all likelihood, Constantine worshipped Mithra as a manifestation of *Sol Invictus*, the Invincible Sun, at the time he became emperor.[299] Mithra was the god of Diocletian, Julian, and Marcus Aurelius and the chief god worshiped by the Roman army. In 307, Diocletian, who was Constantine's immediate predecessor, consecrated a temple to Mithra calling him the "Protector of the Realm."[300]

The cult of Mithra had evolved from Zoroastrianism and was modified by the Greeks to become a mystery cult. Mithra was the Persian's savior god. As we have seen above, the cult of Mithraism predated and shared many attributes with early Christianity, leading scholars to believe it had a strong influence on the formation of the Church of Rome. While there is hot debate on the extent to which this is true, many features of Mithraism came to be equated with the Church of Rome. These included the Eucharist, baptism, the blood sacrifice, and the god's second coming to judge the souls of mankind. So also we must include the Church of Rome's copying of the life of Mithra to describe their version of the life of Christ.

Considered to be *syncretic,* Mithraism allowed for an inclusive approach to religious faith. This proved useful to Constantine in gaining the support of the army for Christianity after he had a miraculous vision that he attributed to Jesus Christ. Constantine finally had the sign he needed as to which deity to worship.

Constantine's Conversion to Christianity

To establish his rule over the western empire, Constantine had to fight another Caesar named Maxentius, which occurred at the Battle of Milvan Bridge on October 28, 312. It was on the day preceding this battle, that Constantine had a vision in which he saw the Christian cross and the message "In Hoc Signo Vinces" (In this sign, you will conquer).[301] According to Church legend, Constantine had his army paint the cross on their shields, which led to their victory.

However, despite Church legend, Constantine did not immediately become a patron of Christianity. After his victory at the Battle of Milvan Bridge, he commissioned a triumphal arch to be built in Rome (the Arch of Constantine) to celebrate his triumph. The arch is decorated with images of the goddess Victoria and at the dedication, sacrifices were made to Apollo, Diana, and Hercules. There were no depictions of Christian symbolism.[302]

Long after his alleged conversion to Christianity, Constantine's coinage continued to carry the symbols of the Sun. Even when Constantine dedicated the new capital of Constantinople, which became the seat of Byzantine Christianity for a millennium, he did so wearing the Apollonian sun-rayed Diadem. Again no Christian symbols were present at this dedication.

Nevertheless, Constantine made his initial headquarters in Rome where he issued decrees to return property to Christians, recall political exiles, and release Maxentius's imprisoned opponents. At the front of the basilica, the large public building where business and legal matters were transacted, Constantine commission a statue of himself holding the Christian symbol (*labarum*) in its hand. This suggests that while Constantine maintained the rituals and made sacrifices to the traditional Roman gods in the name of the people, in his personal life, he added Christ to the Roman pantheon, thus covering all bases.

Within the year of his victory over Maxentius, Constantine had induced Licinius, who was his rival in the Eastern Empire, to sign the Edict of Milan, which granted religious freedom to all Christians in the entire Roman Empire.

In AD 320, Licinius allegedly reneged on the Edict of Milan and began to oppress Christians anew. It has been suggested that Licinius did not trust the Christians in his realm, because he saw them as allies of Constantine. In Rome, Constantine attempted to bring the Christians and the "pagans" (i.e., the followers of Mithra and other Roman gods) into greater accord. In 321, he instructed Christians and non-Christians to unite in observing the venerable day of the Sun, or Sunday.

The conflict with Licinius led to an inevitable civil war in 324. Constantine won an important victory in the Battle of Adrianople and within the year, he became the sole emperor of the Roman Empire.

As emperor, Constantine wanted a new Eastern capital that would represent the integration of the East into the Roman Empire as a whole. He chose to rebuild the Greek city of Byzantium because it already had many Roman buildings and it was strategically located. The city was renamed Constantinople in 330. The Church of Rome (whose supporters now became known as "Catholics," as opposed to Gnostics and other heretics) claimed that the new city was protected by the relics of the True Cross, the Rod of Moses, and other holy relics. In Constantinople, the figures of the old gods were replaced or assimilated into Christian symbolism, many were converted into Catholic saints.[303] Constantine built the new Church of the Holy Apostles on the site of a temple to Aphrodite. It was here that he was buried.

Constantine and the Church of Rome

There is no question that over time Constantine began to favor the Christian religion. As he did so, his role as Pontifex Maximus came into play. If he was to become a Christian, it meant that the religion had to meet the standards of Roman divine law. Constantine's approach was to shape the Christian faith according to the customs already approved by the Roman army and, to some extent, the general population in their acceptance of Mithraism. It is probably during this time that the narrative of the life of Jesus, as presented in the canonical gospels, was firmed up to ensure the identity of Jesus with Mithra. While scholars debate the extent of Mithraism's influence among the general populace, comments from early Christian patriarchs suggest that this marriage had begun much earlier.

Justin Martyr (100-165), a Christian patriarch, in his *First Apology* comments on the identical Eucharist shared between Mithraism and early Christianity:

> For the apostles, in the memoirs composed by them, which are called Gospels, have thus delivered unto us what was enjoined upon them; that Jesus took bread, and when He had given thanks, said, "This do ye in remembrance of Me, this is My body; "and that, after the same manner, having taken the cup and given thanks, He said, "This is My blood; "and gave it to them alone. Which the wicked devils have imitated in the mysteries of Mithras, commanding the same thing to be done. For, that bread and a cup of water are placed with certain incantations in the mystic rites of one who is being initiated, you either know or can learn.[304]

Tertullian (155-ca.240), another Church patriarch, attacked Mithraism in his *The Prescription Against Heretics*, saying:

> The question will arise, by whom is to be interpreted the sense of the passages which make for heresies? By the devil, of course, to whom pertain those wiles which pervert the truth, and who, by the mystic rites of his idols, vies even with the essential portions of the sacraments of God. He, too, baptizes some, that is, his own believers and faithful followers; he promises the putting away of sins by a layer (of his own); and if my memory still serves me, Mithra there, (in the kingdom of Satan) sets his marks on the foreheads of his soldiers; celebrates also the oblation of bread, and introduces an image of a resurrection, and before a sword wreathes a crown.[305]

Despite Tertullian's criticism of Mithraism, he could not bring a charge of plagiarism against the religion because the Mithraic rites preceded the Christian rites.

After the fall of Rome, the consensus rationale among the Church patriarchs was that the "devil" anticipated the advent of Jesus Christ, as predicted in the Jewish scriptures, and caused the Pagans to mimic the Jewish messiah.[306]

Solomon Reinach, writing in *Orpheus*, his classic study of religions, compares the two religions:

> The analogies with Christianity may be summed up as follows; Mithra is the mediator between God and man, he ensures the happiness of mankind by a sacrifice; his worship comprises baptism, communion and fasts, his adherents are called brethren; among the Mithraic clergy there were men and women vowed to celibacy; its moral code was severe, and akin to that of Christianity. The Fathers of the Church were as much impressed by this as the pagans. St. Augustine relates that an Asiatic priest [from the Eastern Empire] told him one day that they worshipped the same god.[307]

From evidence that can be pieced together from various sources, it appears that many of the foundation rites and rituals of the Church of

Rome were copied from Mithraism. Not only did Mithraism contain worship services similar to those that the early Christian Orthodox Church would later include in their rites and rituals, but also we have additional evidence that Constantine, serving in the role of the first Pope, subscribed to Mithraism prior to becoming a Christian. Given Mithraism's pliability as a religion and Constantine's tendency to merge and compromise in the service of the empire, it is highly likely that the Church of Rome assimilated many of Mithra's qualities into its description of Jesus, as well as the rites and rituals of the Mithraic religion. These, of course, had little to do with the message of Jesus Christ or the mystical path. They did, however, serve an important political purpose in establishing Christianity within the Roman Empire.

Constantine's first official act as Pontifex Maximus of Rome and the Pope of the "Catholic" Church was to call the Council of Nicaea in 325. The Gnostics were not invited, of course, but within the Church itself, a conflict regarding a subtle abstraction was surging out of control. The bishops throughout the realm were in a heated confrontation over the question of whether Jesus was equal to God the Father or subordinate to him. A Christian presbyter named Arius, who lived in Alexandria, Egypt (that hotbed of Gnostic dissent), taught that Jesus was the Son of God but that as the Son he did not always exist but was created by the Father. He quoted the Gospel of John in which Jesus tells his apostles, "If you loved me, you would be glad that I am going to the Father, for the Father is greater than I" (John 14:28).

While rational and consistent with monotheism, this argument challenged the mainstream dogma that was forming in the Church of Rome that Jesus was co-equal to the Father and, like the Father, had existed before time itself. This was consistent with their political imperative that brought the authority of the bishops closer to absolute religious power. In a simplified form, the argument was that Jesus is God; the apostles were granted God's powers; and that the Church inherited this power because it represented Peter, the chief apostle. This argument, at a subsequent council, was expanded to include the Holy Ghost as an equal power of the Godhead who inspires human beings to know God. Thus exists the basis for the Church's Trinitarian viewpoint in which God consists of three equal entities, the Father, the Son, and the Holy

Ghost. Arius argued that as God, nothing could be His equal because that would diminish his Absolute nature. Thus God had to create the Son and the Holy Ghost. This point of view became known as Arianism.

The argument was widespread throughout the clergy and the debaters were becoming rancorous in their condemnation of each other. Constantine wanted the issue to be resolved amicably. To address the matter, he called the Christian bishops together in the first Ecumenical Council—the Council of Nicaea.

In the summer of 325, the bishops from all provinces were summoned to Nicaea, a place reasonably accessible to many delegates, particularly those of Asia Minor, Georgia, Armenia, Syria, Palestine, Egypt, Greece, and Thrace. Constantine had invited all eighteen hundred bishops of the Christian church (about a thousand in the east and eight hundred in the west), but a smaller number responded. Estimates given were between two hundred and fifty and three hundred and eighteen.[308]

The participating bishops were given free travel and lodging and each could bring two priests and three deacons, so the total number of attendees could have been above eighteen hundred.

The Eastern bishops formed the great majority. Of these, the first rank was held by three patriarchs: Alexander of Alexandria, Eustathius of Antioch, and Macarius of Jerusalem. Many of those assembled had weathered the persecution and had stood by their faith.

"Resplendent in purple and gold," Constantine made a ceremonial entrance at the opening of the council, but respectfully seated the bishops ahead of himself." As Eusebius described, Constantine "proceeded through the midst of the assembly, like some heavenly messenger of God, clothed in raiment which glittered as it were with rays of light, reflecting the glowing radiance of a purple robe, and adorned with the brilliant splendor of gold and precious stones". The emperor came to oversee and preside, but did not cast any official vote. He organized the Council along the lines of the Roman Senate.[309] This was the first ecumenical council of the Church and set the precedent of the emperor assuming the role of the Pope.

The agenda of the council included:

1. The Arian question regarding the relationship between God the Father and Jesus the Son;

2. The date of celebration of Easter;
3. The Meletian schism[310] (dealing with the readmission of fallen away Christians);
4. Various matters of church discipline;
5. Administrative structure
   a. Ordination at all levels and the suitability of behavior and background for clergy
   b. Readmission to the Church of heretics, schismatics and the "lapsed" (those who gave up their faith under persecution and then wanted readmission to the church): including issues of when reordination and/or rebaptism were to be required;
6. Some minor liturgical concerns.

Arianism: The First of Many Heresies to Come

The greatest issue, and certainly the most contentious, was the issue concerning Arianism. It took almost a month to work things out. The result of the debate was that the Council overwhelmingly concluded that Jesus was the true God, co-eternal with the Father, and begotten from His same substance and not, as Arius and others had argued, that the Son was produced by the Father. The majority decision was codified in the Nicene Creed.

Thereafter, the mainstream branches of Christianity considered Arianism to be heretical. This, of course, did not immediately stop people from believing what they thought was true. Two Roman emperors, Constantius II and Valens, were Arians, as were prominent Goth, Vandal, and Lombard warlords, both before and after the fall of the Western Roman Empire. Constantine, himself, took no official position at the Council of Nicaea, but supported the majority. At the end of his life, however, when he finally became a Christian on his deathbed, he was baptized by an Arian bishop.[311]

While the Arians were considered heretics, Constantine ensured that no harm came to them. Under his son's reign, however, the dispute flared up again. Constantius II (337 to 361) adopted a middle ground between the Trinitarians and the Arians, called "Semi-Arianism," which held that the Son was "of a similar substance" as the Father but not "of the same substance" as him. His advisor in these affairs was Eusebius of Nicomedia, the bishop of Constantinople who supported the Arian belief.

As the Pontifex Maximus, Constantius II removed some bishops and replaced them with those more in keeping with his viewpoint. He did pass laws, however, of great benefit to all Catholics, including exempting the clergy from public service and exempting bishops from being tried in secular courts. Interestingly, he also passed a law stating that Christian prostitutes could only be bought by Christians.

The emperor, however, was not so tolerant of the Jews in his realm. He forbade Jews from marrying Christian women or trying to convert them. A Jew could not own a Christian slave nor circumcise him under penalty of death. Any Christian slaves owned by a Jew were taken away and freed. Conversely, if a Christian converted to Judaism, his property would be confiscated by the state.[312]

Under Theodosius I (379 to 395), a successor to Constantius II, the example of Christian "tolerance" shifted even more toward intolerance of others. It was Theodosius who made the Church of Rome the "official religion" of the Roman Empire. As such, he issued decrees reinforcing the Nicene Creed as the only acceptable dogma. He claimed that only those who believed in this position could be called "Catholics." Others, he considered to be "foolish madmen."[313]

Theodosius I, began a systematic persecution of the traditional Roman religions. Any magistrate (judge) who did not enforce laws against polytheism was punished as a criminal. Non-Christian religious associations were banned. While Theodosius did not torture or kill heretics (this would come later), he neither prevented nor punished Christians who destroyed "pagan" temples and harassed those of other religions. Many classical temples in Greece were also destroyed under his reign. In 393, he banned the "pagan" rituals of the Olympics in Ancient Greece. The Olympics would not be held again until the end of the nineteenth century.[314]

Theodosius I called another ecumenical council, the *First Council of Constantinople,* to reconfirm the Nicene Creed. At this council, the

Holy Ghost was elevated to the same status as the Father and the Son. Consequently, the dogma of the Holy Trinity was established.

Arianism continued to exist in the substratum of Christianity and is still held by existing Christian sects such as the Unitarians, Mormons, and Jehovah's Witnesses. Until about a hundred years ago, it was also a belief of the Seven Day Adventists.[315]

The fact that the dogma of the Trinity became orthodox teaching does not, however, destroy the rational argument that Jesus was born and died as all men are born and die. Because of the magnificence of his existence, however, people had no way of comprehending how a realized master could have come into being, without attributing a preexistent status of Godhood to him. Whether Jesus was a reincarnation of Elisha, or the Teacher of Righteousness, or another spiritual master who realized his divinity while in his lifetime does not really matter. His message would have been the same as that of all spiritual masters. As human beings, we have all led many lives and according to our karmic disposition will continue to lead many more until we evolve into Divinity. As we overcome our attachment to forms of consciousness, our minds gradually lose their distinction and move into pure consciousness. In fact, it is truer said that "The Son becomes the Father." It is the son and the daughter who, through love and self-sacrifice, achieve enlightenment. This is the Way, the Truth, and the Light.

We have taken a little time to describe the process of decision-making within the Catholic Church because it sets the stage for governance that existed throughout the reign of the Church for over seventeen centuries. We have witnessed how a difference of opinion, over a completely abstract concept, could become a basis for determining a heresy. Under the name of orthodoxy, the political elite declared those who did not agree with them *anathema*, (i.e., "something dedicated to evil and thus accursed"). As the power of the Roman priest class congealed, heretics were tortured and put to death for their so-called dedication to evil. In this way, the spiritual message of Jesus Christ was completely destroyed. In its place, a political institution emerged that primarily benefited the priest class, and unbeknownst to the people, they found themselves cut off from the spiritual source of power as manifested by Jesus Christ.

Because the Council of Nicaea, and other such councils, were primarily political assemblies and not spiritual gatherings, the message of Jesus was not embraced in the hearts of Christian devotees. Rather their "belief" became channeled into the establishment of religious doctrines and laws, which were the very legal forms against which Jesus himself had rebelled. In order for a religious institution to develop, dogmas are required, and once established, they must be protected from heresy (false belief). The only way to do this was to punish those who did not agree with the orthodox beliefs.

Institutions of power, as we have seen, cannot exist without dogmas. They cannot exist without what Jesus called "the law" and the enforced subjugation of believers to these dogmas. The warning that Jesus gave to his apostles about being imprisoned by the laws they create came to pass. Dogmas by their very nature deflect from the unity of spiritual reality. When one becomes lost in these contradictions the mental and physical realm becomes the dominant reality and one loses spiritual perspective. This shift in reality forms the main contradiction between spirituality and religions.

Arianism was only one of many "heresies" that was destroyed by the orthodox forces of Christianity. The Catholic Church dealt harshly with all the heretics who opposed their dogmas. It is in the nature of human thought that every concept gives rise to its opposite, so therefore, people were always questioning the religious dogma established by the Church hierarchy. Anything could become a ground for contention. Some people believed that Christians who denied their faith under Roman persecution should not be let back into the Church. Some people questioned whether babies should be baptized when they could not yet decided for themselves to become Catholics. Others questioned the nature of the Holy Ghost or the divinity of Mary. Some argued that Mary was not the Mother of God; she was simply the mother of Jesus, etc. Some believed that Jesus had brothers and sisters, but the Church denied it because it diminished Jesus as a god and made him too human. It sullied the myth of Mary as being the only woman in human history to give birth without having sexual intercourse.

When people are posssessed by a religious socio-sentiment, they succumb to the belief that they are the only ones who "know" and are the only righteous people. Others, who hold different opinions, or worship Divinity under a different guise, represent lesser beings or at worst, Satan's kingdom. This is the fate of all religious fundamentalists, regardless of religion. Religious fundamentalism is the sure sign that the religious believers are lost in the duality of psycho-physical reality and are no longer in touch with spiritual reality. In their spiritual ignorance they remain trapped in their own karma and enslaved by their own ego. For example, Christian fundamentalists are no longer able to intuitively grasp that it is "love," not faith that allowed Jesus to transcend his humanity and become Divine. They fail to grasp the spiritual law that once one has merged with Divine Love, any contradiction between Jesus and God no longer exists. The unit consciousness of Jesus merged with the Cosmic Consciousness as surely as a drop of water, upon contact, merges in the ocean. This is true for anyone on the mystical path. Dogma, as the source of our subconsciously programmed "faith," is merely a mental construct that binds us to an abstract idea of spirituality, the reality of which will never be known without love.

And so it was that a dogma (a mental abstraction) concerning the nature of the Prince of Peace was locked in stone by a group of men who fought and killed each other to have the last word. Today millions of people who are born into Christian churches are taught to believe in a fantasy Jesus in which he is the only God-realized man to ever have walked the earth, and that he was born from a virgin, and that his earthly body was resurrected from the grave. This dogma goes against all the natural laws of the creation. The laws put in place by God as the Creator. It is nothing more than an updated version of an ancient story of an Aryan god who demonstrated superhuman powers and fought imaginary beasts.

The great misfortune of the myth about Jesus, however, is that it was completely unnecessary to create a fantasy to justify his greatness. In fact, the fantasy actually inhibits Jesus's mission to bring love and understanding to the world. Christians who are driven by dogmas and socio-sentiments will never understand Jesus or his message. In their quest for wealth and power, they will continue to siphon from the lives of others to satisfy their own egos. They will put on the name of "Christian" like a wolf puts on sheep's clothing to hide their exploitation of others and the earth. They will use it to oppress women and minorities and to justify killing others out of nationalism or religious pride. This is not to say that only Christians suffer from this programming. The fundamentalists of other religions are also captivated by their dogmas and stand ready to kill those who would challenge them. Only the lovers truly understand what Jesus represents and how he saves humanity. Only the lovers love Jesus regardless of their religion. These are the spiritualists.

Having said this, we must ask ourselves is there any value at all in religions? And if we are truthful, we must certainly conclude that there is. Religion allows the common people to reflect upon a higher reality even though it is presented through a distorted mirror. Religion gives us hope that there is something greater than our backbreaking, often miserable existence. It answers the longing in our hearts for the limitlessness of spiritual reality. It gives us common practices by which we can taste love and harmony, if only for a moment. It builds a sense of community, which is a form of collective love. There is certainly some power and goodness in creating a socio-sentiment in the people even though it is vastly inferior to true spirituality or mysticism.

The evils of religion emerge when church leaders, consciously or unconsciously, begin to manipulate the people's innocent sentiment and keep them in servitude or keep their minds from expanding, or keep them from fighting against oppression. The evils of religion emerge when its leaders denounce those of other nations, creeds, or races; or they preach the control and suppression of women and seek to destroy the lives of people who contradict them. Such a display of authority is a testament to the fact that the church leaders have long forgotten the spiritual roots upon which their religion was initially based. Such behavior should be a wake up call to the faithful that the time has come to overthrow the dogma to which they have long succumbed.

The question that Christians and the followers of every religion must continually ask themselves is: What is the balance between the love of one's own heart and the dictates of the clergy with their scriptures, dogma and rituals?

The Catholic Church claims that, "Outside the church there is no salvation." With even the slightest exploration of this statement, a rational person will see that this is illogical. We must all learn to think rationally. God made human beings rational. This is the cornerstone of our supposed superiority as a species on earth. It is a sin to waste our rationality and to deny our God-given nature.

In our next Volume, we will explore, in depth, the consequences of what happens when we deny our rationality and in its place accept blind faith in an ideology/institution that seeks to take advantage of us for personal gain.

Appendix A: Major Gods and Goddesses in the Greek Pantheon

The Greek gods lived on the top of the highest Greek mountain, Olympus. They were a querulous, back stabbing group. They most likely had their origins in the myths of the Aryans, who made their way west from the Caucasus and down through northern Europe around 2000 BC.[316] The most popular gods include the following:

Aphrodite
Goddess of love, beauty, desire, sex, and pleasure. Although married to Hephaestus, she had many lovers, most notably Ares, Adonis, and Anchises. She was depicted as a beautiful woman and is the only goddess to appear nude or semi-nude. Poets praise the radiance of her smile and her laughter. Her symbols include roses and other flowers, the scallop shell, and myrtle wreath. Her sacred animals are doves and sparrows. Her Roman counterpart was Venus.

Apollo
God of music, arts, knowledge, healing, plague, prophecy, poetry, manly beauty, archery, and the sun. He is the son of Zeus and Leto and the twin brother of Artemis. As brother and sister, they were identified with the sun and moon; both use a bow and arrow. In the earliest myths, Apollo contends with his half-brother Hermes. In sculpture, Apollo was depicted as a very handsome, beardless young man with long hair and an ideal physique. As the embodiment of perfectionism, he could be cruel and destructive, and his love affairs were rarely happy. One example was his fruitless pursuit of the Forest nymph Daphne. Given his large ego, he angered Eros (Cupid), which caused Apollo to be shot with an arrow

of love and Daphne with a lead arrow of hate. The nymph was turned into a laurel bush, leaving Apollo to worship its leaves. His attributes include the laurel wreath and lyre. He often appears in the company of the Muses. Animals sacred to Apollo include roe deer, swans, cicadas, hawks, ravens, crows, foxes, mice, and snakes. His Roman counterpart was also named Apollo.

Ares
God of war, bloodshed, and violence. The son of Zeus and Hera, he was depicted as a beardless youth, either nude with a helmet and spear or sword, or as an armed warrior. Homer portrays him as moody and unreliable, and he generally represents the chaos of war in contrast to Athena, a goddess of military strategy and skill. Ares's sacred animals are the vulture, venomous snakes, dogs, and boars. His Roman counterpart Mars, by contrast, was regarded as the dignified ancestor of the Roman people. He had an affair with his brother's (Hephaestus) wife, Aphrodite, which later Apollo revealed to Hephaestus.

Artemis
Virgin goddess of the hunt, wilderness, animals, young girls, childbirth, plague, and the moon. In later times she became associated with bows and arrows. She is the daughter of Zeus and Leto, and Apollo's twin sister. In art, she was often depicted as a young woman dressed in a short knee-length chiton and equipped with a hunting bow and a quiver of arrows. Her attributes include hunting spears, animal pelts, deer, and other wild animals. Her sacred animals are deer, bears, and wild boars. Diana was her Roman counterpart.

Athena
Goddess of intelligence, skill, peace, warfare, battle strategy, handicrafts, and wisdom. According to most traditions, she was born from Zeus's head fully formed and armored. She was depicted crowned with a crested helm, armed with shield and a spear, and wearing the aegis over a long dress. Poets describe her as "grey-eyed" or having especially bright, keen eyes. She was a special patron of heroes such as Odysseus. She was also the patron of the city Athens (which was named after her). Her symbol

is the olive tree. She is commonly shown accompanied by her sacred animal, the owl. The Romans identified her with Minerva.

Demeter
Goddess of grain, agriculture and the harvest, growth, and nourishment. Demeter is a daughter of Cronus and Rhea and sister of Zeus, by whom she bore Persephone. She was one of the main deities of the Eleusinian mysteries. Demeter held power over the life cycle of plants, which was the main attribute of the Great Goddess. She was depicted as a mature woman, often crowned and holding a sheaf of wheat and a torch. Her symbols are the cornucopia, wheatears, the winged serpent, and the lotus staff. Her sacred animals are pigs and snakes. Ceres was her Roman counterpart.

Dionysus/Bacchus
The ecstatic outsider who appealed to women. To explain his ecstatic personality, Dionysus was often presented as the god of wine. As the effeminate youth who made a trip to India, he is actually a representation of Lord Shiva and explains how mysticism got interpreted as it entered the European theatre thousands of years after Shiva. The point of mysticism is for the most part lost, but the idea of ecstasy, in which one goes beyond the mind and connection to the world, remained.

Hades/Pluto
King of the underworld and the dead and god of regret. His consort is Persephone. His attributes are the drinking horn or cornucopia, key, sceptre, and the three-headed dog Cerberus. The screech owl was sacred to him. He was one of three sons of Cronus and Rhea, and thus sovereign over one of the three realms of the universe, the underworld. As a chthonic god, however, his place among the Olympians is ambiguous. In the mystery religions and Athenian literature, Pluto (Plouton, "the Rich") was his preferred name, with Hades more common for the underworld as a place. The Romans translated Plouton as Dis Pater ("the Rich Father") or Pluto.

Hephaestus
Crippled god of fire, metalworking, and crafts. Either the son of Zeus

and Hera or Hera alone, he is the smith of the gods and the husband of the adulterous Aphrodite. He was usually depicted as a bearded man with hammer, tongs and anvil—the tools of a smith—and sometimes riding a donkey. His sacred animals are the donkey, the guard dog, and the crane. Among his creations was the armor of Achilles. Hephaestus used the fire of the forge as a creative force, but his Roman counterpart Vulcan was feared for his destructive potential and association with the volcanic power of the earth.

Hera
Queen of the gods and goddess of marriage, women, childbirth, heirs, kings, and empires. She is the wife and sister of Zeus and daughter of Cronus and Rhea. She was usually depicted as a regal woman in the prime of her life, wearing a diadem and veil and holding a lotus-tipped staff. Although the goddess of marriage, Zeus's many infidelities drove her to jealousy and vengefulness.His Iconic affair with Alcmene bore him a son, Heracles. There are several versions including one where she sent snakes to kill Heracles and another where she adopts him and nurses him. Her sacred animals are the heifer, the peacock, and the cuckoo. In Rome she was known as Juno.

Hermes
God of boundaries, travel, communication, trade, language, and writing. The son of Zeus and Maia, Hermes is the messenger of the gods, and a psychopomp who leads the souls of the dead into the afterlife. He was depicted either as a handsome and athletic beardless youth, or as an older bearded man. His attributes include the herald's wand or caduceus, winged sandals, and a traveler's cap. His sacred animals are the tortoise, the ram, and the hawk. The Roman Mercury, his counterpart, was more closely identified with trade and commerce.

Hestia
Virgin goddess of the hearth, home, and chastity. She is a daughter of Rhea and Cronus and sister of Zeus. Not often identifiable in Greek art, she appeared as a modestly veiled woman. Her symbols are the hearth and kettle. In some accounts, she gave up her seat as one of the

Twelve Olympians in favor of Dionysus, and she plays little of a role in Greek myths. Her counterpart, Vesta, however, was a major deity of the Roman state.

Poseidon

God of the sea, rivers, floods, droughts, and earthquakes. He is a son of Cronus and Rhea and brother of Zeus and Hades. He rules one of the three realms of the universe as king of the sea and the waters. In classical artwork, he was depicted as a mature man of sturdy build with an often-luxuriant beard and holding a trident. The horse and the dolphin are sacred to him. His wedding with Amphitrite is often presented as a triumphal procession. There are some stories that specify an affair with Medusa, which led to her giving birth to Pegasus from her neck when Perseus sliced her head. His symbols are the trident, horse, dolphin, fish and bull. His Roman counterpart was Neptune.

Zeus

From Dyaus Pita, the Aryan sky god. He is king and father of the gods, the ruler of Mount Olympus, and the god of the sky, weather, thunder, lightning, law, order, and justice. He is the youngest son of Cronus and Rhea. He overthrew Cronus and gained the sovereignty of heaven for himself. In artwork, he was depicted as a regal, mature man with a sturdy figure and dark beard. His usual attributes are the royal scepter and the lightning bolt, and his sacred animals are the eagle and the bull. His counterpart Jupiter, also known as Jove, was the supreme deity of the Romans. Susceptible to female charms, he has a jealous, and sometimes murderous, wife.

Appendix B: Historical Timeline of the Jews

BC	
1200	Thera volcanic eruption
1200	Time of Joshua and Levite tribe
1200	Sea people invade Egypt, Syria, and Palestine
1200-1000	Period of the Judges
1000 BC	Hebrew prophets Samuel and Malachi
1000-587	Monarchial period in Israel – Saul, David, Solomon, etc.
920	Split of kingdom into Judah and Israel
750-700	Israelite prophets Amos, Hosea
722	Assyrians destroy Israel (ten lost tribes)
716	Hezekiah, King of Judah, and the prophet Isaiah resist Assyrian invasion of Jerusalem
620	King Josiah orders scriptural reform. Deuteronomy begins
600-580	Judean prophets Jeremiah and Ezekiel
587	Babylonian Captivity
539	Cyrus, king of Persia, destroys Babylon and frees the Jews
539	Priests have Isaiah praise the Persians and introduce the concept of monotheism, influenced by Zoroastrianism
520-515	Second temple built
520	Judean prophets Haggai and Zechariah
500	Idea of Messiah (military/religion authority) develops
450	Torah (Pentateuch) is recognized as scripture
333-63	Hellenistic period (after Alexander the Great creates empire)
230	Rome comes to east Mediterranean
200	Essenes at Qumran
200	Dead Sea Scrolls written; hidden from Romans
AD	
4	Joshua/Jesus "the Christ" is born
30	Jesus "the Christ" is crucified
36-64	Paul's ministry
63	Pompey of Rome annexes the land of Israel
67	Jewish Revolt against the Romans
70	Rome destroys Jerusalem, Jews and Christians scatter

Appendix C: Stories of the Desert Fathers

Abba Anthony

On attachment
A brother renounced the world and gave his goods to the poor, but he kept back a little for his personal expenses. He went to see Abba Anthony. When he told him this, the old man said to him, "If you want to be a monk, go into the village, buy some meat, cover your naked body with it, and come here like that." The brother did so, and the dogs and birds tore at his flesh. When he came back the old man asked him whether he had followed his advice. He showed him his wounded body, and Saint Anthony said, "Those who renounce the world but want to keep something for themselves are torn in this way by the demons who make war on them."

Abba Arsenius

On the virtue of physical work
Someone said to blessed Arsenius, "How is it that we, with all our education and our wide knowledge, get nowhere, while these Egyptian peasants acquire so many virtues?" Abba Arsenius said to him, "We indeed get nothing from our secular education, but these Egyptian peasants acquire the virtues by hard work."

On the mystical path
A brother questioned Abba Arsenius to hear a word of him and the old man said to him, "Strive with all your might to bring your interior activity into accord with God, and you will overcome exterior passions."

He also said, "If we seek God, he will show himself to us, and if we keep him, he will remain close to us."

Abba Daniel

On humility
Abba Daniel said, "At Babylon the daughter of an important person was possessed by a devil. A monk for whom her father had a great affection said to him, 'No-one can heal your daughter except some anchorites whom I know; but if you ask them to do so, they will not agree because of their humility. Let us therefore do this: when they come to the market, look as though you want to buy their goods and when they come to receive the price, we will ask them to say a prayer and I believe she will be healed.'"

When they came to the market they found a disciple of the old men sitting there selling their goods and they led him away with the baskets, so that he should receive the price of them. But when the monk reached the house, the woman possessed with the devil came and slapped him. But he only turned the other cheek, according to the Lord's Command (Matt. 5.39). The devil, tortured by this, cried out, "What violence! The commandment of Jesus drives me out." Immediately the woman was cleansed. When the old men came, they told them what had happened and they glorified God saying, "This is how the pride of the devil is brought low, through the humility of the commandment of Christ."

On spiritual method
Abba Daniel also said, "The body prospers in the measure in which the soul is weakened, and the soul prospers in the measure in which the body is weakened."

Abba John the Dwarf

On spiritual fantasy
It was said of Abba John the Dwarf, that one day he said to his elder brother, "I should like to be free of all care, like the angels, who do not work, but ceaselessly offer worship to God." So he took off his cloak and

went away into the desert. After a week he came back to his brother. When he knocked on the door, he heard his brother say, before he opened it, "Who are you? " He said, "I am John, your brother." "But," he replied, "John has become an angel, and henceforth he is no longer among men." Then the other begged him saying, "It is I." However, his brother did not let him in, but left him there in distress until morning. Then, opening the door, he said to him, "You are a man and you must once again work in order to eat." Then John made a prostration before him, saying, "Forgive me."

On non-attachment
Abba John the Dwarf said, "If a king wanted to take possession of his enemy's city, he would begin by cutting off the water and the food and so his enemies, dying of hunger, would submit to him. It is the same with the passions of the flesh: if a man goes about fasting and hungry the enemies of his soul grow weak."

On spiritual mindfulness
Some brethren came one day to test him to see whether he would let his thoughts get dissipated and speak of the things of this world. They said to him, "We give thanks to God that this year there has been much rain and the palm trees have been able to drink, and their shoots have grown, and the brethren have found manual work." Abba John said to them, "So it is when the Holy Spirit descends into the hearts of men; they are renewed and they put forth leaves in the fear of God."

On dependence on God
Abba John said, "I am like a man sitting under a great tree, who sees wild beasts and snakes coming against him in great numbers. When he cannot withstand them any longer, he runs to climb the tree and is saved. It is just the same with me; I sit in my cell and I am aware of evil thoughts coming against me, and when I have no more strength against them, I take refuge in God by prayer and I am saved from the enemy."

On being a spiritual warrior
Abba Poemen said of Abba John the Dwarf that he had prayed God

to take his passions away from him so that he might become free from care. He went and told an old man this: "I find myself in peace, without an enemy," he said. The old man said to him, "Go, beseech God to stir up warfare so that you may regain the affliction and humility that you used to have, for it is by warfare that the soul makes progress." So he besought God and when warfare came, he no longer prayed that it might be taken away, but said, "Lord, give me strength for the fight."

On compassion and discriminating truthfulness
One day when Abba John was going up to Sceti with some other brothers, their guide lost his way for it was night-time. So the brothers said to Abba John, "What shall we do, Abba, in order not to die wandering about, for the brother has lost the way?" The old man said to them, "If we speak to him, he will be filled with grief and shame. But look here, I will pretend to be ill and say I cannot walk any more; then we can stay here till the dawn." This he did. The others said, "We will not go on either, but we will stay with you." They sat there until the dawn, and in this way they did not upset the brother.

Macarius the Great (the Egyptian)

On God's love
Now a widow cried out behind us and would not stop weeping. So the old man called the owner of the field and said to him, "What is the matter with the woman that she goes on weeping?" "It is because her husband received a deposit in trust [loan] from someone and he died suddenly without saying where he had hidden it, and the owner of the deposit wants to take her and her children and make slaves of them." The old man said to him, "Tell her to come to us, when we take our mid-day rest." The woman came, and the old man said to her, "Why are you weeping all the time like this?" She replied, "My husband who had received a deposit on trust from someone, has died and he did not say when he died, where he had put it." The old man said to her, "Come, show me where you have buried him." Taking the brethren with him, he went with her. When they had come to the place, the old

man said to her, "Go away to your house." While the brethren prayed, the old man asked the dead man, "So and so, where have you put the deposit?" The corpse replied, "It is hidden in the house, at the foot of the bed." The old man said, "Rest again, until the day of resurrection." When they saw this, the brethren were filled with fear and threw themselves at his feet. But the old man said to them, "It is not for my sake that this has happened, for I am nothing, but it is because of the widow and the orphans that God has performed this miracle. This is what is remarkable, that God wants the soul to be without sin and grants it all it asks." He went to tell the widow where the deposit was. Taking it, she returned it to its owner and thus freed her children. All who heard this story gave glory to God.

On the fruits of doing God's work
It was said of Abba Macarius the Egyptian that one day when he was going up from Scetis with a load of baskets, he sat down, overcome with weariness and began to say to himself, "My God, you know very well that I cannot go any further," and immediately he found himself at the river.

On miracles
A man of Egypt had a paralytic son. He brought him to the cell of Abba Macarius, and put him down at the door weeping and went a good distance away. The old man stooped down and saw the child, and said to him, "Who brought you here?" He replied, "My father threw me down here and went away." Then the old man said to him, "Get up, and go back to him." The child was cured on the spot; he got up and rejoined his father and they returned to their own home.

On the error of criticizing others
The same Abba Macarius said, "If you reprove someone, you yourself get carried away by anger and you are satisfying your own passion; do not lose yourself, therefore, in order to save another."

On non attachment
The same Abba Macarius, while he was in Egypt, discovered a man

who owned a beast of burden engaged in plundering Macarius's goods. So he came up to the thief as if he was a stranger and he helped him to load the animal. He saw him off in great peace of soul, saying, "We have brought nothing into this world, and we cannot take anything out of the world" (1 Tim.6.7). "The Lord gave and the Lord has taken away; blessed be the name of the Lord" (Job 1.2 1).[317]

Notes

1. Harold Walter Bailey *Arya, Encyclopædia Iranica* (New York: Routledge & Kegan Paul, 1989), 2.
2. Julian Jaynes, *The Origins of Consciousness in the Breakdown of the Bicameral Mind* (Boston: Houghton Mifflin Co. 1976), 139.
3. Jaynes, *The Origins of Consciousness in the Breakdown of the Bicameral Mind*, 139
4. Jack Finegan, *Archeological History of the Ancient Middle East* (Boulder: Westview Press, 1979), 4.
5. Georges Roux, Ancient Iraq (London: Penguin Books, 1992), 101.
6. Hans Baumann, *The Land of Ur* (London: Oxford University Press, 1969), 97.
7. Baumann, *The Land of Ur*, 97.
8. George Rawlinson, *The Seven Great Monarchies of the Ancient Asian World* (New York: J.W. Lovell Co., 1880), 224.
9. Alasdar Livingstone, *Mystical and Mythological Explanatory Works of Assyrian and Babylonian Scholars* (Oxford, Clarendon Press, 1986), 71.
10. Jaynes, *The Origin of Consciousness in the Break-Down of the Bicameral Mind*, 105.
11. We will discuss the evolution of the mind in depth in Book II on Ideology.
12. Jaynes, *The Origin of Consciousness in the Break-Down of the Bicameral Mind*, 313.
13. Finegan, *Archeological History of the Ancient Middle East*, 23.
14. Baumann, *The Land of Ur*, p 38.
15. From "Inanna and Enki," quoted in *The Land of Ur*, p. 39.
16. Baumann, The Land of Ur, 41.
17. S. H. Hooke, *Middle Eastern Mythology* (Harmondsworth, England: Penguin Books Ltd. 1963), 110.
18. Finegan, *Archeological History of the Ancient Middle East*, 25-26.
19. Baumann, *The Land of Ur*, 29.
20. Baumann, *The Land of Ur*, 29-30.
21. Baumann, *The Land of Ur*, 31-32.

22 J. V. Kinnier-Wilson, *The Rebel Lands: An Investigation into the Origins of Early Mesopotamian Mythology* (Cambridge: University of Cambridge Oriental Publication 1979).

23 Kinnier-Wilson, *The Rebel Lands: An Investigation into the Origins of Early Mesopotamian Mythology*, 7-8.

24 Kinnier-Wilson, T*he Rebel Lands: An Investigation into the Origins of Early Mesopotamian Mythology*, 10.

25 Kinnier-Wilson, *The Rebel Lands: An Investigation into the Origins of Early Mesopotamian Mythology*, 17.

26 Baumann, The Land of Ur, 36-37.

27 Kinnier-Wilson, *The Rebel Lands: An Investigation into the Origins of Early Mesopotamian Mythology*, 58.

28 Kinnier-Wilson, *The Rebel Lands: An Investigation into the Origins of Early Mesopotamian Mythology*, 58.

29 Kinnier-Wilson, *The Rebel Lands: An Investigation into the Origins of Early Mesopotamian Mythology*, 22.

30 Kinnier-Wilson, *The Rebel Lands: An Investigation into the Origins of Early Mesopotamian Mythology*, 21.

31 Kinnier-Wilson, *The Rebel Lands: An Investigation into the Origins of Early Mesopotamian Mythology*, 25.

32 Baumann, *In the Land of Ur*, 58.

33 Kinnier-Wilson, *The Rebel Lands: An Investigation into the Origins of Early Mesopotamian Mythology*, 82.

34 Baumann, *The Land of Ur*, 62.

35 Baumann, *The Land of Ur*, 62-63.

36 Kinnier-Wilson, *The Rebel Lands: An Investigation into the Origins of Early Mesopotamian Mythology*, 78.

37 Baumann, *In the Land of Ur*, 66.

38 Felix Guirand, ed., *Larouse Encyclopedia of Mythology*, (London: Hamlyn Publishing Group Ltd, 1968), 72.

39 Jaynes, *The Origins of Consciousness in the Breakdown of the Bicameral Mind*, 252.

40 Baumann, The Land of Ur, 108.

41 "Lugalanda," *Wikipedia*, accessed March 26, 2018, http://en.wikipedia.org/wiki/Lugalanda.

42 Gerda Lerner, *The Creation of Patriarchy Vol I* (London: Oxford

University Press, 1986), 62.

43 Lerner, *The Creation of Patriarchy Vol I* , 62.
44 Baumann, *The Land of Ur*, 127-128.
45 Lerner, The Creation of Patriarchy Vol I, 62.
46 Baumann, *The Land of Ur*, 130.
47 Finegan, *Archeological History of the Ancient Middle East*, 41.
48 "Enuma Elish – The Babylonian Epic of Creation – Full Text." *Ancient History Encyclopedia*. Last accessed May 15, 2018. https://www.ancient.eu/article/225/enuma-elish---the-babylonian-epic-of-creation---fu/.
49 Finegan, *Archeological History of the Ancient Middle East*, 43.
50 "Pharaoh," *Ancient History Encyclopedia*. Last modified September 02, 2009. https://www.ancient.eu/pharaoh/.
51 Finegan, *Archeological History of the Ancient Middle East*, 43.
52 Finegan, *Archeological History of the Ancient Middle East*, 44.
53 Finegan, *Archeological History of the Ancient Middle East*, 49.
54 Finegan, *Archeological History of the Ancient Middle Eas*t, 53.
55 Sir Charles Leonard Woolley, *Ur of the Chaldees* (London: Ernest Benn Ltd, 1929), 57.
56 Baumann, *The Land of Ur*, 77.
57 Woolley, *Ur of the Chaldees*, 64-65.
58 Finegan, *Archeological History of the Ancient Middle East*, 54-55.
59. Jacobsen Throkild, *The Treasures of Darkness: A History of Mesopotamian Religion* (New York: Yale University Press, 1976).
60 Finegan, *Archeological History of the Ancient Middle East*, 67.
61 P. Dhorme, La Religion Assyro-Babylonienne (Paris: J. Gabalda & Co, 1910), 199. http://en.wikipedia.org/wiki/Ancient_Mesopotamian_religion#Private_devotions.
62 Finegan, *Archeological History of the Ancient Middle Eas*t, 64.
63 Finegan, *Archeological History of the Ancient Middle East*, 37-39.
64 Lerner, *The Creation of Patriarchy Vol I*, 87.
65 Lerner, *The Creation of Patriarchy Vol I*, 90.
66 Lerner, *The Creation of Patriarchy Vol I*, 107.
67 Lerner, *The Creation of Patriarchy Vol I*, 14.
68 Lerner, *The Creation of Patriarchy Vol I*, 116.
69 Lerner, *The Creation of Patriarchy Vol I*, 117.
70 "The Fall of the Minoans, PBS Special: Secrets of the Dead, 2008,

http://www.pbs.org/wnet/secrets/the-fall-of-the-minoans/61.

71   Olga Krzszkowska, "So Where's the Loot? The Spoils of War and the Archaeological Record," In Robert Laffineur, ed., *Polemos: Le Contexte Guerrier en Egee a L'Age du Bronze. Actes de la 7e Rencontre egeenne internationale Universite de Liège* (Université de Liège, Histoire de l'art d'archeologie de la Grece antique, 1998), Cited in http://en.wikipedia.org/wiki/Minoan_civilization, 489–498.

72   Riane Eisler, *The Chalice and the Blade: Our History, Our Future* (New York: Harper-Collins e-books, 1987), Chapter Three, Kindle.

73   Nicolas Platon, *Crete* (Geneva: Nagel Publishers, 1966), 15.

74   Eisler, T*he Chalice and the Blade: Our History, Our Future,*

75   Jacquetta Hawkes, *Dawn of the Gods: Ninoan and Mycean Origins of Greece* (London: Chatto & Windus, 1968), 73.

76   Platon, *Crete*, 178.

77   "History of Greece: The Dark Ages," *Ancient-Greece.org*, accessed February 20, 2018, ancient-greece.org/history/dark-ages.html.

78   Jaynes, *The Origins of Consciousness in the Breakdown of the Bicameral Mind*, 223.

79   See the chapter on the Double Brain in Jaynes, T*he Origins of Consciousness in the Breakdown of the Bicameral Mind*, 100-125.

80   Jaynes, *The Origins of Consciousness in the Breakdown of the Bicameral Mind*, 104-106.

81   https://www.google.com/search?q=left+brain+right+brain+charts&client=firefox-b-1&tbm=isch&tbo=u&source=univ&sa=X&ved=0ahUKEwirp7fqmIvaAhVFoVMKHVNZDuAQ7AkISQ&biw=1920&bih=943#imgrc=P9aMdU7gJbnZ-M:.

82   Jaynes, *The Origins of Consciousness in the Breakdown of the Bicameral Mind*, 223.

83   Jaynes, *The Origins of Consciousness in the Breakdown of the Bicameral Mind*, 223.

84   Jaynes, *The Origins of Consciousness in the Breakdown of the Bicameral Mind*, 226.

85   Jaynes, *The Origins of Consciousness in the Breakdown of the Bicameral Mind*, 226.

86   Jaynes, *The Origins of Consciousness in the Breakdown of the Bicameral Mind*, 248.

87 Jaynes, *The Origins of Consciousness in the Breakdown of the Bicameral Mind*, 248.

88 Jaynes, *The Origins of Consciousness in the Breakdown of the Bicameral Mind*, 249.

89 Roux, *Ancient Iraq*, 283, 376.

90 Alasdair Livingston, *Mystical and Mythological Explanatory Works of Assyrian and Babylonian Scholars* (University Park, PA: The Pennsylvania State University Press, 2007), 231.

91 Finegan, *Archeological History of the Ancient Middle East*, 104.

92 George Rawlinson, *The Seven Great Monarchies of the Ancient Asian World, An Online Index*, David Wedger, ed., Project Gutenberg Edition, The Second Monarchy, Assyria, Chapter Seven, Manners and Customs, http://www.gutenberg.org/files/16162/16162-h/16162-h.htm#linkD2HCH0001.

93 Joseph Campbell, *Occidental Mythology* (New York: Penguin Books, 2011), 214.

94 "Medes," *Wikipedia*, accessed February 2, 2018, http://en.wikipedia.org/wiki/Medes

95 It is very possible that Yahweh was originally a volcano god, derived from the Thera volcano that destroyed the Eastern Mediterranean region. The Jews date their exodus from Egypt at the same time as the explosion.

96 "Ahura Mazda," *Wikipedia*, accessed Novembe 26, 2018, http://en.wikipedia.org/wiki/Ahura_Mazda.

97 "Zoroaster," *Wikipedia*, accessed November 27, 2018, https://en.wikipedia.org/wiki/Zoroaster.

98 Jayaram V, "Gender Equality and Status of Women in Zoroastrianism," *Hinduwebsite.com*, accessed February 20, 2018, http://www.hinduwebsite.com/zoroastrianism/gender.asp.

99 Jayaram V, "Gender Equality and Status of Women in Zoroastrianism," *Hinduwebsite.com*, accessed February 20, 2018, http://www.hinduwebsite.com/zoroastrianism/gender.asp.

100 Kaufmann Kohler, A. V. W. Jackson, "Zoroastrianism," accessed February 21, 2018, http://www.jewishencyclopedia.com/articles/15283-zoroastrianism.

101 This was a symbolic way of saying in that realm in which heaven

and earth meet. This was the point of the ziggurats; to create a place for meeting the gods and goddesses.

102 Kaufmann Kohler, A. V. W. Jackson, "Zoroastrianism," accessed February 21, 2018.

103 Kaufmann Kohler, A. V. W. Jackson, "Zoroastrianism," accessed February 21, 2018, http://www.jewishencyclopedia.com/articles/15283-zoroastrianism.

104 Bill Yenne, *Alexander the Great: Lessons from History's Undefeated General* (Basomgstple, England: Palmgrame McMillan, 2010), http://en.wikipedia.org/wiki/Alexander_the_Great.

105 "Seleucid Empire," *Wikipedia*, accessed February 13, 2018, http://en.wikipedia.org/wiki/Seleucid_Empire.

106 "Seleucid Empire," *Wikipedia*, modified February 13, 2018.

107 "Semitic people," *Wikipedia*, accesssed January 23, 2018, http://en.wikipedia.org/wiki/Semitic_people.

108 It is difficult to know whether the archeologists who interpreted the stone made a distinction between Hebrew, Jew or Israelite, when they chose the word "Israelite" What is clear, however, is that there is some group of people who have their own identity at this time.

109 "Archaeology of the Hebrew Bible," *NOVA*, November 18, 2008, http://www.pbs.org/wgbh/nova/ancient/archeology-hebrew-bible.html.

110 Mario Liverani, *Israel's History and the History of Israel* (New York: Routledge, 2014), 52-53.

111 See Appendix A for an historical timeline of the Jews.

112 Biblical Mt. Sinai has never been identified archaeologically with any scholarly consensus. Some scholars have identified a volcano in Saudi Arabia, but, to my knowledge, there has been little effort to connect the volcano at Thera as the phenomenon that gives rise to Yahweh. See http://www.biblicalarchaeology.org/daily/biblical-topics/exodus/searching-for-biblical-mt-sinai/, What is certain is that there are no other volcanoes that took place at this time.

113 Dr. llil Arbel, Ph.D. "Jahweh." March 3, 1997, http://www.pantheon.org/articles/y/yahweh.html.

114 Mark, S. Smith, *The Early History of God: Yahweh and Other Deities In Ancient Israel* (Grand Rapids, MI: Eerdmans Publishing, 2002), 7. http://en.wikipedia.org/wiki/Book_of_Judges.

115 "Archaeology of the Hebrew Bible," *NOVA*, accessed November 18, 2008, http://www.pbs.org/wgbh/nova/ancient/archeology-hebrew-bible.html.

116 Raphael Patai *The Hebrew Goddess*, 1967. Referenced at http://en.wikipedia.org/wiki/The_Hebrew_Goddess.

117 Mark Wiley, "Influence of Zoroastrianism on Judaism and Christianity," *The Circle of Ancient Iranian Studies*, access date February 21, 2018, http://www.cais-soas.com/CAIS/Religions/iranian/Zarathushtrian/zoroastrianism_influence.htm.

118 Robert Drews, "Canaanites and Philistines," *Journal for the Study of the Old Testament*, 81 (1998), 48-49.

119 Jaynes, *The Origins of Consciousness in the Breakdown of the Bicameral Mind*, 293.

120 "History of Jerusalem : From Canaanite City to Israelite Capital," *Jewish Virtual Library, Project of AICE*, access February 21, 2018, https://www.jewishvirtuallibrary.org/jsource/Archaeology/canaan.html.

121 Israel Finklestein, Amihay Mazar, Brian B. Schmidt, *The Quest for the Historical Israel* (Society of Biblical Literature, 2007), 14. https://en.wikipedia.org/wiki/Tel_Dan_Stele.

122 "Archaeology of the Hebrew Bible," *NOVA*, November 18, 2008, http://www.pbs.org/wgbh/nova/ancient/archeology-hebrew-bible.html.

123 Yosef Elsen, ''The United Kingdom of Israel and Its Split." *Chabad.org*, accessed February 21, 2018, http://www.chabad.org/library/article_cdo/aid/2837559/jewish/The-United-Kingdom-of-Israel-and-Its-Split.htm.

124 S. David Sperling. "Were the Jews Slaves in Egypt?" *ReformJudaism.org*, http://www.reformjudaism.org/were-jews-slaves-egypt. This article was adapted with permission from *The Original Torah: The Political Intent of the Bible's Writers*, published by New York Univesity Press, 1998.

125 Michaele David Coogan, *The Oxford History of the Biblical World* (London: Oxford University Press, 2001), ISBN 9780195139372, 261. http://en.wikipedia.org/wiki/Battle_of_Megiddo_%28609_BC%29.

126 "Babylonian Captivity," *Wikipedia*, last modified February 8, 2018, http://en.wikipedia.org/wiki/Babylonian_captivity.

127 Niels Peter Lemche, *The Israelites in History and Tradition* (Westminster: John Knox Press, 1998), 85. http://en.wikipedia.org/

wiki/History_of_ancient_Israel_and_Judah.

128 Jill Anne Middlemas, *The Troubles of Templeless Judah* (London: Oxford University Press, 2005), 10. http://en.wikipedia.org/wiki/History_of_ancient_Israel_and_Judah.

129 The practice of circumcision originated from the castration of males in order to become recognized "priestesses" of the Great Goddess. At the time of the Hebrews, well into patriarchy, this act had been modified to circumcision, a sacrifice that was pleasing to a male deity.

130 "History of Ancient Israel and Judah," *Wikipedia*, accessed February 20, 2018, http://en.wikipedia.org/wiki/History_of_ancient_Israel_and_Judah.

131 Demographic history of Jerusalem," *Wikipedia*, accessed Sept. 10, 2018, "https://en.wikipedia.org/wiki/Demographic_history_of_Jerusalem#1st_century_Judea.

132 Stephen M. Wiley, *The Jews in the Time of Jesus: An Introduction* (Mahwah, NJ: Paulist Press, 1996), 25.

133 Lester L. Grabbe, *A History of the Jews and Judaism in the Second Temple Period* (London: Bloomsbury – T&T Clark Publishing, 2004), 154-155.

134 Joseph Blenkinsopp, *Judaism, the First Phase: The Place of Ezra and Nehemiah in the Origins of Judaism* (Grand Rapids, MI: Eerdmans Publishers, 2009), 229.

135 Josephus, *The Jewish War* (London: Penguin Classics. 1959), I.

136 Carol Ann Newsom and Brenna Breed, *Daniel: A Commentary* (Louisville, KY: Presbyterian Publishing Corp, 2014), 26. http://en.wikipedia.org/wiki/Antiochus_IV_Epiphanes.

137 See Appendix B for a description of the gods and goddesses in the Greek pantheon.

138 "List of Greek Mythological Figures," *Wikipedia*, accessed February 22, 2018, https://en.wikipedia.org/wiki/List_of_Greek_mythological_figures.

139 Some Jews do not consider the Hasmonean dynasty a valid kingship by the Jews, since they were not of the lineage of David.

140 Jaynes, *The Origins of Consciousness in the Breakdown of the Bicameral Mind*, 295.

141 Joseph Blekinsopp, *Treasures Old and New: Essays in the Theology of the Pentateuch* (Grand Rapids, MI: Eerdmans, 2004), 1 http://

en.wikipedia.org/wiki/Torah.

142 Peter Enns. *When Was Genesis Written and Why Does It Matter?: A Brief Historical Study*. Published by The BioLogos Foundation. Available at http://biologos.org/uploads/resources/enns_scholarly_essay3.pdf.

143 "Tora," *Wikipedia*, accessed August 5, 2018, https://en.wikipedia.org/wiki/Tora/.

144 "The Elohist," *Contradictions in the Bible.com*, accessed February 22, 2018, http://contradictionsinthebible.com/the-elohist/.

145 "The Deuteronomist," *Contradictions in the Bible.com*, accessed February 22, 2018, http://contradictionsinthebible.com/the-deuteronomist/.

146 "The Priestly Writer," *Contradictions in the Bible.com*, accessed February 22, 2018, http://contradictionsinthebible.com/the-priestly-writer/.

147 "The Priestly Writer", Contradictions in the Bible, accessed February 22, 2018, http://contradictionsinthebible.com/the-priestly-writer/.

148 Torah is sometimes considered just the Pentateuch and at others the entire body of Jewish teachings. Here we are speaking of the teachings of the Jews that appear in the Christian Bible as the Old Testament.

149 Walter Brueggemann, *Theology of the Old Testament: Testimony, Dispute, Advocacy* (Minneapolis: Fortress Press, 1997), 74-75.

150 Count Goblet d'Alviella, *The Migration of Symbols* (New York: University Books, 1956), 153.

151 Count Goblet d'Alviella, *The Migration of Symbols*, 153.

152 The use of capital letters when referring to God and Goddess indicate that the deity is universal in scope, i.e., the supreme Oneness. Any other worship of a deity that is less than this, small letters are used, i.e. goddess and god.

153 Morton Scott Enslin, *Christian Beginnings* (New York: Harper and Brothers, 1938), 91.

154 Marjorie Malvern, *Venus in Sackcloth* (Carbondale, IL: Southern Illinois University Press, 1975), 30.

155 Vern L. Bullough, *The Subordinate Sex* (Chicago: University of Illinois Press, 1973), 114.

156 "Augustine," http://www.womenpriests.org/traditio/august.asp.

157 R.R.Reuther, "Augustine: sexuality gender and women," in J.C.

Stark, ed., *Feminist Interpretations of Augustine* (University Park, PA: The Pennsylvania State University Press, 2007) referenced in http://en.wikipedia.org/wiki/Augustine_of_Hippo, 47–68.

158 Mary Daly, *Beyond God the Father* (Boston; Beacon Press, 1973), 69.

159 Chris Mooney, "The surprising links between faith and evolution and climate denial – charted," The *Washington Post*, accessed May 20, 2015. http://www.washingtonpost.com/news/energy-environment/wp/2015/05/20/this-chart-explains-why-faith-and-science-dont-have-to-be-in-conflict/.

160 "The True Identity of the So-called Palestinians," *Myths, Hypotheses, and Facts Concerning the Origins of Peoples*, accessed February 22, 2018, http://www.imninalu.net/myths-pals.htm.

161 This is an interesting phrase for it implies that the soldiers had to stop thinking about themselves as men i.e. subjectively and give themselves over to a more primal urge. This would indicate that the majority of people at this time already thought subjectively.

162 Alice Laffey, "Deuteronomistic History," in Orlando O. Espín, James B. Nickoloff, *An introductory Dictionary of Theology and Religious Studies* (Collegeville, MN: Liturgical Press. 2007), 337. Referenced at http://en.wikipedia.org/wiki/Book_of_Joshua.

163 "Ecclesiastes," *Wikipedia*, accessed February 18, 2018, http://en.wikipedia.org/wiki/Ecclesiastes.

164 John M. Allegro, *The Dead Sea Scrolls and the Christian Myth* (Amherst, NY: Prometheus Books, 1984).

165 Later in his life Allegro destroyed his career by publishing a book entitled The Sacred Mushroom and the Cross in which he proposes that Jesus in the Gospels was in fact a code for a type of hallucinogen, the Amanita muscaria, and that Christianity was the product of an ancient "sex-and-mushroom" cult.

166 Abegg, Jr, Martin, Peter Flint, and Eugene Ulrich, *The Dead Sea Scrolls Bible: The Oldest Known Bible Translated for the First Time into English* (San Francisco: Harper, 2002).

167 This myth is referred to in the Epic of Gilgamesh and has its roots in Sumerian mythology.

168 Historians know that the Torah was composed over many centuries by various scribes and assembled during the post-exilic period.

169 Hanan Eshel, *The Dead Sea Scrolls and the Hasmonean State* (Grand

Rapids, MI: Eerdmans Publishing, 2008), 117-123. http://en.wikipedia.org/wiki/Alexander_Jannaeus.

170 *Dead Sea Scrolls*, "Jeremiah Apocryphon," trans. Michael Wise, Martin Abegg Jr., and Edward Cook (New York, HarperOne, 2005), 445.

171 "The Dead Sea Scrolls: The Book of Covenant of Damascus, in *Jewish Virtual Library: A Project of AICE*, accessed February 22, 2018, http://www.jewishvirtuallibrary.org/jsource/Archaeology/DamCovenant.html.

172 "Damascus Document," *Wikipedia*, accessed December 2, 2017, https://en.wikipedia.org/wiki/Damascus_Document.

173 Michael Wise, Martin Abegg Jr., Edward Cook, *The Dead Sea Scrolls*, 170.

174 Michael Wise, Martin Abegg Jr., Edward Cook, *The Dead Sea Scrolls*, 170-171.

175 Michael Wise, Martin Abegg Jr., Edward Cook, *The Dead Sea Scrolls*, 182.

176 Michael Wise, Martin Abegg Jr., Edward Cook, *The Dead Sea Scrolls*, 185.

177 Michael Wise, Martin Abegg Jr., Edward Cook, *The Dead Sea Scrolls*, 187.

178 Michael Wise, Martin Abegg Jr., Edward Cook, *The Dead Sea Scrolls*, 180.

179 Michael Wise, Martin Abegg Jr., Edward Cook, *The Dead Sea Scrolls*, 184.

180 Michael Wise, Martin Abegg Jr., Edward Cook, *The Dead Sea Scrolls*, 186-7.

181 Michael Wise, Martin Abegg Jr., Edward Cook, *The Dead Sea Scrolls*, 85.

182 Michael Wise, Martin Abegg Jr., Edward Cook, *The Dead Sea Scrolls*, 243.

183 Michael Wise, Martin Abegg Jr., Edward Cook, *The Dead Sea Scrolls*, 87.

184 Michael Wise, Martin Abegg Jr., Edward Cook, *The Dead Sea Scrolls*, 87.

185 "Yom Kippur," *Wikipedia*, accessed February 20, 2018, https://en.wikipedia.org/?title=Yom_Kippur.

186 Michael Wise, Martin Abegg Jr., Edward Cook, *The Dead Sea Scrolls*, 185.

187 Michael Wise, Martin Abegg Jr., Edward Cook, *The Dead Sea Scrolls*, 482.

188 "Dead Sea Scroll: The Rule of the Congregation," referenced in John M. Allegro, *The Dead Sea Scrolls and the Christian Myth*, 121.

189 Michael Wise, Martin Abegg Jr., Edward Cook, *The Dead Sea Scrolls*, 530.

190 Michael Wise, Martin Abegg Jr., Edward Cook, *The Dead Sea Scrolls*, 531.

191 Michael Wise, Martin Abegg Jr., Edward Cook, *The Dead Sea Scrolls*, 530-531.

192 Michael Wise, Martin Abegg Jr., Edward Cook, *The Dead Sea Scrolls*, 190.

193 John M. Allegro, *The Dead Sea Scrolls and the Christian Myth*, 61.

194 Henry Wace and William Piercy, *A Dictionary of Early Christian Biography* (Peabody, MA: Hendrickson Publishers, 1911), "Ebionites," *Wikipedia*, accessed November 26, 2018, https://en.wikipedia.org/wiki/Ebionites.

195 John M. Allegro, *The Dead Sea Scrolls and the Christian Myth*, 49.

196 John M. Allegro, *The Dead Sea Scrolls*, 117.

197 John M. Allegro, *The Dead Sea Scrolls*, 119.

198 Dr. Sophie Lunn-Rockliffe, "Lost and Hidden Christianity," *History*, February 17, 2011, http://www.bbc.co.uk/history/ancient/romans/losthiddenchristianity_article_01.shtml.

199 *Dead Sea Scrolls*, "The War Scroll," 146.

200 *Dead Sea Scrolls*, "A Vision of the New Jerusalem," 557.

201 The influence of Zoroastrianism on the Pharisees is so conspicuous that some authors as Zaehner have called them "Farsis" or "Persians". Cited at http://firstnewtestament.com/essenes_forerunners_gnostic_christians.htm.

202 John M. Allegro, *The Dead Sea Scrolls and the Christian Myth*, 82. See discussion on a scriptural link between Joshua of Nun and the Teacher of Righteousness.

203 John M. Allegro, *The Dead Sea Scrolls and the Christian Myth*, 95.

204 John M. Allegro, *The Dead Sea Scrolls and the Christian Myth*, 95.

205 *Bulletin of the School of Oriental and African Studies*, Volume 65, Issue 1, 2002, https://en.wikipedia.org/wiki/Christian.

206 "20 Reasons that Jesus Lived in the First Century BC," accessed February 26, 2018, http://lost-history.com/list.php.

207 "Gospel of the Nazarenes," *Wikipedia*, accessed November 16, 2018, https://en.m.wikipedia.org/wiki/Gospel_of_the_Nazarenes.

208 "Hippolytus. Refutations 5.7.1," Referenced in Mark H. Gaffney, *The Gnostic Secrets of the Naassenes: The Initiatory Teachings of the Last Supper. Inner Traditions* (Vermont: Inner Traditions, The First Edition edition, 2004), 55.

209 The use of the name Levi, a Jewish name for Matthew, was also used in the Gnostic Gospel of Mary Magdelene.

210 Jerome, *Lives of Illustrious Men, 392-3 AD* Chapter 3.

211 Elaine Pagels, *The Gnostic Gospels* (New York: Random House, 1979), Introduction, Kindle.

212 "Theodotus," cited in Clemens Alexandrinus, *Excerpta ex Theodoto 78.2.* cited in Pagels, *The Gnostic Gospels, Introduction*, Kindle.

213 Hippolytus, "Refutationis Omnium Haeresium 1." cited in Pagels, *The Gnostic Gospels, Introduction*, Kindle.

214 Pagels, *The Gnostic Gospels, Introduction*, Kindle.

215 Marvin Meyers and James Robinson, *The Nag Hammadi Scriptures* (New York: Harper Collins, 2010), 40.

216 Mark H. Gaffney, *The Gnostic Secrets of the Naassenes: The Initiatory Teachings of the Last Supper. Inner Traditions*, 6.

217 "Elijah," *Wikipedia*, accessed February 23, 2018, https://en.wikipedia.org/wiki/Elijah.

218 This is told in *1 Kings* 19:16, where it says, "And Jehu the son of Nimshi shalt thou anoint to be king over Israel: and Elisha the son of Shaphat of Abelmeholah shalt thou anoint to be prophet in thy room."

219 Mark H. Gaffney, *Gnostic Secrets of the Naassene: The Initiatory Teachings of the Last Supper Inner Traditions*, 16.

220 Irenaeus, "Refutation of All Heresies 5.7.41" quoted in Mark H. Gaffney, *Gnostic Secrets of the Naassene: The Initiatory Teachings of the Last Supper Inner Traditions*, 32.

221 Mark H. Gaffney, *Gnostic Secrets of the Naassene: The Initiatory Teachings of the Last Supper Inner Traditions*, 33.

222 Hippolytus, *Philosophumena*, 5, 4.

223 Hippolytus, *Philosophumena*, 5, 4, https://en.wikipedia.org/wiki/Naassenes.

224 It wasn't until the 5th Century when the Church of Rome, now the Roman Catholic Church, condemned the belief in reincarnation and made it a heresy. Before that time, most Christians believed in what they called the "transmigration of souls", i.e. reincarnation.

225 Mark H. Gaffney, Gnostic Secrets of the Naassene: The Initiatory Teachings of the Last Supper Inner Traditions, 25.

226 Mark H. Gaffney, *Gnostic Secrets of the Naassene: The Initiatory Teachings of the Last Supper Inner Traditions*, 28-29.

227 "Gnosticism," *The New World Encyclopedia*, accessed June 23, 2017, http://www.newworldencyclopedia.org/entry/Gnosticism.

228 Marvin W. Meyers, *The Nag Hammadi Scriptures*, 133.

229 Richard Valantasis, *The Gospel of Thomas* (London; New York: Routledge Publishing, 1997), 12. https://en.wikipedia.org/wiki/Gospel_of_Thomas.

230 *The Nag Hammadi Scriptures*, "The Gospel of Mary," BG8502,1.

231 Marvin W. Meyers, *The Nag Hammadi Scriptures*, 739.

232 Marvin W. Meyers, *The Nag Hammadi Scriptures*, 739.

233 Marvin Meyer, in his introduction to the Gospel of Mary explains the use of the word "adultery" to mean improper attachment to the body and the world of form. By doing so, people are overcome by ignorance and erroneous passions. In doing so they "adulterate" the spirit. See page 738 of 775.

234 As in the Hebrew Gospel, this refers to the Holy Spirit as the Divine Mother.

235 "Historical Reliability of the Gospels," *Wikipedia*, accessed January 23, 2018, https://en.m.wikipedia.org/wiki/Historical_reliability_of_the_Gospels.

236 David L. Turner, Matthew Baker, *Exegetical Commentary on the New Testament* (Ada MI: Baker Pulishing Group, 2008), 6-7.

237 DG Horrell, *An Introduction to the Study of Paul*, 2-15.

238 "Mithraism," *Wikipedia*, accessed February 15, 2018, https://en.wikipedia.org/wiki/Mithraic_mysteries#cite_note-vermaserendec25-54.

239 Hans-Peter Schmidt, "Mitra I: Mithra in Old Indian and Imthra

in Old Iranian," *Encyclopaedia Iranica*, April 2006). https://en.wikipedia.org/wiki/Mitra.

240 "Mithraism," *Wikipedia*, accessed February 15, 2018, https://en.wikipedia.org/wiki/Mithraic_mysteries.

241 M.J. Vermaseren, *The Excavations in the Mithraeum of the Church of Santa Pricsa in Rome* (Leiden, Netherlands: Brill Academic Publishers, 1965), 238. https://en.wikipedia.org/wiki/Mithraic_mysteries.

242 "Mithraism," *Wikipedia*, accessed February 15, 2018, https://en.wikipedia.org/wiki/Mithraic_mysteries.

243 "Mithraism," *Wikipedia*, accessed February 15, 2018, https://en.wikipedia.org/wiki/Mithraic_mysteries.

244 Barbara Walker, *The Woman's Encyclopedia of Myths and Secrets* (San Francisco: Harper Row, 1983), 663.

245 Acharya S. and D.M. Murdock, "Mithra: The Pagan Christ," accessed February 23, 2018, http://www.truthbeknown.com/mithra.htm.

246 J. Angus, *The Mystery-Religions* (New York: Dover Publications, 1975), 168.

247 Christopher Price, "A Thorough Review of the Testimonium Flavianum," *Bede's Library*, accessed December 8, 2009, http://bede.org.uk/Josephus.htm.

248 Christopher Price, "A Thorough Review of the Testimonium Flavianum," *Bede's Library*, accessed December 8, 2009, http://bede.org.uk/Josephus.htm.

249 Andreas J. Kostenberger; L. Scott Kellum and Charles L. Quarles, *The Cradle, the Cross, and the Crown: An Introduction to the New Testament* (Nashville, TN: B&H Publishing Group, 2009), https://en.wikipedia.org/wiki/Historical_Jesus.

250 John P. Meier, "A Marginal Jew, Volume 1," *Anchor Bible*, 2001. cited in Christopher Price, "A Thorough Review of the Testimonium Flavianum," *Bede's Library*, December 8, 2009, http://bede.org.uk/Josephus.htm.

251 John P. Meier, "A Marginal Jew, Volume 1," *Anchor Bible*, 2001, cited in Christopher Price, "A Thorough Review of the Testimonium Flavianum," *Bede's Library*, December 8, 2009, http://bede.org.uk/Josephus.htm.

252 "Cornelius Taxitus, The Annals," printed from Alfred John Church,

William Jackson Brodribb, and Sarah Bryant, eds, *Complete Works of Tacitus* (New York: Random House, Inc. reprinted 1942), accessed February 26, 2018, Wikipedia, http://www.perseus.tufts.edu/hopper/text?doc=Perseus%3Atext%3A1999.02.0078%3Abook%3D15%3Achapter%3D44.

253 Geoffrey Chapman, *The New Jerome Biblical Commentary* (London: Bloomsbury Academic Publishing, 1989), 392-394. https://en.wikipedia.org/wiki/Paul_the_Apostle.

254 "Judaizers," *Wikipedia*, accessed February 22, 2018, https://en.wikipedia.org/wiki/Judaizers.

255 "Council of Jerusalem," *Wikipedia*, accessed February 20, 2018, https://en.wikipedia.org/wiki/Council_of_Jerusalem.

256 "Map of the Roman Empire – Ephesus," from *Bible-History.com*, accessed February 24, 2018, http://www.bible-history.com/maps/roman-empire/Ephesus.html.

257 "Map of the Roman Empire – Ephesus," from *Bible-History.com*

258 "Map of the Roman Empire – Ephesus," from Bible-History.com,

259 "Council of Jerusalem," *Wikipedia*, accesssed February 20, 2018, https://en.wikipedia.org/wiki/Paul_the_Apostle.

260 "Paul's Arrest in Jerusalem," from *Verses About the Apostles*, accessed February 24, 2018, https://www.ccel.org/bible/phillips/CN248ACTSPaulsArrest.htm.

261 Eusebius of Caesarea, "Church History Book II Chapter 25: 5-6," *New Advent Org.*, accessed June 1, 2015.,https://en.wikipedia.org/wiki/Paul_the_Apostle.

262 George Lyons, "Antiquities of the Jews – Book XX, Chapter 9," https://en.wikipedia.org/wiki/James, brother_of_Jesus.

263 "Paul vs the Apostles" *Church Versions of the Relationship Between Peter and Paul*, http://people.uncw.edu/zervosg/Pr236/New%20236/Paul%20vs%20Apostles.htm.

264 Frances Swiney, quoted by Lloyd M. Graham in *Deceptions and Myths of the Bible* (Carol Publishing Group, 1991) 446, http://gnostica.tripod.com/.

265 Stephen L. Harris, *Understanding the Bible* (Palo Alto: Mayfield, 1985), 331, http://en.wikipedia.org/wiki/Paul_the_Apostle_and_Judaism.

266 A.N. Sherwin-White, "Why Were the Early Christians Persecuted? – An

Amendment, Past & Present," Vol 47, No 2 (April,1943: 309, https://en.wikipedia.org/wiki/Persecution_of_Christians_in_the_Roman_Empire.

267 Edward Gibbon, *The History of the Decline and Fall of the Roman Empire* (Hertfordshire, England: Wordsworth Editions, 198), 309, https://en.wikipedia.org/wiki/Persecution_of_Christians_in_the_Roman_Empire.

268 W. H. C Friend, *Martyrdom and Persecution in the Early Church: A study of a Conflict from the Maccabees to Donatus* (Cambridge: James Clarke & Co., 1965), 325. https://en.wikipedia.org/wiki/Persecution_of_Christians_in_the_Roman_Empire.

269 "Credo quia absurdum," *Wikipedia*, accessed March 23, 2018, https://en.wikipedia.org/wiki/Credo_quia_absurdum.

270 Stark, Rodny, *The Rise of Christianity* (New York: Harper Collins Pbk, 1997), referenced in https://en.wikipedia.org/wiki/Early_Christianity#cite_note-Stark1997-49.

271 "Early Christianity," *Wikipedia*, accessed February 17, 2018, https://en.wikipedia.org/wiki/Early_Christianity.

272 "Early Christianity," *Wikipedia*, accessed February 17.

273 Rudolf Pesch, *Simon-Petrus* (Stuttgart: A Hiersemann Publisher, 1980), 29, https://en.wikipedia.org/wiki/Saint_Peter.

274 "The First Council of Nicaea," *Wikipedia*, accessed February 6, 2018, https://en.wikipedia.org/wiki/First_Council_of_Nicaea.

275 "Nicene Creed," *Wikipedia*, accessed February 26, 2018, https://en.wikipedia.org/wiki/Nicene_Creed. Note: the above creed is a slight revision of the Nicene Creed that was authorized at the First Council of Constantinople in 381.

276 Elaine Pagels, *The Gnostic Gospels*, Chapter One, Kindle.

277 Elaine Pagels, *The Gnostic Gospels*, Chapter Two, Kindle.

278 "Emergence of the Four Gospel Canon," *Frontline*, 1998, http://www.pbs.org/wgbh/pages/frontline/shows/religion/story/emergence.html

279 "Valentinus (Gnostic)", Wikipedia, last modified February 14, 2018, https://en.wikipedia.org/wiki/Valentinus_(Gnostic).

280 Barbara Walker, *The Encyclopedia*, 970-971.

281 Douglas Burton-Christie, *The Word in the Desert: Scripture and the Quest for Holiness in Early Christian Monasticism* (Oxford: Oxford University Press, 1993), 7-9, https://en.wikipedia.org/wiki/Desert_Fathers.

282 "Hesychasm," *Wikipedia*, accessed February 1, 2018, https://en.wikipedia.org/wiki/Hesychasm.

283 The meaning is "spiritual teaching of the fathers."

284 Benedict Ward, *The Sayings of the Desert Fathers: The Alphabet Collection* (Collegeville MN; Liturgical Press, 1984), http://www.amazon.com/The-Sayings-Desert-Fathers-Alphabetical/dp/0879079592.

285 "Anthanasius' Life of Anthony," www.newadvent.org, retrieved 2014, 10-15, https://en.wikipedia.org/wiki/Desert_Fathers.

286 Ray Yungen, *A Time of Departing* (Eureka, MT: Lighthouse Trails Publishing, 2006), 42.

287 The following quotes are available from http://www.orthodox-ebooks.org/sites/default/files/pdfs/The Sayings of the Desert Fathers Desert Fathers.pdf.

288 Scetis was a desert monastic settlement in the Valley of Nitria, about sixty miles south of Alexandria, http://legacy.fordham.edu/Halsall/basis/porphyry.asp.

289 Laura Swan, *The Forgotten Desert Mothers: Sayings, Lives, and Stories of Early Christian Women* (Peabody, MA: Paulist Press, 2001.), 39, 43.

290 For additional tales see Appendix C.

291 John Chryssavgis, Kallistos Ware, and Benedicta Ward, *In the Heart of the Desert*, revised Edition : *The Spirituality of the Desert Fathers and Mothers (Treasures of the World Religions)* (Bloomington IN : World Wisdom, 2008), 15. https://en.wikipedia.org/wiki/Desert_Fathers.

292 In the Heart of the Desert: Revised Edition : The Spirituality of the Desert Fathers and Mothers (Treasures of the World Religions), 15.

293 "Glory of Ancient Roman Religion," *Wikipedia*, accessed January 17, 2018, https://en.wikipedia.org/wiki/Glossary_of_ancient_Roman_religion#pax_deorum.

294 Peter Heather, *The Restoration of Rome: Barbarian Popes and Imperial Pretenders* (New York: Oxford University Press, 2013), Part One, Chapter One, Kindle.

295 Peter Heather, *The Restoration of Rome: Barbarian Popes and Imperial Pretenders*, Part One, Chapter One, Kindle.

296 "Pontifex Maximus," *Wikipedia*, accessed February 21, 2018, https://en.wikipedia.org/wiki/Pontifex_Maximus.

297 David Stone Potter, *The Roman Empire at Bay, AD 180-395* (London: Routledge, 2004), 346. https://en.wikipedia.org/wiki/Constantius_Chlorus.

298 "# 107 Constantine's Vision," *Christian History Institute*, accessed February 25, 2018, https://www.christianhistoryinstitute.org/study/module/constantine/.

299 "Sol Invictus," *Wikipedia*, accessed December 29, 2017, https://en.wikipedia.org/wiki/Sol_Invictus.

300 Editors of Encyclopedia Brittanica, "Mithra: Iranian God," *Encyclopedia Brittanica*, updated February 12, 2018, http://www.britannica.com/topic/Mithra.

301 Referred to in Eusebius, *Vita Constantini* 1.28, tr. Odahl, 105. Barnes, Constantine and Eusebius, 43; Drake, Impact of Constantine on Christianity"(CC), 113; Odahl, 105.

302 Robin Lane Fox and Jonathan Bardill, Constantine, *Divine Emperor of the Golden Age* (Cambridge: Cambridge University Press, 2011), 307, note 27, https://en.wikipedia.org/wiki/Constantine_the_Great.

303 "Pagan Saints," *Proto-Indo-European Religion*, February 9, 2012, http://piereligion.org/pagansaints.html.

304 "St. Justin Martyr," *Early Christian Writings*, accessed February 25, 2018, http://www.earlychristianwritings.com/justin.html. See also for access to all early Christian writings including New Testament, Apocrypha, Gnostics, Church Fathers and others.

305 Tertullian, *The Prescription Against Heretics*, Chapter XL, http://www.truthbeknown.com/mithraism.html.

306 Tertullian, *The Prescription Against Heretics*, Chapter XL, http://www.truthbeknown.com/mithraism.html.

307 Salomon Reinach, *Orpheus: A General History of Religions*, translated by Florence Simmonds (New York: G.P. Putnams Sons, 1910), 69.

308 "First Council of Nicaea," *Wikipedia*, accessed February 6, 2018, https://en.wikipedia.org/wiki/First_Council_of_Nicaea.

309 "First Council of Nicaea," *Wikipedia*, accessed February 6, 2018.

310 "Documents Concerning the Meletian Schism, *Fourth Century Christianity*, http://www.fourthcentury.com/documents-concerning-the-meletian-schism/.

311 Justo Gonzalez, *The Story of Christianity* Vol.1 (New York: Harper

Collins, 1984), 176.

312 T. Mommsen and Paul M. Meyer, editors, *Theodosiani Libri XVI Cum Constitutionibus Sirmondianis et Leges Novellae ad Theodosianum Pertinentes* (London: University College, accessed August 25, 2009), 16.8.7. Compiled by Nicholas, revised by Tony Honore for Oxford Text Archive, 1984, https://en.wikipedia.org/wiki/Constantius_II#Paganism.

313 "Medieval Sourcebook: Theodosian Code XVI," *Wikipedia*, accessed February 17, 2018, https://en.wikipedia.org/wiki/Theodosius_I#Nicene_Christianity_becomes_the_state_religion.

314 "Medieval Sourcebook: Theodosian Code XVI", Wikipedia, accessed February 17, 2018.

315 Gerhard Pfandl, "The Doctrine of the Trinity Among Seventh-day Adventists," *Journal of the Adventist Theological Society* 17/1 (Spring 2006), 160-179, http://www.atsjats.org/publication_file.php?pub_id=242.

316 Abstracted from Nigels Rodgers, The Complete Illustrated History of Ancient Greece (Hermes House, internet Publishers, 2013) and also from "List of Greek Mythological Figures", Wikipedia, last modified February 24, 2018, https://en.wikipedia.org/wiki/List_of_Greek_mythological_figures.

317 See "Sayings of the Desert Fathers", from Wikipedia, last modified February 21, 2013, https://orthodoxwiki.org/Sayings_of_the_Desert_Fathers for more quotes.

Illustration Credits

The authors have made every effort to contact the owners of illustrations reproduced in this book. In the few cases where they have been unsuccessful, they invite copyright holders to contact them direct at cpaprocki@gmail.com.

Cover Photo - Gilgamesh.
Source: https://www.flickr.com/photos/internetarchivebookimages/14595392370
Source book page: https://archive.org/stream/mythslegendsofba00spenuoft/mythslegendsofba00spenuoft#page/n200/mode/1up
Author: Internet Archive Book Images
Available at https://commons.wikimedia.org/wiki/File:Myths_and_legens of Babylonia_and_Assria_(1916)_(14595392370).jpg

Map of Ancient Mesopotamia - 3
January 28, 2014
Author: Goran tek-en
File licensed under the Creative Commons Attribution-Share Alike4.0 international license. File is free to share.
https://commons.wikipedia.org/File:N-Mesopotamia_and_Syria_english.svg#metadata

Map of Eastern Mediterranean – 54
Dbachmann at en.wikipedia - Transferred from en.wikipedia to Commons by User:Sumerophile using CommonsHelper. This compound image uses free material land_shallow_topo_east.tif from NASA Visible Earth (formerly "Blue Marble") and world.200407.3x21600x21600.C1.png from JULY, BLUE MARBLE NEXT GENERATION.

Snake Goddess from Heraklion Greece – 58
February 23, 2015
Author: Jebulon Heraklion, Crete, Greece.

This file is made available under the Creative Comons CC0 1.0 Universal Publis Domain Dedication
https://commons.wikimedia.org/wiki/File:Snake_goddess_mother_archmus_Heraklion.jpg

Exterior of the Palace of Knossos – 59
By Mmoyaq - Own work, CC BY-SA 3.0. https://commons.wikimedia.org/w/index.php?curid=51334588.

Interior of the Palace of Knossos –59
mage taken from a Youtube video entitles "Minoan civilization painting murals. Published on Sep 26, 2014 by Kali Travel.

Bull-Leaping Fresco – 60
From the Palace of Knossos, currently in Herakleion museum
Author: ChrisO at English Wikipedia
The official position taken by the Wikimedia Foundation is that "*faithful reproductions of two-dimensional public works of art are public domain*". This protrographic reproduction is therefore also considered to be in the public domain in the United States.
http://www.minoer.net/kult-religion/stiersprung

Volcanic Explosion - 62
Mount Vulcan, Rabaul PNG, Photo:
AustralianGeological Survey Organisation/AusAID
November 6, 2013
Author: Department of Foreign Affairs and Trade
Thsi file is licensed under the Creative Commons Attribution 2.0 Generic license
https://commons.wikimedia.org/wiki/Category:Volcanic eruptions_of_the_Rabaul_Caldera#/media/File:Mount_Vulcan._Rabaul,_PNG_1994._Photo-_Australian_Geological_Survey_Organisation_-_AusAID_(10703427376).jpg

Santorini: Showing the Caldera Left From the Volcanic Explosion on Thera – 63
Santorini island, Greece - EOS photo NASA, public domain 19 April

2011, 06:26 (UTC) Source: Santorini_Landsat.jpg. *This file is in the public domain in the United States.* Available at https://commons.wikimedia.org/wiki/File:Santorini_Caldera_Landsat.jpg.

Altar with king Tukulti-Ninurta I found in the Ishtar Temple of Assur (Qalaat Sherqat) showing the absent god – 65
June 28, 2011
Author: Einsamer Schulze
This file is licensed under the Creative Commons Attribution-Share Alike 3.0 Unported, 2.5 Generic, 2.0 Generic and 1.0 Generic
https://commons.wikimedia.org/w/indes.php?search=Altar+with+king+Tuklti-Nurta+l&title=Special:Search&go=Go&SearchToken=2urdcvx3muxej9b47s6v2o6rc#/media/File:Vorderasiatisches_Museum_Berlin_119.jpg

Functions of the Right and Left Brain – 68
Brain Hemisphere Functions. Free Download ID 34085184 copywrite Nn555 https://www.dreamstime.com/stock-images-brain-hemisphere-functions-vector-illustration-human-s-image34085184.

Expansion of Assyrian Empire– 72
https://www.bible-history.com/studybible/Isaiah/

Persian (Achaemenid) Empire 521-485 BC - 77
August 27, 2009
Author: DHUSMA
This file is in the public domain as original works of the United States federal government and/or military
https://commons.wikimedia.org/wiki/File:Persian_Empire_490_BC.png

Alexander the Great's Empire 323 BC - 89
Kids.britannia.com. Permission requested 8/1/18.

Meneptah Stele known as the Israel stela - 97
From the Egyptian Museum in Cairo
March 15, 2003

Author: Webscribe
This file is licensed under the Creative Commons Attribution-Share Alike 3.0 Unported license

Small Figurine of a Goddess Most Likely Worshiped by the Hebrews – 100
Israel Great Goddess at http://www.pbs.org/wgbh/novba/anvcient/archaeology-hebrew-bible.html. Photo csredit: copyright WGBH Educational Foundation.

Kingdoms of Israel and Judah ca 921 BC – 107
https://www.bible-history.com/maps/images/2_kings_israel_and_judah.jpg.

Timeline of the Major Hebrew Prophets – 130
Chart of Jewish Prophets. Called Bary Bandstra 616-395-7752, email bandstra@hope.edu.

Location of Qumran – 143
Qumran permission requested. John M. Allegro, The Dead Sea Scrolls and the Christian Myth.

Relationship Between the Synoptic Gospels – 205
Relations Between Synoptic Gospels Alecmconoy, November 27, 2007 available at Wiki Commons.

Mithraic Altarpiece- 206
Double-sided 2nd, 3rd Century Mithraic Altarpiece found Newr Fiano Romano, near Rome, and now in the Louvre – 212. For full descriptions, see User:Jastrow's hi-res versions: File:Mithdras tauroctony Louvre MA3441b.jpg (reverse; banquet scene). 2010. Source nl:Bestand:MIthraRelievbert.jpg=cleaned up version of File:MithraReliefvert.jpg.

Map of the Spread of Christianity in Europe, Southwest Asia, and North Africa to the Year AD 600 – 238
Information obtained from Patrick O'Brien , ed. (2003) Atlas of World History, Category: New York: Oxford University Press, pp. 44-5. Permission is granted to copy, distribute, or modify this document

under the terms of the GNU Free Documentation License, Version 1.2 or any later version published by the Free Software Foundation. The file is licensed under the Creative Commons Attribution-Share Alike 3.0 Unported license. Subject to Disclaimers.

INDEX

A

Abel 144
Abraham 17, 105, 116, 117, 118, 122, 124, 145, 214
Abzu 44
Acca Larentia 35
Achaea 224
Acts of the Apostles 166, 219, 220, 227, 241
Adad 45, 73
Adam 9, 87, 125, 126, 127, 191, 201
Adam and Eve 116, 129, 144
Adonis 252, 275
Adultery 51
Aegean 54, 55, 56, 73, 84, 133
Aegean Sea 54, 133, 224
Afghanistan 90
Africa 62, 71
Agag 136, 137
agriculture 3
Ahab 132, 181
Ahriman 78, 79, 85, 86, 123
Ahura Mazda 78, 85, 86
ain Feshkha 147
Airya 87
Akitu Chronicle 73
Akitu Festival 73
Akkad 6, 34, 35, 36, 37, 39, 104
Akkadian 34, 35, 38, 95
Akkadians 2, 6, 13, 17, 34, 43, 44, 46, 99, 111
   established their control over Mesopotamia 34

Akki 13, 14, 34
Al 9
Alexander of Alexandria 267
Alexander the Great 64, 89, 111, 112, 280, 292
   destroyed the Persian Empire 90
   died at the age of thirty-three 90
   king of Macedonia 90
   tutored by Aristotle 90
Amalekites 136
Amarna letters 103
Amar-Sin 39
Amazons 224
Amenhotep IV 103
Ammonites 115, 136, 139
Amorites 38, 42, 44
Amos 131, 138, 139, 140, 280
Amurru 35
Ana 7
Ananus 211, 228
Anat 99
Anata 7, 8
Anath 7, 98, 99
Anatolia 54, 55, 57, 63, 74, 90
Andrew 196
Annals 209
Anshan 42, 43
Anthony the Great 253, 255
Antioch 222, 224, 233, 238, 239, 242
Antiochia 113
Antiochus IV 113, 150
Anu 7, 14, 25, 33, 44, 73
Anuit 9
Anzu 22, 23

Aphrodite 114, 264, 275, 276, 278
Apollo 114, 235, 262, 275, 276
Apophthegmata Patrum 254
Apostolic Decree 223
Apostolic Fathers 239
apostolic succession 239, 240
Apsa 44
Arch of Constantine 262
Ares 114, 275, 276
Arianism 267, 268, 269, 270
Arinna 57
Aristotle 90, 171
Arius 266, 267, 268
Ark of the Covenant 105, 134
Armenia 267
Artemis 114, 225, 275, 276
Aryans 76, 86, 206, 275
  Gutian tribes 37
  Hittites 2
  influence of Shiva on 12
  introduced the worship of Mithra 76
  Medes 2
  Mithra 206
  Persians 2
Asag 22, 27
Ashdod 133, 134, 138
Asherah 98, 99, 135
  consort of Yahweh 99
  Queen of Heaven 99
Ashima 99
Ashkelon 64, 96, 133, 138
Ashurbanipal 71
Ashurnasirpal II 73
Asia Minor 37, 219, 267
Asshur 9

Assur 45
Assyria 1
Assyrians 17, 25, 44, 53, 71, 99
  Assyrian cities 73
  Assyrian law 52
  destroy Marduk 45
  ensuing Dark Age 71
  Eve was the Great Goddess of the Assyrians 126
  excessive brutality 72
  first emperor 73
  invention of total war 74
  sacked Samaria the capital of israel in 722 BC 102
  sense of history 71
Astarte 57, 99
Athena 114, 276
Athens 63, 276
Atlantis 55
Atrahasis 35
Augustine 127, 208, 216, 229, 243, 265
Avesta 78, 79, 86, 87

B

Baal 98, 99, 132, 181, 220
Babylon 7, 44, 46, 71, 75, 87, 90, 104
  Alexander the Great set up his capitol in Babylon 112
  Assyrian armies attack 73
  Persians conquered Babylon in 539 109
  place of Alexander's death 90
  survived the great upheaval after Thera 104
  the creation of slavery as an institution 49

Babylonian
  Babylonian law 51
  Babylonian priest class 47
  creation myth 44
  deities reside in statues 47
  tale of the Great Flood 19
Babylonian Captivity 75, 77, 84, 102, 109
Babylonians 44, 46, 48, 49, 73, 74, 109
  Amorites 44
  bicameral mind 44
  each worshipped a personal god or goddess 46
  Marduk 44
  the Amorites came to be known in history as the Babylonians 44
Baghdad 19
Bahrain 6
baptism
  an evolution in the meaning of 183
  an initiation into divine knowledge (gnosis) 169
  baptism featured in Mithraism 262
  first religious sect to baptize 148
  gains forgiveness of sins and access to heaven 148
  Jesus also baptized John 185
  Jesus instructs his apostles to baptize the faithful 148
  John baptizes Jesus in the Jordan 148
  rules for baptism in Didache 239
  spiritual meaning of water 148
  symbolism of the baptism of Jesus Christ 184
Baranamtarra 31
Battle of Adrianople 263
Battle of Milvan Bridge 262
Bau 31
Beatitudes 216
Bel/Beltis 7
Bel-Nipru 7
Benjamin 106, 134
Bethel 124
Bible 124, 125, 126, 130, 134, 142, 176, 220, 292
  biblical scholars and the Bible 117
  both the Old and New Testament 92
  deluge destroys all people except those saved in ark 87
  historical study of the Bible began when 116
  impact of the Babylonian captivity on 124
  impact on western civilization 116
  Jewish Torah is Old Testament of 92
  mentions deities who competed with Yahweh for people's attention 98
  origins of the biblical Eve 126
  part of the Gilgamesh epic in the 29
  prophets in the 130
bicameral mind 72, 93, 108
  Book of Amos is a book example of the bicameral mind at work 138
  breaks down 65
  consciousness of men and women split after the breakdown of 67
  consistent with Shrii P. R. Sarkar"s Wheel of Creation theory 11
  Julian Jaynes developed the

theory of the breakdown of
the bicameral mind 103
meaning having two chambers 11
psychological counterpart of the
biological 66
subjective consciousness emerges
from breakdown of 71
the transition from the bicameral
mind to the subjective mind 130
the volcano ended a million years
of the bicameral mind 55
Utnapishtim, example of 19
volcanic eruption swept away the
religious tradition based on 64
Bishop of Rome 240, 248
bishops 203, 234, 238, 239, 240, 243, 248, 260, 266, 267, 269
blood sacrifice 163, 164, 221, 237, 252, 262
Book of Enoch 127, 142
Book of Esther 142
Book of Ezra 110
Book of Leviticus 98
Book of Life 159
Book of Secrets 258
Book of Tobit 142
Borsippa 46, 73
bridal chamber 187, 200
bride price 51
Bubonic plague 134
business practices 48

C

Caesarea 227, 228
Cain and Abel 116
Caius 228
Calah 73
Cambyses 111
Canaan 122
collapsed under the pressure of immigrants after volano on Thera 63
Great Goddess of 57
Israelites were native to 106
land area of 102
people were Semites 95
Phoenicia, another name for 102
promised land 222
ruled by the Egyptians 98
significant economic and geopolitical importance 102
canonical gospels 176, 180, 187, 204, 209, 213, 214, 218
canonical gospels were redacted 218
error in the canonical gospels 251
Gospel of the Hebrews once supplemented the 176
Gospel of Thomas predates the 180
identify Jesus with Mithra 264
Irenaeus's justification for choosing the canonical gospels 249
Matthew, Mark, Luke, and John 204
only those accepted as orthodox by the Church of Rome 187
Sermon on the Mount 214
Carchemish 109
Carpocratians 166
Catholics 263, 269
Cerinthians 166
Chaldeans 44, 74, 75, 87
China 6, 48
Christian 102, 112, 219, 235, 236, 238,

239, 248, 249, 250, 262, 264, 270, 272, 303, 304, 305
  Christian church in Jerusalem 223
  Christian in name only 218
  Christian Jews 173
  church-state 170
  comes from the idea of being anointed with sacred knowledge 173
  Desert Fathers/Desert Mothers 253
  earliest gospel 174
  Emperor Theodosius 225
  False Christian 199
  first Christian Emperor 208
  Gnostics 186
  Gospel of Mary 194
  is it Christian to turn the other cheek to institutional greed 258
  Israeli Hebrew for Christian 174
  Jewish-Christian gospels 187
  Jewish religion laid the foundations for their scriptural canon 112
  Mithraic rites preceded the Christian rites 265
  mystics 178
  orthodoxy 229
  Paul founded Christian commuities in Asia Minor and Europe 219
  Pauls communities gave birth to the official Christian church of the Gentiles whose authority was centralized in the Church of Rome 228
  perfect standard of 216
  Peter founded the Christian community in Rome 240
  priests rewrite history 209
  righteousness 218
  sacrament of Confirmation 208
  Sacred kings existed in the early Christian period 252
  schism between Christian spirituality and religious law 229
  the Church of Rome claims leadership of the Christian world 248
  the oldest Christian sect 176
  the oldest Christian treatise dealing with question of leadership 238
  the same trap of dualism 102
  view of sexuality and women in Christian dogma 127
  were baptized as an initiation into their faith 148
Christianity 76, 86, 127, 128, 129, 160, 166, 170, 176, 178, 187, 208, 210, 219, 228, 229, 230, 231, 232, 236, 237, 239, 240, 247, 248, 253, 262, 264, 265, 266, 268, 270, 296, 303, 305, 306
  Apostolic Fathers 239
  apostolic succession 239
  ascetics kept a small flame of mysticism alive within the church 253
  believe evil began with woman 127
  Church of Rome established authority over early Christianity 240
  Constantine's Conversion to 262

early Jewish Christianity and the Gnostics plant the mystical seed of 172
Essenes are largest group of early converts 166
Gnostic scriptures discovered at 170
gospels of Thomas, Philip, Judas and Mary Magdelene 187
It was not Jesus, but the Catholic Church that formed the orthodoxy of 230
Nag Hammadi scriptures 178
Paul's interpretation of Jesus's life and death creates the essential belief of western Christianity 219
reigning authority of orthodox 176
Under Constantine, the Church of Rome builds a power base that has lasted until today 236
Zoroastrianism and Christianity similarities 86
Christians 2
Church expunged the Jews and other mystics from their definition of true 177
Creation myth of Adam and Eve embraces as truth by 125
despised for hating humanity 233
first official persecution of 233
Jewish Christians and 173
Name is from the word chrism 200
original term for 174
question that Christians must continually ask themselves is 273
revolution in consciousness 213
View of Jesus shared by most early Christians 203
viewpoints of early Christians 178
Chronicles 117
Church History 228
Church of Jerusalem 228
Church of Rome 166, 170, 173, 175, 177, 181, 186, 187, 194, 203, 206, 209, 213, 218, 219, 229, 237, 239, 240, 247, 248, 249, 250, 262, 266, 300
a legacy of dominance and persecution 251
assault on reason 206
become the official Church of the entire Roman Empire 239
concerned with the political questions of who would represent the authority of God on earth 173
everyone required to bow the neck to the authority of 249
Gospel of Matthew was largely redacted by priests within the 175
gospels of 187
held to the myth that God is external to the mind of human beings 177
Jesus in the robes of Mithra 219
Mary was not the prostitute that the Church of Rome would later create 180
monasticism 253
mystics and groups of mystics identified as heretics by 186
Patriarchs discarded early scriptures that threatened them 174
Paul the Apostle and the Church

of Rome 219
redacted gospels 209
religious supremacy claimed by 240
scoffed at early Christian mystics 173
spread its domination throughout the West 230
Cimmerians 74
circumcision 110, 113, 123, 150, 175, 222, 223, 242, 294
Clement 176, 239, 248, 249
Code of Hammurabi 50, 51
code of laws 39
College of Pontiffs 260
Commentary on Habakkuk 143, 157, 158
Community Rule 143
concubinage 49
Constantine 174, 208, 236, 239, 243, 247, 259, 260, 261, 262, 263, 264, 266, 267, 268, 305
  became a Christian on deathbed 268
  became sole ruler of the empire in 324 236
  brokered the Edict of Milan in 313 236
  called the First Council of Nicaea 243
  established the Church as a political hierarchy under his control 247
  his role was to enforce dogma and help root our heretics 261
  over time began to favor the Christian religion 264
  provided the church with an army 174
  the first official Pope 260
  the Pax Deorum 260
  worshipped Mithra 261
Constantine the Great 235
Constantinople 262, 263, 269, 303
Constantius 235, 261, 268, 269, 305, 306
Constantius I 235
Corinth 224, 238
Council of Nicaea 266, 267, 268, 271
Covenant of Mercy 166
Covenant of the Eternal Yahad 166
Crete 53, 54, 55, 56, 57, 60, 64
Croesus 74
Crucifixion 151, 165
cuneiform 8, 70, 104, 106
Cyprian 234, 235, 243
Cyprianus 234, 235
Cyrus the Great 89
Cyrus the Great 2, 43, 76, 77, 78, 83, 84, 88, 101, 102, 109, 111
  Babylonian Captivity 77
  Zoroastrianism 77

D

Dagon 98, 134
Damascus 105, 138, 168, 188, 219, 222, 224, 238
Damascus Document 151, 152
Daniel 132, 133, 282
Darius 111
David 104, 105, 110, 133, 134, 137, 214, 280, 294, 305
David Ben-Gurion 115
Day of Atonement 123, 151, 158, 159
deacons 238, 239, 248, 267
Dead Sea 146, 147, 150, 151, 152, 169, 178
Dead Sea Scrolls 142, 143, 152, 156, 157, 158, 160, 161, 165, 166, 167, 170, 245
  Wicked Priest is King Jannaeus in 158
Decius 233

Decretum Gratiani 127
Demeter 114, 277
Demetrius 225
Demetrius III Eukairos 158
Demiurge 186
democracy 60
Desert Fathers 236, 253, 254, 257, 258, 281, 304
Deuteronomist 119, 120, 181, 185
Deuteronomy 110, 116, 117, 118, 120, 139, 231, 280
Devil 1, 80, 82, 199, 208, 254
Dharma 12
dialectical dualism 81
Diana 225, 262, 276
Diaspora 115, 165
Didache 238
Didymus the Blind 176
Dilman 6
Dinah 105
Diocletian 235, 261
Dionysus 114, 252, 277, 279
divine knowledge 148
Domitian 233
Dorians 64
  Aryan tribes who lived in the north, came invaded Greece 64
dowry 51
dragon 8
dualism 1
  Judeo Christian religions 2
  pervaded ancient Greece and Rome 2
  propagated by Zoroaster 1
  United States 2
Dumuzi 14, 15, 16, 28, 46

Good Shepherd 16

E

Ea 44
Early Jewish Christians 172
Eber 37
Ebionites 166
Ebla 37, 39
Ebrum 37
Ecclesiastes 29, 105, 117, 140
Edict of Milan 233, 236, 239, 263
Edom 138, 139
Edomites 87, 115, 136
Edward Gibbon 232, 303
Egypt 36, 54, 55, 57, 76, 83, 96, 98, 100, 102, 103, 184, 280, 285, 291
  Canaan was a colony of 103
  Christian ascetics, monks and nuns lived mainly in the deserts of Egypt 253
  Christian spiritual tracts discovered at Nag Hammadi in Egypt 178
  Desert Fathers/Desert Mothers 253
  Essenes spread into Egypt 168
  first mention of Jews by 96
  Hag Hammadi 168
  instantly hurled into chaos by Thera volcano 54
  Jews not living or enslaved in 96
  myth of Jewish slavery in Egypt 108
  pharaohs of Egypt had begun to equate themselves with gods 36
  Ptolemy took control of Egypt with death of Alexander 113
  the Gnostic Christians held a strong base in Syria and Egypt 228

Thera volcano destroyed the Egyptian Empire 64
Egyptians 1, 237
Ekron 133, 138
Ekur 21, 37, 38
Ekwesh 64
El 98, 99
Elaine Pagles 179
Elam 35
Elamites 42
Eli 133, 134
Elijah 132, 133, 148, 168, 169, 181, 182, 183, 184, 185, 191, 241
  equated with Jesus 133
Elisha 148, 181, 182, 184, 185, 270, 299
elohim 119
Elohim 116
Elohist 119, 120, 121
Emperor Theodosius 225
end of days 145, 167, 172, 181, 190
  forces of good and evil fight during the 149
Enki 13, 14, 16, 18, 35
Enkidu 25, 26, 27, 28
Enkimdu 14
Enlil
  advised the gods in council that they should send a Great Flood 18
  Ekur 21
  Etana 24
  fire and brimstone 21
  gives kingship to Gilgamesh 26
  Great Flood 17
  His temple represented the realm of the netherworld beneath the greatest pillar of fire 21
  justification of male power based on the ruthless behavior of Enlil 43
  lord of the atmosphere 17
  Ninurta 65
  Nippur 21
  ruthless God 23
  seven great lions 21
  subjective consciousness came about through man's attempt to mirror the ruthlessness 23
  Tablet of Destiny 22
  the Dark Lord 17
  the earthquake 20
  Utnapishtim 19
  Yahweh was born in a fashion similar to the birth of Enlil 93
  your me (ordinance) is a me which does not manifest as light 21
Enlil Hymn 21
Enlilship 22
Enmerkar and the Lord of Aratta 20
Enoch 147, 183
Enuma elish 36, 44
Ephesus 224, 225, 232, 238
Epic of Gilgamesh 25
Epic of Marduk 45
Epistle to the Hebrews 219
Eridu 5, 6, 13, 14, 16, 33, 39
Erishkigal 15
Esagila 45
Essenes 280
  add something new to the idea of God 167
  a Jewish mystical community 141

come to be called Gnostics 166
dispersed to many lands 165
Essenes provide prototype of the Last Supper 160
first Judeo-Christian sect to baptize their initiates 148
Jewish Mysticism of the Essenes 142
lived in communal settlements 143
suppressed by Jannaeus 157
Their mother community was called Qumran 143
the sect that trained Jesus 78
the Teacher of Righteousness 148
transmitted the idea of a New Covenant to early Christians 166
wrote many the Dead Sea Scrolls 142
Etana 24
Etham 99
Eucharist 208, 239, 262, 264
Euphrates 2, 5, 6, 8, 109
Europe 62, 219, 275
Eusebius 174, 175, 228, 261, 267, 269, 305
Eustathius of Antioch 267
Eve 8, 87, 126, 127, 128, 129
Exodus 96, 98, 99, 100, 106, 108, 118, 120, 121, 122
Ezekiel 110, 112, 280
Ezra 112

F

faith 223, 230, 232, 235, 243, 258, 267
it was love not faith that allowed Jesus to transcend his humanity 272
Feast of Tabernacles 150
Felix 227, 288

Filiman Kuh 19
First Apology 264
First Council of Nicaea 239, 243, 303, 305
Flood 26, 28
France 233, 249
Freedom 32

G

Gaffney 185
Galatia 224
Galerius 234, 235, 236
Galerius Maximus 234
Galilee 96, 174, 210
Garden of Eden 2, 4, 8, 125, 146, 147, 169
Gath 133
Gathas 78, 79
Gaza 133, 138
Genesis 37, 73, 87, 105, 116, 118, 120, 121, 122, 125
Gentiles 157, 164, 169, 172, 210, 219, 222, 223, 224, 226, 231, 242, 253
George Rawlinson 7
Georgia 267
Gerda Lerner 49
Geza Vermes 142
Gezer 96
Gibil 20
Gilead 138, 181
Gilgal 136, 137
Gilgamesh 25, 26, 27, 28, 29, 31, 36, 55, 85, 296
achieved an integrated sense of self 25
a hero 25
brawl with Enkidu 26

Enkidu 25
Enlil 26
extinguishes one of the burning pillars of fire 27
his mother, Ninsun 26
Humbaba 26
impressed Inanna 28
inspired the warrior kings 29
inspires kings and warriors for millenia 27
in the Bible 29
overcame the bicameral consciousness 25
rise of patriarchal political power 28
son of Lugalanda 25
sought immortality for himself 25
spurns Inanna 28
still unable to develop a worldview that can challenge the matriarchy 28
the God-King 25
the rebel land 21, 26
Uruk 25
Utnapishtim 28
Gnostics 172
　Church of Rome patriarchs set about to systematically discredit the Gnostics 249
　composed of many individuals and groups of early Christians 178
　considered Jesus Christ the reincarnation of Elijah 168
　emphasized spiritual experience as the key to unity with God 186
　included Thomas, Philip, Mary Magdelene and others 178
　killed or driven underground by Catholic Church 174
　Naassene Gnostics 168
　not a homogenous group 186
　see Jesus as one who makes all human beings the sons and daughters of God 179
　the I-feeling had finally identified its highest state of achievement 172
　their name comes from the word gnosis, which means spiritual knowledge 166
　The Roman Church scoffed at the 173
　the secret knowledge of which the Gnostics spoke 179
　Valentinus led the largest school of Gnostics 251
Goliath 137
Gospel of Mary Magdalene 194
Gospel of Matthew 213
Gospel of Philip 197
Gospel of the Ebionites 176
Gospel of the Hebrews 176
Gospel of the Nazarenes 174
Gospel of Thomas 179, 180, 188, 193
Great Flood 17, 19, 21, 24
　Kish 17
　Noah 19
　Shuruppak 17
　Uruk 17
　Utnapishtim 17
Great Goddess 7, 8, 13, 14, 45, 56, 57, 79, 98, 99, 126, 128, 135, 225, 294
　Asherah 99
　Asherah was considered Yahweh's

consort 98
Beltis 8
Beltis became the form in which the Great Goddess was worshipped in Sumer 8
Eve was the Great Goddess who the Jewish priest class blamed as being responsible for the fall of mankind 126
exclusive worship of the Great Goddess 56
figurines were found in earliest evidence of human activity in Middle East 2
Marduk, the Babylonian city god, kills the Great Goddess 36
Paul accused of preaching against the Great Goddess 225
Sumerian pantheon of gods and goddesses each represent an aspect of her being 7
The worship of a loving Goddess created a prosperous economy, a vibrant culture, and a peaceful nation 57
Great Persecution 235
Greece 2, 54, 55, 63, 64, 76, 171, 252, 267, 269, 290, 306
Greeks 55, 56, 60, 63, 83, 90, 113, 114, 145, 149, 157, 168, 169, 237, 260, 261
descended on Minoan civilization after Thera volcano 56
great contribution to western thought 90
In control of Judah until the revolt of Judas Maccabeus in 167 BC 113
introduced the civilized deities of the empire to the rustic Jews 114
learned about democracy from the Minoans 60
Major Gods and Goddesses in the Greek Pantheon 275
The Greeks Enter the Middle East 89
The Mycenaean culture of ancient Greece was also destroyed by Thera volcano 63
Zoroastrian mindset passed to the 83
Gugalanna 28
Gula 9, 31
Gutians 38, 42, 43
Gutian tribes 37

H

Hades 114, 157, 277, 279
Hadrian 233
Halaf 4
Ham 87
Hammurabi 48, 49, 50, 70, 71
Hammurabi's Code
  Babylonian business 48
  crimes vs persons and property 48
  foundations of patriarchal society 51
  men and women relations 49
Hanging Gardens of Babylon 75
Hanukkah 115
Hasmonean 115, 149, 150, 210, 294
Hasmonean Dynasty 115
Hassuna 4
Hathor 57
Hea 8, 9
Hebrew
  word for vagrant in Akkad is

khabiru 104
Hebrews 17, 19, 37, 45, 95, 96, 97, 98, 99, 100, 102, 103, 104, 105, 106, 109, 110, 111, 118, 129, 134, 135, 176, 202, 294
   group emerged from the Hebrews that took a unique identity 104
   a locus of small tribes within a larger landscape of nomadic people 103
   called their newly captured territory Israel 105
   ethnic monotheism 45
   first kingdom of 104
   Hundreds of years later, they would call themselves Jews 104
   Jews in Israel arose out of the 95
   original habitat of 96
   perhaps calling themselves Israelites, ransacked Jericho and later Jerusalem 104
   there's no evidence that Hebrews were slaves in Egypt 106
   were primarily nomads 97
   where did they come from? 102
   worshipped the Great Goddess 99
Hebrew Union College 106
Hegel 81
Hellenizers 115, 158
Hephaestus 114, 275, 277, 278
Hera 114, 276, 278
Hercules 262
Hermes 114, 275, 278, 306
Hermetics 178
Herod 115
Hieros Gamos 15
High Priest 150, 152, 211, 228, 260
Hippolytus 180, 183, 193, 194
Hittites 2, 25, 44, 52, 73, 102
Hoa 8
Holy Ghost 148, 244, 266, 270
Holy of Holies 113
Holy Spirit 86, 176, 199, 200, 202, 283, 300
   as Divine Mother 202
humans 10, 35, 45, 68, 113, 116, 201, 260
   serfs of the gods 23
   subjective consciousness 23
Humbaba 26, 28
Hurki 9
Hurrians 25

I

Ibbi-Sin 42
Ignatius 239, 243
Ignatius of Antioch 239
II Chronicles 109
I Kings 132
Illiad 73
Inanna 9, 14, 15, 16, 18, 20, 28, 37, 39, 46
   Dumuzi 14
   Enkidu 28
   goddess of love 14
   Great Serpent 20
   Gugalanna 28
   Queen of Heaven 16
Inanna and Ebih 20
India 2, 6, 20, 48, 64, 74, 76, 84, 90, 171, 277
Indonesia 62
Indra 9, 76, 78
Indus Valley 1, 2, 55, 74, 76

In Hoc Signo Vinces 262
in the role of 34
Intuition 82
Ionia 224
ira deorum 260
Iran 1, 2
  land of the Aryans 2
Iraq 2, 4, 34
Irenaeus 178, 181, 243, 248, 249
Isaac 105
Isaiah 87, 101, 102, 110, 131, 146, 147, 162, 280
  first to speak of monotheism 101
  praises Cyrus 101
Ishtar 9, 46, 57
Isis 57
Islam 76, 127, 129
Israel 292, 299
  female figurines unearthed in ancient Israel show Asherah the Goddess as a consort of Yahweh 99
  first record that references 64
  Israel fell to the Assyrians 107
  Northern Kingdom of 106
  permanent villages eleven thousand years ago in 3
  Splits into Israel and Judah 106
Israelites 87, 96, 104, 106, 107, 108, 111, 134, 136
Iva 9

J

Jabesh 135
Jack Finegan 42
Jacob 101, 105, 122
James 12, 176, 180, 187, 194, 210, 211, 212, 222, 223, 226, 228, 232, 240, 241, 242, 247, 249, 250, 303
  first Bishop of Jerusalem 175
  Gospel of the Hebrews says that Jesus first appeared to James after his resurrection 176
  Jesus called his brother, James the Just 180
  Most Christians at the time actually looked to James, the brother of Jesus and the Bishop of Jerusalem, as the supreme authority 240
  stoned at the hands of Ananus 211
  the brother of Jesus, became the leader of the Nazarenes in Jerusalem 175
  writes the Apostolic Decree 223
Jannaeus 149, 150, 151, 152, 156, 157, 158, 159, 164, 169, 173
Japheth 87
Jason 150
Jehoiachin 75
Jehoiakim 109
Jemdet Nasr 4, 17
Jeremiah 110, 131, 132, 280
Jericho 104, 111
Jeroboam 106, 119
Jerome 175, 176
Jerusalem 77
  Attacked by Nebuchadnezzar 109
  city chosen by King David to be the capital of the conquered territory 105
  Greek Gods in Jerusalem 112

Greek king Antiochus IV (175-164 BC) captured the city of Jerusalem 113
Hebrews ransacked Jericho and later Jerusalem 104
In 63 BC, the Roman general Pompey conquered Jerusalem 115
James, the Bishop of Jerusalem 228
Jerusalem was a city built by the Canaanites that paid tribute to Egypt 103
King Cyrus freed Jews from their Babylonian Captivity and allowed them to reestablish themselves in Jerusalem 77
King David brought the Ark of the Covenant to Jerusalem 134
King Nebuchadnezzer II (605-562 BC) conquering Jerusalem 75
Paul's trip back to Jerusalem 226
Solomon built the first Temple in Jerusalem 99
symbol to unite Hebrew tribes 105
Jesus ben Sirach 126
Jesus Christ 169, 183, 184, 185, 187, 193, 209, 213, 215, 228, 236, 243, 245, 249, 252, 257, 259, 262, 265, 266, 270
  core message of 179
  Essenes were the sect that trained Jesus 78
  his greatest commandment 217
  how Church dogma paints Jesus 203
  Jesus, as he appears in the gospel of Philip 201
  Jesus Christ introduced human beings to the highest understanding of God 171
  Jesus in the gospel of Mary 195
  Jesus in the gospel of Thomas 188
  Jesus never preached physical resurrection from the dead 221
  Jesus shows the western world how to become God-realized 201
  Jesus was an Essene rabbi 165
  Jesus was born during a time of profound intellectual revolution 236
  Jesus would later instruct his apostles to baptize the faithful 148
  John would baptize Jesus in the Jordan River 148
  Peter denies knowing Jesus 241
  referenced in Antiquities 210
  referenced in Tacitus 212
  scholars of antiquity agree that Jesus existed 205
  tells disciples not to worry about meeting their own basic needs 218
  the common narrative about the life of Christ in the canonical gospels is a plagiarism of the myth of the god Mithra 206
  the earliest Jewish reference to 168
  the God of Jesus was loving and universal 220
  The hard evidence for the existence of Jesus Christ 209
  the love of which Jesus Christ spoke and dedicated his life 153
  the mythology of Mithra was incorporated into the story of Jesus's life 208

The Teacher of Righteousness and Jesus Christ 159
to understand Jesus Christ as more than a mythological figure 144
was always at odds with the established church of his day 191
was an Essene 168
Jewish Antiquities 210
Jewish-Christian 187
Jewish Christianity 172
Jewish Wars 210
Jews 2, 9, 70, 75, 82, 83, 84, 87, 88, 100, 101, 102, 104, 106, 108, 109, 110, 111, 112, 130, 131, 132, 134, 142, 145, 163, 226, 227, 228, 231, 232, 280, 291
  and the Egyptians 96
  as a tribal confederation 96
  as nomads 97
  as Semites 95
  borrowed liberally from Zoroastrianism in the creation of their own religion 84
  Circumcision 222
  covenants of 169
  creation myth of the Jews 125
  Diaspora 165
  Different between Hebrew, Jew, Israelite, and Zionist 95
  discover the source of self-consciousness through the teachings of the Essenes 141
  freed Jews from their Babylonian Captivity 77
  have had a long history 92
  hilltop villages 96
  Jesus and Paul were Jews 223
  Jews and the Rise of Monotheism 92
  Jews did not live in, nor were they enslaved in Egypt 96
  Levites 98
  majority of Jews worshipped Great Goddess in their homes 128
  meaning the people of Judah 111
  myth rooted in a bicameral consciousness 93
  polytheism 98
  promised land 146
  purpose of the Torah was to tell a story to unite the people 117
  resented the forced imposition of the Greek pantheon on their religious and social life 114
  Saul first king of the Jews 137
  Saul their first king 98
  the Exodus 96
  the greatest enemies of the Hebrew Jews were the Philistines 133
  their prophets 98
  their tribal chieftains 98
  the Jews indigenous to Canaan 102
  the story of the prophet Samuel and King Saul 133
  Torah 93
  Who is a Jew? 92
Jews and Constantius II 269
Jews made their covenants with Yahweh at the Jordan River 181
Jews revolted against Roman rule 115
Jezebel 132, 181
John 127, 148, 159, 180, 184, 185, 186, 187, 191, 204, 214, 222, 241, 242, 245, 246, 247, 249, 266, 282, 304

John was a disciple of Jesus 187
namesPeter on three occasions 242
say Mary Magdelene was the first person to see Jesus in a vision after his death 180
writer of one of the four synoptic gospels 159
John Chrysostom 127, 243
John M. Allegro 142
John the Baptist 161, 183, 184, 186, 191, 205, 210, 214, 228, 232, 245
 baptizes Jesus in the Jordan River 148
 Jesus tells John's disciples that their master was a reincarnation of Elijah who was prophesized by Malachi 184
 John asks Jesus, are you the one who is coming, or are we to look for another? 161
 John the Baptist had been beheaded 228
 Mandaeans are followers of John the Baptist 186
 people believed that John was the returned Elijah 184
Jonathan 136, 305
Jordan 102, 168, 182, 183
Jordan River 146, 148, 168, 181, 183, 184, 200
Josephus 113, 151, 152, 156, 174, 209, 210, 211, 212, 213
Joshea 137
Joshua 98, 113, 117, 146, 148, 150, 156, 166, 167, 168, 169, 181, 222, 223, 280
 1200 BC, the Time of Joshua and Levite tribe 280
 Book of Joshua described the time of Thera volcano 98
 Essenes equated the Teacher of Righteousness with Joshua 156
 Joshua becomes Jesus in Greek 166
 Joshua crossed the River Jordan where Qumran situated 146
Jubilees 142
Judah 104, 106, 109, 110, 111, 112, 119, 120, 135, 139, 142, 149, 158, 168, 280
 Jewish kingdom splits into Israel and Judah 106
 once called Canaan 104, 106
Judaism 76, 86, 87, 103, 110, 111, 115, 125, 127, 150, 151, 158, 172, 181, 222, 228, 231, 232, 269, 302
 Antiochus issue a decree banning Judaism in Jerusalem 150
 Hasmoneans forcibly converted tribes in their area to Judaism 115
 Hebrews would eventually develop a religion known as Judaism 103
 Jannaeus campaign to destroy 151
 points of resemblance between Zoroastrianism an 86
 the term 111
Judaizers 222, 226
Judas 113, 115, 178, 187, 188, 251
Judas Maccabeus 113, 115
Judea 112, 115, 117, 143, 149, 165, 168, 175, 210, 224, 228
Judeo-Christianity 168
Judeo Christian religions 2
Judges 98, 103, 117, 130, 131, 133, 280
Julian 66, 103, 261
Julian Jaynes 11, 66, 72, 103

Julius Wellhausen 119
Jupiter 9, 279
jus divinum 260
Justin Martyr 264, 305
J. V. Kinnier Wilson 19

K

Kabir Kub 19
Kaku 35
Kala Nath 7
Kali 7
Kelly 7
king 29
Kingdom of God 169
King Hussein 142
King Josiah 99, 109, 117, 120, 280
kings
  first true 24
Kings 6, 13, 24, 99, 109, 110, 117, 120, 184, 210, 299
Kingu 45
Kirjath-jearim 134
Kish 17, 24, 25, 27, 28, 33, 35
Knossos 55
Kore 7
Kuh Litanor 20
Kuwait 90

L

labarum 263
labyrinth 55
Lagash 30, 31, 32, 33
Land of the Two Rivers 5
Larsa 9, 33, 39
Leah 105
Lebanon 102

Levant 90, 93, 111, 133
Levi 106, 175, 176, 196, 204, 242, 299
Levites 98, 99
Leviticus 52, 108, 109, 118, 121, 122
Libyans 64, 96
Licinius 263
Lord Shiva 12, 171, 277
love 14, 18, 25, 28, 29, 82, 114, 153, 164, 170, 171, 172, 177, 185, 195, 202, 216, 217, 220, 222, 223, 226, 231, 246, 247, 253, 257, 270, 272, 273, 275, 284
  available to all human beings 216
  God is attained through love, selflessness, and the development of the intuition 114
  it is through mercy and love that the Father and the Son are known to each other 177
  Jesus and Mary Magdalan 202
  love as an interpersonal relationship with God 153
  love as a spiritual practice 82
  love is earned by self-sacrifice 223
  love of God or love of neighbor are the same 218
  love of which Jesus Christ spoke 153
  of the Father 216
  Paul said love is the fulfillment of the law 226
  Perfection as universal love 217
  Pharisees placed the law above 220
  the evolution of the idea of love as expressed in the gospels of Jesus Christ 170
Ludlul bel nemegi 68
Lugalanda 25, 30, 31, 32

mentality of a capitalist 31
only interested in wealth 30
Lugalbanda 26
  gas poisoning 26
  Gilgamesh's father 26
  the rebel land 26
Lugalzaggesi 33
  defeated by Sargon 33
  scientific warfare 33
Lugdunum 233
Luglanda
  son of a priest 30
Luke 159, 160, 175, 177, 183, 184, 187, 204, 208, 214, 215, 241, 249
  a follower of Paul and wrote from his perspective 187
  gospel of Luke and Acts were rewritten (redacted) by priests after the fact 241
  not a disciple of Jesus 187
  writer of Luke is dedicated to extolling the accomplishments of Peter and Paul 241
  wrote one of the four canonical gospels 204
Lukka 64
Lydia 63, 73, 76
Lyons 233

M

Macarius of Jerusalem 267
Maccabean Revolt 115, 150
Macedonia 64, 90
Magi 1, 76, 79, 86, 207, 208
Malachi 132, 133, 181, 184, 280
male priesthood
  conflict with the warriors 30
  social class 29
  what they controlled 29
Mandaeans 186
Manichaens 178, 186
Manicheans 235
Manishtushu 34, 35, 36
Marcus Aurelius 233, 261
Marduk 9, 44, 45, 46, 47, 69, 70, 75, 87, 220
  a supreme deity 45
  city god of Babylon 44
  created humans 45
  creation of the universe 45
  destroyed Tiamat 44
  Esagila 45
  festival of the New Year 46
  fifty names 45
  overthrow of Enlil 45
  overthrow of the Great Goddess 45
  storm God 44
Mark 159, 177, 180, 183, 184, 187, 204, 208, 213, 214, 215, 241, 242, 247, 249
  a follower of Paul and wrote from his perspective 187
  Both Mark and John say Mary Magdelene was the first person to see Jesus in a vision after his death 180
  Matthew's gospel and Luke's gospel both drew upon the Gospel of Mark 204
  not a disciple of Jesus 187
  wrote one of the synoptic gospels 177
Mark Gaffney 183
Marriages 51

Mars 9, 276
Marvin W. Meyer 188
Mary Daly 128
Mary Magdalene 186, 194, 202, 242, 249, 251
Mary Magdelene 178, 180, 187, 199, 241, 299
Mashya 87
Mashyana 87
matriarchy 1
Matriarchy 56
Mattathias 115
Matthew 159, 161, 174, 175, 176, 177, 183, 184, 185, 187, 189, 196, 204, 208, 213, 214, 215, 216, 218, 240, 241, 249, 299
   Gospel of the Nazarenes was the original Gospel of Matthew 175
   Jesus tells Sadducees resurrection of the body is impossible 221
   Matthew was a disciple of Jesus 187
   Matthew was also called Levi 175
   Sermon on the Mount only in the gospel of Matthew 214
   source for the Gospel of Matthew 176
   Wrote one of the synoptic gospels 159
Maxentius 261, 262, 263
Maximinus 235
Medes 2, 74, 76, 86
Megiddo 109
Melchizedek 116
Mem-lugal 13
Meno-i-Khard 84
merchant 47, 103
Mercury 9, 278
Merneptah stele 96
Merneptah Stele 64

Mesopotamia 1, 2, 4, 5, 6, 7, 8, 13, 14, 20, 34, 38, 43, 44, 45, 48, 49, 53, 54, 55, 71, 72, 73, 75, 76, 90, 102, 103
   Aryans went south to Iran and ultimately into Mesopotamia 2
   Assyrians ruled Mesopotamia for over 500 years 53
   divided into two parts 6
   earliest cultures 4
   earliest known towns 4
   female slaves became pervasive throughout Mesopotamia 49
   Garden of Eden 4
   Goddess Inanna demanded allegiance from all life in Mesopotamia 20
   In Mesopotamia, empires would rise and fall in succession 43
   oldest towns 5
   Temple 5
   the deeds of Gilgamesh lived in the memory of the Mesopotamian people for more than two thousand years 25
   The Garden of Eden 2
   the Sumerians came to Mesopotamia by boat 6
   Trade routes led from Mesopotamia to India and China 48
   with the overthrow of the Great Goddess, Marduk becomes chief male deity of Mesopotamia 45
   Zagros mountains immediately east of the Mesopotamian plains 19

Messiah 85, 86, 144, 145, 149, 160, 161, 162, 163, 164, 167, 169, 175, 181, 184, 190, 207, 219, 220, 221, 225, 245, 252, 280
- as in previous civilizations, the Jewish Messiah would redeem the world through his sacrifice 163
- Jesus's crucifixion was a continuation and fulfillment of the ancient rite of the Sacred King 252
- Joshua, Elijah, the Teacher of Righteousness and Jesus Christ were all called Messiah 168
- Paul immediately recognized Jesus as the Messiah who was promised by the Jewish prophets to bring a new covenant to the Jews 220
- the Essenes believed that their own Teacher of Righteous was the Messiah 149
- the Essenes studied scripture to predict coming of the Messiah 144
- the Messiah who would save the Jews and usher in the new age 146
- the Messiah would appear at the end of days 145
- under the leadership of the Messiah the Jews would fight all their foes and all the nations would recognize the god of Israel, 149

Michael Wise 152
Middle Assyrian Law 52
Middle East 2, 3, 5, 7, 8, 12, 17, 24, 35, 42, 48, 53, 55, 57, 62, 64, 71, 73, 74, 76, 78, 83, 84, 85, 89, 90, 92, 93, 95, 99, 100, 103, 113, 114, 126, 135, 153, 166, 168, 171, 219, 231, 243, 252, 289
Midrash 118
Millennial Doctrines 85
Minoan civilization 53, 55, 59, 61, 63, 64
Minoans 53, 56, 61, 134, 290
- agricultural civilization 55
- artistic style 57
- Atlantis 55
- centers of commerce and trade 55
- democracy 60
- earliest script 56
- equitable sharing of wealth 57
- islands of Thera 55
- labyrinth 55
- last great matriarchal civilization 53
- Minotaur 55
- palaces 57, 58
- religion 56
- volcanic eruption 54
- volcano 61
- warfare 24, 56, 60
- worship of the Great Goddess 56

minotaur 55
Mithra 76, 144, 206, 207, 208, 214, 219, 261, 263, 264, 265, 266, 305
Mitra 206
Mizpeh 135
Moab 139
Moabites 115, 136
Monoimus 179
monotheism 45, 78, 101, 102, 114, 266, 280
Mosaic law 174, 219, 222, 223, 231

Moses 35, 87, 99, 101, 108, 116, 117, 118, 121, 124, 146, 148, 169, 181, 222, 223, 241, 263
- According to the Torah, in acknowledging the volcano god, Moses, the people's leader, gave them instructions on how to worship this god 99
- after the Babylonian Captivity, when the Torah/Old Testament was written, the first and second commandments were put into the mouth of Moses 101
- Moses did't write Deuteronomy 116
- Moses parallels Zoroaster in many respects regarded his revelation of religion 87
- Pentateuch was not authored by Moses 124

Mother Goddess 56, 99
Mount Nisir 18
Mount Sinai 99
Mt Ebih 19
Mt Krakatoa 62
Mt. Sinai 121, 292
Muhammed 131
Muslim 91
Muslims 125, 128, 131
Myceneans 56
mysticism 82, 163, 166, 170, 171, 172, 179, 196, 199, 203, 249, 253, 277
- a principle of mysticism is that gender is not an issue in spirituality 196
- ascetics kept a small flame of mysticism alive within the church 253
- Jewish Mysticism of the Essenes 142
- mysticism vs the politics of creating a church 178
- Religion vs Mysticism 236
- the Church of Rome suppressed mysticism 203
- the fundamental perspective of mysticism 179
- the onset of western mysticism begins with the Teacher of Righteousness 172
- There is a difference between religions and mysticism 82
- with mysticism, the reality of Oneness began to take root in the minds of men and women 171

mythology 17, 23, 53, 103, 106, 123, 208, 209, 253, 296
- like history 23
- Old Testament 92
- superior forces 23

Mythology
- knowledge of childbirth 35

N

Naassenes 166, 175, 178, 180, 181, 183, 185, 186, 194
Nabi 98, 130, 131, 132
Nabu 45, 46
Nag Hammadi 168, 169, 170, 178, 187, 188
Nanna 39, 40, 42
Naram-Sin 34, 36, 37, 38, 39
Nazarenes 166, 174, 175, 176, 180, 204

Nebo 9, 87
Nebuchadnezzar 75, 109
Nebuchadnezzar II 75
Necho II 109
Nehemiah 112
Nergal 9, 45
Nero 212, 228, 233
New Covenant 148, 163, 166, 168
Nicene Creed 244, 268, 269, 303
Nicolas Platon 56
Nile River 168, 169
Nimrod 7, 8, 73
Nimrud 73
Nineveh 73, 74, 104, 109, 126
Ningal 42
Ningirsu 22
Nin-me-sar ra 20
Ninsun 26, 27
Ninurta 22, 45
  Anzu 22, 23
Nippur 16, 21, 33, 37, 39, 42
Noah 19, 37, 87, 117, 145, 183
Numbers 118, 121, 122

O

Obadiah 132
Odyssey 73
Old Testament 75, 92, 98, 110, 116, 117, 118, 119, 121, 124, 125, 130, 132, 142, 161, 174, 181, 182, 185, 231, 295
  Babylonian Captivity 75
  Book of Genesis and the curse of women 125
  Jewish Torah is the Old Testament 92
  Old Testament written after the Babylonian Captivity 101
  primarily myth with a sprinkling of historical accuracies 93
  story of Elijah and Elisha presents a spiritual lesson without parallel in the Old Testament 182
  story of the Exodus 96
  the Dead Sea Scrolls contain the oldest version of the Old Testament 142
  the Pentateuch 118
  the sin of apostasy in the Old Testament 231
  time period described in the Old Testament Book of Joshua and Book of Judges 98
  Wellhausen's Old Testament scholarship 119
Olga Krzsykowski 56
On the Origin of the World 178
Ophites 186
Origen 175, 176, 193
Orpheus 265, 305

P

Pakistan 90
Palestine 37, 75, 102, 210, 267, 280
Parthians 90
Passover 123, 222
patriarchy 36, 49
Patriarchy 53, 55
Paul 127, 174, 187, 194, 204, 219, 220, 221, 222, 223, 224, 225, 226, 227, 228, 229, 231, 232, 241, 242, 250, 251, 287, 302, 306
  considered himself an apostle because of his mystical

experience of Jesus 220
credited with founding several Christian communities in Asia Minor and Europe 219
excelled at communication and fundraising 219
half of the Book of Acts of the Apostles is dedicated to 219
his conversion 219
known as Saul of Tarsus 219
pax deorum 260
Pentateuch 106, 110, 116, 117, 118, 119, 121, 124, 125, 139, 280, 295
Persia 76, 89, 90, 111, 280
Persian Gulf 6, 8
Persians 2, 43, 44, 74, 76, 91, 111, 112, 209, 233, 237, 280, 298
personal gods 47
Peter 148, 176, 186, 187, 189, 193, 194, 195, 196, 208, 222, 223, 228, 239, 240, 241, 242, 243, 246, 247, 248, 266, 303, 304
   Church of Rome claims Primacy of the Bishop of Rome 240
   Nero executed Peter 228
   Peter and James supported Paul's position that the Gentiles did not need to be circumcised as long as they kept the other covenants of the law 223
   Peter founded the Christian community in Rome 240
   Peter, James, and John looked at Paul as an outsider 222
   structure of Church authority is based on 240
   the Church of Rome vigorously promotes Peter to establish their claim as the reigning authority of orthodox 176
   The First Pope 240
   there are documents attributed to Peter in the Nag Hammadi library 187
Peter Enns 119
Petra 208
Petrine Primacy 240, 243
Pharisees 77, 144, 149, 150, 157, 158, 167, 169, 170, 172, 177, 191, 210, 220, 221, 222, 227, 230, 242, 247, 298
   behavior of king Jannaeus during the Feast of Tabernacles led to a Judean civil war between the middle class Pharisees and the ruling nobility 150
   envisioned an epic battle between good and evil at end of days 170
   Jesus tells the Pharisees that resurrected souls are as the angels of God in heaven 221
   Jesus told the Pharisees that love was more important than the law 247
   Paul was called a blasphemer by the Pharisees 222
   pester Jesus concerning his disregard for Jewish law 177
   Pharisees and Essenes were heavily dependent upon Zoroastrianism for their dualistic interpretation of the world 167
   Pharisees were the middle class or

main stream of the Jews 144
the apostles of Jesus are beaten by the Pharisee priests for preaching in his name 167
were too preoccupied with the rules and rituals of Judaism to explore the idea of having a personal relationship with God 172

Philip 178, 187, 197, 198, 200, 201, 202, 203, 251

Philippi 224

Philippians 226

Philistines 133, 134, 135, 136, 137, 138

Phoenicians 103

pictographs 70

Plato 90, 171

Plotinus 186

Polycarp of Smyrna 239

Pompey 90, 115

Pontifex Maximus 260, 261, 264, 266, 269, 304

Pontius Pilate 205, 209, 210, 244

Pontius Pilatus 212

Pope 237, 239, 240, 248, 260, 266, 267

Presbyters 239

Prescription Against Heretics 228, 264, 305

priest 31, 32, 34, 45, 47, 69, 75, 78, 80, 82, 89, 101, 112, 113, 115, 116, 117, 118, 120, 121, 122, 123, 128, 129, 132, 139, 145, 149, 150, 163, 173, 180, 209, 230, 260, 265
add ceremonies, myths, stories, rules, and dogmas to the teachings of the original master 79

Akkadian priests 37

around 4400 years ago a male priest class had emerged to help the king carry out his religious and civic duties 29

as the male priest class gained ascendency, the role of women was diminished and opportunities curtailed 89

as the power of the Roman priest class congealed, heretics were tortured and put to death for their so-called dedication to evil 270

Babylonians destroyed Jerusalem and the Jewish priest class was taken back to Babylon as slaves 75

care for Marduk 47

Catholic priests 142

creation myth in the Bible 125

Cyrus liberated the Jewish priests 102

during the Middle Ages, the spiritual roots of Christianity were completely cut off because of the church's unquenchable desire for wealth and power 230

ethnic monotheism 45

ethnic monotheism has its origins in the attempt by the priests of ruling cities to place their chief god above all other gods and thus undergird their own supreme authority in the minds of men 45

had power to punish people in the

afterlife 30
high priestess remained more powerful than male priests in Uruk 14
Historical revisionism is how the kings and priests have always justified their rule 209
in Sumer the male priests created the mold for all the priest classes to follow 30
In time, the high priest and the king became rivals 30
In western civilization, women are not allowed to be priests 128
it was necessary for the Levite priests to do this if they were going to institute Yahweh as the only god and gain people's obedience 100
Jesus did not speak as a priest 172
Jewish priests accepted Zoroastria 87
Jewish priests create the Torah or Old Testament and claim it was dictated to Moses by their god 96
Levite priests 100
long term mission of early Jewish priests 98
Magi priests 208
male priesthood 29
Minotaur 55
Pharisaic priests (rabbis) 228
priest class of Zoroastrianism 79
priests of Greek society 114
priests of the Church of Rome 214
ran the machinery of civil government 30
religions always require a priest class to interpret and arbitrate our understanding of the externalized good god 80
religious ideology of the Jewish priests 110
Sharkalisharri, the Akkadian king, was killed by his priests 38
static dualism is the perfect mental state for the imposition of religious dogmas 81
the agenda of the Jewish priests 121
the Babylonian myth, Enuma elish, was created by the Babylonian priest class 36
the Church promoted myth as truth and the spirituality of Jesus Christ was superseded by politics 245
the first bankers and businessmen emerged from the priests of the Temple 48
the god of our priests 81
the Jewish priest class and Adam and Eve 9
the Levites were a hereditary Jewish priest class who instructed the people on how to worship 98
the Magi priest class 1
the main reason that Marduk stayed in his statue at Esagil was that his worship was maintained there by the Babylonian priest class 47
the Median priest class was called

the Magi 76
the priests' insistence upon blind faith lies at the root of religious socio-sentiment in which reason loses all meaning and thus its value 231
the priests interpret the deity's commands 47
the priests of Enlil share his power 21
the priests who created the myth of Adam and Eve were determined to separate the concepts of deity from mother as much as possible. To do so, they eliminated completely the reality of giving birth 126
To suppress the mind with dogma is the typical want of the priest; whereas, to expand the mind is the approach of the mystic or the spiritual teacher 129
Why did the Jewish priests create the myth that the Jews were slaves in Egypt? 107
with the establishment of the Church of Rome, intellectuals, in the guise of a priest class, would rule the western world, beyond the power of kings, for the next seventeen centuries, and would continue to do so until the end of the Middle Ages 170
Zoroastrianism had a profound effect on the Jewish priesthood 77

priestesses 56, 294
Priestly 121, 122, 123
Primacy of the Bishop of Rome 240
Prolegomena to History of Israel 119
Promised Land 164, 166, 167
property 31, 39, 48, 51, 52, 81, 88, 105, 112, 234, 236, 263, 269
prophets 12, 66, 69, 98, 99, 112, 117, 130, 131, 132, 135, 137, 139, 140, 145, 146, 163, 173, 174, 175, 181, 182, 190, 191, 193, 211, 215, 217, 220, 226, 244, 280
according to Jewish legend, prophets were chosen by their god Yahweh to speak on his behalf 130
as subjective consciousness became more commonplace, later prophets were not as sure of "the voice of god" as Samuel 131
at the time of Jeremiah, around 650 BC, the prophets were no longer respected and could be imprisoned for making prophesies 132
authority of the prophets lasted into the period of the kings and, in some cases, as late as the post-exilic period - after 500 BC 130
before Saul became their first king, the Jews were a loose confederation of peoples ruled by their tribal chieftains and by their prophets 98
by the post-exilic period (500 BC to 100 BC), the prophets had

become pariah, rejected and hated by the Jews 132
during the period of the kingdoms (1000 to 500 BC), the prophets are still allowed a voice, but they do not rule 131
Ezekiel 112
Ezra and Nehemiah 112
prophets are presented as models for holiness, wisdom, and closeness to god 130
prophets were feared and revered at the dawn of subjective consciousness 131
prophets were wandering nomads preaching fire and brimstone in a predominantly schizophrenic age 69
the books of the Prophets were added to the Torah after the Babylonian Captivity 117
the Jewish prophets would continue to claim to hear the voice of the gods in their heads for hundreds of years after the dawn of subjective consciousness 66
the movement from Samuel in the twelfth century BC to Zechariah in the fifth century BC reflects the change in Jewish consciousness from the bicameral to the subjective mind 131
the Talmud talks about there being hundreds of thousands of prophets, yet, the scripture only recognizes fifty-five 130
We are told that if parents catch their children saying that they hear the voice of god in their mind, they are ordered to kill their children on the spot 132
Proverbs 105, 117
PR Sarkar 11, 80
Psalms 105, 117, 142, 153, 162, 184
Ptolemy 112, 113

Q

Qalat Jarmo 4
Q source 214
Qumran 143, 146, 148, 149, 165, 167, 169, 178, 280

R

Rabbah 139
Ramses VI 64
rape 49, 52
Rebecca 105
Redemption and Resurrection 161, 167, 245
Red Sea 146, 148, 183
Refutation of all Heresies 180
Rehoboam 106
Remus 35
Riane Eisler 56
Richard Valantasis 194
Rig Veda 12
Rimush 34, 35
River Jordan 146, 148, 181
Robert Carroll 106
Roman Catholic Church 127, 204, 240

Romans 83, 115, 145, 149, 164, 165, 168, 210, 219, 224, 226, 227, 237, 277, 279
Rome 2, 35, 114, 115, 168, 171, 173, 174, 176, 177, 179, 180, 186, 187, 193, 196, 204, 208, 209, 210, 212, 224, 225, 226, 227, 228, 229, 233, 234, 235, 237, 239, 240, 243, 246, 247, 248, 249, 251, 252, 259, 260, 261, 262, 263, 264, 265, 266, 269, 278, 280, 304
   In 63 BC, the Jewish kingdom becomes a colony of Rome 115
Romulus 35
Rosh Hashanah 159
Rule of Saint Benedict 258
Ruth 117

S

Sabbath 110, 113, 123, 150, 158, 159, 222, 258
sacred king 7, 8, 13, 15, 16, 28, 35, 36, 46, 56, 79, 221, 252
  divine consort 17
  marriage with the Goddess 17
Sadducees 121, 144, 149, 169, 191, 210, 211, 227
Saint Sophia 225
Sairima 87
Samaria 110
Sampsaeans 166
Samuel 117, 131, 133, 134, 135, 136, 137, 140, 280
San 9
Sanhedrin 210, 227
Sansi 9
Santorini 55
Saoshyant 85, 86
Sarah 105, 256
Sardmarreh Landslip 19
Sargon 33, 34, 35, 36, 37
  Akkad 34
  first international empire 35
  two sons 35
Sassanid Empire 91
Saturn 9
Saul 98, 104, 133, 135, 136, 137, 280
Saul of Tarsus 219
Savior 85, 128, 145, 164, 173, 183, 196, 202, 207, 252
Sayings of the Desert Fathers 254
Scythians 74
S. David Sperling 106
Seleucid 90, 113, 150, 158
Seleucid Empire 90
  center of Greek culture 90
Seleucus 113
Semite 2, 34, 95
Septinus Severus 233
Sermon on the Mount 160, 168, 214, 216
serpent 8, 29, 56, 126, 127, 277
Sethians 178, 186
Shamash 45
Shanidar 2
Shardana 64
Sharkalisharri 34, 38, 39
Shechem 105, 124
Shekelesh 64
Shem 37, 87
Shiloh 133, 134
Shubad 40, 42
Shubshi-Meshre-Shakken 68
Shulgi 27, 38, 39
Shulshag 31

Shuruppak 17, 33
Shu-Sin 38, 39
Sicily 64
Sin 9, 37, 38, 39, 45, 203
Sin-idinnam 70
Sippara 9
Sir Leonard Woolley 41, 57
slaves 11, 32, 33, 43, 45, 48, 49, 50, 72, 75, 94, 107, 108, 109, 247, 269, 284
 all slaves at this time were women 32
 concubinage became the social institution for integrating captive women into the households of their captors 49
 debt slaves 50
 four thousand four hundred years ago, Baranamtarra, wife of Sumerian king Lugalanda bought and sold slaves 31
 hired out as prostitutes 49
 in Hammurabi's Code, people were classified as nobles, commoners, and slaves 48
 Lugalzaggesi, who followed Urukagina on the Sumerian throne, devised a way to use male slaves for the first time in history 33
 once men had discovered a means to control captive women physically and psychologically, they were eventually able to do so with men and to justify their behavior in "divinely" supported law codes. These laws, in turn, institutionalized and legitimize the practice of slavery for millennia 49
 once the mentality of patriarchy had evolved, fueled by the urge for political power, wealth, and female slaves, it could not be reversed 43
 people thought that humans were the slaves of the gods 45
 social classes in Babylon 48
 the conquered cities were made to supply soldiers for the wars to follow 33
 the process of turning free persons into slaves has always required physical terror and coercion. In regard to male dominance of women, this was accomplished by rape 49
 the socio-psychic imbalances of sexism, racism, and classism, which buttressed the practice of slavery for all those years, are still with us today and provide a large part of our collective, social programming 49
 the Temple of each city owned the lad, grains, slaves, animals, and jewels 48
 Urukagina's wife had 150 female slaves to help with the housework 32
social class 29
Socrates 90
Solomon 24, 99, 105, 106, 158, 280
Song of Songs 105

son of God 172, 246
South Asia 2, 62
statues 47
stele in Tel Dan 105
Steven 232
Strabo 224
Su 42
Subartu 35
subjective consciousness 11, 12, 23, 25, 37, 66, 71, 77, 79, 83, 88, 93, 94, 103, 130, 131, 136, 137, 138, 140, 153
   makes claims on power reserved for the gods 39
   overthrows influence of the gods 23
subjective thought 70
   threshold of 70
Succoth 99
suffering servant 163
Sumer 6, 8, 16, 20, 24, 29, 30, 33, 35, 39, 57
Sumerian King List 6, 13, 17, 24, 38
   chief deity 13
   sacred king 13
Sumerians 2, 6, 7, 9, 12, 13, 14, 19, 20, 23, 25, 34, 38, 39, 43, 44, 46
   earliest records of Sumerian history 13
   Enlil 17
   religious myths 6
   worldview 10
synoptic gospels 159, 177, 187, 204, 206, 207, 208
Syria 4, 37, 63, 71, 73, 102, 138, 158, 171, 187, 228, 267, 280
Syria Palestinia 115

T

Tabernacle 122, 134
Tablet of Destiny 22
Tacitus 209, 212, 213, 233
Tammuz 46, 252
Taurus 224
Teacher of Righteousness 148, 149, 151, 152, 153, 156, 157, 158, 159, 161, 163, 164, 165, 167, 168, 169, 170, 171, 172, 180, 199, 270
   and Jesus Christ 159
   detractors 154
   equated with Joshua 156
   faces death threats 154
   had spiritual experiences 153
   hanged from a tree 156
   interpersonal relationship with the Divine 153
   speaks to deception of the priests 155
   Thanksgiving Hymns 152
   the dawning of mystical consciousness in the Western world 164
   theme of the suffering servant 163
   the new covenant 164
   unique teacher of Essenes 151
   what makes firm his great resolve 156
   Wicked Priest is enemy of 152
Teman 139
Temple 31, 33, 39, 45, 48, 69, 75, 99, 105, 111, 112, 113, 115, 117, 120, 125, 147, 150, 151, 210, 225, 227, 228
   built for a guardian god or goddess 5
   second temple built in Jerusalem 110
   Solomon builds Jewish Temple 105
ten lost tribes 107
Tertullian 127, 228, 237, 246, 248,

249, 264, 265, 305
Tertullus 174
Thanksgiving Hymns 152
The Acts of Peter and the Twelve Apostles 178
The God of My Father 46
The Gospel of Truth 178
The Naassene Sermon 180
Theodosius I 239, 269
Theodotus 178
The Prayer of the Apostle Paul 178
The Preacher 140
Thera 54, 55, 61, 62, 66, 85, 93, 96, 97, 98, 103, 104, 108, 119, 124, 129, 133, 134, 280, 291, 292
 at the time of Thera, Canaan was under Egyptian rule and the Egyptians used the displaced masses of Thera as forced labor to cultivate food for them 108
 civilizations collapsed under the pressure of immigrants from the disaster of Thera 63
 the explosion of Thera rocked the known world and the aftermath was so disruptive of human psychology that it left everyone speechless 54
 the explosion set in motion a three hundred year Dark Age 66
 the Minoan civilization inhabited the small group of islands of Thera, Crete, Santorini, and possibly Atlantis 55
 the patriarchal Greeks (Myceneans) descended on this civilization after 1200 BC 56
 Thera dealt the bicameral mind a mortal wound 66
 the volcano of Thera exploded with such magnitude that scientists believe it was the worst natural disaster ever experienced by human beings 61
 Yahweh was born out of the volcanic eruption that caused the destruction of Thera 93
The Rule of the Blessing 143
the scroll of the covenant 120
The Secret Book of James 178
The Wisdom of Jesus Christ 178
Thomas 175, 178, 185, 186, 187, 188, 189, 190, 194, 197, 203, 204, 241, 242, 251
 excerpts from Gospel of Thomas 187
 Gnostics believed that Thomas and Mary Magdalene received special knowledge from Jesus 186
 the Gospel of Thomas is not a narrative of the life of Jesus but a collection of his sayings and ideas, as well as an attempt to interpret them from a spiritual perspective 197
 the Gospel of Thomas is older than any of the other gospels 179
 the gospels of Thomas, Mary, and Philip provide a look at the mystical core of the teachings of Jesus Christ 203
 Thomas was thought by many to be

the twin brother of Jesus 188
Thrace 267
Thraetaona 87
Tiamat 44
Tiberius 212
Tidnum people 42
Tiglath-pileser I 73
Tigris 2, 6, 8
Timothy 127, 187
Titus 210
Torah 37, 73, 75, 92, 93, 99, 101, 105, 106, 107, 108, 109, 110, 111, 116, 117, 118, 121, 124, 125, 126, 130, 131, 132, 133, 135, 137, 140, 142, 145, 147, 174, 231, 280, 295, 296
- Babylonian Captivity in 585 BC was recorded in Jewish Torah 75
- In the creation myth of the Torah, Eve, the female of the species, is not just stripped of her role as the creator of life, but she is reduced to a sinful woman responsible for the "fall of man" 126
- It was in Babylon, during the Babylonian Captivity that the major sections of the Torah began to be rewritten or written anew 110
- last book in 132
- the Bible is a composite of the Old and the New Testaments 92
- the Jewish Torah is the Christian Old Testament 92
- the Pentateuch 125
- there were three significant periods in Jewish history when the raw materials of the Torah were consolidated and enlarged upon by the priest class 117
- the Torah provides us with an excellent example of the transition in thinking that occurred in the first and second centuries BC between bicameral and subjective consciousness 93, 106

total war 72, 74
Tower of Babel 45, 75
Trajan 233
tsunami 62
Tukulti-Ninurta I 65
Tura 87
Turkey 4, 55, 57, 74, 171, 219
Turkmenistan 90
Tursha 64
Tyrus 139

U

Ubaid 4
Ubaidians 4, 5, 13
Umma 31, 33
United States 2
Upanishads 12
Ur 9, 13, 16, 27, 29, 33, 35, 38, 40, 41, 42, 288
Ur-Nammu 38, 39
Uruk 4, 14, 15, 16, 17, 25, 26, 28, 29, 33, 35, 38, 39
Urukagina 31, 32, 33
- overthrew Lugalanda 31
Urukh 9
Utnapishtim 17, 18, 19, 28, 29

V

Valentinians 178, 186
Valerian 233, 234
Vara 87
Vedas
  and women 88
Venus 9, 275
Vespasian 210
Vohu Manah 78
volcano 55, 61, 62, 73, 85, 98, 99, 102, 119, 291, 292
Vul 9

W

Wadi-en-Natuf 2
Walter Brueggemann 124
warrior 13, 22, 29, 30, 31, 32, 35, 37, 39, 47, 73, 76, 149, 164, 253, 276, 283
War Scroll 143, 149, 170
Wernicke's area 11, 66
Wicked Priest 149, 152, 156, 157, 158, 159
Wisdom of Sirach 142
Women
  Assyrian law 52

Y

Yahweh 17, 77, 87, 93, 95, 98, 99, 100, 101, 105, 107, 108, 109, 110, 111, 113, 116, 118, 119, 122, 126, 130, 135, 145, 172, 173, 181, 182, 183, 186, 201, 209, 220, 222, 291, 292
  a volcano god 98
  enthronement of 17
  introduced to the Hebrew tribes by the Levite tribe 98
  paired with Asherah 99
  the idea of 95
  the Volcano God 95
Yahwist 119
Yano'am 96
Yima 87
yoga 12
Yom Kippur 151, 158, 159

Z

Zababa 35, 45
Zagros Mountains 19, 20, 37, 54
  earthquake 19
  Inanna 20
  Mt Ebih 19
  the rebel lands 19
Zealots 149, 169, 170
Zechariah 131, 147, 149, 280
Zedekiah 75, 109
Zeus 9, 114, 201, 275, 276, 277, 278, 279
ziggurat 6, 21, 39, 45, 75
Zobahites 136
Zoroaster 1, 76, 78, 79, 80, 81, 85, 87, 89, 149, 164, 171, 221
  appalled by the Aryan gods 78
  a revelation 78
Zoroastrianism 76, 77, 78, 79, 81, 83, 84, 85, 86, 87, 88, 101, 102, 110, 123, 167, 170, 172, 206, 207, 208, 209, 261, 280, 298
  and Jews 84
  and Judaism 86
  and women 84
  and Yahweh 77
  animal sacrifices 86
  a static dualist 79

Avesta 78
battle between good and evil 79
dogmatic mindset 81
earliest environmentalists 86
free will 80
Gathas 78
impact on western civilization 83
leap in human consciousness 78
mythology 85
purpose of 85
revolutionary step forward 83
the Magi 79

About the Authors

Charles Paprocki has spent many years working with troubled teenagers, prison inmates, welfare recipients, and migrant workers in the human services system. He also owned a graphics and advertising agency in New York City where he combined his skill and knowledge to create social marketing campaigns. He was one of the core leaders to create the Universal Pre-K program in New York State and the local food movement in Illinois. His last work was to manage an organic farm in southern Illinois. He has consulted with international NGO's on management strategies and participated in the earth Summit in Brazil and the Social Summit in Denmark. He is now retired and living in Herrin, Illinois.

Tom Paprocki has worked several years in social services, including starting a preschool and daycare center in rural southern Illinois and serving as an administrator for a drug education and crisis center. After receiving a Masters in Public Administration, he was hired by the NASA Goddard Space Flight Center as a Presidential Management Intern. He served thirty years at Goddard, which included positions as head of Personnel, Procurement, and Institutional Resources. He spent the last seven years as Director of Management Operations, which included facilities, acquisitions, environmental and health services, security, and logistics for the research and launch facilities at Greenbelt, Maryland and Wallops Island, Virginia.

www.ingramcontent.com/pod-product-compliance
Lightning Source LLC
Chambersburg PA
CBHW021052080526
44587CB00010B/222